AN EXPOSITION ON THE SHORTER CATECHISM

AN EXPOSITION ON THE SHORTER CATECHISM

INCLUDES THE WESTMINSTER CONFESSION
AND THE LONGER CATECHISM

ALEXANDER WHYTE

CHRISTIAN HERITAGE

ISBN 1-85792-250-6

Previously published by T & T Clark as
A Commentary on the Shorter Catechism
by
Alexander Whyte D.D.

Published in 2004
in the
Christian Heritage imprint
by
Christian Focus Publications
Geanies House, Fearn, Ross-shire,
IV20 1TW, Great Britain

www.christianfocus.com

Cover design by Alister Macinnes

Printed and bound by
WS Bookwell, Finland

Contents

Publisher's Introduction

Alexander Whyte (1836-1921) was a leading Scottish churchman of the nineteenth and early twentieth centuries. He occupied the prestigious pulpit of St George's Free Church of Scotland in Edinburgh, where he succeeded the noted preacher and theologian Dr. Robert S. Candlish. From 1909 he was also Principal of New College, Edinburgh.

Whyte was a prolific author. In addition to his *Exposition of the Shorter Catechism* his writings include *Bible Characters* (also published by Christian Focus), *Bunyan's Characters*, *The Life, Walk and Conversation of Jesus*, and *The Apostle Paul*. He also published biographical studies, including books on Samuel Rutherford, James Fraser of Brea, Thomas Goodwin and Thomas Shepherd.

In some ways Whyte is an enigma: although he urged his hearers and readers to read Puritan literature, yet he supported liberal theologians in their studies which undermined much of the previous conservative theological outlook of the Scottish Presbyterian church. In this volume, Whyte includes many comments from Puritan and other Reformed theologians and writers.

Whyte was a strong supporter of the union between the Free Church of Scotland and the United Presbyterian Church which took place in 1900 with the formation of the United Free Church of Scotland.

In this edition of Whyte's *Exposition of the Shorter Catechism*, a few changes have been made. First, the book was initially designed for use in Bible Classes and contained study questions at the end of each chapter; since many of these questions alluded to books now no longer available, it was decided to omit them. Second, in his explanations of the Catechism's Answers, Whyte would direct his reader to consult particular volumes, and since many of these are no longer in print, these directions are also omitted. Third, Whyte often directs his readers to compare the words of the Shorter Catechism with those found under the same theme in the Westminster Confession of Faith and in the Larger Catechism; in order to enable the user to follow Whyte's direction, we have included at the end of the volume the text of both the Westminster Confession and the Larger Catechism.

In connection to the Westminster Confession of Faith, Christian Focus publishes, in its Christian Heritage imprint, Robert Shaw's *Exposition of the Westminster Confession*, and in its Mentor imprint, *The Westminster Confession of Faith in the Twenty-First Century*, a three-volume set in which a range of modern Reformed scholars discuss the teachings of the Westminster Confession.

QUESTION 1

What is the chief end of man?

Answer: Man's chief end[1] *is to glorify God,*[2] *and to enjoy him for ever.*[3]

If an assembly of philosophers had been convened at Athens to compose a catechism of religion and morals for the youth of Greece, to a certainty it would have opened with the very question before us. For almost all the dialogues and discussions of the fathers of moral philosophy revolve around this supreme and everlasting question, What is the final cause and chief end of man? Moral philosophy can put this question, but it is a theology drawn from the Holy Scriptures that can alone supply the answer: Man's chief end is to glorify God, and to enjoy Him for ever.

It has often been pointed out, that full as the Shorter Catechism is of ripe Christian doctrine, it is at the same time cast into a thoroughly scholastic shape. The Westminster Divines who drew this document were deeply-read and scholarly men. 'It is perhaps new to some of our readers to be told, that the profound distinctions of an Aristotle and a Bacon are employed in the construction of that humble primer called The Shorter Catechism' (Macfarlan's Preface to Paterson's Catechism).

Man's chief end ('chief and highest end', Larger Catechism).
Our well-known word *end* most commonly carries the sense of a limit, a boundary, a termination. But it also means an aim, a purpose, an intention, a design. And it is in this latter sense the word is used in the

---

1. So much of every Question, both in the Larger and Shorter Catechisms, is repeated in the Answer as maketh every answer an entire proposition, or sentence, in itself; to the end the learner may further improve it upon all occasions, for his increase in knowledge and piety, even out of the course of catechizing as well as in it (Cornelius Burgess, Prolocutor; Henry Roborough, Scriba; Adoniram Byfield, Scriba).

For an excellent account of the Westminster Assembly, from which the Confession of Faith and the Larger and Shorter Catechisms emanated, the student is recommended to read the introduction to John MacPherson's *Exposition of the Westminster Confession*.

2. 1 Corinthians 10:31: Do all to the glory of God. Romans 11:36: To whom be glory for ever. Amen.

3. Psalm 73:25: Whom have I in heaven but thee? and there is none upon earth that I desire beside thee. Verse 26: God is the strength of my heart, and my portion for ever. Verse 28: But it is good for me to draw near to God.

text. The student will at once see that this question and answer carefully recognize other ends in man besides his 'chief' end. For it could not with propriety be said that man had a 'chief' end unless he had also inferior, secondary and subordinate ends. The Catechism does not concern itself with them, but it is aware of their existence; it implies them in passing by them to pursue man's chief end.

to glorify God

Glory in its scriptural use is a divine word setting forth, struggling to set forth, a divine thing. The divine glory is the revelation of the divine perfections in the works of creation, providence and redemption. God's glory stands originally in His possession of all being, wisdom, power, holiness, justice, goodness, and truth; and He is glorified in the manifestation of Himself to all His receptive and responsive creatures. 'The glory of God,' says Calvin, 'is when we know what He is.' 'Glory is the divinity manifest' (Bengel). In the fourth verse of the seventeenth of John we are supplied with an explanation of this work which will admit of being adapted and applied to the whole creation of God. In our Lord's report and prayer contained in that great chapter, He says, 'I have glorified Thee on the earth.' And then, as if in explanation, He adds, 'I have finished the work which Thou gavest me to do.' Now this same explanation of the word, carried through the whole creation, and adapted to the nature and capacity of each part, will make the meaning of this great word as clear as it is capable of being made. 'Man's chief end,' therefore, is to 'finish the work God has given him to do," and what that work is the Catechism will labour in both its parts to set forth.'

and to enjoy him

Joy is the purest, deepest and most satisfying delight that can possess the heart of man; and the Scriptures continually set forth God as man's chiefest joy. As thus: 'In Thy presence is fulness of joy.... Then will I go to God, my exceeding joy.... Enter thou into the joy of thy Lord.... before the presence of His glory with exceeding joy.' See Answer 38: 'perfectly blessed in the full enjoying of God to all eternity.'

for ever

Never to end, eternal, everlasting. These words *for ever* occur four times altogether in the Catechism. In the answer before us they assure us that our enjoyment of God shall never come to an end. The very same words are found along with the pains of hell in Answer 19; with the continuance of two distinct natures in Christ in Answer 21; and with God's kingdom, power, and glory in Answer 107.

Uses

1. Thomas Carlyle, in speaking against modern materialism in 1876, made this confession: 'The older I grow, and I am now upon the brink of eternity, the more comes back to me the first sentence of the Catechism which I learned when a child, and the fuller and deeper its meaning becomes, "What is the chief end of man? To glorify God, and to enjoy Him for ever." ' And Dr Binnie says: 'Of the numerous excellences that have endeared the Westminster Shorter Catechism to so many churches on both sides of the Atlantic, I am disposed to reckon this among the greatest, that it opens with such a solemn announcement of the nobility of human nature. I know no other Catechism that opens so grandly.'

2. 'Indeed, this seems properly to be an affair of divine revelation. In order to be determined what was designed, in the creating of the astonishing fabric of the universe we behold, it becomes us to attend to, and rely on, what *He* has told us, who was the architect. He best knows His works which He has wrought' (Edwards).

QUESTION 2

What rule hath God given to direct us how we may glorify and enjoy him?

Answer: The word of God, which is contained in the scriptures of the Old and New Testaments[1]*, is the only rule to direct us how we may glorify and enjoy him.*[2]

---

1. 2 Timothy 3:16: All scripture is given by inspiration of God, and is profitable for doctrine, for reproof, for correction, for instruction in righteousness. Ephesians 2:20: Built upon the foundation of the apostles and prophets, Jesus Christ himself being the chief corner-stone.

2. 1 John 1:3-4: That which we have seen and heard declare we unto you, that ye also may have fellowship with us: and truly our fellowship is with the Father, and with his Son Jesus Christ. And these things write we unto you, that your joy may be full.

The student who would understand and appreciate the Shorter Catechism must at every turn attend to the construction and development of this orderly and elaborate work. The foundations of all religion, natural and revealed, have already been laid in the doctrine, 'Man's chief end is to glorify God, and to enjoy Him for ever.' And now the second Question naturally and logically asks: 'What rule hath God given to direct us how we may glorify and enjoy Him?'

The Word

The Word of God is the title of a Divine and Eternal Person before it is applied in a subordinate and historical sense to the communications made through Him, and recorded in the Holy Scriptures (John 1:1, 14; 1 John 1:1; Rev. 19:13). And all the divinity and authority of the written word are ultimately derived from the original divinity and authority of that Divine Person who is the Eternal and Living Word. 'Therefore, as all revelations from heaven are duly designated by the title of the Word of God, so the highest place must be assigned to that substantial Word, the source of all inspiration, which, as being liable to no variation, remains for ever one and the same with God, and is God' (Calvin).

The Word of God in the text, however, does not bear this high sense. 'The Holy Scriptures of the Old and New Testaments are the word of God, the only rule of faith and obedience' (Larger Catechism).

the scriptures

Anything written, writings, documents; but now universally used by way of distinction to describe the canonical books of the Old and New Testaments.

the Old and New Testaments

The word *testament* was originally a term of law. And in legal language it still designates that testifying instrument by means of which a man declares his will as to the disposal of his possessions after his death. The word is used repeatedly in this sense in the Epistle to the Hebrews. To explain fully how it came about that this word *testament* stands as the translation of *covenant*, first in the Latin versions of the Scriptures, and then through the Latin in our own version, would lead us into matter unsuitable for this Commentary. Suffice it to say that the original Greek term is seen passing into our testament through the Scotch law word *disposition*, and that the words *Old and New Testaments* are now appropriated to designate the two collections of canonical books belonging to the two great economies or covenants under which God has successively placed His people (see the Confession, chapter 7: 4-6).

'The Greek word for covenant was never naturalized in the Latin of the Western and African Churches, and the writers of those Churches were for a time undecided as to what equivalent they should use for it, and wavered between *fœdus*, a 'covenant'; *instrumentum*, a 'deed'; and *testamentum*, a 'will'. The earlier Latin writers, such as Tertullian, use both the latter words, but state that the last was the more generally accepted term. As such, it passed first into the early Latin versions of the Scriptures, and then into Jerome's Vulgate, and so became familiar through the whole of Latin Christendom' (Plumptre).

'Tertullian (160-240) is the first writer, I believe, who uses the word "Testamentum" in its ordinary acceptation, though it seems to have been current before his time' (Westcott).

the only rule to direct us how we may glorify and enjoy him

A rule in its proper and original signification is an instrument by means of which we draw the straightest and shortest line from one point to another (Greek, *canon*, a reed or rule, whence come a series of English words, all implying the idea of straightness: cane, canal, channel, cannon, etc.). And accordingly, when the term is used in a moral and religious sense, it imports nothing else than a direction, or instruction, or command, by attending to which a man best attains the end desired. In the polemical phrase, *only rule*, there is a trace left of those burning controversies in which the Reformers and Puritans were engaged with Popish and Prelatic divines. This position was taken up against the Romish and Anglican practice of adding apocryphal writings and oral traditions to the rule of faith as it is contained in the canonical Scriptures. Hooker's *Ecclesiastical Polity*, the greatest work of English theology, and one of the chief ornaments of English literature, rose out of this hot contention. It is a standard work on Anglican doctrine, and as such it is a *via media* between Romanism on the one hand and Puritanism on the other. The Westminster Confession of Faith and the Larger and Shorter Catechisms, on the other hand, are thoroughgoing Protestant symbols on this as on other disputed questions. And the present doctrine of the Catechism is drawn directly against the Romanist position, which maintains that revelation is partly written and partly unwritten; and that the rule of faith includes both Scripture and tradition.

'Tradition is always represented by Romanists as not only the interpreter, but the complement of the Scriptures. The Bible, therefore, according to the Church of Rome, is incomplete. It does not contain all the Church is bound to believe; nor are the doctrines which it does contain therein fully or clearly made known' (Hodge).

But one who once occupied the *via media* on this question, while yet he occupied it wrote thus: 'Scripture has a gift which tradition has not; it is fixed, tangible, accessible, readily applicable, and besides all this, perfectly true in all its parts and relations; in a word, it is a sacred *text*. Tradition gives us little or nothing that can be handled and argued from. We can argue only from a text, we can argue freely only from an inspired text. Thus Scripture is in itself specially fitted for that office which we assign to it in our Article: to be a repository of manifold and various doctrines, a means of proof, a standard of appeal, an umpire and test between truth and falsehood in all emergencies.'

Uses

1. 'Alas! many have the Bible, and use it but little; and many use it amiss, because they know not its right name. It is well warrantably called, from its contents, on its title-page, the Old and New Testaments of our Lord and Saviour Jesus Christ. But how few, in reading this title, mind the use and virtue of the blood of Christ Jesus, which turned the covenant of God's grace into the testament of Christ, and thereby sealed and confirmed all the good words and good things in that covenant!' (Traill).

2. 'Concerning the actual state of man in this world; considering, I say, what he is, any standard of duty which does not convict him of real and multiplied sins, and of his utter inability to please God of his own strength, is untrue; and any rule of life which leaves him contented with himself, without fear, without anxiety, without humiliation, is deceptive; it is the blind leading the blind; yet such, in one shape or other, is the religion of the whole earth beyond the pale of the Christian Church' (Newman).

QUESTION 3

What do the scriptures principally teach?

Answer: The scriptures principally teach what man is to believe concerning God, and what duty God requires of man.[1]

The two first Questions in the Catechism are introductory to the body of the work, as has already been pointed out. And the whole superstructure is exhibited in outline in the present Answer: 'what man is to believe concerning God, and what duty God requires of man.' The Questions from 4 to 38 inclusive, then deal, broadly speaking, with matters of faith (theology), and the Questions from 39 to the end of the work treat principally of duty (morals). These two great divisions contain their own respective sub-divisions, which will be indicated as we meet with them.

principally

There is a great variety of matters treated of in the Scriptures of the Old and New Testaments; but, as this qualifying word points out, their principal intention is to teach 'what man is to believe concerning God, and what duty God requires of man'. Man's chief end is to glorify God, and to enjoy Him for ever, and the Scriptures principally teach him how he is to do so. There are incidental, occasional and subordinate ends that both man and Scripture serve, but their chief and principal end is set forth clearly and correctly in the Catechism.

'Although the Scripture of God, therefore, be stored with infinite variety of matter in all kinds, although it abounds with all sorts of laws, yet the principal intent of Scripture is to deliver the laws of duties supernatural.... The several books of Scripture having each had some several occasion and particular purpose which caused them to be written, the contents thereof are according to the exigence of that special end whereunto they are intended. Hereupon it groweth that every book of Holy Scripture doth take out of all kinds of truth – natural (Eph. 5:29), historical (2 Tim. 3:8), foreign (Tit. 1:12), supernatural (2 Pet. 2:4) – so much as the matter handled requireth' (Hooker).

---

1. 2 Timothy 3:16: All scripture is given by inspiration of God, and is profitable for doctrine, for reproof, for correction, for instruction in righteousness. 2 Timothy 1:13: Hold fast the form of sound words, which thou hast heard of me, in faith and love which is in Christ Jesus.

'It is here intimated that the sacred writings teach some things beside what we are to believe concerning God, and what we are to consider as our duty to Him. The Bible contains a good deal of biography and history, and many genealogies; and all that it contains in unmixed verity, and none of it is without its use. But the word we consider intimates, and the fact is unquestionably so, that some parts of the Scripture are much more important than others. The most important, that is, the principal parts, are those which teach us faith and practice' (Dr Ashbel Green's Lectures).

'Although all Scripture is the word of God, and consequently all equally true, and no part of it undeserving our notice, yet all things in it are not equally important, nor equally connected with eternal salvation. Those things which man is bound to believe and do, as necessary to salvation, are the things which the Scriptures principally teach' (Paterson).

to believe concerning God

Belief is the assent of the mind to what is told us on competent and credible authority. We are said to believe when we are convinced of a fact without our having had immediate and personal knowledge of it. Belief and faith are precisely the same state of mind; the thing is the same, though the names are different. Divines distinguish human faith and divine faith, meaning thereby faith resting on the testimony of man, and faith reposing on the word of God. The latter is the faith or belief of the text. For the broadest and most general description and illustration of divine faith, see Hebrews 11; and for a theological definition of that particular exercise of faith which justifies the sinner in the sight of God, see Questions 33 and 86.

duty

That which we ought to do; that which we are under an obligation to do. We are so constituted in our creation, that when we see anything to be right, we cannot but feel it is our duty to do it. 'An orthodox faith and an obedient life is the whole duty of man.'

Uses

1. 'The general design of Scripture, considered as historical, may be said to be, to give an account of the world, in this single view as God's world; by which it appears essentially distinguished from all other books, so far

as I have found, except such as are copied from it' (Butler).

2. 'Search the Scriptures; for in them ye think ye have eternal life: and they are they which testify of me' (John 5:39).

3. 2 Timothy 3:14-17.

QUESTION 4

What is God?

Answer. God is a Spirit,[1] infinite,[2] eternal,[3] and unchangeable,[4] in his being,[5] wisdom,[6] power,[7] holiness,[8] justice, goodness, and truth.[9]

The compilers of the Catechism have taken our Lord's words to the woman of Samaria as the basis of their answer to the loftiest of all questions, and they have filled up the definition with an enumeration of the divine attributes carefully collected out of Holy Scripture, altogether constructing a statement on this great subject of which Dr Hodge says that it is probably the best definition ever penned by man. The tradition that connected this Answer with a prayer of George Gillespie's in the Westminster Assembly is now discredited by our best authorities.

---

1. John 4:24: God is a Spirit: and they that worship him must worship him in spirit and in truth.

2. Job 11:7: Canst thou by searching find out God? canst thou find out the Almighty unto perfection? Verse 8: It is as high as heaven; what canst thou do? deeper than hell; what canst thou know? Verse 9: The measure thereof is longer than the earth, and broader than the sea.

3. Psalm 90:2: Before the mountains were brought forth, or ever thou hadst formed the earth and the world, even from everlasting to everlasting thou art God.

4. James 1:17: ...the Father of lights, with whom is no variableness, neither shadow of turning.

5 Exodus 3:14: And God said unto Moses, I AM THAT I AM; and he said, Thus shalt thou say unto the children of Israel, I AM hath sent me unto you.

6. Psalm 147:5: Great is our Lord, and of great power: his understanding is infinite.

7. Revelation 4:8: Holy, holy, holy, Lord God Almighty, which was, and is, and is to come.

8. Revelation 15:4: Who shall not fear thee, O Lord, and glorify thy name? for thou only art holy: for all nations shall come and worship before thee; for thy judgments are made manifest.

9 Exodus 34:6: And the LORD passed by before him, and proclaimed, The LORD, The LORD God, ...abundant in goodness and truth, Verse 7: Keeping mercy for thousands, forgiving iniquity, and transgression, and sin, and that will by no means clear the guilty; visiting the iniquity of the fathers upon the children, and upon the children's children.

God

'The old Saxon word "God" is identical with good. God is the good One, personified goodness. There is in that derivation not a mere play upon words, there is a deep truth' (Frederick Robertson). But Webster says: 'As this word and good are written exactly alike in Anglo-Saxon, it has been inferred that God was named from His goodness. But this is probably an idea too remote from the rude conceptions of men in early ages. With the exception of the word Jehovah [see Q. 44], the name of the Supreme Being appears usually to have reference to His supremacy or power, and to be equivalent to lord or ruler. In the present case there is some evidence that this is the sense of this word; for in Persian *Godd* signifies lord, master, prince, or ruler.' And Skeat, our latest and best authority on etymological questions, says: 'God, the Supreme Being.... The name is of unknown origin; quite distinct and separate from good, with which it has often been conjecturally connected.'

God is a Spirit, or better, both in grammar and theology, 'God is Spirit.' 'God is pure Spirit, perhaps better not "a Spirit," since it is His essence, not His personality, which is here spoken of' (Alford). Compare the two other definitions found in 1 John 1:5, 'God is light,' and 4:16, 'God is love', with which this present definition must, in Westcott's words, be 'compared and combined'.

This word Spirit, 'the profoundest word in human language' (Stier), as employed in Scripture and theology, like so much of their vocabulary, bears a figurative or metaphorical sense. The growth of the word is something like this. It first means air, the air that is the atmosphere of the earth, and the breath of all its living creatures. From this it is a short and easy step to become expressive of the life of man, and the life of his soul, as in the cry: 'Into Thine hand I commit my spirit.' And from that highest earthly use the word has been taken up and consecrated to describe for us the manner of God's own life: 'God is Spirit.' And this single expression at once does this great service for us, that it removes God's nature far from all association with material and corporal organization. For, as our Lord said: 'A spirit hath not flesh and bones, as ye see me have.' God, then, is Spirit, such as the Scripture and the Catechism teach us concerning Him.

'RESOLVED upon the question, Hath God any body, or is He to be seen with bodily eyes? – A. God is a Spirit, invisible, without body or bodily parts, not like a man or any other creature. ORDERED. Q. Since you say God cannot be seen, how do you know that there is a God? A. I am sure there is a God, because the things that are in the world could neither have their being nor their preservation, nor be ordered as they are, without God' (*Minutes of Session of Westminster Assembly*, 714, September 22, 1646, Tuesday morning).

infinite

Without limit or boundary. We cannot cross a line and say, 'Now here God is not; here is a limit which He has not passed, and cannot pass.' 'Trismegistus sayd God is a circle, whose centre is everywhere, but His circumference is noe where.' This word is used here, as always in Scripture, in a theological and religious, rather than a philosophical and speculative way. This attitude of God is set forth in Scripture and in the Catechism less for the satisfaction of the intellect than for exercise of the affections, imaginations and consciences of men. And thus the Scriptures bring the awful doctrine of the divine infinitude to bear on us in the most affecting and practical way. 'Am I a God at hand, saith the LORD, and not a God afar off? Can any hide himself in secret places that I shall not see him? saith the LORD. Do not I fill heaven and earth? saith the LORD' (Jer. 23:23, 24). And this attribute rightly and religiously reflected on, will always awaken adoration and godly fear after this manner:

> O LORD, Thou hast searched me and know me.... Thou hast beset me behind and before, and laid Thine hand upon me. Whither shall I go from Thy Spirit, or whither shall I flee from Thy presence? If I ascend into heaven, Thou art there; if I make my bed in hell, behold, Thou art there. Such knowledge is too wonderful for me: it is high, I cannot attain unto it'(Ps. 139:1,5-8).

In this way those for whom the Catechism is designed may be profitably and impressively taught what the greatest minds cannot comprehend. 'Thou hast hid these things from the wise and prudent, and hast revealed them unto babes' (Matt. 11:25).

eternal

As we associate infinitude with unbounded space, so we are compelled to think of eternity as unbeginning and unending time.

'But as the substance of God alone is infinite, and hath no kind of limitation, so likewise His continuance is from everlasting to everlasting, and knoweth neither beginning nor end.... Out of this we gather that only God hath true immortality or eternity, that is to say, continuance wherein there groweth no difference by addition of hereafter unto now; whereas the noblest and perfectest of all beings besides have continually through continuance the time of former continuance lengthened. So that they could not heretofore be said to have continued so long as now, neither now so long as hereafter' (Hooker).

The divine name *The Eternal*, is connected with the great name *Jehovah*, *I am*, He who *is*, He who alone truly and eternally *is*, the Self-existing, the Everlasting. 'The Hebrews attached a higher and more solemn meaning to eternal existence than to creative energy. In Revelation 1:8, God is called the Alpha and the Omega, the beginning and the end, He who was and is and is to come, three epithets signifying eternity, which are followed by one only, – the Almighty, indicating power' (Ewald). The Arabic version of Exodus 3:14 has 'The Eternal who never passeth away,' where the English has 'I AM THAT I AM.'

'In my solitary and retired imagination I remember that I am not alone, and therefore forget not to contemplate Him and His attributes, who is ever with me, especially those two mighty ones, His wisdom and eternity. With the one I recreate, and with the other I confound my understanding. In eternity there is no distinction of tenses; for to His eternity, which is indivisible and all together, the last trump is already sounded, the reprobate is in the flame, and the blessed in Abraham's bosom' (*Religio Medici*).

unchangeable

This also is spoken of only as it bears on our faith and trust. He is 'the Father of lights, with whom is no variableness, neither shadow of turning'. And when it is said that He changes, and repents, and takes back for good or evil that which He has spoken, all that again is but a fuller application of the principle of condescension on which all divine revelations are made: God speaking to man in ways that man can understand.

in his being

The foregoing words – *infinite, eternal,* and *unchangeable* – characterize and describe the being, wisdom, power, holiness, justice, goodness and truth of God. He is infinite, eternal and unchangeable in each and all of these attributes. 'Being' expresses reality of existence as contrasted with non-existence. Thus Jehovah, I AM, signifies BEING; originality, eternity, unchangeableness, and fruitfulness of being. The I AM thus becomes known as the Eternal.

'The true name of Being is proper to God only; the creatures are in themselves but shadows and appearances of beings. God alone is' (Goodwin).

wisdom

'Knowing all things, most wise' (Larger Catechism). When spoken of as an attribute of man, wisdom, while comprehending certain intellectual qualities, gives much more prominence to the moral. Taking its rise necessarily in the mind, wisdom attains its fulness only in the depth and purity of the heart. There cannot, indeed, be wisdom where there is no knowledge; but there may be great stores of learning and knowledge where there is a total absence of wisdom. Knowledge often puffeth up; wisdom always buildeth up. And it is wisdom in its purest and noblest sense that is here applied to God. In the Old Testament, especially in the later and what are called the sapiential books, the Divine Wisdom attains a prominence, and vividness, and distinction among the other attributes of God that prepare the way for the advent of that Divine Person who is afterwards announced as the Wisdom and the Word of God. But here again the gracious, the religious, and the practical aspects of the truth govern and subordinate the philosophical and speculative ideas.

power

Infinite in power. Hence God is often in Scripture spoken of as the Almighty, or the Omnipotent. 'The word Almighty conveys three ideas: that God is omnipotent, His dominion universal, and His essence infinite.'

'God's power is limited only by the workings of His will. He doth not work all things that He might work. "Unto Thee," saith Christ, "all things are possible." God doth not show Himself omnipotent by doing all He can do, but everything that He doth do He showeth an almighty power in it' (Goodwin).

holiness

'This word is nothing but Middle English *hool* (now spelt whole). The original sense is perfect or excellent' (Skeat). Holiness, therefore, etymologically, as well as theologically and religiously, is inward health or spiritual wholesomeness.

'It is instructive to note how the Psalmist dwells upon the holy name of God, as if His holiness were dearest to him, or perhaps because the holiness or wholeness of God was to his mind the grandest motive for rendering to Him the homage of his nature in its wholeness. Babes may praise the divine goodness, but fathers in grace magnify His holiness' (Spurgeon).

'Holiness is intellectual beauty. Divine holiness is the most perfect and the measure of all other.... The divine holiness is the most perfect pulchritude, "the ineffable and immortal pulchritude, that cannot be declared by words or seen with eyes," – they are a heathen's expression concerning it. This may therefore be styled a transcendental attribute, that, as it were, runs through the rest, and casts a glory upon every one. It is an attribute of attributes. Those are fit predications, holy power, holy truth, holy love. And so it is the very lustre and glory of His other perfections, He is "glorious in holiness" ' (Howe).

justice

Integrity and uprightness as of a true judge with whom is no respect of persons. The Scriptures reveal the divine law as the foundation of all God's dealings with men. Whatever else in God is manifested to man, His justice is never set aside or forgotten. Even in justifying the ungodly, the justice of God is magnified.

'Nothing is more precisely according to the truth of things than divine justice; it weighs things in an even balance; it views and estimates things no otherwise than they are truly in their own natures' (Edwards). And the greatest teacher of morals outside the Hebrew dispensation, taught that 'in justice every virtue is summarily comprehended'.

goodness

'Goodness is the genus that comprehends mercy, grace, long-suffering, kindness, truth, etc. in it; these are branches from that as the root' (Goodwin).

'From the beginning of the world till now, all effluxes which have come from God have been nothing but emanations of His goodness, clothed in variety of circumstances. He made man with no other design than that man should be happy, and by receiving derivations from His fountain of mercy, might reflect glory to Him.... And grace is the treasure of the divine goodness, the great and admirable efflux of the eternal beneficence, "the riches of His goodness," which whosoever despises, despises himself and the great interests of his own felicity; he shall die in his impenitence, and perish in his folly' (Jeremy Taylor).

'"For He is good." Is not this the Old Testament of "God is love"?' (Andrew Bonar).

and truth

It is clear that truth as an attribute of God must mean something far nobler than fact or information, a common use of the word in the ordinary speech of mankind. Neither is truth to be taken here merely as opposed to error, falsehood and deceit. When our Lord, addressing His Father, said, 'Thy word is truth,' He had something far greater in His mind than merely that God's word is true and trustworthy. Truth in the text and in our Lord's prayer embraces the whole revelation of God that has been at any time, or in any manner, made to man; all that it is God's glory to reveal, and man's blessedness to believe and enjoy. Truth, the highest and surest truth, is that God is true, and that Jesus Christ is His Truth. 'I am the Way, the *Truth*, and the Life.'

'Truth is grace clad with a promise and put forth in exercise' (Bengel).

'Now there are other spirits besides God: and these are angels and the souls of men. But the difference betwixt God and them lies here, that God is an infinite, eternal, and unchangeable Spirit, and they are not so. The attributes of God, as perfections of His divine nature, are of two sorts, incommunicable and communicable. His incommunicable attributes, whereof there is no vestige in the creation, are His infinity, eternity, and unchangeableness. His communicable attributes again, whereof there are some scantlings in the creatures, are His being, wisdom, power, holiness, justice, goodness, and truth. The difference between these perfections as they are in God and as they are in His creatures, lies here, that they are all infinite, eternal, and unchangeable in God, but in His creatures not so' (Boston).

Use

With this Question we are entering on the doctrinal division of the Catechism. Now it was the teaching of our Lord in His conversation with the woman of Samaria, that all acceptable and profitable worship must rest on the fundamental doctrine so fully set forth in this Answer. Our Lord puts the profoundest of all doctrines just where the Catechism, following His example, puts it, as one of the first principles of faith and worship. And there is not one word in the statement before us that will not sensibly assist an intelligent and devout mind in the worship of God. Rightly used, the Creeds and Catechisms of the Church are really devotional guides. The doctrines of Revelation are coals of heavenly fire on the altar of the religious heart. 'The formula, which embodies a dogma for the theologian, readily suggests an object for the worshipper.... Theology may stand as a substantive science without the life of religion; but religion cannot maintain its ground without theology' (Newman).

QUESTION 5

Are there more Gods than one?

Answer: There is but One only, the living and true God.[1]

Having given us our Lord's definition or description of what God is, and having supplemented that definition by fathering round it a cluster of His scriptural attributes, the Catechism proceeds to ask, God being such, 'Are there more Gods than one?' And the answer is made, 'There is but One only, the living and true God.' 'Thus,' says an eminent teacher of Christian truth, 'we must ever commence in all our teaching concerning the Holy Trinity: we must not begin by saying that there are Three, and then go on to say afterwards that there is One, lest we give false notions of the nature of that One; but we must begin by laying down the great truth that there is One God, in a simple and strict sense, and then go on to speak of Three, which is the way in which the mystery was progressively revealed in Scripture. In the Old Testament we read of the Unity; in the New, we are enlightened in the knowledge of the Trinity.' The Old Testament taught that 'God is a Spirit, infinite, eternal, and unchangeable in His being, wisdom, power, holiness, justice, goodness, and truth.' The

1. Deuteronomy 6:4: Hear, O Israel; The LORD our God is one LORD. Jeremiah 10:10: But the LORD is the true God, he is the living God, and an everlasting King.

unity and spirituality of God formed the article of a standing or falling Church in that early dispensation of grace and truth.

One only

'The words "one" and "only," ascribe to God in Scripture, are not used in contrast to the Son or the Holy Spirit, but rather with reference to those who are not God, and are falsely called so' (Basil).

'One,' in this connection, is not used in the sense of numeration; it points to an absolute aloneness rather than to plurality and accumulation. This has been called a transcendental unity, or the oneness of what is indivisible. Thus it has been said: 'To apply arithmetical notions to God is as unphilosophical as profane.... He is not One in the way in which created things are severally units; for one, as applied to ourselves, is used in contrast to two or three and a whole series of numbers. But God has not even such relation to His creatures as to allow, philosophically speaking, of our contrasting Him with them' (Newman).

'Our divines, therefore, reckon not God, in point of arithmetic, together with us. They cast not God and us into the same numbering. They suffer not creatures to bear or sustain the repute or account of numbers after Him, or when He is spoken of. They say of Him that He is *unicus* [unique], the only One, who stands apart by Himself, out of all arithmetic, as His transcendent being comes not under our logic' (Goodwin).

the living and true God

Living in the supreme sense of having life in Himself, and thus being the Fountain of life to all His creatures. 'For in Him we live, and move, and have our being' (Acts 17:28). 'No name is so free from the taint of anthropomorphism, or of anything incongruous and degrading, as the living God' (Goldwin Smith, *Bystander*, ii. 141). And true as distinguished from all false gods. This doctrine of God was the ground of all the prophetical preaching and controversy in the Old Testament: 'Hear, O Israel, the LORD our God is one LORD' (Deut. 6:4, see Q. 44). And Paul, treating of things offered to idols, made a restatement of this fundamental position of the Hebrew and Christian faith: 'We know that an idol is nothing in the world, and that there is none other God but one. To us there is but one God, the Father, of whom we are all things, and we in Him' (1 Cor. 8:4, 6).

QUESTION 6

How many persons are there in the Godhead?

Answer: There are three persons in the Godhead; the Father, the Son, and the Holy Ghost; and these three are one God, the same in substance, equal in power and glory.[1]

Familiar to us as the doctrine of the Trinity is, yet it must never be forgotten what it cost the early Church to bring this fundamental truth out of the Scriptures and get it inserted in the Creed. There was an immense expenditure of learned theological labour before this doctrine was finally formulated and universally accepted in the Church of Christ. In his chapter on the Trinity, Dr. Hodge maintains that this doctrine is peculiar to the religion of the Bible, and that, like all Bible truths, it is not an abstract, speculative and notional truth, but is most fundamental and vital to the whole Christian faith. And he endorses Meyer's words, to the effect that 'the Trinity is the point in which all Christian ideas and interests unite; at once the beginning and the end of all insight into Christianity.'

There are three persons

'Lat. *per-sona*, a mask used by an actor, a personage, character, part played by an actor, a person. The large-mouthed masks worn by the actors were so called from the resonance of the voice sounding through them' (Skeat). It is a long step from the original sense of the word 'person' to that usage we are most familiar with when it is applied to an individual of the human race. But it is a still longer step from our ordinary usage of the words up to the scriptural and theological acceptation when applied to the Three in the Divine Nature. It is utterly inadequate to set forth the manner of Their subsistence, but the Latin theologians could find no better, no less inadequate word in their tongue, and the modern languages of Christendom have not as yet developed any more adequate term. We must be content to call Father, Son, and Holy Ghost *Persons*; but while we do so, we must always remember that They are utterly unlike any personalities we have ever known.

---

1. Matthew 28:19: Go ye therefore, and teach all nations, baptizing them in the name of the Father, and of the Son, and of the Holy Ghost.

'In modern philosophical usage, the term person means a separate and distinct rational individual. But the Tri-personality of God is not a numerical or essential trinity of three beings, like Abraham, Isaac, or Jacob, for this would be Tritheism; nor is it only, on the other hand, merely a threefold aspect and mode of manifestation in the Sabellian or Swedenborgian sense; but it is a real, objective, and eternal, though ineffable distinction in one Divine Being' (Schaff, *Creeds*, 2:70).

'The scriptural facts are: (a) The Father says I; the Son says I; the Spirit says I. (b) The Father says Thou to the Son, and the Son says Thou to the Father; and in like manner the Father and the Son use the pronouns He and Him in reference to the Spirit. (c) The Father loves the Son; the Son loves the Father; the Spirit testifies of the Son.... The summation of these and kindred facts is expressed in the proposition: The one Divine Being subsists in Three Persons: Father, Son, and Spirit' (Hodge).

the Godhead

'Divinity, Divine Nature.... The suffix is wholly different from English – head, being the same suffix as that which is commonly written – hood. The etymology is from A.S. *hád*, office, state, dignity' (Skeat). By the Godhead is meant the Divine Nature. And a Person in the Godhead is the whole Godhead distinguished by 'personal properties'. The Godhead neither is nor can be divided into parts; each of the Three Persons hath in Himself the one whole indivisible Godhead. But, as has been said, they are distinguished by their personal properties – that is to say, it is the personal property of the Father to beget the Son (Heb. 1:5); and of the Son to be begotten of the Father (John 1:14); and of the Holy Ghost to proceed from the Father and the Son (John 15:26; Gal. 4:6).

'So the personal properties make no inequality among them; forasmuch as these properties are not temporary or accidental, but eternal and necessary, and could not but be; and every one of the three persons is the eternal, the supreme, and the most high God' (Boston).

And, accordingly, just as manhood signifies that human nature, possessing which we are men, so, in some such way, the Godhead is that divine nature which the three divine persons equally possess, and are therefore equally and eternally God. In manhood there are a multitude of persons that no man can number, but in the Godhead there are three persons only –Father, Son, and Holy Ghost.

the Father

The name of father is a relative name, father and son. Paternity is a relation of origin and production, but it is not every kind of production that properly constitutes paternity: paternity is production by generation. Now the Scriptures call the relation that eternally obtains between the First Person and the Second, Fatherhood and Sonship; and they teach that it is originated by a 'begetting'; but here also all earthly figures and phrases utterly fail us when we treat of the Divine Fatherhood and the Divine Filiation. The Son is of the Father; the Father is the Fountain of His Divine Nature; but as to how the Son is generated – before questions like this reason and revelation are alike dumb. Still, there is nothing clearer in Holy Scripture than this, that there is a Person in the Divine Nature who is constantly spoken of as the Father, and Another who is as constantly spoken of as the Son. The First Person calls the Second Person His Son; He treats Him always as His Son; He sends Him forth and sustains Him; and He receives Him back again, and rewards Him as His Son. While, on the other hand, the Second Person calls on His Father, serves Him, obeys Him, puts His trust in Him, and at last returns home to Him. And this is not a mere economical, conditioned and figurative relation; for above and apart from their historical and redemptive relations to us at all, the First Person and the Second are represented in Scripture as eternally existing under the internal relations of the Father and Son.

the Son

The Son is set forth as eternally and continually 'begotten'; or, as an incomprehensible and yet most vivid Scripture says, He is 'in the bosom of the Father'. And this eternal generation of the Son is the ultimate ground of His Godhead; that is to say, He is God because He is the Son of God; and He is the Son because He has His Godhead by a divine and eternal generation. And thus He is able to say, 'I and the Father are one,' and also at the same time to say, 'The Father is greater than I.' One, because begotten of the Father, and therefore the same in substance, equal in power and glory. While the Father is the *greater*, as being before and above the Son in order of existence, and as being eternally and continually the source of the Godhead and Sonship life.

Calvin commends Augustine for the following explanation: 'Christ, as to Himself is called God, but as to the Father He is called Son. The

Father, as to Himself is called God, but as to the Son He is called Father. He who, as to the Son is called Father, is not Son; and He who, as to the Father is called Son, is the same God.'

the Holy Ghost

'The Third Person of the Trinity is called the Spirit by way of eminence, probably for two reasons: first, because He is the power of efficiency of God; and secondly, to express His relations to the other persons of the Trinity. The Son is called the Word as the revealer or image of God, and the Third Person is called Spirit as the breath or power of God. He is also called predominantly the Holy Spirit, to indicate both His nature and operations. He is absolutely holy in His own nature, and the cause of holiness in all creatures. For the same reason He is called the Spirit of Truth, the Spirit of Wisdom, of Peace, of Love, of Glory' (Hodge).

'The Holy Ghost receiveth the same essence from the Father that the Son receiveth, and thereby becometh the same God with the Father and the Word; but though the essence be the same that is communicated, yet there is a difference in the communication: the Word being God by generation, the Holy Ghost by procession; and though everything that is begotten proceedeth, yet everything which proceedeth is not begotten. Wherefore in the language of the Sacred Scriptures and the Church, the Holy Ghost is never said to be begotten, but to proceed from the Father; nor is He ever called the Son, but the gift of God' (Pearson).

'The Spirit of God bears the name of Holy in the New Testament where His more special title is "the Holy Ghost," as our old English hath rendered it to us. But is not the Father holy, and the Son holy, and Both equally holy with the Holy Ghost? Yes, essentially and personally holy in themselves: 'Holy, Holy, Holy,' they are all proclaimed (Isa. 6:3). How is it then that He, the Third Person, should have the peculiar title of Holy? It is neither in a peculiar, neither in a personal or essential respect, but relatively unto that which is His proper and peculiar work, because He sanctifies us and makes us holy, and so merits the name of Holy Ghost as Christ doth of Saviour, and the Father doth of Father' (Goodwin).

these three are one God

'This is the Catholic faith, that we worship one God in Trinity and Trinity in Unity. Neither confounding the Persons nor dividing the substance' (Athanasian Creed).

'It seems to me nothing can be more admirable than the words of Gregory Nazianzen: "I cannot think of the Unity without being irradiated by the Trinity: I cannot distinguish between the Trinity without being carried up to the Unity"' (Calvin).

'The Father is the one simple, entire Divine Being, and so is the Son; they do in no sense share divinity between them: each is whole God. This is not ditheism or tritheism, for they are the same God; nor is it Sabellianism, for they are eternally distinct and substantive Persons; but it is a depth and height beyond our intellect, how that which is Two in so full a sense, can also in so full a sense be One, or how the Divine Nature does not come under number' (Newman's *Notes on Athanasius*).

Where all is mystery, we may not properly speak of any part being more mysterious; but perhaps of all the mysterious aspects of the blessed Trinity as they are presented to us in Scripture, the most mysterious is that which has been called the Mutual Indwelling of the three Divine Persons. Theology, both Greek and Latin, has had to coin terms to set forth this mystery. This intimate union was named by the Greeks the *Perichoresis*, and by the Latins *Inhabitatio*. These scientific terms were struck out to express the scriptural facts that the Son is always in the Father, and the Father in the Son: that the blessed Three dwell in each other. As in all this exposition we here fall back on Athanasius and his annotator Dr. Newman. 'A Perichoresis of Persons is implied in the unity of substance. This is the connection of the two texts so often quoted: "The Son is in the Father, and the Father is in the Son," because "the Son and the Father are one." And the cause of this unity and Perichoresis is the Divine Begetting.' 'The Perichoresis was the test of orthodoxy.'

the same in substance

'Substance' as here used is a scientific or theological term; that is to say, it is not found in Scripture, but has had to be coined by scriptural students for their use, and for the service of the truth. The word 'substance' in its etymology means that which in matter or mind underlies and sustains all phenomenal manifestation. Popularly, we associate the word more with matter than with spirit, but it is equally suitable and serviceable as applied to both. Philosophically taken, substance means that in matter which underlies, and so to speak supports, all the attributes or qualities of matter. Locke gives the primary qualities of matter as extension, figure, divisibility, motion, hardness, softness, fluidity. And accordingly substance, as its name implies, is that mysterious and inaccessible background which stands behind and sustains all these its qualities. And so it is in the spiritual world. The substance treated of in the Catechism is that awful, mysterious essence of which the qualities are not extension, or colour, or figure, or fluidity; but the qualities that the Divine Substance supports are infinite and eternal wisdom, power, holiness, justice, goodness, and truth. These qualities are, so to speak, the phenomena that the inscrutable Divine Substance presents to us. God, then, as to His Substance, is Divine Spirit; and as to the phenomena, or qualities, or attributes of that uncreated, eternal, Divine Substance, they are such as we have already learned.

It was for this phrase, 'the same in substance,' that Athanasius carried on his splendid and successful contention before the Ecumenical Council of Nice in the fourth century. And thus it is that Athanasius leaves his mark on our own Catechism, as on all the symbolical and confessional books of the Christian Church since his day. He saw that this word consubstantial, of one and the same substance, was the only word that would assert without ambiguity or possibility of gainsaying the scriptural doctrine of the perfect and eternal Godhead of Jesus Christ. And by the blessing of God on his great talents and his heroic stand, the Godhead of our Lord has ever since been safely fixed in the Church's Creed; sheltered, so to speak, under the shield of the consubstantiality which Athanasius fashioned and hung up before it. By scriptural, Athanasian, Nicene doctrine then we are taught that there are three Persons in the Godhead, who are the same in substance, and that that same substance sustains in each Person the same properties or attributes of divine wisdom, power, holiness, justice, goodness, and truth.

equal in power and glory

'The divinity of the Father, and of the Son, and of the Holy Ghost is one, the glory equal, and the majesty equal.... And in this Trinity there is nothing prior or posterior, nothing greater or less, but all three Persons are co-eternal and co-equal in themselves' (Athanasian Creed). 'Are the three Hypostases or Persons of the Most Holy Trinity all of equal majesty? Yes; all of absolutely equal divine majesty. The Father is true God; the Son is equally true God; and the Holy Ghost true God; but yet so that in the three Persons there is only one Tri-Personal God' (Eastern Church Catechism).

Q. How doth it appear that the Son and the Holy Ghost are God equal with the Father? A. The Scriptures manifest that the Son and the Holy Ghost are equal with the Father, ascribing unto them such names, attributes, works, and worship, as are proper to God only (Westminster Larger Catechism).

Uses

1. 'The design of all the revelations contained in the word of God is the salvation of men. Truth is in order to holiness. God does not make known His being and attributes to teach men science, but to bring them to the saving knowledge of Himself.... This is specially true of the doctrine of the Trinity' (Hodge).

2. 'What will it avail thee to dispute profoundly of the Trinity, if thou be void of humility, and art thereby displeasing to the Trinity? Surely high words do not make a man holy and just: but a virtuous life maketh him dear to God' (à Kempis).

3. 'May we never speak on subjects like this without awe; may we never dispute without charity; may we never inquire without a careful endeavour, with God's aid, to sanctify our knowledge, and to impress it on our hearts, as well as to store it in our understandings' (Newman).

QUESTION 7

What are the decrees of God?

Answer: The decrees of God are his eternal purpose, according to the counsel of his will, whereby, for his own glory, he hath foreordained whatsoever comes to pass.[1]

The decrees of God

A decree is a determination, an edict, a rule. It is an order from one having supreme authority, deciding what is to be done by a subordinate.

'The word decree, or decrees, in the sense in which it is used in this Answer, is not found in the New Testament. It is a technical term,

---

1. Ephesians 1:4: According as he hath chosen us in him before the foundation of the world. Verse 11: Being predestinated according to the purpose of him who worketh all things after the counsel of his own will. Romans 9:23: The vessels of mercy, which he had afore prepared unto glory.

adopted by theologians to convey a complex idea; that is, to convey a number of ideas by a single term. The express design of the answer is to explain this term, and it is done almost wholly in the words of inspiration' (Green's Lectures).

'The Scripture speaks of God's decrees, condescending therein to the conceptions of men.... Yet, what is in man imperfectly, is to be looked on as an image of God's proceedings herein, in a transcendent way of perfection' (Goodwin).

'God does not do what He does, nor order what He orders, accidentally and unawares; either without or beside His intention. And if there be a foregoing design of doing and ordering as He does, this is the same with a purpose or decree' (Edwards).

'The consideration of this great doctrine runs up into the most profound and inaccessible subjects that can occupy the minds of men – the nature and attributes, the purposes and actings, of the infinite and incomprehensible Jehovah – viewed especially in their bearings upon the everlasting destinies of His intelligent creatures.... Many men have indulged in the most presumptuous and irreverent speculation concerning it. There is probably no subject that has occupied more of the attention of intelligent men in every age.... All that the highest ability, ingenuity, and acuteness can effect has been brought to bear upon the discussion of this subject; but the difficulties attaching to it have never been solved, and we are well warranted in saying that they never will, unless either God give us a fuller revelation, or greatly enlarged capacities, although, perhaps, it would be more correct to say, that, from the very nature of the case, a finite being can never fully comprehend it, since this would imply that he could fully comprehend the infinite mind' (Cunningham).

Archbishop Leighton maintains that the utterances of the Catechism on the divine decrees are worthy of the subject: few, sober, clear, and certain.

his eternal purpose

'The second point included in this doctrine is, that the decrees of God are all reducible to one purpose.... They are not successively formed as the emergency arises, but are all parts of one all-comprehending plan.... As, however, this one purpose includes an indefinite number of events, and as these events are mutually related, we therefore speak of the decrees of God as many, and as having a certain order' (Hodge).

the counsel of his will

'You know counsel referreth to the understanding, to the judgment. It is a considering what one meaneth to do, how to do it, and to do it the best way, and most wisely: that is properly counsel. There is something in counsel which is in man which must not be attributed unto God, and something in man which may be attributed unto God: for we must cut off all imperfection in what we attribute unto God. There are two things in counsel in a man. There is, first, a discourse and inquiry which is best; he setteth his reason a-work, and one thought cometh in after another. And then there is, secondly, a judgment, when he hath considered all, which is best. Now, the first part we must cut off from God; He doth not advise and deliberate as men do, to take this thing, or that thing, one after another, by way of inquiry into His mind. No, for known unto God are all His works from eternity. How then is counsel attributed unto God? Thus: that which is the result, that which ariseth in men's minds or judgments out of inquiry, a mature pitching upon what is best: this view, which is the perfection of counsel, which is the ripening and maturing of it, this is attributed unto God. This is certain *judicium*, a certain judgment of what is best to do' (Goodwin).

for his own glory

'The general end of God's external working is the exercise of His most glorious and most abundant virtues.... Not that anything is made to be beneficial unto Him, but all things for Him to show beneficence and grace in them' (Hooker). See Question 1.

whatsoever comes to pass

With this proviso, which is given in Hodge's words: 'The decretive and the preceptive will of God can never be in conflict. God never decrees to do, or to cause others to do, what He forbids. He permits men to sin, although sin is forbidden. But God cannot decree to make men sin.' See Question 13.

Uses

1. 'The doctrine of this high mystery is to be handled with special prudence and care' (Confession). And Turretine maintains that it should be taught, yet he says it is a subject more proper for the school than the pulpit.

2. 'Doth God work all things according to His will? Then give up thy will to Him. "It is not in man that walketh to direct his steps" (Jer. 10:23). It is God that must direct them for thee, for He works all things according to His will. If any man in the world, if his understanding and will were a rule to mine, and I knew he were infallible, I would certainly go give up all my ways to what he saith. As you say you must be ruled by him who bears the purse, so you must be ruled by him who bears the understanding. Certainly, if any man hath an infallible understanding, I will be ruled by him. God hath: He works all things, and all effectually, by the counsel of His own will. Therefore in all thy ways give up thyself to Him' (Goodwin).

QUESTION 8

How doth God execute his decrees?

Answer: God executeth his decrees in the works of creation and providence.

QUESTION 9

What is the work of creation?

Answer: The work of creation is God's making all things of nothing, by the word of his power, in the space of six days, and all very good.[1]

creation
The act of creating: especially the divine act of bringing all things beyond the Divine Nature into existence. 'In the beginning God created the heaven and the earth' (Gen. 1:1).

out of nothing
'The clause "out of nothing" is vital in defining a creative act' (Shedd). This is directed against those ancient heathen speculations which taught

1. Genesis 1 throughout. Hebrews 11:3: Through faith we understand that the worlds were framed by the word of God, so that things which are seen were not made of things which do appear.

that matter was eternal: that there were two necessary and eternal beings, God and matter. But it is the teaching of the Bible and of the Catechism that there is only one necessary and eternal Being, and that He is the absolute Creator of everything beyond Himself. On Romans 11:36, Goodwin remarks: 'Not so much as a first matter was existing to His hands.' And in his extraordinarily able and suggestive treatise, of the Creatures, he says: 'All things were once nothing, and all afflictions and miseries are smaller vacillations or reelings of the creatures toward their first nothing.... The whole creation is built upon a quagmire of nothing, and is continually ready to sink into it, and to be swallowed up by it, which maketh the whole or any part of it to quake and quiver when God is angry, as Jeremiah then did (10:24).'

'The Divine Father, by the strange fecundity of His omnipotent power, first made the clay out of nothing, and then made man out of that' (Pearson).

in the space of six days

'According to the commonly received chronology, our globe has existed only a few thousand years. According to geologists, it must have existed for countless ages. And again, according to the generally received interpretation of the first chapter of Genesis, the process of creation was completed in six days; whereas geology teaches that it must have been in progress through periods of time that cannot be computed.... It is of course admitted that, taking this account by itself, it would be most natural to understand the word "day" in its ordinary sense; but if that sense brings the Mosaic account into conflict with facts, and another sense avoids such conflict, then it is obligatory on us to adopt that other. Now it is urged that if the word "day" be taken in the sense of "an indefinite period of time", a sense which it undoubtedly has in other parts of Scripture, there is not only no discrepancy between the Mosaic account of the creation and the assumed facts of geology, but there is a marvellous coincidence between them' (Hodge).

all very good

Manes (whence Manichæism), a Persian philosopher, taught the dualistic doctrine of creation. He held that there are two eternal principles or powers, the one good and the other evil; and that all creation, visible and invisible, material and spiritual, has sprung from those two sources. Those two sources, so ran the dualistic doctrine, were eternally and essentially contrary the one to the other, wherefore they were named light and darkness, good and evil, God and matter. This doctrine worked much mischief in patristic times: Augustine's early life was devoted to its promulgation, and the doctrines he preached were only too well illustrated in his life. The Bible doctrine of creation overturns all such speculation. 'The being of God is a kind of law to His working: for that perfection which God is giveth perfection to that He doth' (Hooker).

Use

Butler says that the Scriptures begin with an account of God's creation of the world and man in order to acquaint man with his origin, and to enable him to trace his life and preservation to his Creator, and to connect all men with Him of whom the whole book treats, and of whose laws and revelations the whole book is full. The history of creation has not been written to make scientific research superfluous, but to guide learned and simple to religious contemplation and thought on nature and their own creation and preservation.

QUESTION 10

How did God create man?

> *Answer: God created man male and female, after his own image, in knowledge, righteousness, and holiness, with dominion over the creatures.*[1]

God created man

As if to mark off and signalize the creation of man from that of all the other creatures, there is a striking change in the manner in which the sixth

1. Genesis 1:26-28: And God said, Let us make man in our image, after our likeness; and let them have dominion over the fish of the sea, and over the fowl of the air, and over the cattle, and over all the earth, and over every creeping thing that creepeth upon the earth. So God created man in his own image, in the image of God created he him; male and female created he them. And God blessed them, and God said unto them, Be fruitful, and multiply, and replenish the earth, and subdue it; and have dominion over the fish of the sea, and over the fowl of the air, and over every living thing that moveth upon the earth. Colossians 3:10: And have put on the new man, which is renewed in knowledge after the image of him that created him. Ephesians 4:24: And that ye put on the new man, which after God is created in righteousness and true holiness.

day's work is recorded. Hitherto the Creator had spoken 'by the word of His power', and all things immediately became as He commanded. But when we are introduced to the work of the sixth day, we discover a remarkable modification in the narrative; and instead of a creative command, as on the preceding days, there is heard the language rather of counsel, deliberation and resolution. The Creator now speaks as if a work was about to be wrought altogether distinct from, and immeasurably superior to, all that had hitherto been made. For God said: 'Let us make man in our image, after our likeness.... So God created man in His own image, in the image of God created He him: Male and female created He them.' And with more detail in another place: 'The LORD God formed man of the dust of the ground, and breathed into his nostrils the breath of life; and man became a living soul.' All which produces on the reader, and must have been intended to produce, the impression that man by his peculiar creation is separated off on all sides from connection with the rest of the creatures, except as completing them and being their monarch and their end. In the posture of deliberation and mutual counsel in which God reveals Himself when proceeding to create mankind; in His so signally connecting mankind with the Godhead through putting man in possession of the Divine Image; and in the royal, and, so to speak, divine position He gave Adam over all the rest of creation – in all this there was secured for man a clear and indubitable charter of his divine origin and heavenly relationship.

man

'The sense is thinking animal, from Sanskrit *man*, to think; the animal with mind' (Skeat).

after his own image

An image is any imitation, resemblance, or similitude of another thing. It is anything drawn, painted, sculptured, or otherwise fashioned to represent some person or thing. And such is the capacity of the word 'image', that it is applied in a great number of senses, and is put to a great variety of uses, one of the noblest of which we are now to elucidate. There was a twofold act or process in the creation of man; and accordingly two substances enter into his complex constitution. 'The LORD God formed man of the dust of the ground, and breathed into his nostrils the breath of life; and man became a living soul.' Now in searching in man for the divine image that was impressed upon him in his creation, we at once pass beyond all that in man which was 'made of the dust of the ground'. For no formation of dust, not even when it is refined and elaborated into flesh and blood, can carry an impression of the image of God. It is not therefore in man's body, erect, noble, fair, beaming with intelligence and girded with strength as it is, that the divine image stands; but in his soul, in his mind and conscience and heart, or as the Catechism has it, in his 'knowledge, righteousness, and holiness'. At the same time, the doctrine of divine image in man cannot now be fully and thoroughly studied in Adam: we must see it preserved and exhibited in a yet greater than he, if we would understand it even as it originally existed in him. We must go above Adam to Him who made him, to Him who is eternally 'the express image of the Father's person'. Indeed, most that we know of Adam's state before his fall, we learn afterwards from the provision made in the 'second Adam' to restore and reinstate man in his lost knowledge, righteousness, holiness and dominion.

'So then after all the other things, Moses says that man was made in the image and likeness of God. And he says well, for nothing that is born on the earth is more resembling God than man. And let no one think that he is able to judge of this likeness from the character of the body; for neither is God a being with the form of a man, nor is the human body like the form of God, but the resemblance is spoken of with reference to the most important part of the soul, namely, the mind.... But as it is not every image that resembles its archetypal model, since many are unlike, Moses has shown this by adding to the words, "after His image" the expression, "in His likeness," to prove that it means an accurate impression, having a clear and evident resemblance in form' (Philo).

And in a very remarkable fragment of his lost works the same writer says: 'Why, then, does God use the expression, "In the image of God made I man," as if He were speaking of that of some other God, and not of having made him in the likeness of Himself? This expression is used with great beauty and wisdom. For it was impossible that anything mortal should be made in the likeness of the Most High God, the Father of the universe; but it could only be made in the likeness of the Second God, who is the Word of the other; for it was fitting that the rational type in the soul of man should receive the impression of the Word of God.'

'Spirits only are made in God's image, as if of His race, or as children of His house, since they only can serve Him freely, and knowingly act in imitation of the Divine Nature. One spirit alone is worth more than a whole world, since it not only expresses that world, but knows it also, and is governed in it as God orders. So that it seems, that whilst every substance expresses the universe, other substances express the world rather than God, but spirits express God rather than the world' (Leibnitz).

in knowledge

In man as he came from the hand of God, there was a rich fountain of knowledge springing up within him. There was in him a deep well of intuitional truth, which secretly filled his understanding and heart and conscience. God has all knowledge by intuition, by direct and immediate vision; and He made man in His own image in this respect, that man had immediately and intuitionally a knowledge of God and duty and doubtless of many other things that we now have to toil painfully after if we would attain to it. Men learned in the matters of the mind assure us that there is still a deep well of intuitional truth, a fountain of innate ideas that opens spontaneously in every human soul. Our father Adam drank of this well, and in spite of all that has been done to choke it, it still rises within the soul. The Light that shone so fully on Adam at his creation, still lighteth every man that cometh into the world.

'Adam's heart was the common ark of mankind, and though the tables be lost, yet our ignorance doth not make the law of none effect. For the law of nature for ever binds; that is, all that was written in Adam's heart, because it was thereby then published in him, and to him for us' (Goodwin).

righteousness

In etymology and in fact, the word 'righteousness' means rectitude, obedience. Righteousness is a relation, a relation of conformity in all respects to the law under which any one is made subject. And accordingly the text teaches that man was created in the most perfect conformity to the moral law, under which as a creature of God he was for ever to live. Measured immediately on his creation by that divine law, man was pronounced by His Maker and Lawgiver and Judge 'very good'. It is in this sense that our divines speak of Adam's 'natural justification'.

and holiness

For the root and original meaning of this noble and inward word, see Answer 4.

Man's original righteousness and holiness corresponded somewhat to his justification and sanctification in his redeemed and evangelical estate. His holiness, if it is possible to say so, was something more personal, more inward, and more spiritual than even his righteousness. His holiness was, and was to be, the hidden root of his outward righteousness; his root and sap and fatness as a tree of righteousness, the planting of the Lord. He would stand in righteousness, in fruitfulness, and in acceptance only as his holiness was preserved unimpaired and untainted. Bengel seems to favour this distinction when he says that righteousness corresponds to the Divine Will; holiness, as it were, to the whole of the Divine Nature. 'The parts of the image of God impressed on man's soul were knowledge on his mind, righteousness on his will, and holiness on his affections' (Boston).

dominion over the creatures

This last feature or accompaniment of the Divine Image is borrowed in as many words from God's fatherly and 'prolifical benediction' pronounced over Adam and Eve: 'And God blessed them, and said unto them, Be fruitful, and multiply, and replenish the earth, and subdue it; and have dominion over the fish of the sea, and over the fowl of the air, and over every living thing that moveth upon the earth' (Gen. 1:28; see Ps. 8).

'God appointed man lord of the world, and this authority was given to Adam's posterity as well as to himself. And hence we infer what was the end for which all things were created, namely, that none of the conveniences and necessaries of life should be wanting to man. In the very order of the creation the paternal solicitude of God for man is conspicuous, because he furnished the world with all things needful, and even with an immense profusion of wealth, before he formed man. Thus man was rich before he was born. But if God had such care for us before we existed, He will by no means leave us destitute of food and other necessaries of life, now that He has placed us in this world. And if He often keeps His hand closed toward us, to what is this to be imputed but to our sins?' (Calvin).

Uses

I. 'If a man should be able to assent to this doctrine as he ought, that we are all sprung from God, I suppose that he would never have any ignoble or mean thought about himself. Many incline to their kinship with the animals, which is miserable and mortal, and some few to their kinship with the gods, which is divine and happy. See then that through this kinship with the flesh you do not become savage, and bestial, and untamed' (Epictetus).

2. Every case of conversion is a new act of creation. 'We are His workmanship created in Christ Jesus.'

3. Every thought, word, and deed of sin strikes at the image of Christ in the soul.

QUESTION 11

What are God's works of providence?

Answer: God's works of providence are his most holy,[1] wise,[2] and powerful preserving[3] and governing all his creatures and all their actions.[4]

providence

The word 'providence' belongs to a large and well-known family of English words. The idea that lies under them all is that of foresight: foreseeing what is coming, and making due provision for it. The term 'providence' can scarcely be claimed as a scriptural word; the almost exclusive appropriation of the word to a sacred use is later than our translation, but it is already put to its present high religious use in *Paradise Lost*. In the noble invocation of the Holy Ghost, at the commencement of his first book, Milton says:

'What in me is dark,
Illumine; what is low, raise and support;
That to the height of this great argument
I may assert Eternal Providence,
And justify the ways of God to men.

1. Psalm 145:17: The LORD is righteous in all his ways, and holy in all his works.

2. Psalm 104:24: O LORD, how manifold are thy works! in wisdom hast thou made them all: the earth is full of thy riches. Isaiah 28:29: This also cometh forth from the LORD of hosts, which is wonderful in counsel, and excellent in working.

3. Hebrews 1:3: Upholding all things by the word of his power.

4. Psalm 103:19: The LORD hath prepared his throne in the heavens; and his kingdom ruleth over all. Matthew 10:29-31: Are not two sparrows sold for a farthing? and one of them shall not fall on the ground without your Father. But the very hairs of your head are all numbered. Fear ye not therefore, ye are of more value than many sparrows.

This is the loftiest sense the word ever bears; it occurs in a more familiar sense at the close of the same work:

> The world was all before them, where to choose
> Their place of rest, and Providence their guide.

According to the definition supplied by the Catechism, God's works of providence embrace two distinct functions – preserving all His creatures, and governing all His creatures and all their actions – both functions being fulfilled with divine holiness, wisdom and power.

preserving
'Providence must extend itself as large as creation. For what is providence but a continuance of creation; a preservation of those things in being that God hath given to have a being' (Sibbes).

But Dr. Hodge, one of the ablest of our Calvinistic divines, says: 'Creation, preservation, and government are in fact different, and to identify them leads not only to confusion but to error. Creation and preservation differ; first, as the former is the calling into existence of what did not exist, and the latter is continuing, or causing to continue, what already has a being; and secondly, in creation there is and can be no co-operation, but in preservation there is a concursus of the first with second causes. In the Bible, therefore, the two things are never confounded. God created all things, and by Him all things consist.'

governing
Steering, directing, ruling, from the Latin *gubernare*, to steer a ship. 'It is true indeed that Plato seems to acknowledge a certain plastic or methodical nature in the universe, subordinate to the Deity, or the Perfect Mind, which is the supreme Governor of all things' (Cudworth).

all his creatures
All His creatures are embraced in God's works of providence; but all are not capable of receiving and sustaining the same degree of care and rule. As we rise in the scale of creation, it is clear that more and more care and rule is needed to preserve and govern the nobler creatures. Hence it is

put as a special section of the Confession, that as 'the providence of God doth, in general, reach to all creatures; so, after a special manner, it taketh care of the Church, and disposeth all things to the good thereof.'

and all their actions

The truth as so stated is too high for us. It is too stupendous a thought. We cannot picture it in our imagination. We receive it on the testimony of Scripture, but we cannot reason it out in a thesis so as to compel all men's assent and reverence and trust. It has never been by reasoning that these awful truths have possessed the heart and conscience and imagination and will of man. We must ourselves, one by one, believingly and with a filial heart, live under God's providences in order to realize them aright. But by this means we come, as life goes on, to amass an amount of evidence that no unbelief or doubt can suffice to gainsay. When we are so brought under the power of this great truth, it is with daily increasing awe, wonder and expectation that we watch God's providence preserving and governing us; His searching, penetrating and discriminating dealings with ourselves become a daily worship and solemn joy to us. It seems sometimes as if all other lives were preserved and governed for our good, for our trial and temptation, for our probation and benefit, for our reward or punishment; so completely may we come under this great law of God's government, that we shall seem to ourselves to be the very centre of all God's providential dealings, a centre towards which 'all things work together for good'. It is not so much by a dialectic and philosophical and theological mind that these things are apprehended; it is in the quick and responsive conscience, and in the new and ever wakeful heart, that God makes the clearest discoveries of His holy providences. 'I thank Thee, O Father, Lord of heaven and earth, because Thou hast hid these things from the wise and prudent, and hast revealed them unto babes' (Matt. 11:25).

Uses

1. A great lesson lies for us in the very etymology of the leading word. It speaks to us of One who sees our way before we have trod it. One moreover who has taken on Himself to provide all we need as we travel the way He has appointed us. Even the heathen world had some hold of this truth, and hence the most thoughtful and devout among them taught and practised augury and divination, grounding their inquiries into the mind and will of God on the assurance that He had a mind and purpose about

every man and his lot and way in life. And thus Paul speaks to the Athenians of all nations seeking God, if haply they might find Him. The doctrines and the experience of Providence have taught us that God is not far from any one of us, for in Him we live and move and have our being.

2. For those who say they are waiting on providence to discover their duty. Providences are not appointed as guides in life. They show God's path rather than point out ours. It is not His purpose, hidden in a decree or fulfilled in a providence, that is our rule of faith and life, but His word. 'We are not to go in businesses merely by providences, for we shall find that oftentimes providences do lay fair occasions for sinning. When Jonah was to go Tarshish, he had the fairest providences that could be; he found a ship all ready; ay, but he went against the word of God. Never be ruled by providences, they may be temptations and probations; be ruled by the word alone' (Goodwin).

3. 'The providence of God in the lives of men is to each one in particular a private revelation of His love' (Faber).

4. The Scriptures are full of assurances and illustrations of the consoling truth that grace mingles with all providences, and carries them out to her own blessed ends. In a multitude of passages, we are assured that our Redeemer is our King and Protector (John 17:1, 2; Rom. 8:28; Rev. 7:1-3).

QUESTION 12

What special act of providence did God exercise toward man in the estate wherein he was created?

Answer: When God had created man, he entered into a covenant of life with him, upon condition of perfect obedience; forbidding him to eat of the tree of the knowledge of good and evil, upon the pain of death.[1]

Immediately after the definition of providence given in the eleventh Answer, there is an illustration supplied in the twelfth. 'What special act of providence did God exercise?' and the Answer before us is the reply. See Question 20, Larger Catechism, for a much fuller account of the providence of God toward man in his creation estate.

---

1. Galatians 3:12: And the law is not of faith: but, The man that doeth them shall live in them. Genesis 2:17: But of the tree of the knowledge of good and evil, thou shalt not eat of it: for in the day that thou eatest thereof thou shalt surely die.

a covenant of life

'The word covenant is not to be found in the three first chapters of Genesis, but the spirit of the word is there, and the term itself is expressly predicated of the transactions there recorded when referred to in other parts of the Old Testament; see Hosea 6:7, marg.' (Tayler Lewis).

This covenant is more commonly known as the covenant of works to distinguish it from the coming covenant of grace. Both were covenants of life, in that life was the reward of both. 'And the Holy Ghost calls that blessedness of the old covenant of works life, but never salvation, for you are saved by grace' (Goodwin).

The covenant of life is here called a 'special act of providence', because Adam had many other providential arrangements around him, and duties devolving upon him, besides those specially embraced in this covenant. But amid all his creative abundance and comfort, and over and above his 'original righteousness,' God saw good to lay a positive law on Adam, and to suspend all his blessedness, and even life itself, upon it. That special act of providence was intended to teach Adam self-restraint, self-conquest and unquestioning obedience to the Divine Will. 'The first covenant under which Adam was created is termed by divines *fœdus naturæ*, the covenant of nature; that is, of man's condition, which from and by his creation was natural to him; yet I would rather call it the creation law, *jus creationis*, or that which was equitable between God, considered merely as a Creator on one part, and His intelligent creatures which were endued with will and understanding on the other' (Goodwin). See Larger Catechism, Question 20.

upon condition of perfect obedience

'God will not be honoured with exceptions, nor will He allow us to cut off from His law what is less pleasing to us. It is not said of a part of the law (Jas. 2:10), "This is the way, walk ye in it" ' (Calvin).

'A man is spotted though he have only one stain; a cup is broken, if only the top be broken; one disease will make a man sick; and there are a hundred ways to wander in, but only one to life and immortality' (Jeremy Taylor).

'The solidarity of the law is such, that it does not admit of being broken in one point, and yet kept in the whole' (Alford).

forbidding him to eat of the tree of knowledge

The tree of knowledge of good and evil stood in the midst of the garden as a trial of obedience, and as a sign and a seal of the solemn word, 'in the day thou eatest thereof thou shalt surely die' (Gen. 2:17). Both the tree of life and the tree of the knowledge of good and evil received their names 'not from any virtue in them' of good and evil, but entirely from the will and dispensation of the Lord God. They were set apart from all the other trees not because of anything in their own nature, but solely from their economical and sacramental rank in Adam's covenant. The tree of knowledge was a tree of trial; Adam's probation for good or evil was suspended upon it.

'Now it was very proper to make trial of his obedience by such a command as this, because the reason of it is fetched purely from the will of the lawmaker. Adam had in his nature an aversion to that which was evil in itself, and therefore he is tried in a thing that was evil only because it was forbidden; and being in a small thing, it was the more fit to prove his obedience by' (Matthew Henry).

'Knowledge is here taken disparagingly, in a bad sense, for that wretched experience which man began to acquire for himself' (Calvin).

upon the pain of death

'The wilful sinner has deserved death. Having used the gift of life to revolt against Him from whom he holds it, it is just that this gift should be withdrawn from him. Hence the sentence: In the day thou sinnest, thou shalt die. Every act of sin should thus, in strict justice, be followed by death, the violent and instant death of its author' (Godet).

But death here is something far deeper and more awful than the dissolution of the body. Death in the Bible sense is sinfulness; guilt and inward corruption, with all the unspeakable miseries that flow from them.

'It appears to me that the definition of this death is to be sought from its opposite; we must, I say, remember from what kind of life man fell.... The miseries and evils both of soul and body, with which man is beset so long as he is on earth, are a kind of entrance into death, till death itself entirely absorbs him.... Therefore the question is superfluous, how it was that God threatened death to Adam on the day in which he should touch the fruit, when He long delayed the punishment. For then Adam was consigned to death, and death began its reign in him, until supervening grace should bring a remedy' (Calvin).

Uses

1. 'There is no religion without this idea of a covenant with a personal God, and therefore all such views as those of Comte, Mill and Spencer

are, for all moral and religious purposes, wholly atheistical. They acknowledge no personality in God; they cannot use the personal pronouns in speaking of Him or to Him. It may, in truth, be said that all religion is covenant, even when religion appears in its most perverted form' (Tayler Lewis).

2. 'It is of great importance that the scriptural form of presenting truth should be retained. Rationalism was introduced into the Church under the guise of a philosophical statement of the truths of the Bible free from the outward form in which the sacred writers, trained in Judaism, had presented them. On this ground the federal system as it was called, was discarded.... It is far more than a mere matter of method that is involved in adhering to the scriptural form of presenting scriptural truths' (Hodge).

3. 'Observe, that even Adam in innocency was awed by a threatening. Fear is one of the handles of the soul by which it is taken hold of and held. If he then needed this hedge, much more do we need it now' (Matt. Henry).

QUESTION 13

Did our first parents continue in the estate wherein they were created?

Answer: Our first parents, being left to the freedom of their own will, fell from the estate wherein they were created, by sinning against God.[1]

being left to the freedom of their own will

It is a very mysterious thing that God should so 'innovate upon His own eternity' as to summon into existence a race of creatures, and bestow upon them the perilous gift of free-will: a perilous and in the event a fatal gift: because, as experience proved, the possessor of it might rise up against his Maker, might oppose and obstruct His will, and introduce sin and misery and death where life and love and holiness had been intended to dwell.

---

1. Genesis 3:6: And when the woman saw that the tree was good for food, and that it was pleasant to the eyes, and a tree to be desired to make one wise, she took of the fruit thereof, and did eat; and gave also unto her husband with her, and he did eat. Verse 8: And Adam and his wife hid themselves from the presence of the LORD God amongst the trees of the garden. Ecclesiastes 7:29: Lo, this only have I found, that God hath made man upright; but they have sought out many inventions.

'Freedom of will is a power in the will, whereby it doth of its own accord, without force upon it, choose or refuse what is proposed to it by the understanding. And man hath this freedom of will in whatever state he be. In the state of innocency it extendeth to good or evil; in the state of corrupt nature, to evil only; in the state of grace, partly to good and partly to evil; and in the state of glory, only to good' (Boston).

'The practice of distinguishing, in the exposition of this subject, between the freedom of man's will in his unfallen and in his fallen condition, and indeed of viewing it distinctively with reference to the different stages or periods of his fourfold state – as unfallen, fallen, regenerate, or glorified – has prevailed in the Church in almost all ages. These views were fully brought out and applied by Augustine.... They were embraced and promulgated by the whole body of Reformers, both Lutheran and Calvinistic.... They have a prominent place in the West-minster Confession, the 9th chapter, entitled "Of Free Will," being entirely devoted to the statement of them' (Cunningham's Essay, *Calvinism, and the Doctrine of Philosophical Necessity*).

fell

The Fall is a technical theological term, appropriated to that catastrophe which is described at length in the third chapter of Genesis, and assumed throughout Scripture. The expression in this historical and original sense is not found in Scripture; its earliest use is in Wisdom 10:1.

'fell...by sinning against God.' Judas by transgression fell (Acts 1:25). The words crime and criminal belong to every language; but sin and sinner belong exclusively to the vocabulary of the Christian revelation' (de Maistre).

'The word sin, just because it denotes the Godward side of moral evil, branding it as a transgression of moral law, is excluded from the vocabulary of certain philosophical schools, and is seldom heard from the lips of worldly men' (Binnie).

Uses

1. 'Many there be that complain of Divine Providence for suffering Adam to transgress. Foolish tongues! When God gave him reason, He gave him freedom to choose; for reason is but choosing: he had been else a meer artificiall Adam, such an Adam as he is in the motions' (*Areopagitica*).

2. 'The sovereign will must be granted a right of freedom – that freedom which by putting it into our wills He surely teaches us to honour in His' (Drummond's *Natural Law*).

3. 'The Bible account of the fall and sin, instead of vilifying human nature, implies the highest view of man and his constitution.... It is mere perversion of thought and language, however, to represent man's experience of moral evil as not a fall but a rise' (Laidlaw).

4. Butler shows that the supposition of the fall is the ground of the Christian dispensation.

5. Edward Irving goes further: 'The very end of the fall was to put the proper distance between the Creator and the creatures: and to show the creature that the source and the continuance of its being was from God, and not in any way from itself. And if any one ask me, Could not this without a fall, have been accomplished? I am ready to answer, As to that I cannot tell; but I believe that this was the best way of accomplishing it.'

QUESTION 14

What is sin?

Answer: Sin is any want of conformity unto, or transgression of, the law of God.[1]

Sin
Wickedness, iniquity, crime. Skeat follows Curtius in tracing the root to a Teutonic base, 'to be.' 'Language regards the *guilty* man as the man *who it was*' (cf. Gen. 3:12, 13; 2 Sam. 12:7; Rom. 7:9).

But Wedgewood gives the Norse root *Sund*, sundered, separated, Germ. Sünde; cp. Sound of Mull: ethical, to separate as guilt does. 'Your iniquities have separated between you and your God' (Isa. 59:2). (See Answer 25.)

want of conformity
Whoso committeth sin transgresseth also the law; for sin is the transgression of the law, and where no law is there is no transgression. The law of God is the rule given to man for all his actions, and wherein

1. 1 John 3:4: Whosoever committeth sin transgresseth also the law: for sin is the transgression of the law.

he does not conform his actions to that rule he has committed sin. We may commit sin either by doing what we ought not to do, or by not doing what it is our duty to do. We may become guilty either by commission or omission. Want of conformity here means sins of omission, and transgression means the commission of actual deeds of sin. This two-edged definition is admirably observed and illustrated in the analysis of the Ten Commandments given in the practical parts of the Catechism. Under each commandment it is asked, What is required? and, What is forbidden? In other words, What is 'conformity' here? and what is 'transgression'?

Augustine defines sin as *factum vel dictum vel concupitum aliquid contra æternam legem*, every work, word, or wish contrary to the law of God. And Trench in his *New Testament Synonyms* gathers a 'mournfully numerous' group of words out of Holy Scripture, all of which describe sin in one or other of its many aspects. It is the missing of a mark or aim; it is the over-passing or transgression of a line; it is disobedience to a voice; it is falling where one should have stood upright; it is ignorance of what one ought to have known; it is any diminishing of that which should have been rendered in full measure; it is non-observance of a law; it is a discord, and other evil things and ways 'almost out of number'.

'Sin is no other thing than disagreeableness, in a moral agent, to the law, or rule of his duty. And therefore the degree of sin is to be judged by the rule; so much disagreeableness to the rule, so much sin, whether it be in defect or excess.... Sin is an abominable defect, and appears so to the saints, especially those that are eminent' (Edwards).

Use

'Shall I speak the least evil I can say of sin? It is an evil, which in the nature and essence of it, virtually and eminently contains all evils of all kinds that are in the world, insomuch as in the Scriptures you shall find that all the evils of the world serve but to answer for it, and to give names to it. Hence sin, it is called poison, and sinners, serpents; sin is called a vomit, and sinners, dogs; it is the stench of graves, and they rotten sepulchres; it is mire, sinners, sows; and sin, darkness, blindness, shame, nakedness, folly, madness, death, whatever is filthy, defective, infective, painful.... It is so evil that it cannot have a worse epithet given to it than itself; and therefore the apostle, when he would speak his worst of it, and wind up his expression highest, *usque ad hyperbolem*, calls it by its own name, sinful sin (Rom. 7:13).... It is sinning sin, you cannot call it by a worse name than its own' (Goodwin).

QUESTION 15

What was the sin whereby our first parents fell from the estate wherein they were created?

Answer: The sin whereby our first parents fell from the estate wherein they were created, was their eating the forbidden fruit.[1]

the forbidden fruit

'There was no evil in the fruit itself. The evil of the matter lay in man's eating it against the express command of God. God forbade it to be eaten, for the trial of man's obedience. And the fitness of taking trial of man by that means, appears in that so it was taken in an external thing, in itself indifferent, wherein man's obedience behoved to turn precisely upon the point of the will of God' (Boston).

'The opinion of some of the ancients, that our first parents were allured by intemperance of appetite, is puerile. Augustine is more correct, who says that pride was the beginning of all evils, and that by pride the human race was ruined.... Unbelief was the root of defection, just as faith alone unites us to God' (Calvin).

QUESTION 16

Did all mankind fall in Adam's first transgression?

Answer: The covenant being made with Adam, not only for himself, but for his posterity; all mankind, descending from him by ordinary generation, sinned in him, and fell with him, in his first transgression.[2]

---

1. Genesis 3:6. Verse 12: The woman whom thou gavest to be with me, she gave me of the tree, and I did eat.

2. Romans 5:12: Wherefore, as by one man sin entered into the world, and death by sin; and so death passed upon all men, for that all have sinned. 1 Corinthians 15:21: For since by

The covenant – See Answer 12.

Adam

A Hebrew word signifying red, ground colour. But the generic term Adam becomes in the case of the first man a denominative. The name may possibly have been given to embody the history of his creation. Some scholars hold, on the other hand, that the name comes from a similar Hebrew root, meaning likeness; and that the allusion consequently is to the divine fiat: 'Let us make man after our likeness' (Gen. 1:26).

not only for himself, but for his posterity

'With Adam as a publick person' (Larger Catechism). Read Romans 5:12-19. 'God made and appointed Adam to be a public person, yet not so out of mere will, but that it had also for its foundation so natural and necessary a ground, as it was rather a natural than a voluntary thing.... Now the natural necessity upon which this designation of him to be a public person was made is this: God had, as the author of nature, made this law of nature, that man should beget in his image or likeness.... So then, in this first man the whole nature of man being reposited, therefore what befalls this nature in him by any action of his, that nature is to be propagated from him' (Goodwin).

by ordinary generation

This exception is taken because of the extraordinary generation of our Lord in His incarnation. His birth was so ordered by God that He was the Son of man, one of the human race, and yet that the entail of original sin did not embrace Him. God, in ways we cannot fathom, but at the same time in ways that show us that a singular exception was here made to the otherwise universal traduction of original sin, sent His Eternal Son in our nature, and yet did not send Him through Adam. The birth of Christ was rather a creation of a new humanity than a propagation and sanctification of the old. His flesh was the flesh of Adam's race, sanctified and united to the personality of the Son of God. Adam was the type of Christ, but he was not His father.

---

man came death, by man came also the resurrection of the dead. Verse 22: For as in Adam all die, even so in Christ shall all be made alive.

'The man Christ was not included in that representation which Adam made as head of the covenant of works (1 Cor. 15:22, 45); and that, because Christ came not in virtue of the blessings of fruitfulness, given while the covenant of works stood entire, but in virtue of a special promise made after it was broken (Gen. 1:28; 3:15). Adam's sin, then, could not be imputed to the man Christ, since Adam did not represent Him in the covenant' (Boston).

'The formation of His human nature was the effect of miraculous, supernatural creating power; therefore he was no more liable to Adam's sin, as being man, than a world of men would be, should God create them out of the dust of the ground, which would be no more miraculous or supernatural than it was to form the human nature of Christ in the womb of the Virgin. Now, as Jesus, so formed, would not be concerned in Adam's sin, or fall, whatever similitude there might be of nature; even so our Saviour was not concerned therein' (Ridgely).

all mankind ...sinned in him

That is to say, we were so in Adam that what he did we did, not indeed as to the act, but as to its consequences. Human life is full of this vicarious, solidary way of acting and suffering, and this was the first and most terrible example of it. 'To be guilty of Adam's sin, meant in the Latin anthropology, to be guilty of the Adamic sin. It implied the oneness of Adam and his posterity, and a guilt that belonged to the sum total, only because the sin was the act of the sum total' (Shedd).

fell with him

'Fell with him in that first transgression' (Larger Catechism). 'O thou Adam, what hast thou done? For though it was thou that sinned, thou art not fallen alone, but we all that come of thee' (2 Esdras 7:48).

'It is improper to say, Adam's eating of the forbidden fruit was personally and inherently an act of mine. It was personally his, and imputatively mine: personally his, because he did it; imputatively mine, because I was then in him. Indeed, the effects of his personal eating is found in my person; to wit, defilement and pravity' (Bunyan).

in his first transgression

Those divines who go most deeply into these matters, believe that they have sufficient scriptural and theological ground for holding that Adam's headship ceased with his fall.

Use

'Our very nature is sinful. Herein is the importance of the doctrine of original sin. It is very humbling, and as such the only true introduction of the preaching of the gospel. Men do not like to be told that the race from which they spring is degenerate. We know how ashamed men are of being low born or discreditably connected. This is the sort of shame forced upon every son of Adam. "Thy first father hath sinned" is the legend on our forehead' (Newman).

QUESTION 17

Into what estate did the fall bring mankind?

Answer: The fall brought mankind into an estate of sin and misery.[1]

sin and misery

Sin is both guilt and disease. Man's depravity, therefore, is the object of both vengeance and compassion, as the Catechism proceeds to set forth.

QUESTION 18

Wherein consists the sinfulness of that estate whereinto man fell?

Answer: The sinfulness of that estate whereinto man fell, consists in the guilt of Adam's first sin, the want of original righteousness, and the corruption of his whole nature, which is commonly called Original Sin; together with all actual transgressions which proceed from it.[2]

---

1. Romans 5:12: Wherefore, as by one man sin entered into the world, and death by sin; and so death passed upon all men, for that all have sinned..

2. Romans 5:12: Wherefore, as by one man sin entered into the world, and death by sin; and so death passed upon all men, for that all have sinned. Verse 19: By one man's disobedience many were made sinners. Romans 5:10-20. Ephesians 2:1: Dead in trespasses and sins. Verse 2: Wherein in time past ye walked according to the course of this world ...children of disobedience. Verse 3: ...by nature the children of wrath, even as others. James 1:14: But every man is tempted, when he is drawn away of his own lust, and enticed. Verse 15: Then, when lust hath conceived, it bringeth forth sin; and sin, when it is finished, bringeth forth death. Matthew 15:19: For out of the heart proceed evil thoughts, murders, adulteries, fornications, thefts, false witness, blasphemies

This Question deals with some of the most profound and important matters in the whole range of revealed and experimental religion. And the Answer supplies a clear, careful and every way admirable statement of Pauline, Augustinian, and Calvinistic doctrine. In language the most scriptural and theologically exact, the guilt and corruption of Adam, and through him of all mankind, are here set forth. And the foundations are here laid deep for that noble structure of gospel truth that is soon to rise before us. The most that can be done in the notes to such a condensed mass of doctrine as this Answer contains, is to call the student's attention to the main outlines of the several doctrines here set forth, and especially to indicate where the best teaching is to be found on the profound but most personal and urgent truths here enunciated.

the guilt of Adam's first sin
'Guilt. Properly conduct which has to be atoned for, which has to be paid for. Debt, return of equivalent' (Wedgwood). 'Crime, punishable offence. The original sense was probably a fine or a payment by way of recompense for a trespass; and the word is to be connected with *gyld*, a recompense. Both words are from the Teutonic base *gald*, to pay' (Skeat). But words become shaped and fitted to things; and as human life becomes enlarged and enriched, or again degraded and impoverished, so human language expands or contracts itself to life and experience. And accordingly, while guilt in the text retains all its etymological significance, yet here the further element is necessarily added of representation, suretyship and solidarity. If there is anything fixed in theological language, it is the sense of the word guilt. And if there is anything in which Calvinists are agreed, it is in saying that when they affirm 'that the guilt of Adam's sin has come upon us', they mean exposure to punishment on account of that sin. The first and commonest meaning of this word undoubtedly is that liability to punishment that follows a personal act of illegality. But all history, and literature, and experience sustain the Calvinistic use of the word. We all suffer daily through the wrong-doing of others. And often the guilt of others, of those over us, and in a place to act for us – statesmen, parents, representatives – is imputed to us in exactly the Pauline and catechetical sense. Turretine says that the union or relationship which is to serve as the ground of imputation may be threefold: natural, as between the father and his children; moral and political, as between the king and his subjects; voluntary, as among friends, and

between the guilty and his substitute. The bond between Adam and his posterity is twofold: natural, as he is a father and we are his children; and political and forensic, as he was the prince and representative head of the whole human race. And Owen, in his great work *On Justification*, says that things that are not our own may yet be imputed to us, and that by a rule of perfect righteousness. Things done by one may be imputed to another *propter relationem fœderalem*, because of a covenant relation between them. So the sin of Adam was and is imputed to all his posterity. And the ground of this is, that we stood in the same covenant with him, naturally and morally, who was our head and representative.

the want of original righteousness
The Catechism, following Scripture, here teaches that mankind have now lost that 'righteousness' which as a race we were created with. We are not only a disinherited family, but we are personally depraved and demoralized. We are born in sin; we are born sinners. The image of God is all but obliterated in us; it is altogether obliterated in its best features. Consult Answer 10 as to what we had and what we have lost.

the corruption of his whole nature

'Corruption. The state of being corrupt or putrid; the process of putrefaction; putrescence; taint. Loss of purity and integrity; depravity, wickedness' (Webster). The word is used in morals and religion in a metaphorical sense, and means moral putrescence and pollution.

'If a man is able to do a right action, and does a wrong one, he is personally guilty indeed, but it cannot be said that his nature is corrupt. The passions and affections may be inconveniently strong, and so the nature be at a disadvantage; but no mere strength of the passions and affections shows the nature corrupt so long as the will retains its power.... The test of a sound or corrupt nature, then, is an able or an impotent will; and if a corruption of nature means anything at all, it means the loss of free-will. This was the legitimate advance that was wanted in the Western Church to complete the expression of the doctrine; and this complement it was left to St. Augustine to give' (Mozley).

'The corruption of human nature might be a doctrine of theology, but it was also a fact in natural history. If a naturalist could come from Jupiter or Saturn to describe the inhabitants of this earth, he would say that man alone had instincts and tendencies which were constantly leading him to courses of action injurious and fatal to himself and to the race to which he belonged. This corruption was a fact in natural history' (Duke of Argyll in the House of Lords, June 28, 1883).

'Nor is it any proof to the contrary that men often excel in generosity of disposition, undertake designs apparently honourable, and put forth evidences of virtue.... For all such things which please us with the colour of virtue, are like wine spoiled with the flavour of the cask' (Calvin).

Commenting on Zechariah 14:12, Dr. Moore says: 'The first element of the punishment is corruption, which is set forth by the terrible image of a living death, a fearful, anomalous state, in which the mouldy rottenness of death is combined in horrible union with the vivid, conscious sensibility of life. The soul of the sinner, in its future consciousness of sin, shall feel its loathsome corruption as vividly as now it would feel the slow putrefaction of the body that rotted piecemeal to the grave.'

Accounting for the origin of this corruption of human nature, and defending his doctrines from all misunderstanding and misrepresentation, Edwards says: 'I think a little attention to the nature of things will be sufficient to satisfy any impartial considerate inquirer that the absence of positive good principles, leaving the natural principles of self-love, appetite, etc., to themselves, will certainly be followed with the corruption, yea, the total corruption of the heart.'

whole nature

'There is an intense aversion to the doctrine of total depravity in some men's minds.... The feeling comes in some measure from a misapprehension of its true meaning. It is a term of extensity rather than intensity. It is opposed to partial depravity; to the idea that man is sinful in one moment and innocent or sinless in another; or sinful in some acts and pure in others. It affirms that he is all wrong, in all things, and all the time. It does not mean that man is as bad as the devil, or that every man is as bad as every other, or that any man is as bad as he may possibly be, or may become. But there is no limit to the universality or extent of evil in his soul. So say the Scriptures, and so says every awakened conscience' (Tayler Lewis).

commonly called Original Sin

This theological distinction and nomenclature is derived from Augustine, to whom the Church of Christ owes so much. Now what is original sin? The Shorter Catechism answers that it is the inherited corruption of the whole moral and spiritual nature of man. And the Larger Catechism enlarges that Answer thus: 'Original sin is the corruption of man's nature, whereby he is utterly indisposed, disabled, and made opposite to all that is spiritually good, and wholly inclined to evil, and that continually.' A fearful indictment to be laid against all mankind without exception; but by the confession of the ablest and best of mankind, not one whit exaggerated, or in any point opposed to actual fact and daily experience. If any reader doubts the truth of this terrible doctrine, or is staggered at the tremendous charge it lays against human nature, he is recommended to suspend his judgment till he has read the great masterpiece on this subject, Jonathan Edwards'

Original Sin.

Dr Cunningham admits that it may be doubted, as a mere question of grammatical construction, whether the words, 'which is commonly called Original Sin,' apply only to the 'corruption of his whole nature', which is the immediate antecedent, or include also the other ingredients or constituent elements of the sinfulness of the state into which man fell, which had been previously mentioned, viz. the guilt of Adam's first sin, and the want of original righteousness, but any ambiguity in this respect is removed in the fuller exposition given under the corresponding Question in the Larger Catechism, where it is plain that the statement made as to the common meaning of the words 'original sin', applies it only to the corruption of our nature: the inherent depravity which is the immediate source of actual transgression.

'Original sin, in its full extent, consists of three parts: the guilt of Adam's first sin, the want of original righteousness, and the corruption of our whole nature. This last is commonly called original sin, as being the worst part of it' (Boston).

'After the heavenly image in man was effaced, he not only himself was punished by the withdrawal of the ornaments in which man had been arrayed – viz. wisdom, virtue, truth, justice and holiness, and by the substitution in their place of those dire pests blindness, impotence, vanity, impurity and unrighteousness – but he involved his posterity also, and plunged them in the same wretchedness. This is the hereditary corruption to which early Christian writers gave the name of original sin, meaning by that term the depravation of a nature formerly good and pure' (Calvin).

'The great and original principle in sin is self-love; it is the spirit, the quintessence of original sin' (Goodwin).

actual transgressions
'It is important to notice that the term "actual" applied to sin in this connection is employed in its etymological signification to denote the sin of single choices and distinct acts, in distinction from the sin of the heart, or natural disposition which proceeds from it' (Shedd).

which proceed from it.
'From within, out of the hearts of men, proceed evil thoughts, adulteries, fornications, murders, thefts, covetousness, wickedness, deceit, lasciviousness, an evil eye, blasphemy, pride, foolishness: all these evil things come from within and defile the man' (Our Lord, instructing His disciples).

'Single out the grossest sin thou hast ever committed, which hath brought thee lowest on thy knees, and hath cost thee most sighs and sobs, which thou hast drenched and watered with most tears, and compare it with the evil disposition of thy heart and nature which was the root that cursed fruit grew on.... Take any poisoned root, and you will find the least piece of it hath as much strength of poison in it as all the leaves and branches.... It hath not only been actually the cause of all the sins thou hast committed, but virtually, and radically, and potentially it is the seminal root of millions more even of all manner of sin thou never actedst, God restraining thee, so that thou hast seen the least parts of the villany of it' (Goodwin).

Uses

1. At first sight, and before experience, one might well think that such a work of divine grace in the soul as the new birth implies, would eradicate and expel the corruption and bias to sin that come to us in our natural birth. And there have been, and still are, superficial and heretical schools in the Christian Church that teach this fanciful doctrine, but they teach it in the teeth of all Scripture and experience. The truth is, an unspeakable torture and wretchedness, because of indwelling and ineradicable sin, has always been a mark of the presence of a deep and evangelical work of grace in the soul.

2. 'Adam, before his fall, felt, we may suppose, love, fear, hope, joy, dislike, as we do now: but then he felt them only when he ought

and as he ought.... But, at the fall, this beautiful order and peace was broken up: the same passions remained, but their use and action were changed; they rushed into extremes, sometimes excessive, sometimes reverse. Indignation was corrupted into wrath, self-love became selfishness, self-respect became pride, and emulation, envy and jealousy. Thus his soul became a chaos, and needed a new creation' (Newman).

3. 'If we, as we come into this world, are truly sinful, and consequently miserable, he acts but a friendly part to us, who endeavours fully to discover to us our disease. Whereas, on the contrary, he acts an unfriendly part who to his utmost hides it from us: and so, in effect does what in him lies to prevent our seeking a remedy for that which, if not remedied in time, must bring us finally to shame and everlasting contempt, and end in perfect and remediless destruction hereafter' (Edwards).

QUESTION 19

What is the misery of that estate whereinto man fell?

Answer: All mankind by their fall lost communion with God,[1] *are under his wrath and curse,*[2] *and so made liable to all miseries in this life, to death itself, and to the pains of hell for ever.*[3]

All mankind by their fall
on 'The Fall,' see Answer 13.

---

1. Genesis 3:8: ...Adam and his wife hid themselves from the presence of the LORD God. Verse10: And he said, I heard thy voice in the garden, and I was afraid, because I was naked; and I hid myself. Verse 24: So he drove out the man: and he placed at the east of the garden of Eden cherubims and a flaming sword which turned every way, to keep the way of the tree of life.

2. Ephesians 2:3: ...by nature the children of wrath, even as others. Galatians 3:10: For as many as are of the works of the law are under the curse: for it is written, Cursed is every one that continueth not in all things which are written in the book of the law to do them.

3. Lamentations 3:39: Wherefore doth a living man complain, a man for the punishment of his sins? Romans 6:23: For the wages of sin is death. Matthew 25:41: Then shall he say also unto them on the left hand, Depart from me, ye cursed, into everlasting fire, prepared for the devil and his angels. Verse 46: And these shall go away into everlasting punishment.

lost communion with God

Communion is only possible when there is community of mind, when the communing minds are animated by the same spirit. Now, though the Catechism does not put it in this way, yet the great loss that man suffered by his fall was just the loss and withdrawal of the Holy Spirit, whose indwelling constituted and sustained the image of God in the human heart. Hence it is part of the apostolic benediction that the 'communion of the Holy Ghost' will be all over whom it is pronounced. He left the soul of man at the fall, and he is restored in regeneration and union to Christ our Second Head. 'Communion with God is by faith in the understanding and love in the will' (Goodwin).

wrath and curse

Wrath, Old English, anger, indignation. 'People that are but little acquainted with the terrors of the Divine Wrath are not much afraid of trifling with their Maker. For my own part, I would sooner take Empedocles' leap and fling myself into Mount Etna, than I would do it in the slightest instance, were I in circumstances to make an election. Wrath in comparison with mercy is but slightly touched upon in Scripture, because it is not so much a discovery of wrath as of forgiveness' (Cowper). '*Curse*, Swedish *kors* (cross) ! interjection; *corsian*, to execrate by the sign of the cross' (Wedgwood). 'The verb from which the word comes denotes to cut off, thence to devote, to withdraw from common use, and consecrate to God = *sacrare*. The word itself, used actively, means the devotement of anything by Jehovah, His putting it under a ban, the result of which is destruction.... And passively the word denotes the thing devoted, doomed, laid under the ban.'

miseries in this life

'Miser, an avaricious man, niggard. It sometimes means merely a wretched creature, as in Spencer. Probably connected with Greek *misos*, hatred, from which Latin *miseria*, wretchedness' (Skeat).

'What are the punishments of sin in this world? The punishments of sin in this world are either inward, as blindness of mind, a reprobate sense, strong delusions, hardness of heart, horror of conscience, and vile affections: or outward, as the curse of God upon the creatures for our sakes, and all the other evils that befall us in our bodies, names, estates, relations, and employments: together with death itself' (Larger Catechism).

death itself (Jas. 1:15).

'Men look upon death as the extreme limit of all punishments, but in the view of the divine tribunal it is scarcely the beginning of them' (Philo).

pains of hell for ever

'Pain, French *peine*, pain, penalty, punishment. From *pœna*, retribution, a word which, from the prominence of the idea in religious teaching, would readily be carried into all European languages' (Wedgwood).

'Hell, the place of the dead; the abode of evil spirits.... From a Teutonic base *hal*, to hide. So that the original sense is the hidden or unseen place' (Skeat).

'I wish you could but lay your ears to hell, that standing as it were behind the screen, you might hear sin spoken of in its own dialect by the oldest sons of perdition there; to hear what Cain says of murdering his brother Abel; what Saul says of persecuting David and the priests of Jehovah; what Balaam and Ahithophel say of their cursed counsels and policies; what Ahab says of his oppression of Naboth; and what Judas says of treason; and indeed hear how the least sin is there spoken of' (Goodwin).

QUESTION 20

Did God leave all mankind to perish in the estate of sin and misery?

Answer: God having, out of his mere good pleasure, from all eternity, elected some to everlasting life,[1] did enter into a covenant of grace, to deliver them out of the estate of sin and misery, and to bring them into an estate of salvation by a Redeemer.[2]

With this question we enter on the region of Christology, the doctrine of Christ, or of Soteriology, the doctrine of salvation, 'the Immanuel's Land of theology.'

---

1. Ephesians 1:4: According as he hath chosen us in him before the foundation of the world, that we should be holy and without blame before him in love.

2. Romans 3:21: But now the righteousness of God without the law is manifested, being witnessed by the law and the prophets. Verse 22: Even the righteousness of God which is by faith of Jesus Christ unto all and upon all them that believe. Galatians 3:22: That the promise by faith of Jesus Christ might be given to them that believe.

'We have already sailed over one sea, that of man's corruption, a dead sea, as I may call it; and we are now entering into another, a far vaster and deeper, of God's love and free grace' (Goodwin).

mere good pleasure
'Of His mere love and mercy' (Larger Catechism). The Scriptures always trace up man's salvation to the sovereign grace of God. Christ Himself is the gift of the Father. 'Herein is love, not that we loved God, but that He loved us, and sent His Son to be the propitiation for our sins.'

'The Apostle Paul saw as deeply as any other man the difficulty of making salvation depend on the elective love of God, but he saw more deeply the difficulty of making it depend on anything else.... There may be difficulties in referring salvation to the election of God, but there are still greater difficulties in trying to refer it to the election of man' (Moore).

elected some to everlasting life
The first time this word occurs in the Bible, it is already put to its very highest use. It is applied by Jehovah in Isaiah to the Messiah Himself: 'Mine elect, in whom My soul delighteth' (Isa. 42:1). And another passage taken out of the same prophet is by an apostle applied to our Lord: 'Behold, I lay in Zion a chief corner-stone, elect, precious' (Isa. 28:16; 1 Pet. 2:6). Jesus Christ is thus described in both Testaments as God's elect.

The unfallen angels are also characterized by this lofty title, as in the apostolic commission to Timothy: 'I charge thee before God, and the Lord Jesus Christ, and the elect angels' (1 Tim. 5:21). Israel as God's people are often called by this distinguishing name (Isa. 45:4, 65:9). In the New Testament this designation is applied to all true believers, as in Romans 8:33: 'Who shall lay anything to the charge of God's elect?' And as the designation is made a ground of comfort to the Roman Christians, so it is used as a ground of counsel to the Church at Colossæ: 'Put on therefore, as the elect of God, holy and beloved, bowels of mercies' (Col. 3:12). And lastly, the word is applied to persons eminent for the display of the Christian graces, as in John's Second Epistle: 'The elder unto the elect lady' (2 John 1), and again: 'The children of thine elect sister' (2 John 13).

'Such is the great scheme of doctrine known in history as the Pauline, Augustinian, or Calvinistic, taught, as we believe, in the Scriptures, developed by Augustine, formally sanctioned by the Latin Church, adhered to by the witnesses of the truth in the Middle Ages; repudiated by the Church of Rome in the Council of Trent, received in that Church by the Jansenists, adopted by all the Reformers, incorporated by all the creeds of the Protestant Churches of Switzerland, France, Holland, England, and Scotland, and unfolded in the Standards of the Westminster Assembly, the common representative of all Presbyterians in Europe and America' (Hodge).

some
Dr. Morison's explanation in another connection is applicable here: 'The distinction is not between some and many, but between some and all; for even many are only some, if they are not all.'

a covenant of grace
See under covenant, Answer 12.

Grace means favour, mercy, pardon. Grace and love are essentially the same, only grace is love manifesting itself and operating under certain conditions, and adapting itself to certain circumstances. As, for instance, love has no limit or law such as grace has. Love may exist between equals, or it may rise to those above us, or flow down to those in any way beneath us. But grace, from its nature, has only one direction it can take. Grace always flows down. Grace is love indeed, but it is love humbling itself. A king's love to his equals, or to his own royal house, is love: but his love to his subjects is called grace. And thus it is that God's love to sinners is always called grace in the Scriptures. It is love indeed, but it is love to creatures, and to creatures who do not deserve His love. And therefore all He does for us in Christ, and all that is disclosed to us of His goodwill in the gospel, is called grace.

'The covenant of grace was made with Jesus Christ, as the Second Adam, party-contractor (Ps. 89:3; 1 Cor. 15:45; Rom 5:15-21; Gal. 3:16). And Christ, in this covenant, represented all the elect, as the spiritual race, the parties contracted for. Then the covenant of redemption and the covenant of grace are not two distinct covenants, but two names of one covenant under different considerations. By a covenant of redemption is meant a bargain of buying and selling; and the second covenant was such a covenant to Christ only (1 Pet. 1:18, 19). By a covenant of grace is meant a bargain whereby all is to be had freely; and it is such a covenant to poor sinners only (Isa. 55:1)' (Boston).

'Dear Charles, My dear love to thee, and to my dear Biddy, who is a joy to my heart, for what I hear of the Lord in her. Bid her be joyful and rejoice in the Lord once and again: if she knows the covenant, she cannot but do so. For that transaction is without her: sure and steadfast, between the Father and the Mediator in His blood; therefore, leaning upon the Son, or looking to Him, thirsting after Him, and embracing Him, we are His seed: and the covenant is sure to all the seed. The compact is for the seed; God is bound in faithfulness to Christ, and in Him to us; the covenant is without us: a transaction between God and Christ. Look up to it. God engageth in it to pardon us: to write His law in our hearts: to plant His fear so as we shall never depart from Him' (Oliver Cromwell).

by a Redeemer

By one who is to buy us back, ransom us, make atonement for us. Who He is, and how He does His redeeming work, will immediately appear.

'The doctrines of God's absolute sovereignty and free grace in showing mercy on whom He would show mercy, and man's absolute dependence on the operations of God's Holy Spirit, have very often appeared to me as sweet and most glorious doctrines. These doctrines have been made my delight.... I have loved the doctrines of the gospel; they have been to my soul like green pastures. The way of salvation by Christ has appeared most glorious and excellent, most pleasant and most beautiful. It has often seemed to me that it would in a great measure spoil heaven to receive it in any other way' (Edwards).

Uses

1. 'The doctrine of this high mystery of predestination is to be handled with special prudence and care, that men attending the will of God revealed in his word, and yielding obedience thereunto, may, from the certainty of their effectual vocation, be assured of their eternal election' (Confession, 3:8).

2. 'Chosen to be holy and without blame'; 'ordained unto good works'; 'elect unto obedience.' This is the end of election. It is not to any earthly dignity or worldly glory. It is not to any possession or privilege that other men will envy them, for all men may have the portion of the elect if they choose. Election bars no man from blessedness; it only secures its own subjects that they shall not come short of it. Election is not in

any sense a decree of exclusion; its whole design is to be an instrument of security. Election shuts no one out; but it is so contrived that it shuts the elect effectually in.

3. And just as holiness is a certain issue of election, so holiness is the only sure evidence of election.

4. 'Can you give yourself to Jesus Christ to be saved by Him? Then were you given to Him to be redeemed by Him. Your faith on Him speaks your election in Him. True faith is "the faith of God's elect" (Tit. 1:1). Go on in trusting Him, and in living by faith on Him, and He will make you know that He loved you, and gave Himself for you' (Traill).

QUESTION 21

Who is the Redeemer of God's elect?

Answer: The only Redeemer of God's elect is the Lord Jesus Christ,[1] who, being the eternal Son of God, became man,[2] and so was, and continueth to be, God and man in two distinct natures, and one person, for ever.[3]

The metaphor of purchase, ransom, redemption, runs through the whole of Scripture, and supplies to Scripture much of its most instructive and impressive language. So deeply, indeed, is this idea of redemption seated in the whole conception of our need of salvation, and in the divine way of accomplishing it, that it is of the very essence of the whole transaction. The student will be interested and instructed and impressed by tracing the growth and contents of the name Redeemer from its first Hebrew

1. 1Timothy 2:5: For there is one God, and one mediator between God and men, the man Christ Jesus. Verse 6: Who gave himself a ransom for all, to be testified in due time.

2. John 1:14: And the Word was made flesh, and dwelt among us, (and we beheld his glory, the glory as of the only begotten of the Father,) full of grace and truth. Galatians 4:4: But when the fulness of the time was come, God sent forth his Son, made of a woman, made under the law.

3. Romans 9:5: Christ ...who is over all, God blessed for ever. Amen. Luke 1:35: ...that holy thing, which shall be born of thee, shall be called the Son of God. Colossians 2:9: For in him dwelleth all the fulness of the Godhead bodily. Hebrews 7:24: But this man, because he continueth ever, hath an unchangeable priesthood. Verse 25: Wherefore he is able also to save them to the uttermost that come unto God by him, seeing he ever liveth to make intercession for them.

appropriation by Jehovah down to its fullest Christian application to Jesus Christ. He will take note also of the wealth of argument and illustration and adoration this conception supplies to the New Testament writers.

The only Redeemer
Cf. the Confession, chapter 8, 'Of Christ the Mediator', and Larger Catechism, Question 36.

the Lord
Owner, ruler, master. Our Redeemer is called our Lord for two reasons. First, He has a lordship founded on His Divine Nature. He owns us and commands us because He created us. He made us, and not we ourselves. But He holds another lordship over us that touches us, if possible, still closer than that: a lordship grounded not so much on His divinity as on His humanity. This is something added to His original power over us. He holds a lordship over us as the recompense and result of all He did and does for us as our Redeemer. This lordship is pointed at in such passages as John 3:35, 13:3, 17:2; Acts 2:36; Philippians 2:9, 11. This lordship of Jesus Christ is one of the principal themes of apostolic preaching.

Jesus
The same as the Hebrew name Jeshua (Neh. 8:17), another form of Joshua, which again is contracted from Jehoshua (Num. 13:16), signifying Help of Jehovah, a Saviour. 'Thou shalt call His name *Jesus*; for He shall save His people from their sins' (Matt.1:21). There was no dispute about our Lord's right to bear the name Jesus. Mary called her first-born Jesus, just as Elizabeth called her child John. The 'carpenter's son' was known among the children of Nazareth as Jesus the son of Joseph. He bore a well-known name, but He bore it as no other son of man had ever borne it before Him. Gabriel took Joseph back to the original meaning of the name when he came to command him so to designate the child about to be put under his charge. The angel explained the name, and attached it, in its fresh and original sense, to the child that was to be born in Joseph's house. It had lost all its meaning, as generations of children so named had heard it called and had answered to it; but all its original force was fulfilled, and far more than fulfilled in Him who was henceforth to bear it, and acknowledge it, and glorify it.

Christ

The Greek word *christos* transliterated into English, meaning the Anointed One, from *chiro*, to anoint. Christ is the Greek and English equivalent for the Hebrew term Messiah. The office of the Messiah was so named and described in Old Testament prophecy long before the Person appeared who was to fill the office and bear the name in history. Of the two names Jesus Christ our Lord bears, the one is His personal name and the other is His official name. His official name, the Messiah, the Christ, was as familiar to the Old Testament Church as it is to us; only, they could not in their time attach it to any given person. Their progress accordingly, as Bengel says, was from the Christ to Jesus, from the office to the official person; while, on the other hand, the progress of the apostolic believers was made just the other way. The Jews in our Lord's day saw and heard Jesus of Nazareth; but the question and invitation continually put to them was this: Did they accept and acknowledge Jesus as 'the Christ'? That the Christ is coming was the faith and hope of Moses and Isaiah; that Jesus is the Christ was the preaching of Peter and Paul.

On John 17:3, Stier says: 'The apostolical custom of using Jesus Christ as one double appellative, making Christ also a proper name, had its origin in this word of our Lord. Speak of Him as He spoke of Himself before God – this was the Spirit's suggestion to their minds.'

'Christ is no single term, but in that name which is one is the signification both of Godhead and manhood. Wherefore Christ is called man, and Christ is called God; and Christ is both God and man, and Christ is One' (Athanasius).

who being the eternal Son of God

See Answer 6. 'Theology, led by Origen, introduced the paraphrase of the "Eternal Son", and with strict propriety, since all the interior relations of the Godhead are of necessity eternal' (Pope). 'His Son Jesus Christ is a compressed creed' (Westcott).

Originally and eternally the Redeemer was with God, and was God; but He was God under the character and relation of a Son. There are three Persons in the Godhead: the Father, the Son, and the Holy Ghost. And it is He who is always designated the Son that we have here to do with. 'Thou art my Son' (Ps. 2:7; Acts 13:33), says the eternal Father, 'this day have I begotten Thee' (Heb. 1:5, 5:5). Again, we read that the

Son is eternally in the bosom of the Father, and that as such He is the Father's only begotten. Now all this is plainly designed to teach us that there is a mysterious communication of the Divine Nature from the Father, the First Person, to the Son, the Second; an inscrutable and ineffable communication continually going on, that can only be conveyed to our minds under the figure of human generation. The Holy Ghost points us to earthly fatherhood and earthly sonship as being the entirely inadequate but only available illustration of that eternal relation within the Godhead by which the First Person conveys the Divine Nature to the Second. As the Father hath life in Himself, so hath He given to the Son to have life in Himself. The Son has His Being of the Father, just as, on the other hand, the Father has His Being of Himself alone. The Son therefore is God, because He is begotten of God the Father; and being so begotten, He is revealed to us under the denomination, description, and character of the Son. 'And first they had him into the study, where they showed him records of the greatest antiquity; in which, as I remember my dream, they showed him first the Pedigree of the Lord of the Hill, that he was the son of the Ancient of Days, and came by an eternal generation' (Bunyan).

became man
'And the Word was made flesh' (John 1:14). 'The loftiest sentence ever penned by human hand' (Godet). God sent forth His Son, made of a woman. In theological phrase, the Incarnation.

'Christology has its own distinct range of theological coinage. Its highest achievement here is the term Theanthropos, Deus-homo, God-man; and with this it boldly utters the secret of the whole Bible. It long faltered and hesitated in the choice of a word that should express the holy bond between the Divinity and the manhood; after many experiments it rested on the word Incarnation, which is the slightest possible deviation from the very word of the Holy Ghost, through St John, "He was made flesh" ' (Pope).

We are men, and the children of men, and to say that any one 'became man' just means that he became like us, became one of us. This then is the 'mystery of godliness', this is the Incarnation of the eternal Son; this is the foundation of all our Christian hope, 'The Word was made flesh, and dwelt among us' (John 1:14).

'Still, we must ever remember, that though He was in nature perfect man, He was not man in exactly the same sense in which any one of us is a man. Though man, He was not, strictly speaking, in the English sense of the word, a man; He was not such as one of us, and one out of a number. His Person was not human like ours, but divine. He who was from eternity, continued one and the same, but with an addition. His Incarnation was a "taking of the manhood into God".... He was not a man made God, but God made man' (Newman).

'Our nature in Him, as it is human, is not circumscribed or enclosed with a proper subsistence of its own, but lies like a field unenclosed, not hedged in with personality as all our natures are' (Goodwin).

two distinct natures

'Two natures met together in our Redeemer, and, while the proprieties of each remained, so great a unity was made of either substance, that from the time that the Word was made flesh in the blessed Virgin's womb, we may neither think of Him as God without that which is man, nor as man without that which is God. Each nature certifies its own reality under distinct actions, but neither disjoins itself from connection with the other. Nothing is wanting from either towards other. There is entire littleness in majesty, entire majesty in littleness; unity does not introduce confusion, nor does propriety divide unity. There is one thing passible, another inviolable, yet his is the contumely whose is the glory. He is in infirmity who is in power; the same is both capable and conqueror of death. God then did take on Him whole man, and did so unite Himself unto him, and him unto Himself, in pity and in power, that either nature was in the other, and neither in the other lost its propriety' (Leo).

'In Christ therefore God and man, "there is," saith Paschasius, "a twofold substance, not a twofold Person, because one person extinguisheth another, whereas one nature in another cannot become extinct." For the personal being which the Son of God already had, suffered not the substance to be personal which He took, although together with the nature which He had, the nature also which He took continueth' (Hooker).

'He has two Natures in one Person, plain to be distinguished, impossible to be divided' (Greatheart in Bunyan).

one person

On Personality, see Answer 6. 'The term "Person" as applied to our Lord has a conventional meaning, which is not amenable to science, but is not inconsistent with it. In the true philosophy personality is not nature; it is that in which the nature, with its various developments and forms of exhibition, inheres. The person of a man is the substratum of all that belongs to his nature, as consciously his own, and distinguished from any other. The Person of Christ is Himself, the substratum of all that belongs to the twofold manner of existence' (Pope).

for ever
'Inseparably joined' (Westminster Confession). 'Never to be divided' (Thirty-Nine Articles). 'These Natures, from the moment of their first combination, have been and are for ever inseparable' (Hooker).

'I would not give the truth expressed in these words of the Catechism, "Two distinct natures and one person for ever," for all the truths that by human language have ever been expressed. I would rather have been the humblest defender of this truth in the Four Ecumenical Councils than have been the greatest reformer in the Church, the father of the covenant, or the procurer of the English Constitution' (Edward Irving).

Uses
1. It has been acutely said that one obvious use of the full and symmetrical statement of the doctrine of the Sonship is to facilitate to the imagination the descent of a Divine Person into human nature and human history.

2. 'If any one is tempted to consider such a subject abstruse, speculative, and unprofitable, I would observe in answer, that I have taken it on the very ground of its being, as I believe, especially practical.... What do we gain from words, however correct and abundant, if they end with themselves, instead of lighting up the image of the Incarnate Son in our hearts? In truth, His Divine Sonship is that portion of the sacred doctrine on which the mind is providentially intended to rest throughout, and so to preserve for itself the identity unbroken' (Newman).

QUESTION 22

How did Christ, being the Son of God, become man?

Answer: Christ, the Son of God, became man, by taking to himself a true body,[1] *and a reasonable soul,*[2] *being conceived by the power of the Holy Ghost, in the womb of the Virgin Mary, and born of her,*[3] *yet without sin.*[4]

Christ, the Son of God, became man
'It was not that, being man, He afterwards became God; but, He afterwards became man' (Athanasius). 'While it may be true to say "Man is God," as well as to say "God is man," it is not true to say "Man became God," as it is to say "God became man"' (Newman).

by taking to himself
The phrase is a scriptural one: 'He took part of flesh and blood,' 'He took on Him the seed of Abraham' (Heb. 2:14, 16). But when the Son of God took our nature He did not circumscribe or enclose it with a human personality like ours. He took a true body and a reasonable soul as instruments He might make use of in His manifold work as Mediator between God and man. Our manhood is like a new attribute added to the Godhead of the Second Person; it is a new avenue of access and egress to the Divine Mind and Heart of the Son of God. Since He took our nature, His capacity for feeling and affection has been enlarged, and His ability to act for us has been increased. And hence our nature endowed, ennobled, and glorified in Him above all conception of ours is after all but a means to an end. For nothing of knowledge or experience or sympathy that enters into or is awakened within our Lord's Human Nature remains stored up there, it all passes on to become motive to move the

---

1. Hebrews 2:14: Forasmuch then as the children are partakers of flesh and blood, he also himself likewise took part of the same. Verse 16: For verily he took not on him the nature of angels; but he took on him the seed of Abraham. Hebrews 10:5: Wherefore, when he cometh into the world, he saith, Sacrifice and offering thou wouldest not, but a body hast thou prepared me.

2. Matthew 26:38: Then saith he unto them, My soul is exceeding sorrowful, even unto death.

3. Luke 1:27: To a virgin espoused to a man, whose name was Joseph, of the house of David; and the virgin's name was Mary. Verse 31: And, behold, thou shalt conceive in thy womb, and bring forth a son, and shalt call his name JESUS. Verse 35: And the angel answered and said unto her, The Holy Ghost shall come upon thee, and the power of the Highest shall overshadow thee: therefore also that holy thing, which shall be born of thee, shall be called the Son of God. Verse 42: Blessed art thou among women, and blessed is the fruit of thy womb. Galatians 4:4: But when the fulness of the time was come, God sent forth his Son, made of a woman, made under the law.

4. Hebrews 4:15: ...in all points tempted like as we are, yet without sin. Hebrews 7:26: For such an high priest became us, who is holy, harmless, undefiled, separate from sinners.

Divine Will, and awake the Divine Arm. And hence also the everlasting love that was in the Godhead comes out now on the world in the form of the manhood love of Jesus Christ. He who loved us and loves us is the Eternal and Unchangeable God, but since the Incarnation He loves us with a love that has all those and all their kindred attributes in it, with this new attribute added, that it is now human, made human by rising up within and running toward us through the human heart of the Incarnate Son. All the indescribable attributes of Divine Love, and all the lovely and familiar, tender and yearning attributes of human love are now mingled together to make that new manner of love, the love that passeth knowledge, the love of God which is in Christ Jesus our Lord.

a true body

This phrase is the abiding protest of the Church against an ancient and deadly heresy. Docetism (Greek, 'to seem,' 'to put on the appearance') taught that our Lord took to Him only the appearance of a body. The Docetics were led to take up this position through a ruling opinion they held, that all matter was essentially and irredeemably impure. And accordingly they believed and taught that our Lord's body was not and could not be real and true flesh and blood, like the bodies of sinful men. This great error was already showing its presence in the Church as early as the days of the Apostle John. For it is against this false doctrine that he directs such passages as these: 'We have seen with our eyes, we have looked upon, and our hands have handled the Word of life' (1 John 1:1). And again: 'Every spirit that confesseth not that Jesus Christ is come in the flesh, is not of God' (1 John 4:2). And an early Father combating the same error says: 'If the Incarnation is a phantom, so is salvation.' And hence the phrase coined for the early creeds, and thence incorporated with our own Catechism – Christ took 'a true body'.

'That body which it hath pleased Him to make His own, that body wherewith He hath saved the world, that body which hath been, and is the root of eternal life, the instrument wherewith Deity worketh, the sacrifice which taketh away sin, the price which hath ransomed our souls from death. The leader of the whole army of bodies that shall rise again, His body is a body consubstantial with our bodies' (Hooker).

a reasonable soul

Possessing reason, rational. This clause of the Creed was originally directed against the Apollinarian heresy, a heresy 'held loosely by Arius, but afterwards shaped into consistency by Apollinaris'. No one who has not studied early Church history can have any conception of the struggles the Church had to carry on with all manner of false doctrine concerning the Person of Christ. The Apollinarian heretics admitted, as against the Docetics, that our Lord had a 'a true body', but they contended that the Divine Nature stood Him instead of a soul. They failed to carry out scripturally and symmetrically the whole doctrine of the Incarnation. They could not accept that Christ had a finite intelligence, and human affections, and a human will. They accepted, without demur, the orthodox doctrine of the Incarnation as far as Christ's body went, but they could not accept it in the region of the mind. It was to correct this defective teaching on a fundamental article of her Christological Creed that the early Church inserted the clause, 'a reasonable soul' – a clause that Scripture enabled, and indeed compelled her to insert. For every page of the gospel narrative testifies to the reality of our Lord's humanity in His soul as well as in His body. At one time He rejoiced, and at another time He was in sorrow, and joy and sorrow are affections of a reasonable soul. He had a human will distinct from His Divine Will, for he said, 'Not My will, but Thine be done' (Luke 22:42). He spoke of what He felt when He said, 'My soul is exceeding sorrowful, even unto death' (Matt. 26:38). And teaching us how to die, he said, 'Father, into Thy hands I commend My spirit' (Luke 23:46).

by the power of the Holy Ghost

'The Holy Ghost shall come upon thee, and the power of the Highest shall overshadow thee' (Luke 1:35). These words of the announcing angel point to a forthputting of divine power which had never been exercised before, and has never been repeated since. For Jesus Christ was born, not of blood, nor of the will of the flesh, nor of the will of man, but of the will and operation of the Holy Ghost.

'The same Holy Ghost who at the first creation moved on the face of the waters, when darkness was on the deep, and out of the chaos produced light, and order, and harmony, and beauty, did at the commencement of the new creation, out of the corrupted substance of the Virgin, form a human body, as perfectly separated from all corruption by the divine workmanship as the symmetry, and light, and beauty of the material world were separated from the darkness, confusion, and shapelessness of the desolate abyss. And at the moment when this body was conceived by the divine operation of the Holy Ghost, the power of the Highest united to it a soul, formed also in perfect purity and holiness. And at the same moment too were both body and soul united to the Godhead in the Person of the Son, by a personal union, never to be dissolved' (Marcus Dods in Christian Instructor, 1830).

the Virgin Mary

The Romish Church has much more to tell her people about Mary than the Scriptures have to tell their readers. But the Popish doctrines concerning the immaculate conception, perpetual virginity, and assumption of Mary are wholly unscriptural and legendary. There is not an atom of authentic history about her till we come to the narrative in the opening of the Gospels. We know nothing of Mary till Gabriel discovers her to us. And important and interesting as her history subsequently would be, it is yet told us in the most incidental way. Though it is to be avoided and blamed, yet it is not to be wondered at that Mary has been too much made of in some parts of the Christian Church. Other women have partaken of Christ, have been grafted into Him, and have received of His spiritual fulness; but Mary, while enjoying this grace with a multitude of her fellows, had this transcendent honour, that her Lord and Saviour took His human life of her, was bone of her bone, and flesh of her flesh, and was to her a child and a Son. 'Hers was the face that unto Christ had most resemblance.'

The unhappy way of glorifying Mary, which has issued in such a portentous development of arbitrary dogma as we now see in the Romish creed, took its rise in an orthodox interest, and with a right intention. The Greek Fathers, 'delighting in the happy compositions of their language,' called her *theotokos*, the mother of Him who is God. This epithet was sanctioned by several of the greatest and most orthodox of the early Councils, and it was first used as a 'criterion of a true belief in the Incarnation'. This name was not at all intended to add to her honour; it was rather used as another way of vindicating the true divinity of Him who was her Son. And when scripturally and intelligibly used, the epithet is unchallengeable. But as the event showed, the addition of this Christological designation to the scriptural titles of Mary was speedily productive of great error and superstition. The undoubted fact is that this orthodox definition of the early Councils was a distinct, though unintentional, step toward the deification of the Virgin Mary.

The sum of Scripture teaching about Mary is this: she was blessed among women in being chosen to be the mother of our Lord. And as His mother her name is to be held in love and reverence by all who believe on and worship her Son. Remembering her service to Him, all generations may well call her blessed.

born of her
'O much wished-for birth, without which we ourselves might well wish we had never been born! But do thou thyself, reader, see that thou makest sure of the benefit of that nativity!' (Bengel).

yet without sin
'A eulogium peculiar to Jesus' (Bengel). 'He had a mother, and His mother conceived Him; but she did not conceive Him in sin, because it was not by the way of ordinary generation (Matt. 1:20). He came not under (and it was well for us He did not) the law of ordinary generation; hence He escaped being defiled with original sin' (Goodwin).

To see the full force of this, it must be recollected that till Jesus was born all the children born of women had been born in sin. To be a man hitherto was to be a sinner. Till His advent there was none righteous, no, not one. But He was not only not sinful, He was 'not capable of sinning.'

Uses
1. This then is 'the Redeemer of God's elect'. We do not yet know from our Catechism what this wonderful Person is to do. We are simply told up to this point who and what He is. He is God and He is man. Man, with a true body and a reasonable soul; and as such born without sin. Knowing as we do that He was the eternal Son of God, equal with the Father in power and glory, and that He took a body and soul prepared for Him by the Holy Ghost, we might well expect something surpassingly great to come of a union of Godhead with manhood. Had we not already known, we must have waited with the deepest wonder to see to what this love would grow. Let us follow it out with understanding, faith, and love.

2. Let us learn from this also that man is not necessarily and always a sinner. To be a man and to be a sinner are not necessarily and always one and the same thing. There has been one child born, yet without sin. There

was once a man on the earth who did not need to confess, 'I was shapen in iniquity.' Sin did not reign in the body of Jesus Christ. His garments were never spotted with the flesh. He was sanctified from His mother's womb, and He kept Himself, and the evil one touched Him not.

3. The life of Christ the God-man is, or may be, our life. As Adam was the bitter fountain of original sin, as all infirmity, impurity, languor, and mortality of the body, and all unbelief, ignorance, malice, hatred, falsehood, and selfishness in the soul has its rise in Adam and in his sin, so all our graces, faith, love, peace, holiness, hope: all have their wellspring in Jesus Christ. He is the Vine, we are the branches. He is the Head, we are the members. He is the Son, we are the children. Great is the mystery of godliness; God manifest in the flesh; and then in the flesh made unto us wisdom, and righteousness, and sanctification, and redemption.

QUESTION 23

What offices doth Christ execute as our Redeemer?

Answer: Christ, as our Redeemer, executeth the offices of a prophet, of a priest, and of a king, both in his estate of humiliation and exaltation.[1]

---

1. Acts 3:21: Whom the heaven must receive until the times of restitution of all things, which God hath spoken by the mouth of all his holy prophets since the world began. Verse 22: For Moses truly said unto the fathers, A Prophet shall the Lord your God raise up unto you of your brethren, like unto me; him shall ye hear in all things whatsoever he shall say unto you. Hebrews 12:25: ...him that speaketh from heaven. Compared with 2 Corinthians 13:3: Since ye seek a proof of Christ speaking in me, which to you-ward is not weak, but is mighty in you. Hebrews 5:5: So also Christ glorified not himself to be made an high priest; but he that said unto him, Thou art my Son, to-day have I begotten thee. Verse 6: As he saith also in another place, Thou are a priest for ever, after the order of Melchisedec. Verse 7: Who in the days of his flesh ...offered up prayers and supplications, with strong crying and tears. Hebrews 7:25: Wherefore he is able also to save them to the uttermost that come unto God by him, seeing he ever liveth to make intercession for them. Psalm 2:6: Yet have I set my King upon my holy hill of Zion. Isaiah 9:6: For unto us a child is born, unto us a son is given; and the government shall be upon his shoulder: and his name shall be called Wonderful, Counsellor, The mighty God, The everlasting Father, The Prince of Peace. Verse 7: Of the increase of his government and peace there shall be no end, upon the throne of David, and upon his kingdom, to order it, and to establish it with judgment and with justice from henceforth even for ever. The zeal of the LORD of hosts will perform this. Matthew 21:5: Tell ye the daughter of Sion. Behold, thy King cometh unto thee. Psalm 2:8: Ask of me, and I shall give thee the heathen for thine inheritance, and the uttermost parts of the earth for thy possession. Verse 9: Thou shalt break them with a rod of iron; thou shalt dash them in pieces like a potter's vessel.

The offices

Our English word *office* is derived from the Latin *officium*, and both in derivation and use it means any special trust, duty, or charge laid upon or taken up by one person to perform for another. The name is never applied to what any man does for himself, and at his own instance: the name of an office is applied only to what one does for another. It is a scriptural term, and as such it is of very ancient and frequent employment. Thus we read of Potiphar as an officer of Pharaoh. The elders and judges in Israel also bore this name. We read also of the priests' office, the office of a pastor, and the office of a deacon. Paul says, 'I am an apostle of the Gentiles, I magnify mine office' (Rom. 11:13).

The name is not applied in as many words in Scripture to our Lord's work, or to any part of it, but it is very familiar to us from theological works, and especially from our Catechism. The classification of our Lord's work as the execution of the offices of Prophet, Priest, and King, may be regarded as somewhat arbitrary. It may fairly be said that these three categories do not exhaust the teaching of Scripture concerning all that our Lord has done and is still doing for us. And He certainly bears other official names, and sustains relations toward us that cannot all be included under those three offices. His favourite title of Shepherd, for instance, implies all His offices. Still, this threefold classification has long obtained in our best scriptural theology, and it serves many useful purposes to the student and the preacher. This classification of Christ's work has come to us from the great schoolmen, and it has secured for itself a sure place in all our modern systems of evangelical divinity.

humiliation and exaltation

'The Jews have invented a double Messiah; to the one they attribute all those places which mention His low estate and sufferings; and to the other, such as speak of His power and glory. The one they style the son of Joseph, and the other the son of David' (Pearson).

Use

'How God is to preserve holiness and forgive sin, I am at my wits' end to know; here I stand nonplussed, my faculty of reason serving me not a jot.... Tell me how this is to come to pass, and you shall be my prophet, and priest, and king. For verily to do this pertaineth to Him only who is my Prophet, and Priest, and King' (Irving).

QUESTION 24

How doth Christ execute the office of a prophet?

Answer: Christ executeth the office of a prophet, in revealing to us, by his word and Spirit, the will of God for our salvation.[1]

the office of a prophet

The title *prophet* fits in finely to the definition and description of an office given in the preceding Answer. For as an office is some place or function that some one occupies or performs for another, so a prophet is one who speaks for another, conveying and interpreting his will. 'The office of the prophet in the fullest sense is to make know Another' (Westcott on John 1:7). Examples of the claim that Christ put forth to be a prophet will be found in such passages as John 7:16, 8:28, 12:49, 15:10, 24.

'Christ was, by way of eminence, The Prophet: that Prophet that should come into the world, to declare the Divine Will. He published anew the law of nature, which men had corrupted; and the very knowledge of which, to some degree, was lost among them. He taught mankind, taught us authoritatively, to live soberly, righteously, and godly in this present world, in expectation of the future judgment of God. He confirmed the truth of this moral system of nature, and gave us additional evidence of it: the evidence of testimony. He distinctly revealed the manner in which God would be worshipped, the efficacy of repentance, and the rewards and punishments of a future life. Thus He was a Prophet in a sense in which no other ever was' (Butler).

'He has the whole prophetic life in Himself. The pathos of an Isaiah, the melancholy of an Hosea, the meekness of a Jeremiah, the joy in nature of an

---

1. John 1:18: No man hath seen God at any time; the only-begotten Son, which is in the bosom of the Father, he hath declared him. 1 Peter 1:10: Of which salvation the prophets have enquired and searched diligently, who prophesied of the grace that should come unto you: Verse 11: Searching what, or what manner of time, the Spirit of Christ which was in them did signify, when it testified beforehand the sufferings of Christ, and the glory that should follow. Verse 12: Unto whom it was revealed, that not unto themselves, but unto us, they did minister the things which are now reported unto you by them that have preached the gospel unto you with the Holy Ghost sent down from heaven. John 15:15: Henceforth I call you not servants; for the servant knoweth not what his lord doeth: but I have called you friends; for all things that I have heard of my Father I have made known unto you. John 20:31: But these are written, that ye might believe that Jesus is the Christ, the Son of God; and that believing ye might have life through his name.

Amos, the power of observation of the proverb-writers, the whole world of feeling of the psalmists have all been transferred to Him' (Hausrath).

by revealing

'Neither knoweth any man the Father, save the Son, and he to whom the Son will reveal Him' (Luke 10:22). 'The only-begotten Son, which is in the bosom of the Father, He hath declared Him' (John 1:18). 'The Revelation of Jesus Christ, which God gave unto Him to show unto His servants' (Rev. 1:1).

'The way of salvation made known by Christ is a revelation; it is not a relation of something already known; it is not theory, invention, or speculation. Neither is the way of salvation a discovery of human reason, like scientific discoveries. And hence the absurdity of improvements in religion' (Stewart of Cromarty).

by his word and Spirit

'The Bible may be considered as a consolidation of partial revelation. There were dreams, visions, voices from heaven, Urim and Thummim, in the olden times. Thus, in these "divers manners," and at "sundry times," were revelations made, but God hath in these last days spoken to us by His Son.... Thus the Bible is addressed to the understanding, conscience, affections, to the whole soul. And the influence of the Spirit is co-extensive with the word. It flows into and embodies itself in the word. Bless God for the promise of the Spirit, who commands the light to shine out of darkness, by the authority, omnipotence, and grace of His agency. If ye love not the Spirit of Christ, ye are none of His' (Stewart).

the will of God for our salvation

'At the time appointed He came forth from the Father, and showed Himself in this external world – first as its Creator, then as its Teacher, the Revealer of secrets, the Mediator, the off-streaming of God's glory, and the express image of His Person. Cloud nor image, emblem nor words, are interposed between the Son and the Eternal Father. No language is needed between the Father and Him who is the very Word of the Father; no knowledge is imparted to Him, who by His very nature and from eternity knows the Father, and all that the Father knows' (Newman).

'It is not enough to say of the doctrine of Jesus that it shows a high religious character: this it has in common with many others; but in the doctrine of our Lord a distinctly soteriological character must be acknowledged.... It is not so much religious truth in general, as in an especial sense, the truth as it regards salvation which has been brought to light through Him' (Oosterzee).

Uses

1. 'The main and proper end of one of the offices of Jesus Christ is to cure the defects of the understanding.... If we consider all the instructions, reproofs, and doctrines in the word, what are they but so many plasters which Christ lays to our heads to cure our diseased judgments, and by healing them to heal all the other faculties' (Goodwin).

2. 'The great subject of Christ's instructions, as the Prophet and Teacher of His Church, was the will of God for our salvation. He did not come to teach science or art; He has furnished us with other means of obtaining information on these subjects' (Stewart).

3. 'What is the first instruction hence? That none need be discouraged at their natural weakness if Christ is their teacher (Matt. 11:25)' (Flavel). 'And thus it happens that men of the lowest class and the humblest education may know fully the ways and works of God: far better and more truly than the most sagacious man of this world to whom the gospel is hid. Religion has a store of wonderful secrets which no one can communicate to another, and which are most pleasant and delightful to know. "Call upon me, and I will answer thee, and show thee great and mighty things which thou knowest not of"' (Newman).

QUESTION 25

How doth Christ execute the office of a priest?

Answer: Christ executeth the office of a priest, in his once offering up of himself a sacrifice to satisfy divine justice,[1] and reconcile us to God;[2] and in making continual intercession for us.[3]

---

1. Hebrews 9:14: How much more shall the blood of Christ, who through the eternal Spirit offered himself without spot to God, purge your conscience from dead works, to serve the living God? Verse 28: So Christ was once offered to bear the sins of many.

2. Hebrews 2:17: ...a merciful and faithful high priest in things pertaining to God to make reconciliation for the sins of the people.

the office of a priest
'Salvation is of the Jews' (John 4:22): so much so, that the very vocabulary of our salvation was once the mother-tongue of God's ancient people. Jewish words, Jewish ordinances, Jewish experiences, mingle with all our New Testament and Christian facts and doctrines. In the doctrine of the Christian atonement we still think and speak after the manner of the Jews. The figure of a throne, and a lawgiver and judge sitting upon it, with an atoning priest and intercessor standing beside the throne sprinkling the throne and all those who approach it with atoning blood: all that scenery and nomenclature is taken from the Mosaic ritual. And so divine and necessary is this whole conception, that even when an inspired apostle is labouring to deliver his readers from their bondage to Jewish traditions, he perpetuates that tradition to all coming time. He is compelled to write as a Jew even when he is divinely working his way out of their religious fellowship. There is no book in the Bible more Jewish in its language and modes of thought than the Epistle to the Hebrews, though that epistle is throughout a divinely directed argument to prove that the Jews' day is past, and that the faith and worship of the Jew is decayed and waxed old and ready to vanish away.

'Sacrifice being of divine appointment, the calling and institution of the priesthood was so likewise. The nature of the priest's office implied sin. A priest is radically and essentially a mediator or intercessor, and it is only when there is no sin that there is no need of an intercessor. It was not because of the distance of the Creator from the creature as a creature that the necessity for a mediator arose, but because of his distance as a guilty creature' (Stewart).

offering up of himself
'And since, in every sacrifice, four things are considered: to whom it is offered, what is offered, and for whom it is offered, nor is sacrifice due to any save to God alone, therefore our High Priest offered Himself to God for us, at once the Priest and the Sacrifice' (Ambrose).

'The very soul of the doctrine of atonement is its substitutionary nature: that taken away, the whole circle of New Testament phraseology

---

3. Hebrews 7:24: But this man, because he continueth ever, hath an unchangeable priesthood. Verse 25: Wherefore he is able also to save them to the uttermost that come unto God by him, seeing he ever liveth to make intercession for them.

– not only in the English translation, but in the original – would require to be fundamentally changed: the language of Scripture is adapted to a vicarious intervention, and to no other' (Pope).

sacrifice to satisfy divine justice

'Sacrifice was the centre of worship before Christ. It was that part of the Hebrew service which above all foreshadowed His love, His atonement and sacrifice, and the reconciliation to God by His blood whose merits it pleaded' (Pusey).

'The honour of God does not permit Him to forgive sinners out of His pity; for thereby not only would the unrighteous be made equal to the righteous, and all order in His kingdom overthrown, but even unrighteousness itself would be put upon a level with God, if, like Him, exempted from the authority of the law' (Ritschl).

'The word "satisfaction" is the one which for ages has been generally used to designate the special work of Christ in the salvation of men. Its exact etymological equivalent is "the doing enough". This word has the advantage of being precise, comprehensible, and generally accepted, and should therefore be adhered to' (Hodge).

'That satisfaction by which sins are blotted out, so that we are no longer under the curse and the sentence of death, is to be found nowhere else than in the sacrifice of Christ's death' (Calvin).

and reconcile us to God

To reconcile is to restore to friendship those who have become estranged or hostile. Now this is the work of Christ as a priest. He removes the offence, and makes peace between God and the sinner, and hence Paul calls the gospel 'the word of reconciliation'.

'In vain it is objected that the Scripture saith our Saviour reconciled man to God, but nowhere teacheth that He reconciled God to man; for in the language of the Scripture to reconcile a man to God is in our vulgar language to reconcile God to man, that is, to cause Him who before was angry and offended with him, to be gracious and propitious to him' (Pearson).

'The satisfaction for our sins was accomplished on the cross, and it depended upon the eternal pleasure of God, who would be pacified in this way' (Calvin on Rom. 4:25). 'There was need of reconciling us to God, because by sin we were set at enmity with God (Isa. 59:2). God had a legal enmity against us, such as a just judge hath against a malefactor, whose person he may love notwithstanding (Matt. 5:25). And we have naturally a real enmity against God, inconsistent with love to Him (Col. 1:21)' (Boston).

'The office of a priest differed from all other ecclesiastical offices, in that he was to deal with God on behalf of man. Others, from the inspired prophet or apostle to the evangelist, bishop, elder, or deacon, were appointed by God to deal with man. The priest likewise held his office by the command of God; but his office was God-ward, while that of all the others was man-ward' (Stewart).

making continual intercession for us

To intercede is to come in between two parties at variance, with a view to their reconciliation. And the Scriptures supply us with abundant consolation concerning the intercession of Christ on our behalf. 'Who is he that condemneth?' is the apostle's challenge; 'It is Christ that died, yea rather, that is risen again, who is even at the right hand of God, who also maketh intercession for us' (Rom. 8:34). 'Nor must we look upon this as a servile or precarious, but rather as an efficacious and glorious intercession, as of Him to whom all power is given both in heaven and earth' (Pearson). This intercession is perpetual, unconditional, and all-prevailing. It is not carried on by words and pleadings; Christ's simple presence in our nature at God's right hand secures for us the fruit of His death. Hence the orthodox schoolmen said His intercession was real, not verbal.

There is a relation or correspondence distinctly traceable in Scripture between the various parts of Christ's work for us, and the results of that work in us. It is a frequent scriptural distinction to say that as on earth He gave Himself for our sins, so in heaven He makes intercession for our persons. He died for our sins, He intercedes for our souls. The apostle puts it very clearly in Romans: 'We are justified by His blood; but being reconciled we are saved by His life' (Rom. 5:9,10). Our past sins were the cause of His death; our sanctification and full salvation are the end and fruits of His intercession.

'Christ's intercession in heaven is a kind and powerful remembrance of His people, and of all their concerns, managed with state and majesty: not as a suppliant at the footstool, but as a crowned price on the throne, at the right hand of the Father' (Traill).

Uses

1. 'The essential idea of sin is not that it is merely a debt or an injury, but that it is a violation of God's law, and therefore the leading character or aspect in which God ought to be contemplated when we regard Him as dealing with it, is not that of a creditor, or an injured party, who may remit the debt, or forgive the injury as He chooses, but that of a lawgiver and a judge who has promulgated a just and righteous law, prohibiting sin under pain of death, and who is bound, by a regard to His own perfections, and the interests of holiness throughout the universe, to take care that His own character be fully vindicated, that the honour of His law be maintained, and that His moral government be firmly established; and who, therefore, cannot pardon sin, unless, in some way or other, full and adequate provision be made for securing all those objects' (Cunningham).

2. 'It is Christ considered as clothed with His garments of blood, and the qualifications of a mediator and reconciler; it is this that makes Him so desirable by sinners, and a fit object for their faith, which looks out for justification, to prey and seize upon. Paul preached Christ above all, so Christ *as crucified* above all in Christ' (Goodwin).

QUESTION 26

How doth Christ execute the office of a king?

Answer: Christ executeth the office of a king, in subduing us to himself,[1] *in ruling*[2] *and defending us,*[3] *and in restraining and conquering all his and our enemies.*[4]

---

1. Acts 15:14: Simeon hath declared how God at the first did visit the Gentiles, to take out of them a people for his name. Verse 16: I will return, and will build again the tabernacle of David, which is fallen down; and I will build again the ruins thereof, and I will set it up.

2. Isaiah 33:22: For the Lord is our judge, the Lord is our lawgiver, the Lord is our king; he will save us.

3. Isaiah 32:1: Behold, a king shall reign in righteousness, and princes shall rule in judgment. Verse 2: And a man shall be as an hiding-place from the wind, and a covert from the tempest; as rivers of water in a dry place; as the shadow of a great rock in a weary land.

4. 1 Corinthians 15:25: For he must reign, till he hath put all enemies under his feet. Psalm 110 throughout.

the office of a king
See the amplification of this Answer in Larger Catechism, Answer 45.

subduing us to himself
We are born in a state of rebellion against God and Christ. We all come into the world alienated from our Maker and Redeemer. And accordingly, one of the leading offices of Christ is to subdue us. And hence it is that every conversion is represented as a conquest: to be more and more brought under law to Christ is the very life of grace and the salvation of the soul. Christ's sceptre is not so much the symbol of His power as of our salvation.

'Earthly kingdoms are founded not in justice, but in injustice. They are created by the sword, by robbery, cruelty, perjury, craft, fraud. There never was a kingdom except Christ's, which was not conceived and born, nurtured and educated in sin. There never was a state but it was committed to acts and maxims which it is its crime to maintain, and its ruin to abandon. What monarchy is there but began in invasion and usurpation? What revolution has been effected without self-will, violence, and hypocrisy? What popular government but is blown about by every wind as if it had no conscience and no responsibilities? What dominion of the few but is selfish and unscrupulous? What is military strength without the passion for war? But Christ's kingdom is of another sort. This is the indelible distinction between it and all other kingdoms, that they spring from evil, and depend on evil, but that the life of the Church lies in what would pull down all the empires of the world: in patience, in simplicity, in innocence, in concession, in passiveness, in resignation' (Newman).

in ruling and defending us
Having subdued us, Christ rules us. We are not compelled, but sweetly constrained to take the law of our life in everything from His Word and Spirit. We are proud to confess that we are not our own. Things we would continually do were we our own, we do not do because we are Christ's. 'Your bodies and your souls are His,' says the apostle. And every breach of the covenant in misruling the body or the soul is an act of rebellion against our heavenly King.

But it is the office of a king to defend as well as rule his subjects. It is the experience of this that teaches His subjects to sing: 'The LORD is my rock, and my fortress, and my deliverer; my God, my strength, in whom I will trust; my buckler, and the horn of my salvation, and my high tower' (Ps. 18:2). And our Lord is set before us in Scripture as a priest upon his throne; that is to say, He is an Intercessor whose power is nothing short of the power of a sovereign. And all power in heaven and on earth is in His hand, that by means of it He should subdue, rule, and defend His people.

restraining and conquering all his and our enemies
The enemies of Christ and the enemies of the subjects of Christ are of two kinds, temporal enemies and spiritual. Under temporal enemies may be classed all opposers and persecutors of the cause and people of Christ, with all scoffers and blasphemers of His name. On the other hand, His and our spiritual foes, according to the common classification of Scripture, are sin, Satan, and death. On the restraining and conquering of sin, Pearson uses these weighty words:

> Christ then as King destroyeth the power of sin in all those that belong to His kingdom, annihilating the guilt thereof by the virtue of His death, destroying the dominion thereof by His actual grace, and taking away the spot thereof by grace habitual. But in the reprobate and damned souls, the spot of sin remaineth in its perfect dye, the dominion of sin continueth in its absolute power, the guilt of sin abideth in a perpetual obligation to eternal pains; but in all this, in subjection to His throne, the glory of which consisteth as well in punishing rebellion as in rewarding loyalty.

On the restraining and conquering of Satan see Hebrews 2:14; 1 John 3:8; also the history of the Temptation in the Gospels, and the book of Revelation throughout. 'The last enemy that shall be destroyed is death' (1 Cor. 15:26); '...death is swallowed up in victory (1 Cor. 15:54); 'And death and hell shall be cast into the lake of fire (Rev. 20:14); 'For He must reign till He hath put all enemies under His feet' (1 Cor. 15:25).

QUESTION 27

Wherein did Christ's humiliation consist?

Answer: Christ's humiliation consisted in his being born, and that in a low condition,[1] *made under the law,*[2] *undergoing the miseries of this life,*[3] *the wrath of God,*[4] *and the cursed death of the cross;*[5] *in being buried,*[6] *and continuing under the power of death for a time.*[7]

Christ's humiliation

The Latin is *humilis*, near the ground, and from the same root come also 'human' and 'homage'. This is a Scripture term as applied to our Lord (Acts 8:33; Phil. 2:8). And the successive steps of His humiliation are given in this Answer.

his being born

The Psalmist says of God, that even to 'behold the things that are in heaven and on earth' is to 'humble Himself' (Ps. 113:6). What then must it be to come to earth and pass through all we are in this Answer told He did pass through! The lowness of His condition, and all that fitly followed that, even to His death and burial – all this strikes our imagination, and awakens our sympathy more; but to stoop from heaven and its glory

---

1. Luke 2:7: And she brought forth her first-born son, and wrapped him in swaddling clothes, and laid him in a manger; because there was no room for them in the inn.

2. Galatians 4:4: ...made under the law.

3. Hebrews 12:2: ...endured the cross, despising the shame. Verse 3: Consider him that endured such contradiction of sinners against himself. Isaiah 53:2: For he shall grow up before him as a tender plant, and as a root out of a dry ground: he hath no form nor comeliness; and when we shall see him, there is no beauty that we should desire him. Verse 3: He is despised and rejected of men; a man of sorrows, and acquainted with grief; and we hid as it were our faces from him: he was despised, and we esteemed him not.

4. Luke 22:44: And, being in an agony, he prayed more earnestly: and his sweat was as it were great drops of blood falling down to the ground. Matthew 27:46: And about the ninth hour Jesus cried with a loud voice, saying, Eli, Eli, lama sabachthani? that is to say, My God, my God, why hast thou forsaken me?

5. Philippians 2:8: ...became obedient unto death, even the death of the cross.

6. 1 Corinthians 15:4: He was buried.

7. Acts 2:24: Whom God hath raised up, having loosed the pains of death. Verse 26: My flesh shall rest in hope. Verse 27: Because thou wilt not leave my soul in hell, neither wilt thou suffer thine Holy One to see corruption. Verse 31: His soul was not left in hell, neither his flesh did see corruption.

and blessedness to earth and its misery, that was humiliation it hath not entered into the heart of man to conceive. For the eternal Son of God to be 'born of a woman' was a humiliation that might lead to any depth, as it did lead to depths that pass our imagination.

a low condition

'She brought forth her first-born Son, and wrapped Him in swaddling clothes, and laid Him in a manger, because there was no room for them in the inn' (Luke 2:7). 'How was it with Christ, the Son of the living God? Where was He born? In a stable. I suppose not many men suffer an indignity so great: born, not in quiet and comfort, but amid the brute cattle. And what was His first cradle, if I may so call it? A manger. Such were the beginnings of His earthly life; nor did His condition mend as life went on. He says on one occasion: "Foxes have holes, and birds of the air have nests, but the Son of man hath not where to lay His head." "Ye know the grace of our Lord Jesus Christ, that though He was rich, yet for your sakes He became poor, that ye through His poverty might be rich"' (Newman).

made under the law

'Christ was born under the moral law as a creature and a Son of Adam, and under the ceremonial law as a Son of Abraham' (Goodwin).

'The law to which Christ subjected Himself was (1) The law given to Adam as a covenant of works, that is, prescribing perfect obedience as a condition of life; (2) the Mosaic law which bound the Jewish people; (3) the moral law as a rule of duty. And the subjection to the law was voluntary and vicarious' (Hodge).

undergoing the miseries of this life

'For sad occurrences and events befalling Him from the dispensations of providence, and the enmity of the creatures, there was more befell Him than ever befell any man. He was *vir dolorum*, a "man of sorrows," which did all wear and waste Him, as griefs use to do us, so that in the judgment of those that saw Him, He looked nearer fifty years old than thirty, as that known speech may seem to impart. Furthermore, we never read that He once laughed in His lifetime.... Nor was there, or ever could there be supposed, any man so put to it as He: wisdom to converse with folly, perfect holiness with sin and impurity, truth with errors and mistakes. In converses of near relations, contrarieties, and antipathies of dispositions, how burdensome are they! He could have had much better and more suitable company in heaven; yet Christ with an unwearied patience bore all this' (Goodwin).

the wrath of God
The word 'wrath' is the familiar scriptural term to express any manifestation of the displeasure of God against sin. Christ, although in Himself perfectly holy, bore our sins (2 Cor. 5:21; Isa. 13:12).

'The wrath of God did operate on His soul, filling it with troubles, sore amazement, heaviness, and exceeding sorrow, and casting Him into an agony, even to His sweating great drops of blood, and at length bringing over it a total eclipse of all comfort, and as it were melting it within Him (John 12:27; Mark 14:33, 34; Luke 22:44; Matt. 27:46; Ps. 22:14). This was a spiritual death, such as a holy soul was capable of. Now the wrath of God could justly fall upon Christ, a person perfectly innocent, inasmuch as He stood surety for sinners (Heb. 7:22, with Prov. 6:1, 2; 2 Cor. 5:21)' (Horsley).

the cursed death of the cross
'Curse' and 'cross' are at the bottom the same word and mean the same thing. To curse originally meant to execrate by the sign of the cross.

'The curse denounced in the law, on those hanged on a tree, was a ceremonial curse, not hindering the salvation of penitents (Luke 23:33, 43). But the curse that lay on Christ in His humiliation was a real and substantial one, whereof the tree of His cross was but the badge and sign (Gal. 3:13)' (Boston).

'The love of Christ led Him to unite Himself to us, and He completed the union by His death' (Calvin). But let the truth taught in the somewhat technical language of theology never be forgotten: The Vital Union was severed for a time by death, but the Personal Union never. (See under 'for ever,' Answer 21.)

continuing under the power of death for a time
This clause in the Catechism is intended to cover all that is taught in the Apostles' Creed by the words 'He descended into Hell.'

Note
The clause in Philippians 2:8, 'He humbled', or better, 'emptied Himself', is a crucial passage in Christological doctrine. There is a

great body of commentators and divines who hold that the eternal Son literally and actually 'emptied Himself' of His divine power and glory during His period of humiliation, and only recovered and resumed after His ascension what He had laid aside. But opposed to them there is another and better body of theologians, who earnestly and anxiously contend against all such impossible explanations, and who assert that the apostle must be read metaphorically, and not literally, or rather must be read as referring to our Lord's condition and experiences in His human nature, and not in His Divine Nature, when he says that the unchangeable and eternal Son 'emptied Himself.' For to read that text literally, and of the Divinity, say they, would be the contradiction and overthrow of the very first principles of the doctrines of the Divine Nature and the Divine Sonship. The Divine Nature, they contend, is eternal and unchangeable in each of the Three Divine Persons, and, therefore, in the Second of the Three; and not even the Incarnation, not even the cross or the grave, can in any way suspend or impair the Son's possession and exercise of the whole Godhead power and glory. And they teach, accordingly, that the 'emptiness', of which Paul undoubtedly speaks, stood only, and could only stand, in the humanity of our Lord, and is to be understood and affirmed of the humanity alone. 'Remaining what He was, He became what He was not.' When the eternal Son of God became man, He extended rather than contracted Himself, He added to rather than took from Himself, He added humanity and its humiliating attributes to Himself rather than emptied Himself of divinity and its glorious attributes. And consequently, His human 'emptiness', which was no metaphor, but an awful reality, was continually supported on earth, and is still eternally supplied in heaven out of His own divine and everlasting and unchangeable Fulness.

Use

'Homer expresses the Greek idea of greatness in these words: "Ever to lead the van, and to surpass others." Quite otherwise was it with the Lord Jesus. His path was not upwards, but downwards. He was great, not by ascending, but by descending; hence his was not a brilliant, but a silent greatness. The aim of his every action was to draw near to the mean and the despised, to seek the lost, to minister to others, instead of being ministered unto' (Ullman).

QUESTION 28

Wherein consisteth Christ's exaltation?

Answer: Christ's exaltation consisteth in his rising again from the dead on the third day,[1] *in ascending up into heaven,*[2] *in sitting at the right hand of God the Father,*[3] *and in coming to judge the world at the last day.*[4]

Christ's exaltation
See Larger Catechism, Questions 51-56.

his rising again from the dead on the third day
The conception of the resurrection of Christ is almost confined, in modern times, to the fact that 'after three days he rose again.' In St. Paul it has a much wider import; it is a new life of Christians as well as Christ: a resurrection of the believer at the same time with his Lord. Altogether, there are four ways in which the resurrection of Christ is spoken of in the Epistles of St. Paul, the ethical or spiritual meanings often blending with the literal facts. First, the resurrection is spoken of as an outward fact, of which there were many witnesses. Secondly, as an idea or doctrine, forming a part also, or aspect, of the inner life of the gospel. Thirdly, as the figure or condition, almost the cause, of the resurrection of believers, which is identified with the resurrection of Christ as the Christian himself is with Christ Himself. Fourthly, as the figure, or condition, or principle of spiritual resurrection.... These four series, as points of view in which the resurrection of Christ is spoken of, easily pass into one another (condensed from Jowett on Galatians 1:1).

'The death of Christ is the principal agency toward our reconciliation; but His resurrection is the real assurance that we are truly reconciled to God' (Lange).

---

1. 1 Corinthians 15:4: He rose again the third day according to the scriptures.
2. Mark 16:19: He was received up into heaven, and sat on the right hand of God.
3. Ephesians 1:20: Which he wrought in Christ, when he raised him from the dead, and set him at his own right hand in the heavenly places.
4. Acts 1:11: This same Jesus, which is taken up from you into heaven, shall so come in like manner as ye have seen him go into heaven. Acts 17:31: Because he hath appointed a day, in the which he will judge the world in righteousness by that man whom he hath ordained; whereof he hath given assurance unto all men, in that he hath raised him from the dead.

ascending up into heaven
It was in His human nature that Christ ascended, not in His Divine Nature, because it was always in heaven.

'Heaven, that place of all places in the universe of things in situation most eminent, in quality most holy, in dignity most excellent, in glory most illustrious, the innermost sanctuary of God's temple above' (Barrow).

'The heaven into which Christ ascended is not the atmospheric or stellar heaven; the term is an emblematical expression for the invisible residence of God, the seat of perfect order, whence emanates every manifestation of righteousness upon the earth, every victorious struggle of good against evil. The visible heavens, the regularity of the motions of the stars, the lifelike and pure lustres of their fires: this whole great spectacle has always been to the consciousness of man the invisible representation of the divine order' (Godet).

> From God the Father He proceeds,
> To God the Father back He speeds;
> Proceeds as far as very hell,
> Speeds back to light ineffable (Ambrose).

sitting at the right hand of God the Father
'A similitude borrowed from princes, who have their assessors, to whom they commit the office of ruling and issuing commands. Thus Christ, in whom the Father is pleased to be exalted, and by whose hand He is pleased to reign, is said to have been received up, and seated on His right hand, as if it had been said that He is installed in the government of heaven and earth, and formally admitted to possession of the administration committed to Him, and not only admitted for once, but to continue until he descend to judgment.... All that the apostles intend, when they so often mention His seat at the Father's right hand, is to teach that everything is placed at His disposal' (Calvin).

'Oh, methought, Christ! Christ! There was nothing but Christ that was before mine eyes. I was not now for looking upon this and that benefit apart, as of His blood, burial, resurrection, but considered Him as a whole Christ, as He in whom all these, and all other His virtues, relations, offices, and operations met together, and that as He sat on the right hand of God in heaven' (Bunyan).

and in coming to judge the world at the last day
God in His pure Godhead is not to be our judge, but Christ in His Godhead and manhood. We are to be judged by man. And man's feelings, affections, passions; His pity, compassion, tenderness, will all operate in the judgment, as well as His wrath, scorn, loathing, and contempt. Our judgment will be as near, and direct, and personal as if we were arraigned before a judge in an earthly court, and as searching and immediate as if God Omniscient and All-righteous sat on our case. The man Christ Jesus will judge every one of us (Acts 17:31).

'Between His ascension and His coming in glory no event intervenes equal in importance to each of these two events; therefore these two are joined together. Naturally, therefore, the apostles, before the giving of the Apocalypse, set before them the day of Christ as very near. And it accords with the majesty of Christ, that during the whole period between His Ascension and His Advent He should, without intermission, be expected' (Bengel).

In Paul's words, 'God shall judge the secrets of men by Jesus Christ, according to my gospel.' Bengel remarks: 'The gospel is the whole preaching as to Christ, and Christ will be the judge.... All the articles of evangelical doctrine, and the article concerning the final judgment, greatly illustrate one another; and moreover this very article, even in respect of believers, is altogether evangelical (Acts 10:42; 1 Pet.4:5).'

Uses

1. 'To none of the great truths relating to the two natures of our Lord is it more necessary to adhere firmly in the present age than to that of His resurrection. A hearty belief in the literal and local ascent of our Lord's humanity is in itself a belief in the whole mystery of the union of Godhead and manhood' (Ellicott).

2. 'Human nature is at this moment the highest of created natures, and more intimately united to the Godhead than any other; and where our Head is, there shall all His members in due time be. Whoever, then, thou art that turnest thine eye on this one page, our message to thee is, that in a few short years thou must occupy that place to which angels may look up with admiration, or that on which devils may look down, with the conviction that they have been less guilty than thee. Higher than heaven is the fate of him whom the Saviour of the world became man to redeem; and lower than hell must be the fate of him who has even at such a price refused to be redeemed' (Dods in Christian Instructor, 1830).

3. 'It is consolatory to think that judgment is vested in Him who has already destined us to share with Him in the honour of judgment; so far is it from being true that He will ascend the judgment-seat for our condemnation. How could a most merciful prince destroy his own people? how could the head disperse its own members? how could the advocate condemn his own clients?... It certainly gives no small security that we shall be sisted at no other tribunal than that of our Redeemer, from whom salvation is to be expected; and that He who now in the gospel promises eternal blessedness, will then as judge ratify His promise. The end for which the Father honoured the Son, by committing all judgment to Him, was to pacify the consciences of His people when alarmed at the thought of judgment' (Calvin).

4. 'Coming to judge the world.' 'The thing is true, but the time appointed is long' (Dan. 10:1).

QUESTION 29

How are we made partakers of the redemption purchased by Christ?

Answer: We are made partakers of the redemption purchased by Christ, by the effectual application of it to us[1] *by his Holy Spirit.*[2]

The student will be rewarded who keeps his eye on the structure of the Catechism. Note that as Question 20 introduced Christ and His redeeming work, so the Question now before us in like manner introduces the Holy Spirit. The logical method of this document is one of its most notable features.

The redemption purchased by Christ

A redemption, from the very etymology of the word, is a purchase. And hence He who purchased in this case is called the Redeemer. See Answer 20. 'The Son of man came to give His life a ransom for many' (Matt. 20:28; Mark 10:45). Now a ransom is a price paid to redeem those who

---

1. John 1:12: But as many as received him, to them gave he power to become the sons of God, even to them that believe on his name.

2. Titus 3:5: According to his mercy he saved us, by the washing of regeneration, and renewing of the Holy Ghost. Verse 6: Which he shed on us abundantly through Jesus Christ our Saviour.

are held in bondage or captivity. And Scripture everywhere teaches that the fallen state of man is a state of guilt and bondage, from which Christ has redeemed His people by laying down His life as a ransom for them. 'Ye are bought with a price' (1 Cor. 6:20, 7:23), saith Paul; and Peter says, 'We are not redeemed with corruptible things as silver and gold, but with the precious blood of Christ' (1 Pet. 1:18). 'The redemption purchased' is thus an entirely scriptural expression.

'Two things are principally to be considered in the respect that forgiveness hath to the blood of Christ: (1) the way of its procurement; (2) the way of its administration by Him. The first is deep, mysterious, dreadful. It was by His blood, the blood of His cross, the travail of His soul, His undergoing wrath and curse. This also adds to the mysterious depth of forgiveness, and makes its discovery a great matter. The soul that looks after it in earnest must consider what it cost.... To see the mystery of the love of the Father, working in the blood of the Mediator, to consider by faith the great transaction of divine wisdom, justice, and mercy therein – how few attain unto it! To come unto God by Christ for forgiveness, and to behold the law issuing all its threats and curses in His blood, and losing its sting, putting an end to its obligation unto punishment, in the cross; to see all sins gathered up in the hands of God's justice, and made to meet in the Mediator, and eternal love springing forth triumphantly from His blood, flourishing into pardon, grace, mercy, forgiveness – this the heart of a sinner can be enlarged into only by the Spirit of God' (Owen).

'Look what salvation thou dost design, saith Christ, that I will purchase, and notwithstanding my purchase thou shalt give it all freely. Grace shall not be robbed one whit by me, but advanced; the ransom of it shall not be one whit impaired by me; no, the giving of me, and that I die by grace (Heb. 2), shall magnify grace so much the more, and make it double grace. So that now the grace that was in God hath a Saviour for us fitted to His own heart' (Goodwin).

effectual application

'There are three sorts of works whereby our salvation is completed and accomplished. (1) Immanent, in God toward us, as His eternal love set and passed upon us, out of which He chose us, and designed this and all blessings to us. (2) Transient, in Christ done for us; in all He did or suffered representing of us, and in our stead. (3) Applicatory, wrought in us and upon us, in the endowing us with all those blessings by His Spirit, as calling, justification, sanctification, glorification' (Goodwin).

by his Holy Spirit

'The Father provides the Saviour, and the purchase is made of Him; the Son is the purchaser and the price, and the Holy Ghost is the great blessing or inheritance purchased, as is intimated, Galatians 3:13, 14. This inheritance was the grand legacy which Christ left His disciples and the Church in His last will and testament, John 14, 15, 16. This is the sum of the blessing of eternal life which shall be in heaven.'

'Christ made His will by His death (Heb. 9), but the Spirit is His administrator. Christ's blood and purchase gave us, by His redeeming us, *jus ad rem*; but the Holy Ghost, by applying it, *jus in re*; He gives us possession, livery, and seisin' (Goodwin).

Use

'We might as well strike from the Bible the name and doctrine of God, as the name and office of the Spirit. In the New Testament alone He is mentioned not far from three hundred times.... The work of the Spirit in applying the redemption of Christ is represented to be as essential as the redemption itself. It is therefore indispensable that we should know what the Bible teaches concerning the Holy Ghost, both as to His nature and office' (Hodge).

QUESTION 30

How doth the Spirit apply to us the redemption purchased by Christ?

Answer: The Spirit applieth to us the redemption purchased by Christ, by working faith in us,[1] *and thereby uniting us to Christ in our effectual calling.*[2]

1. Ephesians 1:13: In whom ye also trusted, after that ye heard the word of truth, the gospel of your salvation: in whom also, after that ye believed, ye were sealed with that holy Spirit of promise, Verse 14: Which is the earnest of our inheritance, until the redemption of the purchased possession, unto the praise of his glory. John 6:37: All that the Father giveth me shall come to me: and him that cometh to me I will in no wise cast our. Verse 39: And this is the Father's will which hath sent me, that of all which he hath given me I should lose nothing, but should raise it up again at the last day. Ephesians 2:8: For by grace are ye saved through faith; and that not of yourselves: it is the gift of God.

2. Ephesians 3:17: That Christ may dwell in your hearts by faith; that ye, being rooted and grounded in love, etc. 1 Corinthians 1:9: God is faithful, by whom ye were called unto the fellowship of his Son Jesus Christ our Lord.

The Spirit applieth
The word literally means to join or fold together, also to lay on, as of an emollient on a diseased or injured part. In the scriptural and doctrinal use of the word in the text, it describes that blessed work of the Holy Ghost by which the fruits of Christ's redemption are laid upon the soul, and effectually and indissolubly made ours. In Hooker's great sermon on justification the following passage occurs, and it is here quoted as stating in noblest words the doctrine both of Christ's purchase of redemption and the manner of its application to us:

> Christ hath merited righteousness for as many as are found in Him. In Him God findeth us, if we be faithful; for by faith we are incorporated into Him. Then, although in ourselves we be altogether sinful and unrighteous, yet even the man which in himself is impure, full in iniquity, full of sin; him being found in Christ through faith, and having his sin in hatred through repentance, him God beholdeth with a gracious eye, putteth away his sin by not imputing it, taketh quite away the punishment due thereunto by pardoning it; and accepteth him in Jesus Christ as perfectly righteous, as if he had fulfilled the whole law? I must take heed what I say; but the apostle saith, "God made Him to be sin for us, who knew no sin, that we might be made the righteousness of God in Him" (2 Cor. 5:21). Such we are in the sight of God the Father, as is the very Son of God Himself. Let it be counted folly, or frenzy, or fury, or whatsoever. It is our wisdom and our comfort; we care for no other knowledge in the world but this, that man hath sinned, and God hath suffered; that God hath made Himself the sin of men, and that men are made the righteousness of God.

redemption
The act of redeeming or buying back, effecting a ransom. Thus we speak of the redemption of prisoners taken in war, and of the redemption of an estate that had been mortgaged. In the scriptural and theological language before us, it means the deliverance of sinners from the bondage of sin and from the sentence of condemnation. (See Answers 21, 29.)

purchased by Christ
Christ effected the redemption, paid the ransom, and hence He is called the Redeemer. His work is called a purchase because He died and paid all that

God's justice demanded for our pardon and release. 'Christ hath merited to make us just; but as a medicine that is made for health doth not heal by being made, but by being applied; so, by the merits of Christ, there can be no justification without the application of His merits' (Hooker).

by working faith
For faith, see Question 86.

uniting us to Christ
To unite is to make two or more into one. Now the text teaches that the subjects of effectual calling are made one with Christ. This union is set forth under many beautiful and instructive figures in Holy Scripture.

Uses
1. 'Let us apply ourselves to the Holy Ghost, let us glorify Him in our hearts, let us dart forth beams of special and peculiar love to Him, let us converse with Him, and fear to grieve Him.'

2. 'Is He the author of conversion? Then lament and bewail the hardness of thy heart, which, though it hath so often had good motions put into it by the Spirit, yet hath not followed them, but given a deaf ear to them' (Goodwin).

QUESTION 31

What is effectual calling?

Answer: Effectual calling is the work of God's Spirit,[1] *whereby, convincing us of our sin and misery,*[2] *enlightening our minds in the knowledge of Christ,*[3] *and renewing our wills,*[4] *he doth persuade and enable us to embrace Jesus Christ, freely offered to us in the gospel.*[5]

---

1. 2 Timothy 1:9: Who hath saved us, and called us with an holy calling, not according to our works, but according to his own purpose and grace, which was given us in Christ Jesus before the world began. 2 Thessalonians 2:13: ...salvation through sanctification of the Spirit, and belief of the truth. Verse 14: Whereunto he called you by our gospel, to the obtaining of the glory of our Lord Jesus Christ.

2. Acts 2:37: Now when they heard this, they were pricked in their heart, and said unto Peter, and to the rest of the apostles, Men and brethren, what shall we do?

3. Acts 26:18; To open their eyes, and to turn them from darkness to light.

Effectual calling

Cruden gives a table setting forth fourteen different uses of this word in Scripture, beginning with the first and simplest use, 'And God called the light Day' (Gen. 1:5). And the highest sense of this familiar word is seen in such scriptures as these, 'God hath saved us, and called us with an holy calling' (2 Tim. 1:9). 'Give diligence to make your calling and election sure' (2 Pet. 1:10). Dr. Hodge, in his exhaustive and excellent chapter on 'Vocation,' says: 'The work of the Spirit is in the scriptures called VOCATION. It is one of the many possible, scriptural terms for scriptural doctrines.... The words of Scripture are the words of the Spirit, and it is becoming and important that they should be retained.'

Effectual means producing, or having adequate power or force to produce, an intended effect. As frequently in Paul, 'a great door and effectual is opened to me;' 'By the effectual working of His power,' etc. 'Calling, in the sense in which Paul uses it, cannot fail, or remain ineffectual. In truth, calling and election are, with him, one and the same thing, with the one exception of the different epochs, which man necessarily assigns to the two acts in question' (Reuss).

the work of God's Spirit

In the Larger Catechism it is called 'the work of God's almighty power and grace'; and in the Confession the work of God's 'word and Spirit'. A work like sanctification, not an act like justification and adoption. And the stages of the work are given in varied detail in the text and in the two documents named. 'Spirit, as the word is used to signify the Third Person in the Trinity, is the substantive, from which is formed the adjective spiritual in the Holy Scriptures. Thus Christians are called spiritual persons because they are born of the Spirit, and because of the indwelling and holy influences of the Spirit of God in them' (Edwards).

---

4. Ezekiel 36:26: A new heart also will I give you, and a new spirit will I put within you; and I will take away the stony heart out of your flesh, and I will give you an heart of flesh. Verse 27: And I will put my Spirit within you, and cause you to walk in my statutes, and ye shall keep my judgments, and do them.

5. John 6:44: No man can come to me, except the Father, which hath sent me, draw him. Verse 45: It is written in the prophets, And they shall be all taught of God. Every man therefore that hath heard, and hath learned of the Father, cometh unto me. Philippians 2:13: For it is God which worketh in you, both to will and to do of his good pleasure.

convincing us of our sin and misery

The first step the Spirit takes in our effectual calling is to convince us of sin. To convict, in ordinary speech, and especially in legal usage, is to prove an accused person guilty of the charge that has been laid against him. To convince, again, though originally and really the same work as to convict, has by long usage been restricted to intellectual and moral processes. To convince is to conquer the mind; it is to subdue anyone by reason and argument; it is to force truth home on the understanding and heart. The phrase before us, conviction of sin, is an expression often made use of by experimental writers to set forth that conquest of divine grace when the soul of a sinner is so overcome that he feels and confesses himself corrupt, guilty, and lost. And that divine work – for a divine work it always is – is here set in the very forefront of the process of 'effectual calling'.

The Holy Ghost, so to speak, frames an indictment, and carries a conviction in their consciences against sinners. He is always and above all the Spirit of God, the Spirit of truth and of holiness, and if He is to enter our hearts effectually as the Spirit of grace and salvation, He must begin His work in truth. And the first stage of His work is finished when our mouth is shut under a sense of guilt and shame. But while conviction of sin is properly put in the foreground of our effectual calling, yet we are not to understand by that that the Spirit's convicting work is past and finished when conversion is first effected. On the contrary, it is only the truly converted and spiritually enlightened man who sees or can see what Scripture calls the sinfulness of sin. It is not under the heavy and prostrating hand of the Spirit of bondage, but rather under the healing and sanctifying hand of the Spirit of adoption, that we become spiritually and adequately convinced of sin.

sin and misery

For misery, see Answers 19, 20, and 27. All men feel the widespread suffering that is in the world, but this doleful word misery is reserved in religious language to describe the experience of persons under the Spirit's hand in effectual calling. See the Psalms throughout, and such books of experimental and evangelical religion as Bunyan's *Grace Abounding*.

enlightening our minds in the knowledge of Christ

'Savingly enlightening their minds' (Larger Catechism); 'enlightening their minds savingly and spiritually to understand the things of God'

(Confession). Darkness and light are terms which continually occur to describe a state of grace in the Scriptures. Heathenism is a life of darkness; Judaism, if not darkness, has its eyes under a dense veil; while an unregenerate state in Jew and Gentile is slavery in a kingdom of darkness. Believers alone are children of the light and of the day. They are light in the Lord. Nay, they are the light of the world.

In this part of His work the Holy Ghost turns the sinner's attention, for a time at least, off himself and toward Christ and His salvation. And the knowledge of Christ now attained just corresponds to the soul's new knowledge of sin; and these true branches of knowledge grow mutually and correspondingly to the end of life. Let a sinner be once truly convinced of sin, and let his eyes be also enlightened in the knowledge of Christ, and just in the measure of his conviction of sin and misery, the revelation of Christ will prove inexhaustible in its power, beauty, attractiveness, and grace. Yea, doubtless, such a man will count all things but less for the excellency of the knowledge of Jesus Christ his Lord.

renewing our wills

'renewing and powerfully determined their wills' (Larger Catechism); 'renewing their wills, and by his almighty power determining them to that which is good' (Confession).

There is a vast literature, ancient and modern, philosophical and theological, connected with the will, and the study is one of the profoundest on which the mind of man can enter. This deep and difficult subject cannot be entered on here. The religious and experimental outcome of the scriptural and confessional doctrine of the will is familiar to many through a well-known work of Scottish divinity: Thomas Boston's *Fourfold State*. The fourfold state, that is, of the human will: its state in Adam before the Fall; its state in his descendants before regeneration; the state of the will in the regenerate; and lastly, its state in the glorified. This is an old division; both the Schoolmen and the Fathers recognized it and made use of it.

All the parts of man's nature have suffered each their own peculiar injury by the catastrophe of the Fall, but it is those parts that have more immediately to do with God and His revealed will that have suffered most. And no part has suffered such a shock and hurt as the will. It is now by nature and in every unregenerate man turned away from God, and in bondage to sin and evil. It is not that man would do good, would return to God if he could; it is not that he cannot, he will not. 'Ye will not come to me that ye might have life' (John 5:40). There was no hand holding them back, no cord binding them but the bands of their evil will. This is what is meant when learned divines treat of the bondage and inability of the will.

The work of the Spirit in renewing the will and setting it free is secret, spiritual and mysterious. 'The wind bloweth where it listeth, and thou hearest the sound thereof, but canst not tell whence it cometh, and whither it goeth; so is every one that is born of the Spirit' (John 3:8). At the same time the work of the Spirit is in a man, and though much of that work is necessarily mysterious and inscrutable, yet its results are such as by attention and care may be noted and known, as thus: 'First,' says one whose name occurs often in these notes, 'I felt my soul, and all the powers of it, as in an instant, to be clean altered and changed in the disposition of them. Secondly, I found from the same time the works of the devil to be dissolved in my heart in an eminent manner, my understanding enlightened, my will melted and softened, and of a stone made flesh, disposed to receive, and disposed to return to God. And, thirdly, I found my spirit clothed with a new nature, naturally inclining me to good; whereas before it was naturally inclined to evil. And I found in me henceforth two contrary principles, spirit against flesh, and flesh against spirit. And this difference I found, not by reading or hearing any one speak of it, but, as Austin did, I perceived it of myself, and wondered at it; for I may say of this combat, that it is proper and peculiar to men that are regenerate.' Then follows an account of the influence that this great change had on his views of truth and on his way of preaching. And preaching on this very subject afterwards, he says: 'When God turneth any man to Himself, He fasteneth that man's will. The Holy Ghost sits there, at the centre of his soul, and hath a chief hand upon the stern of a man's spirit. My brethren, your wills are the slipperiest things in the world, the fullest of a lubricity, of a fickleness.... Therefore, above all, desire the Lord to fasten your wills, to hold His hand upon that stern always to guide you.'

'The will,' says Manton, 'is more corrupted than the mind: the understanding is much blinded, but the will is more depraved.... We are convinced often when not converted.'

doth persuade and enable

To persuade is to operate on the feelings and affections, and to draw the mind to a determination by presenting sufficient motives. 'My brethren, it is not the offers of eternity; it is not all the persuasions of men or angels, nor of the Holy Ghost Himself, if they be but mere moral persuasions, will make a man part with a bird in the hand for two in the bush. My meaning is, that will make a man part with his lusts, or his pleasures and sins, and take and accept the offers of eternity; but it must be the power of God, with whom all things are possible, and He must put forth as much power to work this, as He putteth forth to work all things else' (Goodwin).

to embrace Jesus Christ, freely offered to us

Em, and *bras*, the arm; to clasp in the arms, to cling to with warmth and earnestness: to cherish with affection. 'Paul called unto him the disciples, and embraced them' (Acts 20:1). 'Having seen and embraced the promises' (Heb. 11:13).

in the gospel

'The gospel call is universal in the sense that it is addressed to all men indiscriminately to whom the gospel is sent. It is confined to no age, nation, or class of men.... If therefore any one holds any view of the decrees of God, or of the satisfaction of Christ, or of any other scriptural doctrine, which hampers him in making the general offer of the gospel, he may be sure that his views or his logical processes are wrong. The apostles were not thus hampered, and we act under the commission given to them' (Hodge).

Uses

1. 'I had rather feel compunction, than understand the definition thereof' (à Kempis).

2. 'Consider, then, thou called soul, called with an holy calling, that through that little chink, or narrow passage from death to life, thy effectual calling, which was thy first entrance into thy eternity, thou mayest first contemplate that purposing grace of God's will set on thee; for by calling election is made sure.... A saint's being called is the immediate fruit and breaking forth of purposing and electing grace. Whom He hath predestinated, them He also called' (Goodwin).

3. 'We were safer in slighting the Incarnation and Atonement of the Son of man, against whom sins may be forgiven, than in slighting the work of the Spirit, against whom, if we persevere in sin, it shall neither be forgiven in this life, nor in the world to come' (Irving).

4. A minister writes: 'When I catechise my children or my servants, I ask them, What is effectual calling? and they answer me according to what is written in their book. But now I am retired to catechise myself, must I not be careful to answer according to what is written in my heart? O my soul, what a difference there is betwixt answering this question by the words of the book, and from the experience of my own heart!'

QUESTION 32

What benefits do they that are effectually called partake of in this life?

Answer: They that are effectually called do in this life partake of justification,[1] *adoption,*[2] *and sanctification, and the several benefits which in this life do either accompany or flow from them.*[3]

effectually called
See Answer 31.

in this life
See Answer 36. In this life, God, of His free grace and by His Holy Spirit, justifies, adopts, and sanctifies every soul He effectually calls (Rom. 8:30).

The attentive student will observe that this Question is introductory to the six Questions that follow. He will do well to study and trace the connection and sequence of thought between Question 29 and Question 38.

---

1. Romans 8:30: Moreover, whom he did predestinate, them he also called; and whom he called, them he also justified; and whom he justified, them he also glorified.

2. Ephesians 1:5: Having predestinated us unto the adoption of children by Jesus Christ to himself.

3. 1 Corinthians 1:26: For ye see your calling, brethren, how that not many wise men after the flesh, not many mighty, not many noble, are called. Verse 30: But of him are ye in Christ Jesus, who of God is made unto us wisdom, and righteousness, and sanctification, and redemption.

QUESTION 33

What is justification?

Answer: Justification is an act of God's free grace, wherein he pardoneth all our sins,[1] and accepteth us as righteous in his sight,[2] only for the righteousness of Christ imputed to us,[3] and received by faith alone.[4]

We owe the full and clear exhibition of the great Christian doctrine of justification, as we here possess it, to the labours of the Reformation divines. The Greek Fathers, after centuries of study and discussion, bequeathed to the Church universal the noble inheritance of the doctrines of God, of the Trinity, and of the Person of Christ, as all the orthodox Churches now possess them. The Greek Church, the Latin Church, and the Reformed Church all substantially accept the same answer to the questions, What is God? How many Persons are there in the Godhead? and How did the Son of God become man? And happily, the agreement that extends thus far extends still farther. For as there is no confessional disharmony among the Churches on the Person of Christ, neither is there any schism among them on the great evangelical doctrine of His atoning and redeeming work. But when we come to treat of the work of the Holy Ghost in 'applying the redemption purchased by Christ', errors the most serious, if not fatal, are taught by the Church of Rome.

---

1. Romans 3:24: Being justified freely by his grace, through the redemption that is in Christ Jesus; Verse 25: Whom God hath set forth to be a propitiation through faith in his blood, to declare his righteousness for the remission of sins. Romans 4:6: Even as David also describeth the blessedness of the man, unto whom God imputeth righteousness without works, Verse 7: Saying, Blessed are they whose iniquities are forgiven, and whose sins are covered. Verse 8: Blessed is the man to whom the Lord will not impute sin.

2. 2 Corinthians 5:19: God was in Christ, reconciling the world unto himself, not imputing their trespasses unto them; and hath committed unto us the word of reconciliation. Verse 21: That we might be made the righteousness of God in him.

3. Romans 5:17: The gift of righteousness. Verse 18: By the righteousness of one the free gift came upon all men unto justification of life. Verse 19: By the obedience of one shall many be made righteous.

4. Galatians 2:16: Knowing that a man is not justified by the works of the law, but by the faith of Jesus Christ, even we have believed in Jesus Christ, that we might be justified by the faith of Christ, and not by the works of the law: for by the works of the law shall no flesh be justified. Philippians 3:9: And be found in him, not having mine own righteousness, which is of the law, but that which is through the faith of Christ, the righteousness which is of God by faith.

And as the development and vindication of the theological doctrine of God and Christ made the fourth and fifth centuries for ever famous, so the sixteenth and seventeenth centuries stand out above all that went before them in their full and clear exhibition and promulgation of the doctrines of grace. And among the cloud of witnesses God has from time to time raised up to preach His truth, Luther and Calvin and Knox and Owen and Bunyan stand in the front rank beside Athanasius and Cyril and Augustine. All those men, each in his own age and church, proved themselves the true successors of the apostles in the drawing out and defence of scriptural and saving truth.

Justification

In entering on this great subject, it must be clearly seen and understood that the whole idea and conception of justification rests and operates on the ground of the divine law. And the divine law is an eternal ground, eternal and unchangeable as God Himself. And all law to be law must have its inseparable sanctions; that is to say, it must be adequately supported and unflinchingly enforced. Now both nature in conscience and revelation in Scripture testify that we are in all things and at all times under law to God, under a law moreover that has sanctions of reward and punishment corresponding to the greatness of our trespass or the merit of our obedience. The apostolic and Protestant sense of this word is not the same as its strict etymological sense. According to its root, the word literally means to make just or righteous. But in its secondary and scriptural sense it means to count and pronounce just or righteous. In gospel justification, God treats a sinner as if he were a just man. How God can be both a just God and a Saviour, we are on the way to see. But let the student always remember that justification is the antithesis of condemnation, and he will never go wrong on this essential truth of the gospel. This contrast and the true sense of the terms are to be seen in such passages of Scripture as Romans 8:1, 33, 34. Condemnation is the act of a judge, so is justification. If this simple and clear distinction is kept before the mind, there will be little danger of error or mistake in what follows on justification, and sanctification, and saving faith.

an act

As distinguished from a work. Even a child, if he is intelligently taught, should never mistake and say that justification is a work. A judge's sentence is an act; it is uttered and executed at once. A teacher's work and a physician's extend from day to day, and year to year. Now God's act in justification is the sentence of a judge, while the Spirit's work in sanctification is that of a heavenly Teacher and Healer sent from God. 'Q. Why do you call justification an act and not a work? A. Because it is a thing done all at once, as the sentence or declaration of a judge; and not a work of time, carried on by degrees, as effectual calling and sanctification are' (Willison's Catechism).

of God's free grace

'If it be asked, How it is an act of free grace by which we are justified, since it is through the redemption that is in Christ? The answer is this: The redemption that is in Christ is the channel through which justifying grace freely flows to us. It was free grace that provided a Saviour.... To the Saviour Himself, it is indeed an act of strict justice, that His people should be justified, since He has paid the full price of it. But to His people who receive the benefits of redemption, it is grace from the foundation to the copestone' (Green). See Larger Catechism, Answer 71.

pardoneth all our sins

Forgiveth, remitteth a penalty; *per-donare*: thoroughly to forgive. So far true and scriptural. But gospel justification is more and better than mere pardon. Pardon is an act of grace where no reparation or satisfaction has been made. But in the gospel, forgiveness of sin is offered and bestowed on the ground of a reparation and satisfaction having been made to the broken law. If a criminal expiates his crimes, and exhausts his sentence, it is not a pardon he receives when his chains are struck off and his prison door is thrown open. He can claim his freedom as an act of justice. And the Scripture asserts that it is but an act of 'faithfulness' and 'justice' to the penitent believer when God bestows forgiveness upon him. True; in gospel justification, the sinner has not in himself made satisfaction or endured the penalty, but then the whole gospel goes on this, that Another has done all this for him; his Surety has met the bond and accusation, and on the ground of that offered and accepted satisfaction the sinner is righteously absolved and set free. Pardon is an act, but it is a continued, a constantly-repeated act. We 'daily break the commandments of God in thought, word, and deed.' And to meet this, our Lord hath taught us to pray for the daily forgiveness of sin.

'Nor do I dislike the remark of Chrysostom, that the verb in the present tense, who taketh away, denotes a continued act; for the satisfaction that Christ once made is always in full vigour' (Calvin on John 1:29).

and accepteth us

Acceptance is a Scripture word, 'He hath made us accepted in the Beloved' (Eph. 1:6). And the fact that this definition of justification embraces this element, goes to prove our contention above, that justification is more and better than mere pardon. A sovereign may pardon a criminal, but the pardoned man may be abhorred and eschewed by him to whose clemency or statesmanship he owes his pardon. To see how different it is with a justified man, read the context of the above scripture.

as righteous

We are not in ourselves righteous, for, *ex hypothesi*, we are condemned sinners; but the way of salvation through Christ meets all our case, and the justification which is here under discussion has this as its essential feature, that it 'justifies the ungodly' (Rom. 4:5). In effectual calling and sanctification, God makes us righteous; in justification He accepteth us as righteous. By infusing or implanting righteousness, He renews and sanctifies us; by imputing righteousness, He justifies us. He never does the one without in the same subject doing the other; but they are separate operations or acts of His, and those acts and operations are clearly set forth in the Answers immediately before us.

in his sight

'This expression is a continuation of the forensic scenery. God is on His judicial throne. Men are standing at the bar. The justification referred to is the justification that is realizable in a court of justice.... The therapeutical production of inherent righteousness is also and amply provided for. Justification is really in order to sanctification. It is a steppingstone to something beyond itself. And it is no disparagement to the greater blessing, which is realized in the production of inherent righteousness or holiness, that it is ruled under a different rubric than the term justification' (Morison).

only for the righteousness of Christ

The prophetic and apostolic conception of righteousness differs fundamentally from all those conceptions of this noble idea that have ever been entertained in the world of religion and morals outside the sphere of divine revelation. Righteousness, as the writers of Holy Scripture set it before us, is first a divine attribute, manifested as the supreme order and law of heaven; and then after and under that it is a condition of created character, a state of rectitude and uprightness the alone source and supreme standard of which is God Himself. 'I will fetch my knowledge from afar,' says the prophet, 'and I will ascribe righteousness to my Maker' (Job 36:3). So far all is clear and plain. But what is this 'righteousness of Christ' of which such things are said in Scripture and Confession and Catechism?

The righteousness of Christ is the result of His life of voluntary, sponsorial, and perfect obedience to the whole law of God under which He with and for us was born; His life of obedience and then His death of atonement for our sins. Jesus, as the *Christ*, the second Adam, the Surety, the Lamb of God, wrought out a righteousness and acquired a merit, 'finished a work,' which according to the convenant of grace is made over to those who by repentance and faith are found in Him. He was 'made under' our law; He magnified it, and made it honourable; and we were represented by Him in all He did. From the first breath of humiliation He drew in the manger of Bethlehem to the last sigh of resignation He heaved on the cross of Calvary, in both and in all that came to Him between them, Jesus was acting for God and for us as *the Christ*. And now because of Christ's work, God is the justifier of the ungodly, and in Christ and before God the sinner becomes the justified. This, then, is 'the righteousness of Christ' of which we read so much in the Epistles of Paul. There is no subject the apostle deals with with such pains and power and joy. There is nothing that gives Him such gladness as to be able to offer to sinners the 'gift of righteousness'. And there is nothing that arouses His power of rebuke and exposition like seeing this divine gift despised and rejected.

'Do we ask of Paul what is the great want of man? He will answer it is righteousness. Ask what is gained for man by redemption? Again he answers, righteousness. What is the subject of gospel preaching? Jesus died and rose again, that we might be made righteous. What is the purport of the gospel? To declare to men that henceforth there is a way by which they may attain to righteousness. What is that which redounds most to the glory of God? It is that He has revealed the possibility of His being at once just and a justifier. We do not need to multiply these examples;

as the reply to all questions, the substance of all arguments, the basis of all definitions, we shall find righteousness' (Reuss).

imputed to us

Imputare, to reckon or credit with, to set down to any one's account. Imputation is a scriptural word which the Holy Ghost has used, and designs us to use, in describing one of the divine steps in the act of justification. The word literally means to set down to any one's account, to lay to any one's charge. At the same time, to impute may mean either of two things. It may either mean to lay to the charge of any one what he himself has actually done, as in Psalm 32:2 and 2 Corinthians 5:19; or it may mean to lay to one's charge, and reckon to one's account, what another has done as representing him, and as standing and acting in his room and stead. This latter is the fixed and invariable sense of the word in all those scriptures and scriptural creeds that treat of Adam and his posterity and of Christ and His people. To impute in the Adamic and Christian sense is to account to the children what has been done by their father acting in their name; it is to count and treat with the members as one with their covenant Head. This physical, moral, and spiritual law runs through the whole scheme and constitution of human life on the earth. National life, social life, family life, are all full of illustrations of this federal principal, and the scriptural and catechetical doctrines of the oneness of Adam and his children and of Christ and His people are but divine revelations of the universality and depth of the federal and solidary law of human life. There are but two men, says Thomas Goodwin, who are seen standing before God, Adam and Jesus Christ; and these two men have all other men hanging at their girdles. (See this same subject treated under Question16.)

As was to be expected, this word is frequently found in Paul, he being the apostle who was appointed and enabled to set forth most clearly and fully the divine way of justification. (See Reuss above.) Indeed, so fundamental and ever present is this idea with the apostle, that an exegetical author writing on this subject is able with perfect truth to say: 'I know of no passage in the New Testament in which the doctrine of imputation is more distinctly and unequivocally expressed than in a text where the word imputation is not used. It is this: "For He hath made Him to be sin for us who knew no sin, that we might be made the righteousness of God in Him" (2 Cor. 5:21). *Justificatio* must be taken as the old Protestant dogmatists rightly took it, *sensu forensi*, i.e. *imputatively*.... All interpretations that overlook the fact of imputation, such as the Roman Catholic, are erroneous' (De Wette in Alford, Rom. 1:17).

'The more strictly we attach the character of a legal and judicial procedure to the act of God in justification, so much the better.... We can scarcely err in the direction of viewing justification too forensically – casting it too strongly into the mould of what passes, or may be supposed to pass, in a court of law.... Then, indeed, grace shines forth in it conspicuously: grace providing the substitute; grace making us one with the substitute; grace receiving us and dealing with us as one with the substitute. Thus to conserve its gracious character, it is indispensably necessary to hold fast and firm the forensic character of justification' (Candlish).

received by faith alone

'To the objection that the exclusive term alone is not found in Scripture, it is replied that though the word be not found syllabically used with this purpose, yet there are exceptive expressions equivalent unto it' (Owen).

'At some point or other it was necessary to draw a line between the Catholic and Reformed doctrines of justification. Was it to include works as well as faith? but, if not, was love to be a coefficient in the work of justification? They felt this difficulty, and tried to preserve the doctrine from the alloy of self-right-eousness and external acts by the formula of faith only' (Jowett).

'Luther and his apologists were taunted as being solifidians (faith-alone-ians) and fide solarians. They accepted the taunt, so far as the matter of justification is concerned, and gloried in it. But they ever contended that faith must not, and does not, remain solitary in the soul. Their maxim was that "faith never exists without works, although it justifies without works." "No works," says a Latin writer, "have place in the justification of man before God. Men are justified by faith alone, without works, moral, ceremonial, or judicial, of any law whatsoever, whether natural, Mosaical, or evangelical." It is altogether uncalled for to deny that an unbeliever may be in some, or perhaps in many respects a noble man: noble in honesty, noble in honour, noble in patriotism, noble in philanthropy. Yet his nobility of character has no justifying element in it. Perfect nobility in all relations, to ending of his probationary career, would be requisite, if man were to be justified by works of law' (See Dr. Morison's fine Monograph on Romans Third.)

'But you will say, Is not faith an act? It is true, it is, in a grammatical signification, an act; but in the true, real import of it, it is merely passive. Faith doth not give anything to God, as love doth; faith only suffers God to be good to it; it takes in that salvation which grace would bestow upon it. My brethren, the hands of all the other graces are working hands, but the hands of faith are merely receiving hands; now saith the apostle, Not to him that worketh, but believeth' (Goodwin).

Uses

1. 'I cannot but think it best for those who would learn or teach the doctrine of justification in a due manner, to place their consciences in the presence of God, and their persons before His tribunal, and then, upon a due consideration of His greatness, power, majesty, righteousness, holiness, to inquire what the Scriptures and a sense of their own condition direct them unto as their relief and refuge, and what plea it becomes them to make for themselves' (Owen).

2. 'God did, from all eternity, decree to justify all the elect; and Christ did, in the fulness of time, die for their sins, and rise again for their justification; nevertheless they are not justified, until the Holy Spirit doth in due time actually apply Christ unto them' (Confession of Faith).

3. 'We seldom sit down to meat but we eat and leave; so there is in Jesus Christ more merit and righteousness than the whole world has need of' (Interpreter's aphorism in *Pilgrim's Progress*, ii.).

4. 'The condescending goodness of Scripture, which speaks of the righteousness of the pious, ought not to be treated as if it were in opposition to the doctrine of justification by faith' (Bengel).

5. 'At that time, while I was greatly reproached for defending this doctrine in the pulpit, and just upon my suffering a very open abuse for it, God's work wonderfully broke forth among us, and souls began to flock to Christ, as the Saviour in whose righteousness alone they hoped to be justified. So that this was the doctrine on which this work, in its beginning, was founded, as it evidently was in the whole progress of it' (Jonathan Edwards' *Thoughts on the Revival in New England*).

QUESTION 34

What is adoption?

> *Answer: Adoption is an act of God's free grace,*[1] *whereby we are received into the number, and have a right to all the privileges of the sons of God.*[2]

Adoption is an act whereby a man takes into his family one who was not originally a member of it, and gives him the standing and privileges of a son. 'Neither is there only a natural, but also a voluntary and civil foundation of paternity; for the laws have found a way by which a man may become a father without procreation, and this imitation of nature is called adoption' (Pearson). Adoption is a scriptural expression made use of to set forth the sonship relation in which all true believers stand to God the Father on after their union to His Son Jesus Christ.

an act

On such passages as Romans 8:23, 1 John 3:2, the old divines have founded the distinction of *adoptio incompleta* or *imperfecta*. Compare what has been said above on justification as an act.

received into the number

See Answer 20. They are 'a multitude which no man could number' (Rev. 7:9), but they are all well known to God. 'The LORD shall count, when He writeth up the people, that this man was born there' (Ps. 87:6).

a right

At first sight it may seem strange to say that a sinner, even a justified sinner, can have any rights as before God. But if the matter is fully considered, it will be seen that the Catechism is true both to legal and domestic usage, as well as to Scripture, in so speaking. For a right at law can be established on proof of adoption as well as on descent; on a donation as well as on conquest, or a personal and original possession.

---

1. 1 John 3:1: Behold what manner of love the Father hath bestowed upon us, that we should be called the sons of God!

2. John 1:12: But as many as received him, to them gave he power to become the sons of God, even to them that believe on his name. Romans 8:17: And if children, then heirs; heirs of God, and joint-heirs with Christ: that we may be also glorified together.

all the privileges
'Liberties and privileges' (Larger Catechism). (For an admirable enumeration of the 'liberties and privileges of the children of God,' see Confession, chapter 7.)

the sons of God
'There is one degree of sonship founded on creation, and that is the lowest, as belonging unto all, both good and bad; another degree above that there is grounded upon regeneration, or adoption, belonging only to the faithful in this life; and a third above the rest founded on the resurrection, or collation of the eternal inheritance, and the similitude of God, appertaining to the saints alone in the world to come (1 John 3:2). And there is yet another degree of filiation, of a greater eminency and a different nature, appertaining properly to none of these, but to the true Son of God alone, who among all His brethren hath only received the title of His own Son.... Christ therefore hath called God after a peculiar way His own Father' (Pearson).

Note
The position taken up by Principal Candlish in his eloquent work, *The Fatherhood of God*, is this. The original condition and standing of man, with all its gifts and privileges, was not that of true sonship. It contained the germ and potency of sonship, and it would have issued in sonship but for the dreadful catastrophe of the fall. But as his hour of temptation found Adam, his standing toward God was still simply that of an honoured and trusted servant. It was as yet purely a relation of Creator and creature, Lawgiver and subject; it rested on divine and creative right on the one hand, and on human responsibility on the other. It was all embodied in a covenant of works, and a covenant of works is utterly incompatible with a full Fatherhood on the one hand, or with a secure sonship on the other. Man's standing as constituted in creation was altogether noble, and 'very good', and over and above its present nobility and goodness it had in it the seed of sonship and the prelude of a Divine Paternity. But that seed was trodden down before it had taken proper root, and the yearnings of the Divine Fatherhood had to seek their scope in another object than Adam, and their sphere in another creation than that of which he was the high priest and the head.

But the Fatherhood that embraces and possesses regenerate men is no figure; it is as real and true as that Fatherhood which eternally generates and lovingly embraces the Divine Son Himself. It is as real and true, for it is one and the same. The Fatherhood of God toward believers is grounded on, and indeed is nothing else than an extension of that Fatherhood that followed, and acknowledged, and sustained the descending and redeeming Son Himself. Our Sonship now is not figurative and fugitive, as it was in Adam; it is clear and full, safe and abiding as is the Sonship of Christ Himself. 'I have not hesitated,' says Dr. Candlish, 'to avow my belief in the substantial identity of the relation.' In his fifth lecture, 'On Adoption as connected with Regeneration and Justification,' the same author says: 'I think it of as much consequence to maintain the thoroughly unforensic character of God's act in adopting, as it is to maintain the strictly forensic character of His act in justifying. All is legal and judicial in the latter act. If it were not so, there would be no grace in it at all. Nothing is legal or judicial in the other; if there were anything of that sort in it, all its grace would be gone.' (See the kindred note under 'Justification,' above.) The student who will do justice to that characteristically acute, original, and soaring book will be repaid with lifelong elevation and quickening of mind.

Uses

1. It is a law of nature that like produces like. And that law of a reproduction of likeness happily obtains in the new creation also. It is the heart and the mind that are made new in regeneration, and it is in the 'renewed mind' and in the 'new heart' that the new family features reveal themselves. It is in their actions and in their affections that the children of God discover themselves, and give evidence of their new birth and supernatural descent. Even a foundling, who cannot give an account of himself, may have his parentage traced by his features and his complexion; and a child of God will easily be discovered among the children of the devil by his holy actions and heavenly affections.

2. In the Sermon on the Mount, assurance in prayer is grounded on the Fatherhood of God and the sonship of disciple. See also Question 100.

3. The Divine Paternity is also set forth as the proper ground of Christian patience (Deut. 8:5; Ps. 103:13; Heb. 12:9, 10).

QUESTION 35

What is sanctification?

Answer: Sanctification is the work of God's free grace,[1] *whereby we are renewed in the whole man after the image of God,*[2] *and are enabled more and more to die unto sin, and live unto righteousness.*[3]

The word *sanctification*, with its cognates saint, sanctuary, and such like, occurs a great number of times, and in a great variety of senses, in the Holy Scriptures. The word, like the work it describes, grows from less to more; from small beginnings at first to a great fulness and depth of meaning in the end. Beginning in the most outward, conventional, and ceremonial sense, it ends, as in the text, by containing and setting forth the most inward, spiritual, and exalted realities.

Sanctification

Let no student miss consulting Cruden's most valuable analysis and classification. Calvin, on 1 Corinthians 1:2, says: 'now the term sanctification notes separation. This takes place in us when we are regenerated by the Spirit of newness of life, that we may serve God and not the world.' And Godet, on John 17:17: 'The Greek work to sanctify is not synonymous with the word to purify. The holy is not opposed to the impure, but merely to the natural. To sanctify is to consecrate to a religious use anything pertaining to common life. From an Old Testament point of view, consecration was an external and ritual act; under the New Covenant, where all is spiritual, the seat of consecration is first in the heart, the will of the person sanctified.'

---

1. 2 Thessalonians 2:13: Salvation through sanctification of the Spirit, and belief of the truth.

2. Ephesians 4:23: And be renewed in the spirit of your mind; Verse 24. And that ye put on the new man, which after God is created in righteousness and true holiness.

3. Romans 6:4: Therefore we are buried with him by baptism into death; that like as Christ was raised up from the dead by the glory of the Father, even so we also should walk in newness of life. Verse 6. Knowing this, that our old man is crucified with him, that the body of sin might be destroyed, that henceforth we should not serve sin. Romans 8:1: There is therefore now no condemnation to them which are in Christ Jesus, who walk not after the flesh, but after the Spirit.

the work

Not, like justification and adoption, an act, but a work; a process, having its beginning in regeneration and its consummation and completion in glory. (See Answer 33 under act.) Sanctification is often called a work in Scripture, and from the nature of the case the student will see that this is the proper term to apply to it. For regeneration does not all at once make of a sinner a new man, in the sense of extirpating sinfulness from his heart and filling his life with the fruits of righteousness. The seed is planted in the new birth, but it must spring up and grow; it must be watched and watered, digged about and pruned, before it will become a tree of righteousness. That great change makes the sinner a child of God, but long years may have to pass before he attains the stature of a perfect man in Christ Jesus.

God's free grace

'Grace is not of merit, but merit of grace.' The Latin Father here means that no work of ours, even our working out our own salvation, will merit aught at God's hand; but that if we have any merit, if we do aught worthy of praise or reward, it is all of grace. In the old language of divines, 'grace prevents merit.' And all grace is 'free grace'. The student will note that this phrase 'free grace' occurs three times in succession in this part of the Catechism. Justification is an act of God's free grace; adoption is an act of God's free grace; sanctification is the work of God's free grace. For grace see Answer 20, and mark what Goodwin says on the characteristically Pauline expression, free grace: 'Romans 3:24. The word freely is to show that it is merely grace; it is without cause, it is grace dyed in grace, as I used to say, gracious grace.' 'To make a man a saint, grace is absolutely necessary; and whoever doubts this does not know what a saint is, nor what a man is' (Pascal).

renewed

Dr. John Duncan's daughter tells us in her diary that having heard a good sermon on one occasion on the words, 'For the will of God is your sanctification' (1 Thes. 4:3), and having spoken well of it to her father, he at once replied, 'Did it begin with regeneration?' This question of Dr. Duncan's goes to the very root of the matter. For sanctification is no mere reformation or refinement of manners or morals. It is a maxim even in ethics, that the morality of the man must precede the morality of his actions. Much more is it a law of Christ and His Church. 'Make the tree good.' Reformation and sanctification differ, says Dr. Hodge, as clean clothes differ from a clean heart. It is as essential to a truly holy life as it is to a good sermon on a holy life, that it begin with regeneration. (Confession, chap. 13.) Connect 'renewed' in this Answer with 'renewing' in Answer 31.

in the whole man
'I pray God your whole spirit, and soul, and body be preserved blameless unto the coming of our Lord Jesus Christ' (1 Thes. 5:23). It is the teaching of Scripture and the Catechism that sin has corrupted the whole man in every man, and it is the corresponding offer and promise of God in the gospel that He will make the whole man in spirit, and soul, and body blameless. As deep, and wide, and inward as is the taint and infection of sin, so universal and so thorough will the work of sanctification be.

after the image of God
On God's image see Answer 10. No man hath seen God at any time, but Christ is His express image, and we are renewed after the image of God, when we are made and make ourselves after the image of Christ. The Holy Spirit who wrought all His graces in Christ, and made Him after the image of God, works in us in like manner. He works in us a conformity to the graces that are in Christ, and we put on a conformity to His example. Holy dispositions and heavenly affections are the features and complexion of Christ formed in us. In adoption we are taken into the family of God, and in sanctification we take on us the family features in tone and manners.

'It is the office of the second Adam to give back to a lapsed race the forfeited image of God. Nor is he, as the Son of God, the renewer only of the miserable state of man, but equally the type and model of the new creation. Such he is, both with respect to personal purity, and to his eternal filial relation' (Candlish, *Fatherhood of God*).

enabled
'In which war, although the remaining corruption for a time may much prevail, yet, through the continual supply of strength from the sanctifying Spirit of Christ, the regenerate part doth overcome: and so the saints grow in grace, perfecting holiness in the fear of God' (Confession, 13:3).

more and more to die unto sin

A familiar form of thought with all the more spiritual Scripture writers, with the psalmists and prophets, with John, and Peter, and Paul. To die unto anything is to become indifferent to it, to shake off its power, to be superior to its attractions. A dead man hears not, sees not, tastes not, smells not, feels not; and a soul spiritually dead to sin would be in a world of sin dead to it all. A little reflection and imagination will enable the student to apprehend and appreciate this vivid and impressive scriptural metaphor.

'Such are my feelings; and every day of my life I bless my Redeemer, who has inspired me with them, and who, from a man full of weakness, misery, lust, pride, and ambition, has made me a man exempt from all these evils by the power of His grace, to which all the glory is due, as of myself I have nought but misery and error' (Pascal).

and live unto righteousness

There is, no doubt, a striking and instructive resemblance between a death-bed and one aspect of the work of sanctification; but there is a fundamental and essential contrast also. Death, it may be said, drives out and destroys life in a dying man, but in a godly man it is the new life that expels and destroys sin and death. The wisest physicians do not content themselves with striking at the special disease to which their attention has been called. They aim also at strengthening the enfeebled constitution, sure, as they are, that returning strength will be their best ally in rooting out any local and particular evil. And in like manner evil habits and evil affections will overcome less by ascetic mortification of the body, and close incarceration of the mind and heart, than by attracting the mind and captivating the heart by whatsoever things are true and lovely and of good report. 'Walk in the Spirit, and ye shall not fulfil the lusts of the flesh' (Gal. 5:16). As we study this doctrine we may well say with the prophet, 'The thing is true, but the time is long' (Dan. 10:1). Compare Antoninus: 'Consider thyself to be dead, and to have completed thy life up to the present time: and live according to Nature the remainder which is allowed thee.'

The student who has mastered the teaching of the Answer on Justification will be in a position at once to understand what is meant by 'righteousness' in the text. In the former case it was the righteousness of Christ, here it is the righteousness of the sanctified believer. 'We have already showed that there are two kinds of Christian righteousness: the one without us, which we have by imputation; the other in us, which consisteth of faith, hope, charity, and other Christian virtues.... God giveth us both the one justice and the other: the one by accepting us for righteous in Christ; the other by working Christian righteousness in us' (Hooker).

Uses

1. From a multitude of scriptures, and from the whole course of the life of sanctification in the Church, this sure deduction has been drawn: the more sanctification, the more sense of sin. Before sanctification commences there is little or no knowledge of sin; but as sanctification deepens and spreads through the whole man, so does the sense of sin spread and deepen within it, till this strange and disheartening paradox is realised; the less actual sin, the more indwelling sinfulness; and the less outward transgression, the more inward corruption. And thus it is that the life and work of sanctification are continually delivering over such companies of submissive souls to the type of doctrine set forth in the Answer on Justification. And thus it is that the great and vital and blessed doctrine of imputed righteousness has always had such blameless ornaments and determined defenders in the foremost ranks of scripturally taught and spiritually sanctified men.

2. 'Woe to him that is wholly renewed: that is, that thinks himself to be so. That man, without doubt, has never so much as begun to be renewed, nor did he ever taste what it is to be a Christian' (Luther).

3. One of Bunyan's Puritan contemporaries expounds 'prudence' in Ephesians 1:8 of sanctification. In connection with this read the dialogue between Prudence and Christian commencing: 'Do you not think sometimes of the country from whence you came?'

4. May great sinners be sanctified? Yes, the Spirit of God can sanctify the vilest heart (1 Cor. 6:11). And such were some of you, but ye are washed, but ye are sanctified (Flavel).

5. 'After the greatest mortification, I always find the greatest comfort' (Edwards).

QUESTION 36

What are the benefits which in this life do accompany or flow from justification, adoption, and sanctification?

Answer: The benefits which in this life do accompany or flow from justification, adoption, and sanctification, are, assurance of God's love, peace of conscience,[1] joy in the Holy Ghost,[2] increase of grace,[3] and perseverance therein to the end.[4]

The benefits – compare Psalm 103:2-5.
These benefits are first mentioned in Answer 32, and they are there connected with effectual calling. What benefits do they that are effectually called partake of in this life? Justification, adoption, and sanctification are the great foundation benefits; but these being possessed, certain other benefits accompany or flow from them, and some, though not yet all of these, are now enumerated. And the first is

assurance of God's love
Those students who have any acquaintance with the riper fruits of scriptural and experimental truth will at once recognize the wide field that opens before us at the mention of the word assurance. The Larger Catechism condenses whole treatises of practical divinity into its 80th and 81st Answers. Can true believers be infallibly assured that they are in the estate of grace? and are all true believers at all times assured of their present being in the estate of grace, and that they shall be saved? The only safe and scriptural way by which a believer can attain to assurance is by observing in himself the evidences of a saving change, by discerning in himself those spiritual graces to which the promises of eternal life are made. Assurance is a scriptural word. It is found in the sense of the

---

1. Romans 5:1: Therefore being justified by faith, we have peace with God, through our Lord Jesus Christ: Verse 2. By whom also we have access by faith into this grace wherein we stand, and rejoice in hope of the glory of God. Verse 5: And hope maketh not ashamed; because the love of God is shed abroad in our hearts by the Holy Ghost, which is given unto us.

2. Romans 14:17: For the kingdom of God is not meat and drink; but righteousness, and peace, and joy in the Holy Ghost.

3. Proverbs 4:18: But the path of the just is as the shining light, that shineth more and more unto the perfect day.

4. 1 John 5:13: That ye may know that ye have eternal life. 1 Peter 1:5: Who are kept by the power of God through faith unto salvation, ready to be revealed in the last time.

text in Isaiah 32:17: 'The effect of righteousness shall be quietness and assurance for ever.' 1 John 3:18, 19: 'My little children, let us not love in word, neither in tongue; but in deed and in truth. And hereby we know that we are of the truth, and shall assure our hearts before Him.' At the same time, assurance is not of the essence of faith: that is to say, a man may have a true faith, and sufficient true faith to justify him and finally save him, and yet may not have enough of faith or of its fruits to enable him to attain to assurance. (See Answer 81, Larger Catechism.)

The divine decree may be conducting a particular person by sure steps all his life through to final glory, and yet he may not be aware of it: he may act without much contemplating himself, or, if he does, he may distrust himself. Predestinarians accordingly, both Augustine and his school, and modern ones, have disowned the doctrine of assurance, so far as it is maintained in it, that assurance is absolutely necessary for a Christian. In modern language, they held that 'assurance is not of the essence of faith', and consequently that a man might be in a state of grace and yet not possess the assurance of it.

Bunyan in his *Grace Abounding* tells in his incomparable way how the 'assurance of God's love' manifested itself in his soul:

> Then I began to give place to the Word, which, with power, did over and over make this joyful sound within my soul, Thou art my Love, thou art my Love; and nothing shall separate thee from my love: and with that Rom. viii. 39 came into my mind. Now was my heart filled full of comfort and hope, and now I could believe that my sins should be forgiven me: yea, I was so taken with the love and mercy of God, that I remember I could not tell how to contain till I got home. I thought I could have spoken of his love and of his mercy to me, even to the very crows that sat upon the ploughed land before me, had they been capable to have understood me.

peace of conscience

Every man's conscience is a kind of court of justice; a court that has been set up by the authority and letters patent of our Divine Sovereign; a court that never rises, and never goes on circuit. It sits in the same place summer and winter, daylight and darkness. A strange and an awful court, surpassingly strange in this, that each man among us holds all its offices; for every man is judge, witness, and accused in the inner house of his own heart.

'The conscience is in a man what the snout is in a bear, and the mouth in a horse, a tender part to tame them by. Conscience is acutely sensible to God's wrath, and hell-fire could not take hold of the soul but at this corner. Conscience is the channel by which the streams of fire and brimstone enter the soul. Conscience, accordingly, hath its fullest dominion in hell, and will be at the highest of its power there' (Goodwin).

> O Conscience, who can stand against thy power?
> Endure thy gripes and agonies one hour?
> Stone, gout, strappado, racks whatever is
> Dreadful to sense, are only toys to this.
> No pleasures, riches, honours, friends, can tell
> How to give ease to this, 'tis like to hell (Flavel).

How great a benefit then must 'peace of conscience' be! And how important to learn early how it is to be attained and preserved! And how essential that we be taught to hold clear scriptural truth on this all-important subject! This distinctly evangelical subject has never had a fuller, or clearer, or more suggestive preacher than Dr. Thomas Goodwin, whose name occurs so often in these pages. Writing on this subject in his book on The Holy Ghost, he says: 'The Scripture knows no such phrase as "peace of conscience." It is indeed peace of conscience subjectively, conscience being the principle as to which peace is spoken. But when it is spoken, it is so spoken as that it is the peace of God, and not peace with God only. I will hear what God the Lord will speak; for He will speak peace unto His people and to His saints' (Ps. 85:8).

joy in the Holy Ghost

This is a spiritual expression. In Romans 14:17, we read of 'righteousness, and peace, and joy in the Holy Ghost'. The Holy Ghost is that Divine Person who enters our hearts and makes them His home and His temple. Now the heart is the proper seat of joy, as the conscience is of peace; and as all our solid peace comes to us from God through Christ, so all holy joy comes when the love of God is shed abroad in our hearts by the Holy Ghost which is given unto us. We cannot indeed say with the Ephesian converts that 'we have not so much as heard whether there be any Holy Ghost', but few have attained to much of his joy. We continually vex and grieve the Holy Spirit, and we do not aright and earnestly pray, 'Take not Thy Holy Spirit from me; restore to me the joy of Thy salvation' (Ps. 51:11,12). Hopeful, describing the work of the Holy Ghost in his heart to Christian, says: 'Now was my heart full of joy, mine eyes full of tears and mine affections running over with love to the name, people, and ways of Jesus Christ.... It made me love a holy life, and long to do something for the honour and glory of the name of the Lord Jesus; yea, I thought that had I now a hundred gallons of blood in my body, I could spill it all for the sake of the Lord Jesus.'

increase of grace

Our salvation is of grace, and it is all of grace. It begins in grace, and it is built up in grace, and the headstone is brought out with shoutings of 'Grace, grace unto it'. 'By grace ye are saved, not of works, lest any man should boast' (Eph. 2:8). There are few finer things in a book full of good things than when the dreamer describes Old Honest's character, and then tells us of his passage of the river. 'Mr. Honest in his lifetime had spoken to one Good Conscience to meet him there, the which he also did, and lent him his hand, and so helped him over. The last words of Mr. Honest were, Grace reigns. So he left the world.'

Pauline, Augustinian, and Calvinistic divines, of which John Bunyan was one of the best, have all conspired to magnify the grace of God in the salvation of men. And this indeed is the distinguishing mark of their theology, that they attribute all our salvation in all its parts to the free grace of God. Thus they make much of prevenient grace, meaning by that, as the etymology of the word teaches, the grace that goes before or precedes and excites all our efforts after or interest in divine things. The second stage in the growth of grace is when that grace becomes internally and effectually operative. (See Answers 30, 31.) And lastly, co-operating or habitual grace is the name given to that indwelling and assistance of the Holy Ghost whereby all that has been attained in grace is secured, and new progress is made from grace to grace. These three great stages have of course all manner of modifications and fluctuations in the individual soul, till it is made a partaker of the grace that is to be brought to it at the appearing of Jesus Christ.

the perseverance therein to the end

Steadfastness, constancy, endurance, progress, final perseverance. This is the crowning 'benefit' we receive 'in this life'. And of all the graces, it is the most precious, because it is the one which makes all the others of lasting value. 'The only sure sign that any man is one of the elect is his perseverance in the Christian life; for he is elected to holiness as well as happiness. Perseverance, like faith, is the gift of God, and Augustine denominates it *donum perseverantiae*, the gift or grace of perseverance' (Shedd).

The Larger Catechism gathers up the teaching of Scripture on this subject with its usual clearness and fulness: 'True believers, by reason of the unchangeable love of God, and His decree and covenant to give them perseverance, their inseparable union with Christ, His continual intercession for them, and the Spirit and seed of God abiding in them, can neither totally nor finally fall away from a state of grace, but are kept by the power of God through faith unto salvation.' At the same time it is the believer who perseveres, and not another for him. He must work out his own salvation. He must endure, and press on, and remain steadfast. He must resist unto blood, striving against sin. The greatest work in our language on this subject is John Owen's *Perseverance of the Saints*. It is sadly disfigured in form through its polemical character, but it is a great work, and will well repay any man who reads it.

'One leak will sink a ship, and one sin will destroy a sinner' (Bunyan).

'The evening praises the day, and the chief grace of the theatre is the last scene. Be faithful unto death, and I will give thee a crown of life' (Joseph Hall).

Uses

1. A believer should have his best benefits in daily recollection. Blessed be the Lord who daily loadeth us with benefits. They are new every morning: great is Thy faithfulness.

2. 'The technicalities of the controversy are somewhat altered, while its substance remains the same. The grave question still is, as it has always been, Is it practicable, obligatory, or expedient that believers should be assured of their justification and salvation?... We believe that the prevailing practical disregard of the privilege and duty of having assurance, is, to no inconsiderable extent, at once the cause and the effect of the low state of vital religion amongst us; one main reason why there is so little of real communion with God as our reconciled Father, and so little of real, hearty devotedness to His cause and service' (Cunningham).

3. 'When we want the faith of assurance, we must live by the faith of adherence' (Matthew Henry).

4. 'Serve your God day and night faithfully, walk humbly; there is a promise of the Holy Ghost to come and fill your hearts with joy unspeakable and glorious, to rear you up to the day of redemption. Sue this promise out, wait for it, rest not in believing only, rest not in assurance by graces only; there is a further assurance to be had' (Goodwin).

5. The use and intent of the whole of the First Epistle of John is to lead the soul to joy in the Holy Ghost. 'These things write we unto you, that your joy may be full' (1 John 1:4). Keep conscience well enlightened as to the alone ground of its peace. See Answers 33, 86, 87.

6. Psalm 138:8: 'The LORD will perfect that which concerneth me.'

7. Learn to think of your hearts as the true and only home of the Holy Ghost, and trace all holy and happy affections to His indwelling, and to the effusions of His grace.

QUESTION 37

What benefits do believers receive from Christ at death?

Answer: The souls of believers are at their death made perfect in holiness,[1] *and do immediately pass into glory;*[2] *and their bodies, being still united to Christ,*[3] *do rest in their graves*[4] *till the resurrection.*[5]

Questions 37 and 38 occupy the department of theology which is designated Eschatology, or the doctrine of the Last Things. The benefits

---

1. Hebrews 12:23: The spirits of just men made perfect.

2. 2 Corinthians 5:1: If our earthly house of this tabernacle were dissolved, we have a building of God, an house not made with hands, eternal in the heavens. Verse 6: Therefore we are always confident, knowing that, whilst we are at home in the body, we are absent from the Lord. Philippians 1:23: For I am in a strait betwixt two, having a desire to depart, and to be with Christ. Luke 23:43: And Jesus said unto him, Verily I say unto thee, To-day shalt thou be with me in paradise.

3. 1 Thessalonians 4:14: ...them also which sleep in Jesus will God bring with him.

4. Isaiah 57:2: ...they shall rest in their beds . . .

5. Job 19:26, 27: And though after my skin worms destroy this body, yet in my flesh shall I see God; Whom I shall see for myself, and mine eyes shall behold, and not another; though my reins be consumed within me.

that the effectually called partake of in this life having been set forth in Questions 32–36, the Catechism now passes on to deal with the benefits believers receive at death.

The souls of believers are at their death made perfect in holiness
While teaching the doctrine of the word of God on the matter in hand, this Answer is so drawn as to deny the Romish doctrine of a purgatorial state between death and resurrection. The Underworld of the Fathers and the Purgatory of the Papists are both opposed by the teaching of the Catechism. Were we only to employ natural reason in dealing with such a mysterious matter, we might well be staggered at the assertion that what has taken so long time to make so little progress, should be in a moment made perfect; that our growth in holiness, which has been so slow and fitful, should all at once leap into immediate and everlasting perfection. But in this whole region of things, we must go by the word of God alone, and its teaching all points to the doctrine of the Reformed Churches, that 'the souls of believers are at their death made perfect in holiness, and do immediately pass into glory'. Nor are we without actual examples in Scripture of great and sudden changes wrought in the spiritual state of men by the power and grace of God analogous, at least, to what is here promised to believers at their death. The immense and immediate transformation that the disciples underwent on the day of Pentecost, was, if not equal, at least analogous and initial to that consummating change they underwent at the hour of death. Paul also underwent a more radical change at the gate of Damascus than even that which he passed through at his abundant entrance into glory, 'when, like a northern midnight, the rose of evening became suddenly and silently the rose of dawn.'

At the same time there is room both in Scripture and Protestant doctrine for the observation of Calvin: 'Although those who have been freed from the mortal body do no longer contend with the lusts of the flesh, and are, as the expression is, beyond the reach of a single dart, yet there will be no absurdity in speaking of them as in the way of advancement, inasmuch as they have not yet reached the point at which they aspire; they do not enjoy the felicity and glory which they have hoped for, and, *in fine*, the day has not yet shone which is to discover the treasures which lie hid in hope. And in truth, when hope is spoken of, our eyes must always be directed forward to a blessed resurrection as the great object in view.'

and do immediately pass into glory
'Their souls immediately return to God who gave them.... Besides the highest heavens and hell, besides these two places for souls separated from their bodies, the Scripture acknowledgeth none' (Confession, chap. 32).

and their bodies being still united to Christ
The apostle arguing against sensuality in his First Epistle to the Corinthians, says: 'Know ye not that your bodies are the members of Christ' (1 Cor. 6:15)? and it is his doctrine in all his epistles that Christ has redeemed our whole man, and that we are His, body, soul, and spirit. The believer is united in regeneration to Christ, soul and body, and soul and body are both henceforth in Christ's keeping; and He will present both without spot or blemish at the great day. It is not the soul, but the body, that 'sleeps in Jesus.' Their very dust to Him is dear.

> God, my Redeemer lives,
> And often from the skies
> Looks down and watches all my dust,
> Till He shall bid it rise (Watts).

do rest in their graves till the resurrection
Rest is one of the sweetest words in the language of men, and the rest that remaineth for the weary body is only a rest as in sleep before the glorious awakening. 'This body shall not be buried, but sown,' sown as seed to spring up to eternal life.

> Death, thou wast once an uncouth, hideous thing:
> But since our Saviour's death
> Has put some blood into thy face,
> Thou hast grown sure a thing to be desired
> And full of grace (Herbert).

Uses
1. If all this is so, then death, as Herbert says, is a thing to be desired, as it would be did our faith and hope aright realize it. A gracious soul should live in a constant and hopeful outlook for the approach of such an awful yet glorious change.

2. When death comes, and it may come any moment, all our gracious opportunities will be for ever past. And the thought of this ought to make death to the youngest ever imminent, just as Scripture, because of the transcendent importance of Christ's coming, always speaks of it as just at hand.

3. What is the fourth inference? Saints should not fear death. What is the last inference? Employ your bodies for good now (Flavel).

QUESTION 38

What benefits do believers receive from Christ at the resurrection?

Answer: At the resurrection, believers being raised up in glory,[1] shall be openly acknowledged and acquitted in the day of judgment,[2] and made perfectly blessed in the full enjoying of God[3] to all eternity.[4]

At the resurrection

The resurrection of the dead is exclusively a doctrine of the Word of God. It nowhere appears in the religions of paganism. That the soul should continue to live after death was the faith and hope of many of the best men in heathendom; but that there should be a resurrection of the body, and a reunion of soul and body for ever, this is a doctrine derived wholly from the Word of God. The Athenians in Paul's day believed in the existence of God. They raised no opposition even when he preached the unity, spirituality, providence, and fatherhood of God; but when he went on from these things to preach Jesus and the resurrection, that was a 'new doctrine' to them, and some mocked, though others said, 'We will hear thee again of this matter.'

---

1. 1 Corinthians 15:43: It is raised in glory . . .

2. Matthew 25:23: Well done, good and faithful servant; thou hast been faithful over a few things, I will made thee ruler over many things: enter thou into the joy of thy lord. Matthew 10:32: Whosoever therefore shall confess me before men, him will I confess also before my Father which is in heaven.

3. 1 John 3:2: Beloved, now are we the sons of God; and it doth not yet appear what we shall be: but we know that, when he shall appear, we shall be like him; for we shall see him as he is. 1 Corinthians 13:12: For now we see through a glass, darkly; but then face to face: now I know in part; but then shall I know even as also I am known.

4. 1 Thessalonians 4:17: ...so shall we ever be with the Lord.

There is nothing taught in the text touching the resurrection of unbelievers, because the Catechism is engaged in tracing the benefits that 'believers' receive from Christ; and though all the dead shall rise again, all shall not 'attain to the resurrection' set forth in the text.

believers being raised up in glory

This is the last time 'believers' shall bear that name. From the day of their effectual calling to the day of their resurrection they have been 'believers', but after their resurrection there is no more room for faith; then and thereafter they shall know even as they are known. At the resurrection Christ shall change their vile body, that it may be fashioned like unto His glorious body. But what the glory shall consist in we cannot in this life tell; we are 'believers' in the resurrcction and the resurrection life.

'Therefore some of our divines say that our Saviour Christ did not simply merit the resurrection of the dead, for that apart from Him they must have risen again and been brought to judgment: but these glorious qualifications the saints have at the resurrection, which is the preparation to the glory in heaven – these He merited, this some divines say' (Goodwin).

shall be openly acknowledged and acquitted in the day of judgment

God had secretly acknowledged and acquitted them on the day of their first justification. But both their faith in Christ and their acceptance before God had been hidden with Christ in God. The whole transaction of their renewal, union to Christ, pardon, and acceptance was unknown to the world in which they dwelt: in many cases true believers themselves had never come to a clear assurance that they possessed these saving benefits. But all that will then be made manifest both to themselves and to all men. What had been spoken in secret shall then be told from the house-tops.

'Christ hath not all His members up to Him, nor are they out of all danger, as I may so express it; for though at the day of judgment to the saints there is no real danger, yet they are to give an account of their actions, and there remaineth a final sentence to be pronounced upon them by the Great Judge, and in that sense there is a forgiveness of sins then; therefore Paul prayeth that he may find mercy at that day' (Goodwin).

Jesus, Thy blood and righteousness
My beauty are, my glorious dress:
'Midst flaming worlds in these arrayed,
With joy shall I lift up my head.

Bold shall I stand in that great day:
For who aught to my charge shall lay?
Fully, through these, absolved I am
From sin and fear, from guilt and shame.

made perfectly blessed
See in *Pilgrim's Progress* the talk that the Shining Ones held with the pilgrims about the glory of the place.

in the full enjoying of God
'But especially in the immediate vision and fruition of God the Father, of our Lord Jesus Christ, and of the Holy Spirit, to all eternity' (Larger Catechism). 'To sit down with Abraham, Isaac, and Jacob was the phraseology of the Old Testament, but to sit down with Us – with the Father, Son, and Holy Ghost – this is Christ's language, this is New Testament language' (Goodwin).

'Man's chief end' is now attained. (See Question 1.) The Scriptures constantly teach that man's only true happiness is in God, and that his full happiness in God cannot be attained in this life, but that believing men have that happiness assured to them in the life to come. Commenting on John 14:6, Godet says: 'Jesus here substitutes the Father for the Father's house. For it is not in heaven that we are to find God, but in God that we are to find heaven.'

to all eternity
'When time and sin together cease.' 'Both a prophet and an apostle join in teaching us that eye hath not seen, nor ear heard, nor man's heart conceived, what God has prepared for those that love Him. When the bodies of the just rise at the general resurrection, with their senses spiritualized and rendered capable of pleasures which do not fall within their province now, and with perhaps many new senses developed in the immortal body which were unknown in its mortal days, the pure pleasures of their glorified senses must be

something quite beyond the power of our imagination to picture to itself' (Faber).

Uses

1. 'As Christ would have us to be certainly persuaded that there shall be a day of judgment, both to deter all men from sin, and for the greater consolation of the godly in their adversity; so will He have that day unknown to men, that they may shake off all carnal security, and be always watchful, because they know not at what hour the Lord will come: and may be ever prepared to say, Come, Lord Jesus, come quickly. Amen' (Confession).

2. Luther warns us: 'The flesh ever seeks to be glorified before it is crucified: exalted before it is abased.'

3. It is often ignorantly and frivolously charged against Christian men that it is selfish in them to seek heaven and glory for their own souls; but no man who is truly seeking salvation will be moved by that accusation. When men really begin to seek their salvation, and to turn their faces to the glory of heaven, then it is that all selfish and ignoble desires receive their death-blow. It is not selfish, surely, for the diseased to seek healing, or the hungry food, or the prodigal his father's house. So far from this being a sign that the heart is selfish, there is no surer sign that it is being sanctified.

4. '*Pliable.* The hearing of all this is enough to ravish one's heart; but are these things to be enjoyed? How shall we get to be sharers hereof?

'*Christian.* The Lord, the Governor of the country, hath recorded that in this book; the substance of which is, If we be truly willing to have it, He will bestow it upon us freely.'

Having seen what
the Scriptures principally teach us to believe concerning God,
it follows to consider what they require as the duty of man.

QUESTION 39

What is the duty which God requireth of man?

Answer: The duty which God requireth of man, is obedience to his revealed will.[1]

The duty which God requireth of man

Duty means what is due, what is owed as a debt: that which we ought to do. In seeing anything to be right, we see at the same time that it is our duty to do it. Duty is that act, or word, or thought, or feeling, or wish to which a man is bound. The following is Kant's celebrated apostrophe: '*Duty*! thou great, thou exalted name! Wondrous thought, that workest neither by fond insinuation, flattery, nor any threat, but merely by holding up thy naked law in the soul, and so extorting for thyself always reverence, if now always obedience – before whom all appetites are dumb, however secretly they rebel – whence thy original? and where find we the root of thy august descent, thus loftily disclaiming all kindred with appetite and want? To be in like manner descended from which root is the unchanging condition of that worth which mankind can alone claim for themselves.'

obedience to his revealed will

To reveal signifies to make known what has hitherto been concealed. At its root the word means to draw back a veil. The name of the last book of the New Testament, called in Greek the Apocalypse, has the same root and meaning. It contains the Revelation which God gave to Jesus Christ, that He might again discover it to John, and through John to the Church. The word is also used in a wider sense of the whole of Scripture, or of that economy of gracious manifestation and interposition of which Scripture is the written record. Hence the distinction, Nature and Revelation.

God's will is for many purposes sufficiently revealed to us in the constitution of nature and in the experiences of life. Prior to and apart from Scripture, there is a binding revelation of God written on every man's

---

1. Micah 6:8: He hath showed thee, O man, what is good and what doth the LORD require of thee, but to do justly, and to love mercy, and to walk humbly with thy God? 1 Samuel 15:22: And Samuel said, Hath the LORD as great delight in burnt-offerings and sacrifices, as in obeying the voice of the LORD? Behold, to obey is better than sacrifice, and to hearken than the fat of rams.

conscience and heart. And hence Paul teaching that the very heathen are a law unto themselves. Hooker and Butler have made the thought familiar to us, that revelation itself, in many of its parts, is but a republication and expansion of the law of Nature. At the same time, and after the fullest recognition has been taken, and the frankest acknowledgement made of all that nature and experience can teach to man, there is still a vast field left unoccupied that only revelation can fill. Let the student consider how much nature or experience could have taught him of the transcendently important truths the first half of the Catechism has set before him: as also how much the Catechism rests on Scripture in what it has still to teach.

'The secret things belong unto the LORD our God; but those things which are revealed belong unto us, and to our children for ever, that we may do all the words of this law' (Deut. 29:29).

From this and kindred scriptures divines have learned to speak of God's will as decretive and preceptive, absolute and conditional. God's decretive will embraces His eternal purposes. (See Answer 7.) Which will, so far as it is revealed, is to be believed and reverenced, but His perceptive will is to be received and obeyed. His preceptive will is the rule of life to us. (Answer 2.)

Uses

1. 'If I were asked in what book a clear outline of the Christian faith might be found and studied, I would at once say, "In the first thirty-eight Questions of the Assembly's Shorter Catechism." But if I were asked for a practical guide, to lead men to Christ, and to train them to holiness, I would say, "Begin at the thirty-ninth Question, and be guided with those that follow onward to the end"' (Macfarlan's Preface to Paterson).

2. 'An orthodox faith and an obedient life is the whole duty of man' (Newman).

3. 'The standard of right and wrong is eternal in the heavens, unchangeably one and the same. But here on earth it is perpetually variable; it is one in one age or nation, another in another. Every profession has its conventional morality, current nowhere else.... And in all these cases the temptation is to live content with the standard of a man's own profession or society; and this is the real difference between the worldly man and the religious man. He is the worldling who lives below that standard, or no higher; he is the servant of God who lives above his age' (Frederick Robertson).

QUESTION 40

What did God at first reveal to man for the rule of his obedience?

Answer: The rule which God at first revealed to man for his obedience, was the moral law.[1]

the moral law

Mos, a Latin word signifying manners, conduct, hence *morals, morality*. Philosophers sometimes call the conscience the *moral sense*, because it concerns itself with matters of conduct and character.

The etymological sense of law is 'that which lies', or is in due and proper order. The word varies in its meaning according to the subject treated of. When we speak about natural objects, such as the constitution of the world, and the life of man and beast in it, we use the word 'law' of a divinely established order and uniformity in the sequence of events. Thus we speak of the law of gravitation, the laws of mechanics, chemistry, health, and such like. Again we use the same word for the enactments and regulations which hold society together in families and states. We speak of the law of the family, and the law of the land. But the moral law is that which the Creator and Lawgiver and Judge of all men hath laid on every man's conscience, and according to which all men are commanded to live, and according to which all shall at last be judged. 'That which doth assign unto each thing the kind, that which doth moderate the force and power, that which doth appoint the form and measure of working, the same we term a law.... All things therefore do work after a sort according to law: all other things according to a law, whereof some superior, unto whom they are subject, is author; only the works and operations of God have Him both for their worker, and for the law whereby they are wrought. The being of God is a kind of law to His working; for the perfection which God is, giveth perfection to that He doeth.... Therefore of law there can be no less acknowledged, than that her seat is the bosom of God, her voice the harmony of the world;

1. Romans 2:14-15: For when the Gentiles, which have not the law, do by nature the things contained in the law, these, having not the law, are a law unto themselves: Which show the work of the law written in their hearts, their conscience also bearing witness, and their thoughts the meanwhile accusing or else excusing one another. Romans 10:5: For Moses describeth the righteousness which is of the law, That the man which doeth those things shall live by them.

all things in heaven and earth do her homage, the very least as feeling her care, and the greatest as not exempted from her power; both angels and men and creatures of what sort soever, though each in different sort and manner, yet all with uniform consent, admiring her as the mother of their peace and joy' (Hooker).

But the special line of thought more immediately before us is well carried out in the corresponding part of the Larger Catechism, where we are taught that the moral law is the declaration of the will of God to mankind, directing and binding every one to personal, perfect and perpetual conformity and obedience thereunto, in the frame and disposition of the whole man, soul and body, and in performance of all those duties of holiness and righteousness which he oweth to God and man; promising life upon the fulfilling, and threatening death upon the breach of it.

Note.

In our day the scientific conception of law has so possessed and intoxicated many of us, that the still truer and nobler conception of GOD has all but passed out of mind. The conception of a Creator and Preserver has become absorbed and lost in that stately order and most regular and harmonious law of nature which He has instituted, and which He constantly sustains. The operation is so majestic, that it has cast the Operator into a passing shadow. The instrument is so intricate and complex, that it has for the moment almost hidden the Hand that holds it. But surely science is not to continue to dispense with the great First Cause and Author of all. For that noblest and most fruitful of conceptions gives dignity and depth, elasticity and spirituality to the otherwise hard and sterile idea of natural law. To the truest philosophy LAW is that divine order and harmony that reigns over, penetrates, and sustains all things, human and divine; and to discover which is the wisest pursuit and noblest crown of human wisdom, as to submit, to confess, and ally ourselves to it is the sum of our duty and the source and guarantee of our blessedness.

Uses

1. For the use of the moral law to all men, and for its particular use to the unregenerate, and its special use to regenerate men, be careful to consult Answers 95, 96, and 97 in Larger Catechism.

2. What is the first inference from hence? That God will proceed with

men by different rules in the day of judgment, according to the different laws they have lived under in this world (Rom. 2:12).

3. What is the second inference? That those who have sinned against the clearest light and best helps will, if they die impenitent, be judged to the greatest misery (Matt. 23:23; Heb. 2:3).

4. What is the third inference? That as we are to prize the moral law highly as a rule of life (Ps. 119:105), so we are to bless God for the gospel dispensation, by which only we can attain to justification and salvation (Flavel).

QUESTION 41

Where is the moral law summarily comprehended?

Answer: The moral law is summarily comprehended in the ten commandments.[1]

summarily comprehended

We have in the text and context first the moral law, then the summary of that law in the ten commandments, and then the ten commandments again summarized.

Now where was the moral law published *in extenso* before it was summarized in the Decalogue? Moses received the two tables containing a summary of the moral law at Sinai, and we accordingly call it the Law of Moses, and we do not speak misleadingly if we know what we say. The moral law then became the law of Moses, but it was the law of God to all mankind long before Moses was born. The moral law was first published, not when the tables of stone were graven at Sinai, but when the Holy Ghost wrote the law of God on the tables of Adam's heart. The moral law is the 'light which lighteth every man that cometh into the world' (John 1:9), and that light burned its brightest when it was first kindled in the soul of man. Moses was not that light, but he came to bear witness of that light. Moses was merely commissioned to refurbish the tarnished lamp of the moral law, and to feed its dying flame with fresh

1. Deuteronomy 10:4: And he wrote on the tables, according to the first writing, the ten commandments, which the LORD spake unto you in the mount, out of the midst of the fire, in the day of the assembly; and the LORD gave them unto me. Matthew 19:17: ...if thou wilt enter into life, keep the commandments.

oil. He did not kindle the light, he only set it in a candlestick, so that it might give light to all that were in the house of Israel. It was the moral law of human nature, the law of conscience, the law of creation that was summarized and republished in the ten commandments.

the ten commandments

The oldest form of the ten commandments is found in the twentieth chapter of the book of Exodus; another form is found in the fifth of Deuteronomy. There are some slight differences between the two forms, but the differences do not touch anything essential or important. The Scriptures repeatedly tell us that the commandments are ten in number, but the commandments are nowhere tabulated or numbered so as to fix for us where each and every separate commandment begins and ends. And thus it is, that while all schools of interpretation accept the same number of commandments, they have not all classified the commandments in the same way. Thus the Jewish doctors took what we call the preface to the commandments and reckoned it a commandment, making it the first of the ten. And then, in order to keep the proper number, they ran our first and second commandments into one. The Trent Catechism follows them in giving the 'Exordium' as the first commandment, but adds both first and second as merely exegetical, and then divides the tenth into two. The classification that obtains in the Shorter Catechism is as old as the days of our Lord; it was adopted by many of the Fathers; it is the classification accepted by the Greek Church, and it has the approval of nearly all the Reformed divines. 'The four first commandments contain our duty to God, and the other six our duty to man' (Larger Catechism).

QUESTION 42

What is the sum of the ten commandments?

Answer: The sum of the ten commandments is, To love the Lord our God with all our heart, with all our soul, with all our strength, and with all our mind; and our neighbour as ourselves.[1]

1. Matthew 22:37-40: Jesus said unto him, Thou shalt love the Lord thy God with all thy heart, and with all thy soul, and with all thy mind. This is the first and great commandment. And the second is like unto it, Thou shalt love thy neighbour as thyself. On these two commandments hang all the law and the prophets.

The sum
The sum of a summary. (See Answer 41.) The pith and marrow of the moral law.

to love the Lord our God with all our heart, soul, strength, and mind
The original of this answer is found in Deuteronomy 6. This passage formed part of the great creed of Israel which was written on the phylacteries of all the people, and was committed to memory by all their children. It is remarked by Dean Plumptre that there is something striking and instructive in the fact that words from this passage in Deuteronomy were the weapons with which our Lord baffled the attacks of the tempter, and that they throughout formed the keynote of His teaching.

The anatomy of the inner man here given is not perhaps of that exact and scientific character that modern psychology would sustain, but it is after the rich and impressive manner of Holy Scripture. 'Thou shalt love the Lord thy God with all thy heart, that is, kindly and affectionately; with all thy soul, that is, wisely and discreetly; with all thy might, that is, stedfastly and constantly. Let the love of thy heart inflame thy zeal towards Him; let the knowledge of thy soul guide it; let the constancy of thy might confirm it. Let it be fervent, let it be circumspect, let it be invincible' (Bernard).

'Without the heart, obedience is nothing, obedience is impossible. Without the heart, a man's external acts are no more than the motions of the limbs of a wooden image; have no more of the nature of obedience.... We must love God as much as our capacity will allow.... And though it is not easy precisely to fix the limits of man's capacity to love God, yet in general we may determine that his capacity of love is co-extended with his capacity of knowledge; the exercise of the understanding opens up the way of the exercise of the heart' (Edwards).

and our neighbour as ourselves
'And to do to others what we would have them do to us' (Larger Catechism). Neighbour: *neah*, nigh, and *boor*, a husbandman; the man whose field lies next to ours.

The need for this commandment is seen from the fact that all men by nature live 'in malice and envy, hateful and hating one another'. 'Hateful,' says Goodwin, 'every man is to another man, more or less; he is hated of another, and he hateth another man more or less. And if his nature were let out to the full, there is that in him, his hand would be against every man, as is said of Ishmael, *Homo homini lupus*.' 'All men,' says Pascal, 'naturally hate one another.' Now it is into the human heart thus hating and hateful that this holy law enters: Thou shalt love thy neighbour as thyself. The Apostle James calls this 'the royal law', because it is the supreme and master law, and because it comes as a new commandment from Jesus Christ our heavenly King. 'This is the whole law,' said Rabbi Hillel, 'all else is interpretation.' And John Locke, in his *Conduct of the Understanding*, says, 'Our Saviour's great rule, that we should love our neighbour as ourselves, is such a fundamental truth for the regulating of human society, that I think by that alone one might without difficulty determine all the cases and doubts in social morality.'

Uses

1. 'What a man's love is,' says Augustine, 'that he is. Lovest thou earth? thou art earth. Lovest thou God? what shall I say? Thou shalt be god.... Nought else maketh good and evil actions, save good or evil affections.'

2. 'True virtue essentially consists in Benevolence' (Edwards).

3. 'Are all men to be loved alike, and with the same degree of love? No; though we must love all men with the love of benevolence, yet the saints only with the love of complacence (Ps. 15:4, 16:3; Gal. 6:8)' (Flavel).

QUESTION 43

What is the preface to the ten commandments?

Answer: The preface to the ten commandments is in these words, I am the Lord thy God, which have brought thee out of the land of Egypt, out of the house of bondage.[1]

1. Exodus 20:2

QUESTION 44

What doth the preface to the ten commandments teach us?

Answer: The preface to the ten commandments teacheth us, That because God is the Lord, and our God, and Redeemer, therefore we are bound to keep all his commandments.[1]

The preface
A preface is something spoken before; the introduction to a book; something the author wishes the reader to know before he commences to read. The Gospel of Luke and the Revelation of John are both introduced by prefaces. The preface to the ten commandments is a simple statement of a historical fact. The children of Israel were in bondage, and by a mighty hand and a stretched out arm Jehovah delivered them. And the preface before us but states that historical fact in a single word.

I brought thee out
Mark the individualizing manner in which the preface is set forth, and according to which all the subsequent commandments are drawn. The Decalogue is a national covenant, but it is only so because it lies on the heart and conscience of every Israelite. 'We must say, therefore, that he is desirous here to teach that most excellent lesson to those who read the sacred Scriptures, that each separate individual by himself, when he is an observer of the law and obedient to God, is of equal estimation with a whole nation, be it ever so populous, or, I might rather say, with all the nations upon earth' (Philo).

I am the Lord thy God, ...because God is the Lord
The English Bible neither translates nor transliterates the original Divine Name in Exodus 20:2; it follows a questionable custom of the Jewish doctors in substituting LORD for JEHOVAH. JAH or JEHOVAH is the

---

1. Luke 1:74, 75: That he would grant unto us, that we, being delivered out of the hand of our enemies, might serve him without fear, In holiness and righteousness before him, all the days of our life. 1 Peter 1:15-19: But as he which hath called you is holy, so be ye holy in all manner of conversation; Because it is written, Be ye holy; for I am holy. And if ye call on the Father, who without respect of persons judgeth according to every man's work, pass the time of your sojourning here in fear: Forasmuch as ye know that ye were not redeemed with corruptible things, as silver and gold, from your vain conversation received by tradition from your fathers; But with the precious blood of Christ, as of a lamb without blemish and without spot.

original : I AM. I AM THAT I AM is the translation; and LORD is simply the substitution of another name or title in room of a transliteration or translation of the original.

Note

Shaddai or El-Shaddai, translated God, was the name by which their Maker and Ruler and Guide was known to the pre-Mosaic patriarchs. Perhaps the best modern equivalent of this ancient and august name is our somewhat vague and remote epithet, the Deity. This name recognized the existence of the Divine Nature, and it described that Nature in the broadest and most general way. El-Shaddai, Almighty God, called Abraham, and pledged the fulfilment of His covenant promises on His announced and accepted name. The name El-Shaddai kept before the patriarchal mind the unity, spirituality and omnipotence of God, and on these great truths, as a bridge on its piers, the subsequent revelations of God all reposed. And when some further but still kindred titles were added to this great name; when God successively announced Himself as the God of Abraham, and Isaac and Jacob, and the God of Bethel, in all these amplifications and applications of El-Shaddai the sacred writer but embodies in a memorable phrase this and that man's lifelong experience of the divine power and helpfulness.

But a new epoch in the publication of the Divine Name occurred in the time of Moses. For when God was giving His commission to His chosen servant to put himself at the head of the tribes of Israel, and when Moses raised the difficulty that the people might doubt his authority, and demand his credentials, and ask him in whose name he came, he was told to say to them, JEHOVAH, I AM, hath sent me unto you. The Hebrew student at once recognizes this to be in the circumstances an immense step onward in the progressive revelation of the Divine Name; and even the most unlearned may, on due consideration, see something of its great importance. El-Shaddai was God's primitive and first published name, and JAH, JEHOVAH, reposed on and was an extension of that.

The name Jehovah, as everyone knows who has paid any attention to the composition, contents and characteristics of the book of Genesis, was by no means an unknown name to the pre-captivity patriarchs. All commentators are agreed that the words in Exodus, 'by my name Jehovah was I not known to them' (Exod. 6:3), are to be understood with a certain latitude. It is not meant that no such name as Jehovah was ever heard by the forefathers of the Hebrew people in the divine announcements made to them, but the meaning is that the full import of that name had not been opened up to them. There is an economical and contemporary sense and usage, as well as an essential and permanent truth connected with the great name JEHOVAH, I AM. When God said I AM, He thereby said, there is no other.

El-Shaddai as a name might be supposed to be borne, as a matter of fact it was borne, by the divinities of other nations, just as the idolaters of our own day call their idols gods. Egypt and Assyria insisted that El-the Almighty was with them, if not exclusively, yet truly; and therefore now, when Israel was to be so much in contact and collision with other nations and other religions, it was necessary that the true and only God should take to Himself a name that taught and asserted HIS ALONE GODHEAD. The God of Abraham and Isaac and Jacob is now by a succession of mighty acts to prove to Israel and to all the nations that HE ALONE IS, and that all other gods are but dumb and dead idols, the imagination of men's darkened hearts, and the work of their impious hands. Neither Baal nor Ashtoreth, neither Jupiter nor Mercurius, could say I AM, for, in the apostle's words, 'we know that an idol is nothing in the world.' But when a Hebrew worshipper came to his God, he could believe and be sure that He is, for I AM is His very name.

But this is not all. For as to the Abrahamic name, the Almighty God, the Revealing Spirit in process of time added the names and titles, God of Isaac and Jacob, and God of Bethel, so, to the Mosaic name I AM, there was immediately added, 'Merciful and gracious, long-suffering, and abundant in goodness and truth.' The thirty-fourth of Exodus is one of the very fontal passages of revelation. This great well-spring, high up in the hill of God, always recalls to the mind the saying of the wise man: 'All the rivers run into the sea; into the place from whence the rivers come, thither they return again.' All the previous proclamations of the Divine Name were but well-springs sent up to water the earth from this as yet undiscovered sea. And from this supreme Old Testament scripture, as from a perennial and everlasting fountain, all succeeding prophets and psalmists come hither to draw. And as God's name JAH is worthily written in our largest letters, so that parent passage might well be printed in letters of gold a finger deep, if only to arrest the unthinking reader, and make him tarry to inquire what this supreme scripture may mean, and to learn on what holy ground he here ignorantly stands: 'And JEHOVAH passed before Moses, and proclaimed, JEHOVAH, JEHOVAH-El, merciful and gracious, long-suffering, and abundant in goodness and truth, keeping mercy for thousands, and forgiving iniquity and transgression and sin' (Ex. 34:6,7). Like doves to their windows, like the heart to the water-brooks, so do all the prophets and psalmists in Israel turn back to this scripture till the coming of Christ.

and God
JEHOVAH, not Baal, nor any of the gods of the heathen, is our God, confessed the devout Hebrew. 'To take the Lord for our God is the natural part of the covenant; the supernatural part is to take Christ for our Redeemer. The former is first necessary and implied in the latter' (Baxter).

and Redeemer
This great and expressive name which our Lord bears in the New Testament, was first borne by Jehovah in the house of Israel. The word literally means one who pays a ransom, and thus buys back any person or thing that has been in the possession of another. From this the word comes to mean a deliverer by conquest, as in Exodus: 'I will bring you out from under the burdens of the Egyptians, and I will rid you out of their bondage, and I will redeem you with a stretched out arm, and with great judgment' (Exod. 6:6). In the captivity and post-captivity prophets the redemption promised and celebrated is that which Jehovah wrought for His people in the overthrow of Babylon. (See the marginal note on Hosea 9:3, in which it is pointed out that in the days of that prophet Egypt had come to stand for Assyria and Babylon, as in our day it often stands for our unregenerate estate. And thus a language was developed and a memory accumulated in the Old Testament that were divinely adapted to illustrate and describe the great redemption accomplished by our Lord.) (See Answer 20.)

therefore we are bound to keep all his commandments
'Therefore we are bound to take Him for our God alone, and to keep all His commandments' (Larger Catechism). (See Answer 52, under reasons annexed.)

Uses

1. From this exposition we must see the absolute necessity for sacred learning in all competent expositors of the divine word. In studies of

this kind, and especially in all studies connected with the development of revelation and the progress of Scripture, it is indispensable that the expositor be a student, and that as a student he possess some acquaintance with the sacred tongues in which the Holy Scriptures were originally written.

2. There is no name and no assemblage of names so necessary for us to know and understand as the names of God, and yet there is no group of names in all our vocabulary that we utter so loosely, listen to so languidly, and consider so little what they discover, connote, and convey. What is His name, and what is His Son's name, if thou canst tell?

QUESTION 45

Which is the first commandment?

Answer: The first commandment is, Thou shalt have no other gods before me.[1]

QUESTION 46

What is required in the first commandment?

Answer: The first commandment requireth us to know and acknowledge God to be the only true God, and our God;[2] *and to worship and glorify him accordingly.*[3]

---

1. Exodus 20:3.

2. 1 Chronicles 28:9: And thou, Solomon my son, know thou the God of thy father, and serve him with a perfect heart, and with a willing mind; for the Lord searcheth all hearts, and understandeth all the imaginations of the thoughts: if thou seek him, he will be found of thee; but if thou forsake him, he will cast thee off for ever. Deuteronomy 26:17: Thou hast avouched the Lord this day to be thy God, and to walk in his ways, and to keep his statutes, and his commandments, and his judgments, and to hearken unto his voice.

3. Matthew 4:10: Then saith Jesus unto him, Get thee hence, Satan: for it is written, Thou shalt worship the Lord thy God, and him only shalt thou serve. Psalm 29:2: Give unto the Lord the glory due unto his name; worship the Lord in the beauty of holiness.

QUESTION 47

What is forbidden in the first commandment?

Answer: The first commandment forbiddeth the denying,[1] *or not worshipping and glorifying the true God as God,*[2] *and our God;*[3] *and the giving of that worship and glory to any other, which is due to him alone.*[4]

QUESTION 48

What are we specially taught by these words 'before me' in the first commandment?

Answer: These words 'before me' in the first commandment teach us, That God, who seeth all things, taketh notice of, and is much displeased with, the sin of having any other god.[5]

This is the first commandment, and it was of the first necessity at the time it was published. For the whole human family having fallen from the knowledge of God and from all communion with Him, and a God being indispensable to every conscience and heart, men had conceived and manufactured all manner of gods for themselves. Each separate tribe and nation had created its own divinity according to its own character. And accordingly the first thing to be done in beginning to establish the true religion in Israel, and through Israel in the whole earth, was to sweep all superstitious and mischievous notions about local and contending deities

1. Psalm 14:1: The fool hath said in his heart, There is no God.

2. Romans 1:21: Because that, when they knew God, they glorified him not as God, neither were thankful; but became vain in their imaginations, and their foolish heart was darkened.

3. Psalm 81:10, 11: I am the Lord thy God, which brought thee out of the land of Egypt: open thy mouth wide, and I will fill it. But my people would not hearken to my voice; and Israel would none of me.

4. Romans 1:25: Who changed the truth of God into a lie, and worshipped and served the creature more than the Creator, who is blessed for ever. Amen.

5. Ezekiel 8:5, to the end of the chapter. Psalm 44:20, 21: If we have forgotten the name of our God, or stretched out our hands to a strange god; Shall not God search this out? for he knoweth the secrets of the heart.

clean out of the mind. Israel must learn to hold and teach that there is no God but Jehovah only. And He was not a new or unknown God who gave to Israel this comprehensive and exclusive law. He was the God of Adam and Abel, of Enoch and Noah, of Abraham and Isaac and Jacob. He was the God of Moses and Aaron; it was He who by the hand of Moses had just delivered them out of the land of Egypt. It was He who said to the whole house of Israel, and to every individual Israelite, Thou shalt have no other gods before me.

In Calvin's *Institutes* there is an admirable analysis which gathers out all those things in this commandment that make it common to Israel and to us. The commandment came to them, and it still comes to us, carrying the divine demand on all our adoration, trust, invocation and thanksgiving. And these affections, attitudes and acts, rightly understood and spiritually performed, fulfil and satisfy this first and fundamental commandment.

The first commandment
'In duties themselves there is an order, which it is of much importance to observe. There is scarcely a greater or more mischievous error than one which has found advocates, even among some who profess a regard to revealed truth; namely, that the principal service which God requires of us, and which of course we need to be much concerned about, is the performance of social duties: the duties of justice and benevolence to our fellow-men. Now, that social duties constitute an indispensable part of all true religion, we both admit and inculcate. But we maintain that the duties first in rank and importance are those we owe immediately to God, our Creator and Redeemer; that He is infinitely the greatest and best of all beings, and that if reverence, love, service, and worship be due to Him at all, our obligations to these must of necessity be higher and more sacred than any other' (Green).

requireth
Conformity to. (See Answer 14.)

to know and acknowledge
'This is life eternal, that they might know Thee the only true God, and Jesus Christ whom Thou hast sent' (John 17:3). 'In all thy ways acknowledge Him, and He shall direct thy steps' (Prov. 3:6).

'The true knowledge of God includes the love of God. "To love man, we must know him: to know God, we must love Him." They who will not love God, cannot even aright know of God. To know God is to know by experience that God is good, and this God makes known to the soul He loves, while it meditates on Him, reads of Him, speaks to Him, adores Him, obeys Him' (Pusey).

only true God

See Answer 5. The epithet only, as Meyer says, bears upon the whole phrase 'true God'. The term true shows that this God alone perfectly answers to the great idea expressed by the word GOD.

worship and glorify him accordingly

Worship means to put proper worth upon: to value supremely: to adore, love, and serve. 'The God of glory is the sum of the divine praise' (Bengel).

In her beautiful book on the Commandments, Miss Rossetti calls this commandment the Catholic basis on which the Christian structure can alone be raised. What is Catholic underlies what is Christian. And to that fundamental doctrine of the divine unity from which the Christian doctrine is developed there has been granted a freer currency: so that while the Jewish Church knew it by revelation, multitudes of the Gentile world knew it, or at least surmised it, by intellectual or spiritual enlightenment.

forbiddeth

Want of conformity to or transgression of. (See Answer 14.)

the denying

This commandment forbiddeth *atheism*, speculative and practical. For speculative atheism is the looking upon nature and man as coming into existence and being sustained without God; while practical atheism is just vulgar irreligion: living 'without God in the world'. Many who would shudder at the name of atheist are yet to all intents and purposes living an atheist's life. How many atheistic hours we all spend, and how many atheistic acts we all perform, let each man say for himself.

giving that worship to any other

This is directed against all idolatry, and this sin is treated more fully in and under the second commandment. Milton makes idolatry the first result of Eve's eating the forbidden fruit:

> So saying, from the tree her steps she turned,
> But first low reverence done, as to the Power
> That dwelt within, whose presence had infus'd
> Into the plant sciential sap.

before me
In my presence, which is omnipresence. There is no place where man may set up or worship another God. (See Psalm 139:1-12.)

seeth, taketh notice of, and is much displeased with
Note the progress in these clauses. 'How doth the idolatry forbidden in the first, differ from that forbidden in the second commandment? The idolatry forbidden in the first commandment is a sin respecting the Object of worship, when we set up anything in the place of God, which by nature is not God. But that against the second commandment is, when we pretend to worship the true God, but do it by such means, and in such a manner as He hath not required, or hath forbidden' (Flavel).

QUESTION 49

Which is the second commandment?

Answer: The second commandment is, Thou shalt not make unto thee any graven image, or any likeness of any thing that is in heaven above, or that is in the earth beneath, or that is in the water under the earth: thou shalt not bow down thyself to them, nor serve them; for I the LORD thy God am a jealous God, visiting the iniquity of the fathers upon the children unto the third and fourth generation of them that hate me: and showing mercy unto thousands of them that love me, and keep my commandments.[1]

1. Exodus 20:4-6.

QUESTION 50

What is required in the second commandment?

Answer: The second commandment requireth the receiving, observing, and keeping pure and entire, all such religious worship and ordinances as God hath appointed in his word.[1]

QUESTION 51

What is forbidden in the second commandment?

Answer: The second commandment forbiddeth the worshipping of God by images,[2] *or any other way not appointed in his word.*[3]

---

1. Deuteronomy 32:46: And he said unto them, Set your hearts unto all the words which I testify among you this day, which ye shall command your children to observe to do, all the words of this law. Matthew 28:20: Teaching them to observe all things whatsoever I have commanded you: and, lo, I am with you alway, even unto the end of the world. Amen. Acts 2:42: And they continued stedfastly in the apostles' doctrine and fellowship, and in breaking of bread, and in prayers.

2. Deuteronomy 4:15-19: Take ye therefore good heed unto yourselves; for ye saw no manner of similitude on the day that the Lord spake unto you in Horeb out of the midst of the fire: Lest ye corrupt yourselves, and make you a graven image, the similitude of any figure, the likeness of male or female; The likeness of any beast that is on the earth, the likeness of any winged fowl that flieth in the air, The likeness of any thing that creepeth on the ground, the likeness of any fish that is in the waters beneath the earth: And lest thou lift up thine eyes unto heaven, and when thou seest the sun, and the moon, and the stars, even all the host of heaven, shouldest be driven to worship them, and serve them, which the Lord thy God hath divided unto all nations under the whole heaven. Exodus 32:8: They have turned aside quickly out of the way which I commanded them: they have made them a molten calf, and have worshipped it, and have sacrificed thereunto, and said, these be thy gods, O Israel, which have brought thee up out of the land of Egypt.

3. Deuteronomy 12:31, 32: Thou shalt not do so unto the Lord thy God: for every abomination to the Lord which he hateth have they done unto their gods; for even their sons and their daughters they have burnt in the fire to their gods. What thing soever I command you, observe to do it: thou shalt not add thereto, nor diminish from it.

QUESTION 52

What are the reasons annexed to the second commandment?

Answer: The reasons annexed to the second commandment are, God's sovereignty over us,[1] his propriety in us,[2] and the zeal he hath to his own worship.[3]

The unity and sole supremacy of Jehovah is the subject of the first commandment, and in the same manner the spirituality of the Divine Nature is taught and guarded in the second. Locality, limitation, shape, and all suchlike creaturely conditions, are to be put out of our minds when we would think aright about God. These things are never in any way to be associated with God. The worship of God is to be purely spiritual, and lest its spirituality should be invaded or infringed, it is here fenced round with a most explicit and rigorous commandment against the worship of images, and even their manufacture. The unity and spirituality of God are accordingly the two cornerstones of the Decalogue, and indeed of all divine revelation, Mosaic and Christian. The law that came by Moses, and the grace and truth that came by Jesus Christ, all alike rest on those eternal and immutable truths of our holy faith.

Thou shalt not make unto thee any graven image

Aldis Wright in *Smith's Bible Dictionary* tells us that there are no fewer than twenty-one different Hebrew words that have been rendered in the Authorized Version either by idol or image. Nothing could be more instructive and significant than this multiplicity and variety of words designating the incentives, instruments and objectives of idolatry. At the same time, stringent and indispensable as this commandment was in such circumstances, it gives no countenance to the superstitious position that

---

1. Psalm 95:2: Let us come before his presence with thanksgiving, and make a joyful noise unto him with psalms. Verse 3: For the Lord is a great God, and a great King above all gods. Verse 6: O come, let us worship and bow down; let us kneel before the Lord our maker.

2. Psalm 45:11: ...he is thy Lord, and worship thou him.

3. Exodus 34:13, 14: But ye shall destroy their altars, break their images, and cut down their groves. For thou shalt worship no other god: for the Lord, whose name is Jealous, is a jealous God.

some have taken up against all works of art even for purposes of culture and pleasure. Referring to this misreading of the second commandment, Calvin says: 'I am not so superstitious, however, as to think that all visible representations of every kind are unlawful. But as sculpture and painting are gifts of God, what I insist on is, that both shall be used purely and lawfully. We think it unlawful to give a visible shape to God, because God Himself has forbidden it, and because it cannot be done without in some degree tarnishing His glory.'

'It may be admitted,' says Kalisch in his commentary on Exodus, 'that the prohibition expressed in our text has exercised a retarding influence upon the progress and development of the plastic arts among the Hebrews, as a similar interdiction in the Koran has produced a similar effect among the Arab tribes.... But it is an incomprehensible mistake, if it is believed that the plastic arts in general, sculpture and painting, are forbidden in our text. Josephus tells us that the Jews would not even suffer the image of the emperor which was represented on the eagles of the Roman soldiers, and a temple in Tiberias was, by decree of the Sanhedrin, burnt down, merely because it was ornamented with figures of animals (Josephus' Life, 12). Such a barbarous and irrational law could not possibly emanate from a legislator who erected a holy tent, furnished with all adornments of art and beauty, and who even ordered two cherubims to be placed in the Holy of Holies. In the first temple as well as the second, was an abundance of plastic works, which nobody has found to be at variance with the spirit of Mosaism.'

'The commandment which forbade the making of graven image or likeness was not observed in the sanctuary itself. By this exception it was made evident that the enactment was directed against accidental abuses of imitative art, and not against the art itself' (Westcott).

any likeness of anything that is in heaven above

'Left to themselves, to their own appetites, fears, caprices, imaginations, men made originally capable of discriminating truth from falsehood sought out many inventions. Sun, moon and stars, from being accounted symbols, came to be rated as gods; rivers were deified; beasts, birds, fishes, reptiles, all were adored; trees waxed oracular, mountain-tops grew sacred, light and darkness engrossed each its representative deity; fire had its own formidable divinity, and the world of the dead its own.

Mere attributes, mere operations, became embodiments capable of undergoing invocation and receiving worship; and destruction claimed its horrid ritual of human sacrifice, and fruitfulness was adored with such rites as it is a shame even to speak of' (Miss Rossetti's *Letter and Spirit*).

for I the Lord thy God am a jealous God
In the scientific language of theology, this is called an anthropopathic or economical manner of speech. God here speaks to man after the manner of men. He takes the human passion of jealousy to himself in a figure. But while making this explanation, it must be made in a reverent, guarded, believing manner. To say God is jealous is to say that while all human infirmity and evil are to be taken out of the expression, yet, at the same time, we are to receive it as the truest mode of conveying to us what, owing to the imperfections of the human mind and human language, cannot otherwise be impressed upon us. All Scripture, at least all Revelation, is and must be more or less anthropomorphic and anthropopathic. And the text is but an arresting and solemn example of this necessary and universal manner of divine communications. When Jehovah represents Himself as the husband of the Church in Israel and as having loved her with an everlasting love, her infidelity and idolatry come then in awful impressiveness to be spoken of as kindling jealousy in the divine bosom. The thoughtful reader of the Old Testament will recall many passages where these figures of speech are powerfully employed. But let it here and in all such passages be remembered that the scriptural metaphors never exaggerate or in any way misrepresent the reality; the prophetic figures never overstate the facts. Nahum is within the truth when he utters his burdensome vision: 'God is jealous, and the LORD revengeth; the LORD revengeth, and is furious; the LORD will take vengeance on His adversaries, and He reserveth wrath for His enemies' (Nah. 1:2).

visiting the iniquity of the fathers upon the children
Mozley in his able work, *Ruling Ideas in Early Ages*, exhibits the operation of this judicial principle in the old dispensation, and points out that while the second commandment and its sanctions of terror and of comfort remain entirely valid to this day, yet that it is to be read now in a providential and didactic sense rather than in a judicial and penal. Children

are not now punished for their fathers' sins though they still suffer in many ways on account of them.

'That God doth [or did] so is certain, because He saith He doth [or did]; and that this is just in Him to do so, is also certain therefore because He doth it. For as His laws are our measures, so His actions and His own will are His own measures. He that hath right over all things and all persons, cannot do wrong to any thing. He that is essentially just, it is impossible for him to be unjust' (Jeremy Taylor's Sermon on 'The Entail of Curses cut off').

keeping pure and entire

Flavel's warning not to invent ceremonies to make God's institutions 'more decent than Christ left them', should be laid to heart and pondered by those who have the charge of public worship.

appointed in his word

'Particularly prayer and thanksgiving in the name of Christ; the reading, preaching, and hearing of the word; the administration and receiving of the sacraments; Church government and discipline; the ministry and maintenance thereof; religious fasting; swearing by the name of God, and vowing unto Him' (Larger Catechism).

forbiddeth the worshipping of God by images

Mr. Robson tells that in India there are three views of image worship: the philosophical, that the image is an aid to devotion; the mystical, that some particular deity is present in or with the image; and the literal, that the material image is the Deity.

'The natural and obvious meaning of the second commandment is, that God there, in regulating the mode in which He is to be worshipped, forbids the making of the likeness of any object with the view of introducing this likeness into religious worship, or paying unto it any of the external marks of religious honour and veneration. And so sensible are Romanists that this is the natural and obvious meaning of the second commandment, that they have been accustomed to exclude it wholly, while professing to quote the Decalogue, from the Catechisms commonly used in the instruction of their people' (Cunningham).

How far popular Romanism has declined not only from apostolic spirituality in public worship, but even from that of the Old Testament, anyone who has seen a modern Popish cathedral or chapel, and will compare it with the following testimonies, will see. Milman tells us that the heathen world beheld with astonishment a whole race whose deity was represented under no visible form or likeness. The conqueror Pompey, when he entered the violated temple, was filled with wonder at finding the sanctuary without image or emblem of the deity: and Tacitus, 'the philosophic historian, whose profound mind seems struggling with hostile prejudices, defines, with his own inimitable compression of language, the doctrine, to the sublimity of which he has closed his eyes. The worship of the Jews, he says, is purely mental; they acknowledge but one God, and that God supreme and eternal, neither changeable nor perishable.'

The reasons annexed

In his learned sermon 'Of the Nature of Pride', Hooker has an introductory passage which will be the best note on the annexing of reasons to a commandment: 'The nature of man, being much more delighted to be led than drawn, doth many times stubbornly resist authority, when to persuasion it easily yieldeth. A law simply commanding or forbidding, is but dead in comparison of that which expresseth the reasons wherefore it doth the one or the other. And, surely, even in the laws of God, although that He hath given commandment be in itself a reason sufficient to exact all obedience at the hands of men, yet a forcible inducement it is to obey with greater alacrity and cheerfulness of mind, when we see plainly that nothing is imposed upon us more than we must needs yield unto, except we will be unreasonable. In a word, whatsoever we be taught, be it precept for direction of our manners, or article for instruction of our faith, or document any way for information of our minds, it then taketh root and abideth, when we conceive not only what God doth speak, but why.'

The reasons annexed to the second commandment as here drawn out are three: (1) God's sovereignty over us; He is our King, and we are His subjects, and therefore we are bound to obey His laws: (2) His propriety in us – an obsolete form; property has taken its place in modern English – His property in us; we belong to Him, He created us, and He hath redeemed us, and therefore we are not our own, least of all in our worship of our Maker and Redeemer: and (3) the zeal or jealousy He has to His own worship. The prophets and psalmists are full of that zeal and jealousy. For example, Isaiah 1:10-15; Ezekiel 14:1-11.

Uses

1. Though we do not build our places of worship with niches to hold images, yet this commandment is not on that account an obsolete precept, or the study of it the study of an antiquarian topic. The iconoclastic Puritanism of our fathers removed the temptation to idolatry from us. But they bequeathed to us a very spiritual law: a law that does not so much search our sanctuaries for statues and images as it turns its scrutiny into our own hearts. 'Know ye not that ye are the temple of God, and that the Spirit of God dwelleth in you? If any man defile the temple of God, him shall God destroy; for the temple of God is holy, which temple ye are' (1 Cor. 3:16,17).

2. But if the law against images in divine worship came by Moses, then the grace that obviates the supposed necessity for them – the grace that meets and answers the craving in the human heart to see God – that grace came by Jesus Christ. For it is one of the noblest and most expressive of the scriptural titles of our Lord to call Him the Image of God. For just as a man's face is the image of his soul; just as we address ourselves to a man's face in addressing his mind and heart; so is it when we seek God in Christ. 'No man hath see God at any time; the only begotten Son which is in the bosom of the Father, He hath declared him' (John 1:18).

3. 'The sins of fathers descend very often to their children, both in way of nature, that the children inherit strong temptations to their father's sins; and by way of example, that they greedily imitate, and often exaggerate them. Wouldest thou not have children whom thou wouldest wish unborn, reform thyself.... Parents who are careless as to themselves, and as to their own lives, still long that their children should not be as themselves' (Pusey).

4. 'I am to consider what remedies there are for sons to cut off the entail of curses.... The heirs and sons of families are to remove from their house the curse descending from their father's loins – (1) by acts disavowing the sins of their ancestors; (2) by praying for pardon; (3) by being humbled for them; (4) by renouncing the example; (5) quitting the affection to the crimes; (6) by not imitating the actions in kind, semblance, or similtude; and lastly (7) by refusing to rejoice in the ungodly purchases, in which their "fathers did amiss, and dealt wickedly" '(Jeremy Taylor).

QUESTION 53

Which is the third commandment?

Answer: The third commandment is: Thou shalt not take the name of the Lord thy God in vain: for the Lord will not hold him guiltless that taketh his name in vain.[1]

QUESTION 54

What is required in the third commandment?

Answer: The third commandment requireth the holy and reverent use of God's names,[2] *titles,*[3] *attributes,*[4] *ordinances,*[5] *word,*[6] *and works.*[7]

---

1. Exodus 20:7.

2. Matthew 6:9: After this manner therefore pray ye: Our Father which art in heaven, Hallowed be thy name. Deuteronomy 28:58: If thou wilt not observe to do all the words of this law that are written in this book, that thou mayest fear this glorious and fearful name, THE LORD THY GOD.

3. Psalm 68:4: Sing unto God, sing praises to his name: extol him that rideth upon the heavens by his name JAH, and rejoice before him.

4. Revelation 15:3, 4: And they sing the song of Moses the servant of God, and the song of the Lamb, saying, Great and marvellous are thy works, Lord God Almighty; just and true are thy ways, thou King of saints. Who shall not fear thee, O Lord, and glorify thy name? for thou only are holy.

5. Malachi 1:11: For from the rising of the sun, even unto the going down of the same, my name shall be great among the Gentiles; and in every place incense shall be offered unto my name, and a pure offering: for my name shall be great among the heathen, saith the Lord of hosts. Verse 14: But cursed be the deceiver, which hath in his flock a male, and voweth, and sacrificeth unto the Lord, a corrupt thing: for I am a great King, saith the Lord of hosts, and my name is dreadful among the heathen.

6. Psalm 138:2: I will worship toward thy holy temple, and praise thy name for thy lovingkindness, and for thy truth: for thou hast magnified thy word above all thy name.

7. Job 36:24: Remember that thou magnify his work, which men behold.

QUESTION 55

What is forbidden in the third commandment?

Answer. The third commandment forbiddeth all profaning or abusing of any thing whereby God maketh himself known.[1]

QUESTION 56

What is the reason annexed to the third commandment?

Answer. The reason annexed to the third commandment is, That however the breakers of this commandment may escape punishment from men, yet the Lord our God will not suffer them to escape his righteous judgment.[2]

Thou shalt not take the name of the Lord thy God in vain

The first commandment teaches us that Jehovah is God alone: He has no equal and no rival. The second commandment goes on to instruct us that

---

1. Malachi 1:6, 7: A son honoureth his father, and a servant his master: if then I be a father, where is mine honour? and if I be a master, where is my fear? saith the Lord of hosts unto you, O priests, that despise my name. And ye say, Wherein have we despised thy name? Ye offer polluted bread upon mine altar; and ye say, Wherein have we polluted thee? In that ye say, The table of the Lord is contemptible. Verse 12: But ye have profaned it, in that ye say, The table of the Lord is polluted; and the fruit thereof, even his meat, is contemptible. Malachi 2:2: If ye will not hear, and if ye will not lay it to heart, to give glory unto my name, saith the Lord of hosts, I will even send a curse upon you, and I will curse your blessings; yea, I have cursed them already, because ye do not lay it to heart. Malachi 3:14: Ye have said, It is vain to serve God; and what profit is it that we have kept his ordinance, and that we have walked mournfully before the Lord of hosts?

2. 1 Samuel 2:12: Now the sons of Eli were sons of Belial; they knew not the Lord. Verse 17: Wherefore the sin of the young men was very great before the Lord; for men abhorred the offering of the Lord. Verse 29: Wherefore kick ye at my sacrifice, and at mine offering, which I have commanded in my habitation; and honourest thy sons above me, to make yourselves fat with the chiefest of all the offerings of Israel my people? 1 Samuel 3:13: For I have told him, that I will judge his house for ever, for the iniquity which he knoweth; because his sons made themselves vile, and he restrained them not. Deuteronomy 28:58, 59: If thou wilt not observe to do all the words of this law that are written in this book, that thou mayest fear this glorious and fearful name, THE LORD THY GOD; Then the Lord will make thy plagues wonderful, and the plagues of thy seed, even great plagues, and of long continuance, and sore sickness, and of long continuance.

God is a spirit, and that we are not to set up any supposed similitude of God before our eyes. He has no shape or similitude, but He has a Name. That is to say, He has taken a name to Himself under which He wills that we know Him, think of Him, speak of Him, and address ourselves to Him. And accordingly He issued through Moses this warning commandment, the third.

'The literal meaning of this command is doubtful. It may mean, Thou shalt not utter the name of God in a vain and irreverent manner; or, Thou shalt not utter the name of God to a lie, thou shalt not swear falsely. It is urged as an objection to the second interpretation, that perjury is an offence against our neighbour, and therefore belongs to the second table of the law: and that it is in fact included in the ninth commandment, Thou shalt not bear false witness against thy neighbour. Bearing false testimony and false swearing are, however, different offences' (Hodge).

in vain

'I suppose the primary meaning of the phrase points to indifferentism at least as obviously as to antagonism. "In vain" suggests not irreverence only, but voidness, nothingness, the bringing in for no cause but to round a sentence or fill up a gap, of that Name which was proclaimed before Moses in majesty and mercy; to utter simply for the sake of saying something, that Name which Isaiah foresaw as coming from far burning with divine anger. It is to pronounce that Name as though it were a mere word, not standing for any person, to bring it in when another word would actually serve our purpose as well' (Christina Rossetti).

Note

Oaths. An oath is a solemn appeal taken from the weakness, untruthfulness and mistrust of men to the omniscience, truth and power of God. At bottom all oaths are of the same nature and design, and they come into use in this way. If I am forming any important engagement, and my self-interest leans against the likelihood of my performing it: or if I am called to bear witness or give judgment in a matter that tests my integrity, and if my neighbour doubts my will, my ability, my sincerity, then, conscious of all these in myself, I am permitted to swear by the name of God that I am true in my words, and just in my judgments, and sincere in my purposes. In taking an oath for his assurance, I as good as say to my neighbour: Were this matter between you and me only, the temptation to me rising out of it might be too strong for me; but since this transaction is so important for you, to give you the best possible security I can supply, I hereby carry this transaction into the presence of God: I hereby open my whole mind and heart in this matter to Him, and I solemnly affirm that as He is just and true in all His ways, so am I in this thing; and that as He will bring every secret thing to judgment, so I protest to you against that day that there is nothing false or unjust in my mind or heart toward you. I know that of every word I speak now I shall have to give an account at last; and I swear to you that I am speaking nothing now that I will repent of when I meet you before God in judgment.

Now all this, instead of being doubtful or wrong, is both most rational and indeed religious. It is most rational in that it accepts the facts and conditions of human life, as these facts and conditions are found in ourselves, and in our fellows around us. For an oath enables a weak, self-seeking, self-sheltering creature to take up a firm, open and honourable stand both toward himself and toward his neighbour. It enables a man to meet the most difficult duties and most searching demands of this life with his mind girt about with a strongly-wrought girdle of truth.

Nor does the Confession of Faith go any too far when it teaches that 'a lawful oath is a part of religious worship'. The Confession indeed but borrows Calvin's very words. 'An oath,' he says, 'when duly taken, is a species of divine worship.' Which it surely is, in so far as it is a most solemn acknowledgement of God as our lawgiver and our judge. It openly acknowledges His omnipresence, omniscience, justice and power. It connects the second table of His law most closely with the first. It confesses also, that my neighbour has but too good reason to fear that I do not love him as I love myself; it is a confession that my heart and lip are not necessarily above suspicion, and that I do not rebel against giving any legitimate guarantee that my help to secure my just and honourable treatment of my neighbour, and my jealous and conscientious watchfulness over myself. And the oath rises above both of us in that it binds fast the engagements of moral and social life to the throne of divine righteousness and truth. When a man takes an oath in the name of God, he at once humbles and ennobles himself thereby. He humbles himself, in that he takes his place among a race of fallen and false-hearted men; among men hateful and hating one another; deceitful and deceiving one another. And he ennobles himself, in that he acknowledges his evil nature and kinship, and at the same time seeks divine help, and promises, with

God's help, to speak only what is true, and to do only what is right. An oath accordingly, in the mouth of a devout juror, is nothing less than an act of divine worship. It turns a court of justice for the time into a church, and elevates its solemn procedure into an earthly figure and forecast of the day of judgment.

But we are not left to our own reasonings to guide and vindicate our practice in this matter of oaths. The Scriptures afford us endless examples, and some of them examples of the most solemn kind, of this method of ascertaining and reassuring the doubtful and anxious mind. At the very opening of the Hebrew history, Jehovah Himself swears by His own awful Name that He will perform to His people such and such things that confessedly lie beyond the pale of past experience and future likelihood. And when the things so promised were actually accomplished, they were thus celebrated in a psalm: 'O ye seed of Abraham His servant; ye children of Jacob His chosen: remember the covenant made with Abraham, and His oath unto Israel; He confirmed the same to Jacob for a law, and to Israel for an everlasting covenant' (Ps. 105:6, 9, 10). Again: 'Jehovah hath sworn, and will not repent, Thou art a priest for ever, after the order of Melchizedek' (Ps. 110:4). And again: 'For men verily swear by the greater, and an oath for confirmation is to them an end of all strife. Wherein God, willing more abundantly to show unto the heirs of promise the immutability of His counsel, confirmed it by an oath' (Heb. 6:16, 17). And our Lord also, when put on oath before the high priest, took the adjuration as made under the law, and thus both recognized and established the lawfulness and propriety of the judicial custom. All which is surely sufficient to disprove the somewhat fanatical position that oaths are unlawful; that judicial swearing is a breach of the third commandment.

But it will to a certainty occur to some readers to say at this point, What then is to be made of our Lord's words in the Sermon on the Mount: 'I say unto you, Swear not at all: neither by heaven; for it is God's throne: nor by earth; for it is His footstool: but let your communication be Yea, yea; Nay, nay: for whatsoever is more than these cometh of evil' (Matt. 5:34, 35, 37)? That is a most instructive example of our Lord's popular teaching, but it has little or nothing to do with the matter in hand. He is here dealing with one of the most common vices among His fellow-countrymen. The whole sermon, and eminently this part of it, is directed against the perversions and exaggerations, the glosses and refinements under which it may almost be said the moral law lay buried in our Lord's day; and hence the paradoxical and startling words He sometimes makes use of, as if just to set men to think what the law of God really is, and what obedience to it really implies. And accordingly our Lord is not so much dealing in the passage quoted with the legal practice of courts of justice, or even with the solemn assurances exchanged between man and man among the important concerns of daily life, as with the too familiar and irreverent use of God's name and attributes in their common conversation. And besides, the casuistical teaching of the ecclesiastical schools had laid down a mass of entangling, vexatious and demoralizing rules, measuring out the degrees of responsibility and solemnity that attached to this and that form of oath. Swearing by heaven meant so much; swearing by the temple meant so much; swearing by one thing you were not absolutely bound to keep your word; while swearing by another kept you firm; all this was sapping the foundations of truth and reverence in the land, and it was against all such rabbinical glosses and popular abuses of the third commandment that our Lord thus emphatically protested.

The third commandment requireth the holy and reverent use of God's names, etc.
'Men do not begin by intending to dishonour God; but they are afraid of the ridicule of others; they are ashamed of appearing religious, and thus they are led to pretend that they are worse than they really are.... They think contemptuously of God's ministers, sacraments, and worship; they slight His word, rarely looking into it, and never studying it. Thus they are in heart infidels; though they may not formally be such, and may attempt to disguise their own unbelief under pretence of objecting to one or other of the doctrines or ordinances of religion. And should a time of temptation come, when it would be safe to show themselves as they really are, they will almost unawares throw off their profession of Christianity, and join themselves to the scoffing world' (Newman).

forbiddeth all profaning
This commandment among other things denounces the sinful and degrading habit of profane cursing and swearing. It is distressing to think of the hold this coarse and vulgar habit has taken of certain classes of people. You can scarcely pass a field in seed-time or harvest, you will not walk far along any frequented highway without hearing men uttering savage bursts of cursing at the mute creatures God has given them to assist them

in their work, and even at the very implements they hold in their hands. In every knot of workmen there are usually some whose mother-tongue is blasphemy, whose mouth is filled with cursing and bitterness. And sometimes seriously-minded men, such is the strength of example, or of an early bad habit, will be surprised into this lamentable language, and that long after they have begun to set a watch on the door of their lips. Peter's explosion in the palace of the high priest is no doubt an example of the long survival of an early evil habit. 'Once,' says Bunyan, in his *Grace Abounding*, 'when I was in the height of vanity, yet hearing one to swear that was reckoned for a religious man, it had so great a stroke upon my spirit that it made my heart to ake.'

We have reason to be thankful that this sinful and indecent habit has almost entirely disappeared from among educated men. For there are certain kinds of historical and social literature that survive to show us how common and almost universal this abominable practice was at one time even among the more cultivated classes of society. Addressing working men in the twentieth letter of *Fors Clavigera*, Mr. Ruskin says: 'I wish you to think over the meaning of this habit of yours very carefully with me. I call it a habit of yours, observe, only with reference to your recent adoption of it. You have learned it from your superiors; but they, partly in consequence of your too eager imitation of them, are beginning to mend their manners.... And first, it is necessary you should understand the difference between swearing and cursing, vulgarly so often confounded. They are entirely different things; the first is invoking the witness of a spirit to an assertion you make, the second is invoking the assistance of a spirit to a mischief you wish to inflict. When ill-educated and ill-tempered people clamorously confound the two invocations, they are not, in reality, either cursing or swearing, but merely vomiting empty words indecently. True cursing and swearing must always be distinct and solemn.'

And Dr. Newman calls all this kind of language 'a sort of vocal worship of the evil one, to which he listens with especial satisfaction. He goes to and fro upon the earth, and walks up and down in it, hearing and rejoicing in that light and profane talk which is his worship.'

or abusing of anything whereby God maketh himself known

The Bible word blasphemy is just Greek for this which is forbidden in this commandment. And Bengel excellently defines blasphemy thus: 'Blasphemy is committed when (1) anything unworthy of God is attributed to Him; (2) when things worthy of God are denied to Him; (3) when the incommunicable attributes of God are attributed to others.'

God will not suffer them to escape his righteous judgment
'Jehovah alone, according to the ancient constitution, was King in Israel, so that the crime of high treason could only be committed in respect of Him, and as the ten commandments would lead us to expect, the penalty for blaspheming His name was death. The book of Leviticus (24) relates how on one occasion a semi-Israelite in a brawl reviled and cursed HIS NAME, and how the community, shocked at the unlooked-for event, sought counsel of the oracle, and how this commanded the man to be stoned' (Ewald).

Uses
1. The holy and reverent use of God's name 'implies right faith to call upon Him as He Is; right trust in Him, leaning upon Him; right devotion, calling upon Him as He has appointed; right life, ourselves who call upon Him being, or becoming by His grace, what He wills' (Pusey).

2. 'Whenever you hear the name of God mentioned, accustom yourselves to make a reverential pause, and form within yourselves an inward act of adoration, whereby you will be less apt to profane that venerable name in your more solemn addresses' (A Father's Advice to his Children).

3. Certain classes of men have already been named whose transgression of this commandment is notorious and scandalous. But this commandment, like all God's commandments, is very broad and very spiritual. And those who are farthest from the profane habits of speech referred to may fall into another profanity not less displeasing to God and injurious to themselves. There is a professional, a familiar, a conventional way of addressing God in prayer and praise, as also in speaking of Him in preaching and writing and debating, that is a grievous breach of this holy commandment. 'We are apt to act toward God and the things of God as toward a mere system, a law, a name, a religion, a principle; not as against a Person, a living, watchful, present, prompt and powerful Eye and Arm. That all this is a great error is plain to all who study Scripture' (Newman).

QUESTION 57

Which is the fourth commandment?

Answer: The fourth commandment is, Remember the sabbath day, to keep it holy. Six days shalt thou labour, and do all thy work: but the seventh day is the sabbath of the Lord thy God: in it thou shalt not do any work, thou, nor thy son, nor thy daughter, thy man-servant, nor thy maid-servant, nor thy cattle, nor thy stranger that is within thy gates: for in six days the Lord made heaven and earth, the sea, and all that in them is, and rested the seventh day: wherefore the Lord blessed the sabbath day, and hallowed it.[1]

QUESTION 58

What is required in the fourth commandment?

Answer: The fourth commandment requireth the keeping holy to God such set times as he hath appointed in his word; expressly one whole day in seven, to be a holy sabbath to himself.[2]

Remember the sabbath day

Sabbath is from the Hebrew *Shabath*, to rest, the day of rest, the Sabbath day. This name is the most ancient name of the day, and till New Testament times it was the only scriptural and ecclesiastical name. The Lord's day is the New Testament and Christian name (Rev. 1:10). In the early Church the weekly commemoration of Christ's resurrection was observed on that day, hence the Greek Church still calls it Resurrection day. Another familiar name of the day is Sunday. This is an astrological and heathen designation, and comes down from times when Sol or Apollo, the Sun god, was worshipped on that day of the week, just as Saturn was worshipped on Saturday and the Moon on Monday. The Puritans and Presbyterians tried hard to get this pagan title removed from the first

1. Exodus 20:8-11.

2. Deuteronomy 5:12-14: Keep the sabbath day to sanctify it, as the Lord thy God hath commanded thee. Six days thou shalt labour, and do all thy work: But the seventh day is the sabbath of the Lord thy God: in it thou shalt not do any work.

day of the week, but in this as in many other things they were overborne. In their own Confessions and Catechisms, however, they use the only defensible names, Christian Sabbath or Lord's day.

The Sabbath day is the oldest religious institution in the world. It existed long ages before the Mosaic legislation, into which it was afterwards incorporated. Baptism and the Lord's Supper, circumcision and the Passover, public worship, nay, the Holy Scriptures themselves, all these ordinances and possessions are ancient and venerable, but none of them all can compare with the Sabbath day for hoary antiquity. It is the noble and beautiful representation of the most ancient page of Scripture, a representation, in Ewald's words, of 'unsurpassable truth', that the first morning that rose on Adam and Eve was the morning of the Sabbath day. And in spite of the fall, the Sabbath has kept its place among mankind as one of the two sweet relics of Eden, and is week by week sent down among us as an earnest of heaven, a foretaste of the rest that remains for the people of God. The second great epoch of sabbatical development and legislation was in the time of Moses. Standing at the head of human history and looking down the long vista, we hardly ever, even among the most darkened nations, lose sight of a Sabbath day. But it is only at the time of the exodus that the Sabbath becomes a permanent national and ecclesiastical ordinance, a political and religious institution of first-rate importance.

Sinai was not the birth-place of the Sabbath day. The law of the Sabbath as it was published in the fourth commandment was not a new thing on the earth, any more than the law of reverence for the name of God, or the law commanding honour to parents. The law of the Sabbath, like the laws of worship and parental honour, was rather a reinforcement and republication of a law that had been written on the human heart from the beginning. The Sabbath was first appointed by the Creator of mankind, and it was issued anew by Him when He became the Redeemer and Lawgiver of Israel. And within this holy field of time, within and around this hallowed day, all the holiest practices of religion, and all the best blessings of national, domestic and individual life gathered in Israel. By this commandment a space was cleared in the daily life of that ancient people for the study and pursuit of divine things, and among all the debts that modern Christendom owes to ancient Israel, and they are many and irrequiteable, after Christ Himself and the Holy Scriptures, the Sabbath day is the greatest.

It is well known that the Hebrew Sabbath began at sunset on Friday and ended at sunset on Saturday. And from the Holy Scriptures themselves, as well as from the expository and ecclesiastical writings of the Jews, we gather a pretty full acquaintance with the habits of Sabbath observance that obtained among that people. Perfect rest from all manual and mental toil was the original and fundamental idea of the institution. The Sabbath was literally and universally the day of quiet and repose. And to signalize and fix that idea in every mind, the commandment became unusually explicit and minute. 'The seventh day is the rest of the Lord thy God. In it thou shalt not do any work: thou, nor thy son, nor thy daughter: thy man-servant, nor thy maid-servant, nor thy cattle, nor thy stranger that is within thy gates.' And though troublesome and vexatious rules about this and that personal and domestic habit rose up among the later Jews, still this matter of rest was and is to them and to us the fundamental law of the Sabbath day.

But it did not follow that this weekly vacation from ordinary labour was to be left void of all occupation. The law of holy rest did not leave the day open to be wasted in sloth and idleness. Indolence of body and vacancy of mind are not the divine rest designed for the physical, intellectual and spiritual natures of man. And hence it was that in Israel, the Sabbath, without ceasing to be a day of real repose, became at the same time a day of special occupation with divine things. On the Sabbath the daily sacrifices were doubled in the tabernacle and temple. On the Sabbath the priests made ready the new display of shewbread, changing last week's preparation, and setting forth the new service upon the sacred table. On that day also the new relays of priests relieved the exhausted occupants of the holy office: the refreshed and recruited functionaries commenced their weekly terms on the seventh day.

And throughout the whole nation the same special religious aspect was given to the Sabbath day. The seventh day was the day of holy convocation. On that day the pious people resorted to their prophets to hear their new revelations, and their expositions and applications of the divine law. In later times, when the prophetical office had come to a standstill, the people gathered into the synagogues on the Sabbath day for reading the Scriptures, and for mutual exhortation and prayer. At home also, in the more devout households, all light and foolish as well as all anxious and worldly thoughts were banished from the mind, and quiet meditation and communion with the highest subjects was devoutly cultivated.

'And,' as one of their own writers has said, 'it is to this intellectual and religious observance of the Sabbath day that the Jewish nation owes the gratifying and auspicious fact that ignorance never spread among them as among many other nations and sects, and that every Israelite was, in consequence of the instruction given to him on the Sabbath day, enlightened in the principles of his faith, so that, even in the Middle Ages, when everywhere the deepest darkness of ignorance and superstition prevailed in Christendom, immortal philosophers and poets flourished in Israel.'

Remember
'This unique verbal form suggests that our liability to transgress the command is increased by a danger of its slipping our memory. Not that the day itself is likely to elude observation: on the contrary, temporal affairs are in Christian lands regulated and modified in reference to its occurrence. But we must not merely start in the morning under a conviction that Sunday is Sunday: we must bear the circumstance in mind all day long, doing or not doing in intentional subordination to that dominant circumstance, or else we shall not hallow the hallowed day. Wandering thoughts and a wandering heart desecrate it' (Christina Rossetti).

thou shalt not do any work, thou, nor thy son, nor thy daughter, thy man-servant, nor thy maid-servant, nor thy cattle, nor thy stranger that is within thy gates
'In this I go so far that I would not have the rest of the Sabbath day broken up even by too large demand for public worship. We should have time for both body and mind to come into a state of repose.... All letters of business, all messengers of business, and all conversations of business, and all books which treat of business we should exclude.... And as the commandment is upon our servants and the stranger within out gates, so we should hinder our workmen from doing anything on our account, and we should require nothing of them save what is necessary for our own health and the health of the cattle. We should not encourage any traffic, nor employ any Sabbath vehicles. Our Sabbath journeys should be indeed Sabbath-day journeys; and if we employ the services of our servants and cattle, it should be to them after Sabbath-day measure, for health or refreshment sake, by no means for labour or for profit.... I have no ascetic views of the Sabbath, and grudge not to myself or the

people whatever may comfort and refresh their minds. And if they find that end to be served by walking abroad to meditate and muse upon the handiworks of God, to escape from the noisy city, and rest in some retired rural plain, I commend them to that or any other method which they find best for fulfilling the purposes of God. But sure I am, a crowded vehicle, whether by land or water, or a public inn, or a crowded garden, or a bustling highway, or a park parade, are not the places most fitting for repose and retirement: and they who so spend the Sabbath, and call it keeping the commandment, do but lie unto the Lord and their own soul' (Edward Irving).

QUESTION 59

Which day of the seven hath God appointed to be the weekly sabbath?

> *Answer: From the beginning of the world to the resurrection of Christ, God appointed the seventh day of the week to be the weekly sabbath; and the first day of the week ever since, to continue to the end of the world, which is the Christian sabbath.*[1]

From the beginning of the world

The opening of the book of Genesis contains the account of the appointment of the seventh day of the week to be the weekly Sabbath, and though there is no direct reference to the keeping of a Sabbath in Patriarchal times, yet the repeated reference to a septenary division of time not only among the Hebrews, but also among the Assyrians, Egyptians, Arabians and Persians, is a remarkable, and on any other theory than that of Scripture, an inexplicable one. In his *Antiquities of Israel* Ewald says: 'Many ancient nations were acquainted with a weekly circle of seven days, which is quite in accord with the fact that such a week is spoken of in the primitive history of Jacob. These traces leave no doubt that the division

1. Genesis 2:2, 3: And on the seventh day God ended his work which he had made; and he rested on the seventh day from all his work which he had made. And God blessed the seventh day, and sanctified it. 1 Corinthians 16:2: Upon the first day of the week let every one of you lay by him in store, as God hath prospered him, that there be no gatherings when I come. Acts 20:7: And upon the first day of the week, when the disciples came together to break bread, Paul preached unto them.

into weeks of seven days, and all subsequent distributions of time, were widely extended over the earth long before the time of Moses.'

The first day of the week ever since the resurrection of Christ

The notorious deterioration and scandalous abuses of the Mosaic Sabbath in the days of our Lord were overruled so as to become a kind of providential preparation for the great change that shortly after took place as to the time and manner of observing the fourth commandment. The Sabbath of Moses was utterly and irrecoverably demoralized. A dense web of foolish, fantastic and immoral traditions had been spread over it, and had become grave-clothes to the mind and a snare to the conscience. Though our Lord was made under the law, and fulfilled all its righteousness, yet He took pains again and again to break through the puerile, harassing and demoralizing teaching of the scribes and doctors concerning the Sabbath day. And He who was the Lord of life and the Lord of the Sabbath lay in the grave all that fatal seventh day, and we may say that the dead Sabbath of Judaism was buried beside Him, and, unlike Him, never saw a resurrection. But when He rose from the dead, a new Sabbath, a better rest, a true Lord's day rose with Him. Our Lord rose from the dead on the first day of the week. For the whole of that week He was again lost to His disciples, but appeared to them again on the first day of the second week, as if to signalize that day and make it memorable. Again, on the day of Pentecost, which that year fell on the first day of the week, when the followers of Christ were all met together in one place, as if it were their peculiar Sabbath, the Holy Ghost fell on them as never before. Our blessed Lord had finished His work, He had entered into His rest from the labours of our redemption; and as the first man began life on the Sabbath day, so the new man in Christ Jesus counted His Sabbath days, calling them by a new name, counted them from the resurrection of Christ, and called them the Lord's day, the Christian Sabbath.

Never, perhaps, in the history of any sacred institution did Divine Revelation so clearly devote her functions on her sister Providence as in the origin and establishment of the Christian Sabbath. There is nothing in this department of sacred studies more striking and suggestive than the kindred and parallel histories of the obsolescent Jewish Sabbath and the new Christian Sabbath during the generations immediately succeeding the resurrection of Christ. The quietness with which that great innovation of the Lord's day was brought into the Church; the gradual decay of the sacredness that had been divinely and from such an antiquity attached to the Jewish Sabbath; the slow, but at last the complete assimilation by the first day of the week of all that had for so long been gracious, beneficent and sacred in the seventh; and the consequent bequest to all succeeding times of the Christian Sabbath: all this is a triumph of providential patience, watchfulness and wisdom that has never been sufficiently studied or extolled in the Church of Christ.

QUESTION 60

How is the sabbath to be sanctified?

Answer: The sabbath is to be sanctified by a holy resting all that day,[1] even from such worldly employments and recreations as are lawful on other days;[2] and spending the whole time in the publick and private exercises of God's worship,[3] except so much as is to be taken up in the works of necessity and mercy.[4]

The sabbath is to be sanctified by a holy resting

The question of what constituted and what invaded and broke up this holy rest was a frequent cause of dispute between our Lord and the scribes and doctors of His day. The unlearned reader of the New Testament would easily see that there was something very far wrong in the habits and practices as well as the teaching about the Sabbath in the time of our Lord, but without some historical reading he could form no conception of the mass of arbitrary regulations, and fantastic and impossible prohibitions

---

1. Exodus 20:8: Remember the sabbath day to keep it holy. Verse 10: But the seventh day is the sabbath of the Lord thy God: in it thou shalt not do any work, thou, nor thy son, etc. Exodus 16:25-28: And Moses said, Eat that to-day; for to-day is a sabbath unto the Lord: to-day ye shall not find it in the field. Six days ye shall gather it; but on the seventh day, which is the sabbath, in it there shall be none. And it came to pass, that there went out some of the people on the seventh day for to gather, and they found none. And the Lord said unto Moses, How long refuse ye to keep my commandments and my laws?

2. Nehemiah 13:15-22.

3. Luke 4:16: As his custom was, he went into the synagogue on the sabbath day, and stood up for to read. Acts 20:7: And upon the first day of the week, when the disciples came together to break bread, Paul preached unto them. Psalm 92 [title, A psalm or song for the sabbath day]. Isaiah 66:23: From one sabbath to another, shall all flesh come to worship before me, saith the Lord.

4. Matthew 12:1-31. Verse 12: It is lawful to do well on the sabbath days.

that were withering the hearts and exasperating the consciences of men when our Lord began to teach. And it made matters worse and more irreconcilable between Him and the leaders in Israel, that He did not aim merely to restore the Mosaic law to its primitive purity. He had come, among other things, to make Moses' law not less a law, but more a life. He had come to exhibit in His own walk and conversation the original and essential freshness and spirituality, the perennial richness and flexibility of the law of God. It was an advance on Moses rather than a return to him that our Lord was carrying on by word and example. And hence we possess not only the record of His example, but also such penetrating and fruitful utterances as these: 'The Sabbath was made for man, and not man for the Sabbath' (Mark 2:27,28), and, 'The Son of man is Lord also of the Sabbath' (Luke 6:5) – utterances fitted and intended to teach His hearers and all men that the Sabbath law is not the heavy and galling yoke they were making it, but is rather an ancient and divine badge and seal of liberty, an inalienable franchise and a permanent privilege granted to man by his Maker and Redeemer.

'Therefore I go not to assign to you any course of employment for the Sabbath; I plead simply for the fulfilment of the ordinances, that you work not and think not of your vocations, and allow your minds to come into repose from this world's agitations. Then nature and the Spirit of God will direct you to proper occupations. You will go to the house of prayer out of choice; you will go to your closet out of choice; you will read the holy page out of choice; you will shun intrusive company out of choice; and out of choice you will turn your thoughts to holy and spiritual subjects. All I ask is, keep the intrusion of the world out, shut your door upon worldly men, shut your ear upon worldly talk, shut your eye upon all ephemeral and worldly reading. Fulfil the statute, and see that those in your household do, and it will come to pass that ere long you will derive the benefit of the statute, both as to bodily and spiritual refreshment. Your soul will make progress toward heaven; you will learn to live above the world; and from all the weariness of the week you will run like a tossed and tempest-driven vessel to the haven of your Sabbath rest' (Edward Irving).

the whole time

'Q. Is it the whole day, or only some hours of the day that are set apart for God? A. Not a part, but the whole day is the Lord's, and it is as dangerous to halve it with God in point of time, as it was for Ananias and Sapphira to halve their dedicated goods and bring in but a part. Remember that thou keep holy the Sabbath day is the command' (Flavel).

'He who keeps the day most strictly, most religiously, he keeps it best, and most consonant to the designs of the Church, and the ends of religion, and the opportunity of the present leisure, and the interests of his own soul' (Jeremy Taylor).

in the public and private exercises of God's worship
The student will observe that the Confession embraces 'Religious worship and the Sabbath day' in one chapter, the twenty-first.

'Attendance on a Sunday may, through God's mercy, avail even in the case of those who have not given themselves up to Him – not to their salvation (for no one can be saved by one or two observances merely, or without a life of faith), but so far as to break in upon their life of sin, and give them thoughts and notions that may be the germs of future good. Even to those, I say, who live to the world, the mere Sunday attendance at church is a continual memento on their conscience, giving them a glimpse of things unseen, and rescuing them in a measure from the servitude of mammon or of Belial. And therefore it is that Satan's first attempt, when he would ruin a soul, is to prevail on him to desecrate the Lord's day' (Newman).

'What a man is in his private duties, that he is in the sight of God, that and no more' (Owen).

'*Non est religio, ubi omnia patent*. Religion doth not lie open to the eyes of all men. Observed duties maintain our credit, but secret duties maintain our life' (Flavel).

except so much as is to be taken up in the works of necessity and mercy
The Confession does not make works of necessity and mercy an exception to, or an intrusion on the exercises of God's worship; it rather co-ordinates them, and ranks them together: 'The whole time in the public and private exercises of His worship, and in the duties of necessity and mercy.' And the Directory specifies as Sabbath-day duties 'visiting the sick, relieving the poor, and such-like duties of piety, charity, and mercy, accounting the Sabbath a delight.' Even the Talmud taught that danger to life always supersedes the Sabbath law. Even for the sake of the tiniest babe it may be broken, 'for the babe will keep many a Sabbath yet for that one that was broken for it.'

Uses

1. 'Every rightly constituted man has his time of retreat, so that in the face of the onset of tasks and impressions brought on him by the outer world, he may be, and may continue to be, himself; and may maintain by dint of rest and recollection his proper personality as the fixed point round which his world must range itself' (Keim). This was not written to enforce the keeping of the Lord's day, but the student will at once see its excellent application to that duty and privilege.

2. 'Besides his particular calling for the support of this life, every one has a concern in a future life, which he is bound to look after. This engages his thoughts in religion; and here it mightily lies upon him to understand the reason right. Men therefore cannot be excused from understanding the words, and framing the general notions relating to religion aright. This one day of seven, besides other days of rest, allows in the Christian world time enough for this, if they would but make use of these vacancies from their daily labour, and apply themselves to improvement of knowledge.... There are instances of very mean people who have thus raised their minds to a great sense and understanding of religion' (Locke).

3. 'I am always well pleased with a country Sunday; and think, if keeping holy the seventh day were only a human institution, it would be the best method that could be thought of for the polishing and civilizing of mankind' (Addison's *Sir Roger at Church*).

4. 'We are on this day specially to meditate upon and celebrate the work of redemption. We are with special joy to remember the resurrection of Christ, because that was the finishing of that work. This was the day of gladness of Christ's heart; it was the day of His deliverance from the chains of death, and also of our deliverance; for we are delivered in Him who is our head.'

5. 'Works of mercy and charity are very proper and acceptable to Christ on this day. They especially become the Christian Sabbath, because it is a day kept in commemoration of the greatest work of mercy and love towards us that ever was wrought' (Edwards).

QUESTION 61

What is forbidden in the fourth commandment?

Answer: The fourth commandment forbiddeth the omission or careless performance of the duties required,[1] *and the profaning the day by idleness, or doing that which is in itself sinful,*[2] *or by unnecessary thoughts, words, or works, about our worldly employments or recreations.*[3]

forbiddeth ...profaning the day by idleness

'Freedom from all occupation, both physical and mental and moral, is indolence, and thoughtlessness, and apathy, which cannot possibly produce that sanctification which is the ulterior aim of all human aspirations. The rest of God is our prototype; but God watches and rules, and is a perfect Spirit at all time; to approach Him is the end of the Sabbath; but mental and moral indolence would remove us from Him; and the Sabbath, instead of being the greatest blessing of mankind, would be its greatest curse' (Kalisch).

'To rest and not to sanctify is to keep the Sabbath of an ox or an ass' (Nicholson).

Boswell tells us that Dr. Johnson, in his forty-sixth year, wrote in his journal the following scheme of life for Sunday: 'Having lived not without an habitual reverence for the Sabbath, yet without that attention to its religious duties which Christianity requires: I resolve henceforth – 1. To rise early, and in order to it, to go to sleep early on Saturday. 2. To use some extraordinary devotion in the morning. 3. To examine the tenor of my life, and particularly the last week; and to mark my advances in religion, or recessions from it. 4. To read the Scriptures methodically

---

1. Ezekiel 22:26: Her priests have violated my law, ...and have hid their eyes from my sabbaths, and I am profaned among them. Amos 8:5: Saying, When will the sabbath be gone, that we may sell corn, and that we may set forth wheat? Malachi 1:13: Ye said also, Behold, what a weariness is it! and ye have snuffed at it, saith the Lord of hosts: and ye brought that which was torn, and the lame, and the sick; thus ye brought an offering: should I accept this of your hand? saith the Lord.

2. Ezekiel 23:38: Moreover, this they have done unto me: they have defiled my sanctuary in the same day, and have profaned my sabbaths.

3. Jeremiah 17:24: Bring in no burden through the gates of this city on the sabbath day, but hallow the sabbath day, to do no work therein. Isaiah 58:13: If thou turn away thy foot from the sabbath, from doing thy pleasure on my holy day, and call the sabbath a delight, the holy of the Lord, honourable; and shalt honour him, not doing thine own ways, nor finding thine own pleasure, nor speaking thine own words.

with such helps as are at hand. 5. To go to church twice. 6. To read books of divinity, either speculative or practical. 7. To instruct my family. 8. To wear off my meditation any worldly soil contracted in the week.'

'To lie late, to go holidaying, to doze in pew or arm-chair, or smoke, is not resting. Such rest deserves not the name of rest when tried by the sacred standard of God's fourth commandment' (Christina Rossetti).

unnecessary thoughts, words, or works

'This day was specially consecrated to devout occupation with holy thoughts. In earlier periods the people visited the prophets to listen to their instructions and exhortations (2 Kings 4:23). It was also a day of holy assembly; the religious service was, especially in later times, most solemn, and in the synagogue the law was read to the congregation (Joseph. Antiq. xvi. 2. 4, Ap. i. 22; Luke 4:16, 31; Acts 13:42, 16:13). Even light, thoughtless, everyday conversations were avoided on Sabbath. It was intended to induce the Israelite to reflect on the state of his soul, and on the nature of his conduct, and thus to be a day of self-examination, of true repentance, and internal reformation' (Kalisch).

worldly employments or recreations

Bunyan tells us in his *Life and Death of Mr. Badman*, that 'even as a child that unhappy man could not endure the Lord's day because of the holiness that did attend it. The beginning of the day was as if he were going to prison, except he could get out from his father and mother and lurk in bye-holes among his companions till holy duties were over.'

Uses

1. The prophet Ezekiel said that the Sabbath in his day was a 'sign' between Jehovah and His people, a sign whereby they might know that He acknowledged and sanctified them. And what the Sabbath was in his day, it remains still in our day. It is an infallible sign of the state of true religion in a land, in a church, in a family, and in a man's own heart and life. It may be said of the Sabbath among divine institutions what Luther said of justification by faith among divine doctrines: it is the sign of a standing or falling church. There is perhaps no surer sign of a falling Christian than a growing neglect of Sabbath-day ordinances, and an indolent and profane abuse of its sacred and priceless hours. There is no bulwark that parents can build up around their children's religion and morality like

a well-kept Sabbath day; and there is no surer sign that a young man is declining from faith and personal religion than when he begins to find his own pleasure and go his own way on the Lord's holy day. And conscience fastens with peculiar poignancy on the breaking of the Sabbath day. It is as if she instinctively saw that that day was the stronghold and the tower of her strength. Many of us, like young Bunyan, have been early awakened to a sense of sin through youthful acts of Sabbath-breaking.

2. 'See that they have some profitable, moving book (beside the Bible) in each family; if they have not, persuade them to buy some of small price and great use. If they be not able to buy them, give them some, if you can; if you cannot, get some gentleman, or other rich persons that are willing to do good works, to do it, and engage them to read them at night when they have leisure, and especially on the Lord's day. The life of religion lieth much in this, because poor people have no other free considerable time; and therefore if they lose this they lose all, and will remain brutish and ignorant. So should the master of the family every Lord's day at night cause all his family to repeat the Catechism to him, and give him some account of what they have learned in public that day' (Baxter).

QUESTION 62

What are the reasons annexed to the fourth commandment?

> *Answer: The reasons annexed to the fourth commandment are, God's allowing us six days of the week for our own employments,*[1] *his challenging a special propriety in the seventh, his own example, and his blessing the sabbath day.*[2]

his challenging a special propriety in it

'And so a sin, which for the outward act is small, may in regard to the inward of it be a great one. As that act of the man gathering sticks on the Sabbath day, a small thing in appearance, to get a few sticks to make a fire; but he doing it in contempt of Moses, so as to put Moses into a strait, since if for so small a thing he executed or inflicted any punishment, he

1. Exodus 20:9: Six days shalt thou labour, and do all thy work.
2. Exodus 20:11: The Lord blessed the sabbath day, and hallowed it.

would have been thought a cruel governor by all the people; but on the other side, if he should pass it by, he opened a way to have the Sabbath broken; so as it was done in high contempt of both God and Moses, and this God took notice of especially' (Goodwin).

'Let us not grudge at this requisition of God, that the seventh day be unoccupied, as if He made an invasion of our liberty, and grudged us the enjoyment of our time, or sought to dispossess us of a seventh part of our gains. The Sabbath was made for man, not for God. We are to benefit from it, not He. And the only part the Almighty hath in the matter is to interpose His authority against our doing ourselves any harm' (Edward Irving).

And besides, the Sabbath comes to ourselves clothed with the very noblest and most commanding traditions and associations, both national and domestic, that would of themselves be a royal law to us, though we had had none other. For such is the solicitude and submissiveness of the Christian conscience, and such is the congruity, propriety, and blessedness of the Lord's day, that had the law of the day been published in no more ancient and authoritative document than our own confessional and catechetical symbols, these, with the subsequent experiences and testimonies of a Sabbath-keeping people as sanctions, would have been sufficient to have made the Sabbath day to us 'a delight, the holy of the LORD, and honourable' (Isa. 58:13).

his blessing the sabbath day

'If Sunday had not been observed as a day of rest during the last three centuries, I have not the smallest doubt that we should at this moment have been a poorer and less civilized people than we are' (Macaulay).

But no historian could attempt to tell the spiritual and saving blessings that have for millennia descended on the Church through this venerable and holy institution. The soul of every believing and Sabbath-keeping man contains for him the best commentary on this clause.

Use

If the Sabbath day is all this – and the half of its authority, dignity and blessedness hath not been told – we may well say with the scholarly and devout Bengel: 'Let us weigh well the caution to whosoever shall break the least part of this commandment, or shall teach men to break it; a caution which can never be too much recommended to critics, teachers, and sacred orators.'

QUESTION 63

Which is the fifth commandment?

Answer: The fifth commandment is, Honour thy father and thy mother; that thy days may be long upon the land which the Lord thy God giveth thee.[1]

QUESTION 64

What is required in the fifth commandment?

Answer: The fifth commandment requireth the preserving the honour, and performing the duties, belonging to everyone in their several places and relations, as superiors,[2] *inferiors,*[3] *or equals.*[4]

QUESTION 65

What is forbidden in the fifth commandment?

Answer: The fifth commandment forbiddeth the neglecting of, or doing any thing against, the honour and duty which belongeth to every one in their several places and relations.[5]

---

1. Exodus 20:12.
2. Ephesians 5:21: Submitting yourselves one to another in the fear of God.
3. 1 Peter 2:17: Honour all men. Love the brotherhood.... Honour the king.
4. Romans 12:10: Be kindly affectioned one to another with brotherly love; in honour preferring one another.
5. Matthew 15:4-6: For God commanded, saying, Honour thy father and mother: and, He that curseth father or mother, let him die the death. But ye say, Whosoever shall say to his father or his mother, It is a gift, by whatsoever thou mightest be profited by me, and honour not his father or his mother, he shall be free. Thus have ye made the commandment of God of none effect by your tradition. Romans 13:8: Owe no man any thing, but to love one another: for he that loveth another hath fulfilled the law.

QUESTION 66

What is the reason annexed to the fifth commandment?

Answer: The reason annexed to the fifth commandment, is a promise of long life and prosperity (as far as it shall serve for God's glory and their own good) to all such as keep this commandment.[1]

Honour thy father and thy mother
All revealed religion reposes on the first four commandments of the Decalogue, and in like manner all our best domestic, social and political life has its earliest, deepest and most fruitful roots in the fifth commandment. Natural conscience, indeed, supplies to all men some knowledge of God, and sanctions a certain worship toward Him, and in like manner nature herself teaches every child to love and honour his parents. But just as the natural conscience requires to be corrected, guided and reinforced by revelation, so the filial instinct must be watched over, its growth promoted, and its fruits secured.

Of all the commandments in the Decalogue, perhaps none was so well observed in the house of Israel as the commandment to honour father and mother. Of all the beautiful and winning pictures of patriarchal life that have been handed down to us, there are none so uniformly sweet and beautiful as those of parental love and solicitude on the one hand, and those of filial love and honour on the other. The union between parent and child was both by divine law and universal custom much closer and much more lasting than in our day would be either desirable or possible. But apart from the local, primitive and temporary forms which this natural relation and divine precept took in the patriarchal communities, the parental care and love, and the corresponding filial reverence and obedience in the house of Israel are set before us as ensamples worthy of all admiration and imitation.

The honouring of our parents comes in the order of the commandments after the honouring and worship of God; but in the order of nature,

1. Deuteronomy 5:16: Honour thy father and thy mother, as the Lord thy God hath commanded thee; that thy days may be prolonged, and that it may go well with thee, in the land which the Lord thy God giveth thee. Ephesians 6:2-3: Honour thy father and mother, (which is the first commandment with promise,) that it may be well with thee, and thou mayest live long on the earth.

and in our actual lives, the fifth commandment is the first fulfilled. A child's father is more than a father to him; his father is both his father and his god. A little child cannot rise above his father. It is impiety to him to think that there can be anywhere any one greater or better than his own greatest and best of fathers. To every child his father is the man of men. There is nothing he cannot do. There is no valour, no nobleness, no resources, no wisdom with which he is not clothed. The pious heart that will afterwards rise to everlasting adoration and love of its Father in heaven, for a long time knows him not, and feels no need of Him. What child cares for more than just to have his father ever near to him to love and worship? And in all this, 'earthly fathers learn their craft from God.' For God for a time clothes every father among us with His own attributes, and prerogatives, and dues. The divine throne, the divine sceptre, the divine sword, are immediately made over to the house of every man into whose keeping and care a little child is committed.

The honour due to parents, and to all superiors set over us in the Lord, is thus expanded and explained in the Larger Catechism, that incomparable commentary on the Shorter: 'This honour consists in all due reverence in heart, word, and behaviour; prayer and thanksgiving for them; imitation of their virtues and graces: willing obedience to their lawful commands and counsels; due submission to their corrections; fidelity to, defence, and maintenance of their persons and authority; bearing with their infirmities, and covering them in love,' and such like. Honour, indeed, is a noble, rich and inexhaustible word. Honour is more than love, and it is more than fear; for it is both love and fear. There may be a love where there is no affection; but he who has true honour in his heart toward any one, has toward him both love and fear. The highest and noblest love always contains an element of fear. No one truly loves another who does not feel reverence toward him. And this is the love that is due from a child to his parents; love with fear; honour, which contains both love and fear. A child without honour is worse than no child at all. Such a child, says Calvin, is a monster, and not a man.

'Children, obey your parents in the Lord' (Eph. 6:1), adds Paul; that is to say, obey and honour your parents as *Christian children* should; as the child Jesus did, and as He commands. With all Old Testament commands and counsels and examples, exalted and spiritualized as the New Testament exalts and spiritualizes all Old Testament duties and commands.

that thy days may be long upon the land
'The Lord spoke to the Israelites specially of the land which He had promised them for an inheritance. But as the whole earth is blessed to believers, we justly class the present life among the number of divine blessings. It is not promised to us, nor was it promised to the Jews, as if in itself it constituted happiness, but because it is an ordinary symbol of the divine favour to the Jews. Wherefore, if any one who is obedient to parents happens to be cut off before mature age (a thing which not unfrequently happens), the Lord nevertheless adheres to His promise as steadily as when He bestows a hundred acres of land when He had promised only one' (Calvin).

'In my Father's house are many mansions; ...I go to prepare a place for you. And if I go and prepare a place for you, I will come again and receive you unto myself; that where I am, there ye may be also' (John 14:2,3).

as far as it shall serve for God's glory and their own good
'It is a received rule among divines, that all temporal promises are to be understood *cum exceptione crucis*; that is to say, not absolutely, but with this reservation, unless the Lord in His holy wisdom shall see it good for us to have it otherwise' (Sanderson).

Uses

1. The graces with which we are clothed in our childhood will remain with us to be our ornament and defence in manhood, and amid its manifold relationships. To honour our father and mother is the first step toward honouring all men and adoring and serving God. Our Lord is but recognizing this original law of nature, when He says that we must become little children again if we would enter His Father's house. That is to say, we must become simple, reverent, devout, obedient, as we were long ago when we were little children.

2. Every well-organized, well-ruled household is a very seminary of good morals and good manners to society, as well as a pillar of stability to the State. All the virtues thrive in a family where the children are ruled by a pious, loving, conscientious hand. Every son who has been brought up in that nurture and admonition which produces honour, respect and obedience, is a gift to society and the State of a priceless kind.

3. In the Memoirs of Jonathan Edwards we read largely of his wise and saintly wife, and of her success in the upbringing of her children. As

thus: 'She had need to speak but once, and she was cheerfully obeyed; murmuring and answering again were not known among her children. In their manners they were uncommonly respectful to their parents. When their parents came into the room, they all instinctively rose from their seats, and never resumed them till their parents were seated; and when either parent was speaking, no matter with whom they had been conversing, they were all immediately silent and attentive.'

4. 'The justice of God falls more severely on those who degenerate from a holy parent than on those who have no incitement to good from the piety of their homes.'

5. 'Distaste will vitiate our observance of the fifth commandment.... Our elders speak and we wish they would be quiet; their manners are old-fashioned, their taste is barbarous. Their opinions are obsolete, their standard is childish, they know nothing available, they do not even aim at knowing any person or any thing worth knowing. We habitually stand in an attitude of endurance or of self-defence; we are censors and not children, at best we tolerate what we cannot reform. Bystanders may see ever so clearly that our father's little finger outweighs our whole self, but we see nothing of the sort.... Nor is our own day exempt from even an exceptional temptation to this sin of distaste; for now it is common enough in some ranks for children to be better taught than their parents, and those who acquire that dangerous thing, a little learning, are more likely to be puffed up by the little they know than ballasted by the much they know not; conceit spurns at reverence and submission, and the undermining of natural piety is too often followed by the repudiation of spiritual loyalty' (Christina Rossetti).

QUESTION 67

Which is the sixth commandment?

Answer: The sixth commandment is, Thou shalt not kill.[1]

1. Exodus 20:13.

QUESTION 68

What is required in the sixth commandment?

Answer: The sixth commandment requireth all lawful endeavours to preserve our own life,[1] *and the life of others.*[2]

QUESTION 69

What is forbidden in the sixth commandment?

Answer: The sixth commandment forbiddeth the taking away of our own life, or the life of our neighbour unjustly, or whatsoever tendeth thereunto.[3]

Thou shalt not kill

Were this all that the sixth commandment contains, it might surely be passed without comment. It is not to be thought that any one who reads this page will ever imbrue his hands in his brother's blood. Were the whole moral law concerning human life fully expressed, fully applied, and fully illustrated in the letter of this commandment, then it need not detail us long. But when we find a Psalmist saying, 'Thy commandment is exceeding broad' (Ps. 119:96), and when we hear the apostle crying out because of the pain in his own heart, 'We know that the law is spiritual' (Rom. 7:14), and especially, when we read our Lord's gloss and comment on this commandment, we come to see that it has more to say to us than at first sight we had thought. No expositor dare pass by the sixth commandment in silence after reading this utterance of his Divine

---

1. Ephesians 5:28, 29: So ought men to love their wives as their own bodies: he that loveth his wife loveth himself. For no man ever yet hated his own flesh; but nourisheth and cherisheth it.

2. 1 Kings 18:4: For it was so, when Jezebel cut off the prophets of the Lord, that Obadiah took an hundred prophets, and hid them by fifty in a cave, and fed them with bread and water.

3. Acts 16:28: But Paul cried with a loud voice, saying, Do thyself no harm; for we are all here. Genesis 9:6: Whoso sheddeth man's blood, by man shall his blood be shed: for in the image of God made he man.

Master: 'Ye have heard that it was said by them of old time, Thou shalt not kill;... and whosoever is angry with his brother without a cause shall be in danger of the judgment: and whosoever shall say to his brother, Raca! shall be in danger of the council: but whosoever shall say, Thou fool! shall be in danger of hell fire' (Matt. 5:21, 22). That authoritative interpretation lifts the sixth commandment into a new world; the student sees now something of what the Psalmist meant when he said, 'The commandment is exceeding broad.' And if any more were needed to open up the manifold fulness of this commandment, it would be found in the commentary supplied by the Catechism itself, in which we are taught that this commandment 'requireth all lawful endeavours to preserve our own life, and the life of others', and 'forbiddeth the taking away of our own life, or the life of our neighbour unjustly, or whatsoever tendeth thereunto'.

requireth all lawful endeavours to preserve our own life

This implies that there may be such a thing as an unlawful and impolitic endeavour to preserve our own life, according to our Lord's apposite sayings: 'Whosoever shall seek to save his life shall lose it; and whosoever shall lose his life shall preserve it' (Luke 17:33); 'He that loveth his life shall lose it, and he that hateth his life in this world shall keep it unto life eternal' (John 12:25). The paradoxical saying of Dr Witt has an important bearing on this matter also: 'Be careful of your health, but be careless of your life.'

forbiddeth the taking away of our own life, or the life of our neighbour unjustly

This conditioning word *unjustly* suggests, and indeed teaches, that there is a taking away of life that is done justly. War and capital punishment come under the shelter of this limiting and constraining clause. They are permitted and indeed enjoined by this commandment when it is correctly interpreted. Judicially to take away the life of a murderer is not only lawful, but obligatory. This commandment does not say to the judge, 'Thou shalt not kill;' it does not bid him put back the sword of justice into its sheath, for then he would bear the sword in vain, and would become a protection to evil-doers, and a terror to them that do well.

War also, a just and necessary war, is not only not forbidden, but is rather sanctioned and enjoined by this commandment. Religion does not annul the right and duty of self-defence. Civilized nations must protect the life and property and liberty of their citizens. This indeed is one main end of national life. At the same time, all rulers and judges, all statesmen who guide public and international affairs, and all citizens whose suffrages install statesmen, should remember the noble words of Edmund Burke: 'The blood of man should never be shed, but to redeem the blood of man. It is well shed for our family, for our friends, for our God, for our country; the rest is vanity; the rest is crime.'

Uses

1. As interpreted and reissued by our Lord, this commandment is directed against all causeless, unjust, ungoverned and cherished anger. There is an anger that is natural, proper and even praiseworthy; and again there is an anger so different from all that, that it is in danger of the judgment. Anger is an emotion of the human heart that slumbers in silence till it is kindled and flames up in the presence of any wrong. Anger, in this sense, is a gift of God. It is a quick instrument designed to protect life and life's interests against whatever would destroy or injure them. No passion that God has implanted in the human heart can be in itself evil. In excess, unrestrained, unchastened, put to evil ends, our best affections and emotions are injurious and sinful; but there is a legitimate and divinely appointed scope and sphere for all the passions that God hath implanted in the heart of man. And eminently so of anger. Sudden anger is simply a natural instinct. It springs up before reflection, and is independent of it. Anger is up in arms in a moment before a man has time to ask whether or no he does well to be angry. The hand is instinctively and immediately lifted to protect the body from a sudden blow, and anger is as quick in its movements, and is directed to the same end. But as we best study the doctrine of anger in the teaching of our Lord, so do we find in His conduct its safest and best illustration. He was made man; that is to say, He had in His heart all our passions and affections, and again in His words and deeds we see this passion of anger burning up against wrong, and burning up for our example. 'Be angry,' says the apostle, 'and sin not. Let not the sun go down upon your wrath' (Eph. 4:26).

2. But it is a very different thing when instinctive anger and righteous indignation become settled hatred and invincible malice. Now that this sin is both natural and universal among men, the apostle teaches us in the confession he makes about himself. 'We ourselves,' he says, 'sometimes lived in malice and envy, hateful, and hating one another'

(Tit. 3:3). And this fearful indictment is not any too dark, as every man must confess with shame and guilt who reads aright what goes on in his own heart. Hatred is an inveterate and bitter dislike at any one, a dislike that is always accompanied with a more or less explicit, a more or less acknowledged and fostered desire to hurt the hated person. 'Hates any man,' cries Shylock, 'the thing he would not kill!' Murder, in the teaching of our Divine Master, and in the teaching of the greatest master of the human heart that has ever risen among the sons of men, is not alone, is not at all in the act, it is in the wish and intention. And when we have the wish, though the murderous act is securely hindered, yet in God's sight we are red all over with our brother's blood. 'The heart is deceitful above all things, and desperately wicked: who can know it? I the LORD search the heart, I try the reins, even to give every man according to his ways, and according to the fruit of his doings' (Jer. 17:9, 10).

3. Our Lord counts scorn also under the same murderous category with anger and hatred. But here also a distinction must be taken. Scorn, like anger, may sometimes be most fitting, most just, and most praiseworthy. There is in all noble hearts a divinely implanted and noble scorn wherewith to blight and burn up all meanness and selfishness, all despicable and contemptible persons with all their mean and despicable deeds. The Scriptures, and especially the prophetical scriptures, abound in this divine and magnanimous scorn. But, on the other hand, there is the satanic scorn of a proud, hard, cruel heart. A scorn very far indeed from that exhibited by Isaiah and Jesus Christ. This scorn is full of contumelious and bitter words. It despises and humiliates men out of sheer ungodliness and pride of heart. And if it is too proud to show itself scornful, it is not less, but more hateful in the sight of God. It is far easier and far more natural for all of us to look down, and find fault, and despise, and scorn, than it is to look up, and find excellence, and then to honour, and reverence, and praise.

QUESTION 70

Which is the seventh commandment?

Answer: The seventh commandment is, Thou shalt not commit adultery.[1]

1. Exodus 20:14

QUESTION 71

What is required in the seventh commandment?

Answer: The seventh commandment requireth the preservation of our own and our neighbour's chastity, in heart, speech, and behaviour.[1]

QUESTION 72

What is forbidden in the seventh commandment?

Answer: The seventh commandment forbiddeth all unchaste thoughts, words, and actions.[2]

There are two principal and indeed essential relationships in every household and home of the human kind, in every house that is also a home. There is first the relationship of parent and child, and there is also the relationship of husband and wife. Other relationships may attach themselves to these, such as that of brother and sister, master and servant, magistrate and citizen, sovereign and subject. But the relationships that constitute and are essential to every complete human home are the parental and conjugal relationships. The fifth commandment protects the integrity and sanctity of the parental and filial relationships, and the seventh, in like manner, protects the yet more sacred relationship, the supreme and inviolable union between a man and a woman in marriage.

'The communion of the sexes is the complete giving up and appropriating of each party as the property of the other; hence where it is not the fruit of an already accomplished, morally-personal, spiritual unity, it is then an immoral throwing away of one's moral personality,

---

1. 1 Corinthians 7. Colossians 4:6: Let your speech be alway with grace, seasoned with salt, that ye may know how ye ought to answer every man. 1 Peter 3:2: While they behold your chaste conversation coupled with fear.

2. Matthew 15:19: For out of the heart proceed evil thoughts, murders, adulteries, fornications. Matthew 5:28: But I say unto you, That whosoever looketh on a woman to lust after her, hath committed adultery with her already in his heart. Ephesians 5:3, 4: But fornication, and all uncleanness, or covetousness, let it not be once named among you, as becometh saints; Neither filthiness, nor foolish talking, nor jesting, which are not convenient.

an irremediable ruining of the moral personality of the other. Lost innocence is irrecoverable, love that is not moral love is a defamation' (Wuttke).

'There is no ancient religion which is so sternly opposed to misconduct in these relations, and is yet so free from unnatural limitations of their due rights as Jahveism, the religion of Jehovah. What importance it attached to their purity, and how it sought to protect real marriage as the primary basis of all true life in common among human beings, is at once shown by its stringent laws on the subject. Chastity is an equal good with life itself.... The fair type of true matrimony in Isaac and his Rebecca does no more than represent with little alteration marriage as it really existed in the majority of families during the best days of the nation. Simple fidelity, pious love and attachment, and hence a certain amount of foresight in the choice of a wife from a worthy race, were not less in reality than they are in that type, the foundation on which a new family in Israel was created. All else that we know from history was in harmony with this; and here, too, we may clearly recognize the mighty working of an elevated religion' (Ewald).

Uses

1. 'There is a perfect harmony between obligation to God and all the sources of pleasure and happiness God has provided, so that there is no real collision between the statutes over us and the conditions within us. It is only false pleasures that are denied us, those that would brutalize the mind, or mar the health of the body, or somehow violate the happiness of fellow-beings around us' (Bushnell).

2. 'Amongst all sins, the sin of uncleanness lies heaviest upon the conscience; for no other sin is so directly contrary to holiness; no sin quenches the Holy Ghost like this' (Burkitt).

3. 'How should our festered sores be cured, but that God hath delivered a law as sharp as the two-edged sword, piercing the very closest and most unsearchable corners of the heart, which the law of nature can hardly, human laws by no means possibly, reach unto? Hereby we know even secret concupiscence to be sin, and are made fearful to offend though it be in a wandering cogitation' (Hooker).

4. In the Larger Catechism, intemperance in eating and drinking, immodest apparel, idleness, listening to filthy and corrupting conver-

sation, lascivious songs, books, pictures, and all other provocations to sin are denounced. There is a great lesson to all men who would keep themselves pure in heart and life in the old classical story in which Cupid complains to Jupiter that he could never fasten upon the Muses, because he could never find them idle. And as regards our literature, pure as on the whole it is, still there is room for Cowley's lament, that

> Still the old heathen gods in numbers dwell,
> The heavenliest thing on earth still keeps up hell.

Concerning immoral thoughts Dr. Johnson said: 'To attempt to think them down is madness.' And again: 'Be not solitary when you are idle, be not idle when you are solitary.'

5. 'True, all our lives long we shall be bound to refrain our soul, and keep it low: but what then? For the books we now forbear to read, we shall one day be endued with wisdom and knowledge. For the music we will not listen to, we shall join in the song of the redeemed. For the pictures from which we turn, we shall gaze unabashed on the Beatific Vision. For the companionship we shun, we shall be welcomed into angelic society, and the communion of triumphant saints. For the amusements we avoid, we shall keep the supreme jubilee. For all the pleasure we miss, we shall abide, and for evermore abide, in the rapture of heaven' (Christina Rossetti).

6. 'Think,' says Cornelius à Lapide, 'when lust goads thee, in thy hand and choice are heaven and hell, salvation and damnation, bliss or misery everlasting. Choose. Think. A moment which delighteth, eternity which tortureth; on the other hand, a moment which tortureth, eternity which delighteth.'

7. Q. What is the first inference hence? A. What cause those have to bless God that have been kept from sin: though the best ought to be humbled for their heart's pollutions. Q. What is the second inference from hence? A. Let it warn parents to do what in them lies to prevent the ruin of their children by this sin. (1) By filling their heads and hands with lawful business. (2) By keeping them from vain and tempting company. (3) By serious admonition and prayers for them. (4) By disposing them seasonably in a suitable marriage (Flavel).

QUESTION 73

Which is the eighth commandment?

Answer: The eighth commandment is, Thou shalt not steal.[1]

QUESTION 74

What is required in the eighth commandment?

Answer: The eighth commandment requireth the lawful procuring and furthering the wealth and outward estate of ourselves and others.[2]

QUESTION 75

What is forbidden in the eighth commandment?

Answer: The eighth commandment forbiddeth whatsoever doth or may unjustly hinder our own or our neighbour's wealth or outward estate.[3]

---

1. Exodus 20:15.

2. Genesis 30:30: For it was little which thou hadst before I came, and it is now increased unto a multitude; and the Lord hath blessed thee since my coming: and now, when shall I provide for mine own house also? 1 Timothy 5:8: But if any provide not for his own, and specially for those of his own house, he hath denied the faith, and is worse than an infidel. Leviticus 25:35: And if thy brother be waxen poor, and fallen in decay with thee, then thou shalt relieve him; yea, though he be a stranger, or a sojourner: that he may live with thee. Deuteronomy 22:1-5. Exodus 23:4, 5: If thou meet thine enemy's ox or his ass going astray, thou shalt surely bring it back to him again. If thou see the ass of him that hateth thee lying under his burden, and wouldest forbear to help him; thou shalt surely help with him. Genesis 47:14: And Joseph gathered up all the money that was found in the land of Egypt, and in the land of Canaan, for the corn which they bought: and Joseph brought the money into Pharaoh's house. Verse 20: And Joseph bought all the land of Egypt for Pharaoh; for the Egyptians sold every man his field, because the famine prevailed over them: so the land became Pharaoh's.

3. Proverbs 21:17: He that loveth pleasure shall be a poor man; he that loveth wine and oil shall not be rich. Proverbs 23:20, 21: Be not among wine-bibbers; among riotous eaters of flesh: For the drunkard and the glutton shall come to poverty; and drowsiness shall clothe a man with rags. Proverbs 28:19: He that tilleth his land shall have plenty of bread: but he that followeth after vain persons shall have poverty enough. Ephesians 4:28: Let him that stole steal no more: but rather let him labour, working with his hands the thing which is good, that he may have to give to him that needeth.

All questions connected with the sanctity and inviolability of human life are covered by the sixth commandment, and all dangers and duties that arise in connection with the preservation of personal purity are searched out by the breadth and inwardness of the seventh; and then in the ethical development and excellent order of the Decalogue comes the eighth commandment securing and consecrating each man's property and possessions. The divine law here sets a hedge about every man, and about his house, and about all that he hath on every side. Second only to the commandments protecting life and honour comes the commandment which covers all matters connected with the earning, saving, spending, inheriting and bequeathing of money and property. The eighth commandment enters a quite new field of human life, but this commandment is not less broad, or less deep, or less spiritual than those that have gone before it, as we shall soon see.

All a man's possessions, go back to the beginning of them, go down to the bottom of them, will always be found to represent so much self-denial, labour, industry. Obscure as may be the origin, history and growth of this or that particular estate, yet it must in its beginning have been due to some man's obedience to the Creator's law of labour and reward. 'Be fruitful, and multiply, and replenish the earth, and subdue it' (Gen. 1:28). This is the original charter of the right of property. But the world is old in our day, and the primitive conditions of personal labour and direct reward are somewhat overlaid and correspondingly obscured. And fundamental and rigorous as the law of labour is, there are nowadays many other ways in which men come into the possession of property. If each man among us held only what he had himself earned and made, the world's wealth would be incalculably less than it is, and what there would be of it would be very differently distributed. Even in the house of Israel, much nearer as human life then was to its original foundations, the ultimate ground of all personal property and family wealth was not so much that it was the fruit of personal exertion as that it was the direct donation of their covenant God. Jehovah, who had made earth and sea, could enrich or impoverish, could give or withhold as seemed to Him good. And this gracious, and, so to say, supernatural ground of Israel's possession penetrated all the economy of domestic, ecclesiastical and political finance. Still, there was room left in the theocratic and patriarchal system of the Hebrews for the free and full play of those laws of labour and reward on which the Creator had constructed human society on the earth; so much so, that we find principles and rules and illustrations in the Old Testament that are wisely applicable to all varieties of human life in all its modern developments and relationships.

Uses

1. 'These things are linked and as it were chained one to another; we labour to eat, and we eat to live, and we live to do good, and the good which we do is as seed sown with reference unto a future harvest' (Hooker).

2. Industry is one of the prime virtues of human life upon the earth: work is both a necessity and a virtue in man. But hard work is seldom divorced from its due and proper fruits: labour is lightened and sweetened by the hope of its proper wages. And well-directed and successful labour enriches the labourer in more and better ways than in the mere accumulation of his wages, or in the collection and possession of riches. For the possession of this world's good things enlarges and ennobles the possessor's whole life. Human existence on the earth becomes a better and more desirable thing when hard work has once had its proper reward, and a man has been put in possession of the garnered fruits of his past diligence and industry. Enlarging possessions expand and enrich a man's earthly existence; according to their amount they increase his power for good; they multiply his opportunities, and they help to make his earthly existence sheltered, and refined, and full of manifold means of good-doing and delight.

3. Akin to the habit of industry is the sister habit of frugality and forethought. And this virtuous habit cannot be commenced too soon. Even children should be exercised in little ways of frugality and self-denial. They should be taught to spare something of playthings and sweetmeats, which, when sufficiently accumulated, would purchase a piece of dress for themselves, or a birthday present for father or mother, sister or brother. The immediate object of such youthful frugality is of less importance than the formation of the virtuous and fruitful habit. Then again, every young man on the expiry of his appenticeship should open an account with a savings bank. If his wages are as yet small, then perforce his savings will be small also: but at their smallest they will grow, and he will grow alongside of them in carefulness, temperance, frugality and forethought. And then, when the time comes that he takes up a house of his own, he will not need to lie down on a borrowed bed, or eat his meals out of a dish he is in debt for. All men should honourably save something against a rainy day. If these and suchlike 'minor moralities' are despised, then

the chances are that other people will have to pay for it. There are other ways of robbing our neighbours besides garrotting them in the dark: and the worst and most barefaced thieves a man ever meets with are usually those of his own reckless and improvident household. This commandment also is exceeding broad.

4. 'Of great riches,' says Lord Bacon, 'there is no real use, except it be in the distribution. There is a custody of them; but beyond distribution there is no solid use of them to their owner. Seek not therefore,' adds the essayist, 'proud riches, but such as thou mayest get justly, use soberly, distribute cheerfully,and leave contentedly.'

And accordingly, in all systems of morals – Pagan, Hebrew and Christian – liberality is esteemed among the noblest of the virtues. 'Property,' says Aristotle, in the fourth book of his *Ethics*, 'is evidently a thing to be used. The very essence of property is its use, and liberality is that quality or virtue which enables us to make the best use of property.... However, as all virtues have a noble end in view, mere giving freely is not enough to constitute liberality. Special regard must be had to three conditions: a noble motive, due consideration of the occasion and amount of the gift, and cheerfulness on the part of the giver. The absence of any of these conditions destroys the liberality of the gift.'

'Munificence,' the same master in morals tells us, 'differs from liberality in the largeness of the sums in which it deals. Its general character is magnitude. There is a sort of scientific skill implied in the munificence. The occasion must be worthy of the expenditure, and the expenditure worthy of the occasion. There must also be a desire after what is noble. There is a grandeur of manner which imparts a special lustre to the acts of a munificent man. We pass now,' he continues, 'to the occasions which are fitting for the display of munificence. And we notice, first, the service of religion, and next the great and rare occasions in private life, such as a wedding, works of public and general interest, entertaining strangers, making and returning presents; or, again, the furnishing and ornaments of one's house; and, generally, permanent rather than perishable objects. There is a greatness in any work that is perfect of its kind, even in toy presents to children. Even in the smallest matters the munificent man will act munificently.' But while munificence is possible to only a very few men, liberality, on the other hand, is open to all. For liberality is in the mind and in the manner more than in the amount. 'If there be first a willing mind, it is accepted according to that a man hath, and not according to that he hath not.'

QUESTION 76

Which is the ninth commandment?

Answer: The ninth commandment is, Thou shalt not bear false witness against thy neighbour.[1]

QUESTION 77

What is required in the ninth commandment?

Answer: The ninth commandment requireth the maintaining and promoting of truth between man and man,[2] *and of our own and our neighbour's good name,*[3] *especially in witness-bearing.*[4]

QUESTION 78

What is forbidden in the ninth commandment?

Answer: The ninth commandment forbiddeth whatsoever is prejudicial to truth, or injurious to our own or our neighbour's good name.[5]

---

1. Exodus 20:16.

2. Zechariah 8:16: These are the things that ye shall do, Speak ye every man the truth to his neighbour; execute the judgment of truth and peace in your gates.

3. 3 John 12: Demetrius hath good report of all men, and of the truth itself: yea, and we also bear record; and ye know that our record is true.

4. Proverbs 14:5: A faithful witness will not lie: but a false witness will utter lies. Verse. 25: A true witness delivereth souls: but a deceitful witness speaketh lies.

5. 1 Samuel 17:28: And Eliab his eldest brother heard when he spake unto the men: and Eliab's anger was kindled against David, and he said, Why camest thou down hither? and with whom hast thou left those few sheep in the wilderness? I know thy pride, and the naughtiness of thine heart; for thou art come down that thou mightest see the battle. Leviticus 19:16: Thou shalt not go up and down as a talebearer among thy people; neither shalt thou stand against the blood of thy neighbour: I am the Lord. Psalm 15:3: He that backbiteth not with his tongue, nor doeth evil to his neighbour, nor taketh up a reproach against his neighbour.

The Larger Catechism, in discussing this commandment, calls special attention to unseasonable speech or loquacity, tale-bearing, backbiting, detraction, aggravating small faults, discovering infirmities, impairing our neighbour's credit, and rejoicing in their disgrace and infamy. The whole analysis is a terrible indictment laid against the tongue of sinful man.

A loquacious man is one who speaks much, and the preacher says that 'in the multitude of words there wanteth not sin'. True, a multitude of words is not necessarily of itself a sin. A multitude of words is more a matter of temperament and constitution than of morals or religion. But then, mankind being what they are, a talkative tongue becomes to many a temptation and a snare. Were all men's minds full of wisdom and knowledge, then a full and free utterance would cause no injury; but a talkative tongue, rooted in a selfish, corrupt, unloving heart, cannot but utter much folly and sin. Butler points out that loquacity springs from 'that original disease of the mind, an eager desire to engage attention'. In his sermon *On the Government of the Tongue*, this great ethical writer points out that one of the main mischiefs of a loquacious habit of speech is this, that the necessity to be always talking tends to produce tale-bearing.

The strong idiomatic word 'backbiting' is full of expressiveness

This word brings out strongly the meanness, the cowardice, and the treachery of the conduct it condemns. Pascal says that if everybody knew what one says about another behind his back, there would not be four friends in the whole world. Detraction, 'envy's abhorred child,' is a very common kind of backbiting. The etymology here also is very expressive and instructive. Detraction is literally to *draw away something from some one*, and in this case it is to draw some praise, or honour, or esteem from the good name of an absent man. Butler warns us that the 'giving of characters' makes up too much of our conversation. And no doubt it is so, since depreciation of our neighbour's merits is so pleasant to us. There are many men of whom it may be said without much exaggeration, 'At every word a reputation dies.'

'Party feeling, whether called religious zeal, or national antagonism, or political creed, becomes simple malice, and is simply devilish when it leads us not only to condemn opponents, but to wish that they may be really as unworthy as history or rumour makes them, to court and hug and blaze abroad every tittle of evidence which tells against them, and to turn a dull ear to everything which tells in their favour. Charity rejoiceth not in iniquity, but rejoiceth in the truth' (Christina Rossetti).

This evil spirit poisons much of our spoken and printed criticism and polemic. Dr. William Cunningham was one of the ablest theological and polemical writers that our Church and country has ever seen, and he did much to expound and establish evangelical truth, and to chastise its opponents, but he never wrote a nobler passage than that in which he introduced a second castigation of Sir William Hamilton, who had died immediately after the publication of a most powerful and unanswerable paper against him. 'The knowledge,' Dr. Cunningham wrote, 'if we had possessed it, that he was to die so soon, would assuredly have modified somewhat the tone in which the discussion was conducted, would have shut out something of its lightness and severity, and imparted to it more of solemnity and tenderness; and the knowledge which we did possess, that he, as well as ourselves, was liable every day to be called out of this world, and summoned into God's presence, ought to have produced this result.'

Uses

1. 'Man is nothing but insincerity, falsehood and hypocrisy, both in regard to himself and in regard to others. He does not wish that he should be told the truth; he shuns saying it to others: and all these moods, so inconsistent with justice and reason, have their roots in his heart' (Pascal).

2. 'What is almost all conversation almost everywhere, but a breach of the law of love? Word follows word, chasing one another, sweeping over one another, like wave on wave; and what remains in the memory? How few call themselves really, evening by evening, to any account! It were not too much to say of most men, that they are "curious to know the lives of others, slothful to amend their own" ' (Pusey).

3. Eschew as much as possible the 'giving of characters.'

4. Garrulous Plutarch winds up his essay on Garrulity with these words: 'Before we speak, and at the very moment when the words are ready to break out of our mouths, we should thus address ourselves, What is this which I would say? What is this which presses so hard to be uttered? For what reason would this tongue of mine so fain be talking?

What mischief shall I incur by holding my peace? We ought always to bear in remembrance, and have at our tongue's end, that saying of the philosopher that he had often repented him of talking, but never once of keeping silence.'

5. Augustine tells us in his *Confessions* how much his mother abhorred everything like slander, and the fruit of her counsels and example on her great son was, that long after her death, he caused these lines to be carved on the table at which his guests sat: 'He that is wont to slander absent men, may never at this table sit again.'

6. 'Judge not without knowledge, charity, or necessity; yet a dog is to be accounted a dog, and a swine a swine' (Bengel).

QUESTION 79

Which is the tenth commandment?

Answer: The tenth commandment is, Thou shalt not covet thy neighbour's house, thou shalt not covet thy neighbour's wife, nor his man-servant, nor his maid-servant, nor his ox, nor his ass, nor any thing that is thy neighbour's.[1]

QUESTION 80

What is required in the tenth commandment?

Answer: The tenth commandment requireth full contentment with our own condition,[2] *with a right and charitable frame of spirit toward our neighbour, and all that is his.*[3]

---

1. Exodus 20:17

2. Hebrews 13:5: Let your conversation be without covetousness; and be content with such things as ye have: for he hath said, I will never leave thee, nor forsake thee. 1 Timothy 6:6: But godliness with contentment is great gain.

3. Job 31:29: If I rejoiced at the destruction of him that hated me, or lifted up myself when evil found him. Romans 12:15: Rejoice with them that do rejoice, and weep with them that weep. 1 Timothy 1:5: Now the end of the commandment is charity out of a pure heart, and of a good conscience, and of faith unfeigned. 1 Corinthians 13:4-7.

QUESTION 81

What is forbidden in the tenth commandment?

Answer: The tenth commandment forbiddeth all discontentment with our own estate,[1] *envying or grieving at the good of our neighbour,*[2] *and all inordinate motions and affections to any thing that is his.*[3]

A peculiar interest attaches to the tenth commandment, from the fact that it was the chief instrument employed by the Holy Ghost in the awakening and conversion of the Apostle Paul. In that priceless fragment of his religious autobiography contained in the seventh chapter of his Epistle to the Romans, the apostle tells us that, notwithstanding all his religious upbringing, and notwithstanding all his sacred studies in Gamaliel's school, he never discovered that he himself was a sinner, he did not so much as know what sin was, till the tenth commandment came home to him, saying, 'Thou shalt not covet.' 'I was alive,' so his famous confession runs, 'I was alive without the law once, but when the tenth commandment came home to me, sin revived, and I died. And ever since then, and until now, I have known that the law is spiritual, but I am carnal, sold under sin. O Wretched man that I am!' Saul of Tarsus, the scrupulous, studious, ambitious young Pharisee, could make answer to all the other commandments in the Decalogue, 'All these have I kept from my youth

1. 1 Kings 21:4: And Ahab came into his house heavy and displeased because of the word which Naboth the Jezreelite had spoken to him; for he had said, I will not give thee the inheritance of my fathers: and he laid him down upon his bed, and turned away his face, and would eat no bread. Esther 5:13: Yet all this availeth me nothing, so long as I see Mordecai the Jew sitting at the king's gate. 1 Corinthians 10:10: Neither murmur ye, as some of them also murmured, and were destroyed of the destroyer.

2. Galatians 5:26: Let us not be desirous of vainglory, provoking one another, envying one another. James 3:14: But if ye have bitter envying and strife in your hearts, glory not, and lie not against the truth. Verse 16: For where envying and strife is, there is confusion, and every evil work.

3. Romans 7:7, 8: I had not known lust, except the law had said, Thou shalt not covet. But sin, taking occasion by the commandment, wrought in me all manner of concupiscence. For without the law sin was dead. Romans 13:9 For this ...Thou shalt not covet; and if there be any other commandment, it is briefly comprehended in this saying, namely, Thou shalt love thy neighbour as thyself. Deuteronomy 5:21: Neither shalt thou desire thy neighbour's wife, neither shalt thou covet thy neighbour's house, his field, or his man-servant, or his maid-servant, his ox, or his ass, or any thing that is thy neighbour's.

up' (Matt. 19:20; Luke 18:21). But the tenth commandment came to him like a two-edged sword, discerning the thoughts and intents of his heart. Humanly speaking, we owe the Apostle Paul, with all his writings, to the awakening and searching power of the tenth commandment.

'The universal prohibition of theft seemed weighty enough to occupy the eighth place in the ten fundamental commandments of Jehovahism; and as the true religion felt that there was more to be required than the avoidance of open transgression, it also prohibited in the tenth and last fundamental law every sinful desire for whatever was the property of another, and thus condemned the first step to countless open or secret offences which no law can enumerate and punish' (Ewald).

requireth full contentment with our own condition

Like so many other moral and spiritual expressions, this term contentment has a physical basis, a material origin and root. We speak of one thing being contained in another when it is held within it, and does not exceed or overflow its bounds. The contents of a vessel, for instance, are just what the vessel is able to hold. And our scriptural and Catechism term contentment has just the same meaning. A contented mind is a mind that does not overflow, push itself out of, and wander beyond the conditions and limits within which it is providentially placed. A contented mind has all it wants; or if it has some wants still unsupplied, it surrenders its desires without rebellion or complaint, and wishes for nothing it has not been permitted to possess. And thus it comes about that if the contented mind has not full and perfect satisfaction in its outward possessions, it has what is far better, it has inward detachment, acquiescence and peace.

> 'Now as they were going along and talking, the espied a Boy feeding his Father's sheep. The Boy was in very mean cloathes, but of a very fresh and well-favoured countenance, and as he sat by himself he sung. Hark, said Mr. Greatheart, to what the Shepherd's Boy saith. So they hearkened, and he said:-
>
> He that is down needs fear no fall;
> He that is low, no pride:
> He that is humble, ever shall
> Have God to be his Guide.

I am content with what I have,
Little be it or much:
And, Lord, contentment still I crave,
Because Thou savest such.

Fulness to such a burden is
That go on pilgrimage:
Here little, and hereafter bliss,
Is best from age to age.

Then said their Guide, Do you hear him? I will dare to say, that this Boy lives a merrier life, and wears more of that herb called Hearts-ease in his bosom, than he that is clad in silk and velvet.'

a right and charitable frame of spirit
'When those two quarrelling pronouns, meum and tuum (mine and thine), have no more use, as in heaven, then we shall fully rejoice in one another's gifts and graces, and what others enjoy will be our comfort' (Manton).

forbiddeth envying or grieving at the good of our neighbour
The Bible gives to envy its true etymology when it calls it 'an evil eye.' For this 'worse of the passions' is kindled through the eye, the eye of the body or the eye of the mind. The envious eye sees the welfare of another with an evil grudge. Thomas Adams, in his *Soul's Sickness*, tells us of a certain philosopher who, on seeing an envious man dejected, asked him whether some evil had happened to himself, or some good to his neighbour.

all inordinate motions and affections
Inordinate, out of order, dis-orderly, excessive. The word occurs twice in the Scriptures, Ezekiel 23:11; Colossians 3:5. Motions also occurs in Romans 7:5.

Uses
1. All moralists, Pagan and Christian, tell us that contentment with his own estate is not natural to any human being. Indifference, asceticism, stoicism, despondency, despair: these states of mind are all quite natural to man, but none of all these approach to true contentment. True contentment must rest on a religious foundation. And it is only when from

a religious resignation a devout and patient man rises to true Christian contentment, only when he sees that all his times are in the hand of Jesus Christ, only then does contentment come to its maturity and fruitfulness. 'I have learned,' says the apostle, 'in whatsoever state I am, therewith to be content.... I can do all things through Christ which strengtheneth me' (Phil. 4:11,13).

2. Rich men, talented men, successful men should alleviate as much as possible the temptations they cause to their less able and less fortunate fellows. And this they can largely do by studying humbleness of mind, by a steady and habitual consideration of the circumstances and feelings of others, and by making as much as may be made of the talents and performances of their neighbours.

3. This commandment is of the greatest use as a test and gauge of an awakened heart and a spiritual mind. When an envious feeling or an inordinate desire springs up suddenly and involuntarily in the soul, and when it is struggled against till it is cast out, and when after being cast out it still leaves a stain and a wound behind it, and drives us to the blood and righteousness of Christ, what could be a surer mark of the reality and depth of the work of grace in the heart? Nothing.

QUESTION 82

Is any man able perfectly to keep the commandments of God?

Answer: No mere man since the fall is able in this life perfectly to keep the commandments of God,[1] *but doth daily break them in thought, word, and deed.*[2]

---

1. Ecclesiastes 7:20: For there is not a just man upon earth, that doeth good, and sinneth not. 1 John 1:8: If we say that we have no sin, we deceive ourselves, and the truth is not in us. Verse 10: If we say that we have not sinned, we make him a liar, and his word is not in us. Galatians 5:17: For the flesh lusteth against the Spirit, and the Spirit against the flesh: and these are contrary the one to the other: so that ye cannot do the things that ye would.

2. Genesis 6:5: And God saw that the wickedness of man was great in the earth, and that every imagination of the thoughts of his heart was only evil continually. Genesis 8:21: The imagination of man's heart is evil from his youth. Romans 3:9: What then? are we better than they? No, in no wise: for we have before proved both Jews and Gentiles, that they are all under sin. And so on to verse 21. James 3:2: For in many things we offend all. If any man offend not in word, the same is a perfect man, and able also to bridle the whole body. And so on to verse 13.

No mere man

'That admirable discrimination, united with conciseness and perspicuity, which characterizes the whole of our Shorter Catechism, is strikingly visible in the Answer before us' (Ashbel Green). It would not have been scriptural to have said no man since the fall, because our Lord was a man. But then He was not a mere man, for He was God and man. This limiting term corresponds to the third clause in Answer 16, 'all mankind descending from Adam by ordinary generation.' (See also Answers 21, 22.)

since the fall

It was necessary also that this clause should stand here, because man and mere man, Adam and Eve namely, were able perfectly to keep the commandments of God, and for a season they did actually keep them. (See Answer 10.) But no mere man since they fell has even approximately kept the commandments of God. (See Answers 16, 17, 18.)

is able in this life

Here again we see the discrimination, conciseness and perspicuity celebrated above. For a multitude that no man can number of mere men will in the life to come be able to keep in thought and word and deed all the commandments of God. (See Answer 38.) But the doctrine of the Catechism is a sad truth, and it is put still more explicitly in the Larger Catechism Answer: 'No man is able, either of himself, or by any grace received in this life, perfectly to keep the commandments.'

perfectly to keep the commandments of God

This well-chosen phrase recognizes the cheering and inspiring truth that God's people are enabled and endeavour to keep His commandments increasingly, while on the other hand it teaches the humiliating fact that no complete or adequate success is ever in this world attained by any man with his best endeavour. The language of Richard Hooker is found in the mouth of every child of God: 'The little fruit which we have in holiness, it is, God knoweth, corrupt and unsound; we put no confidence at all in it; we challenge nothing in the world for it; we dare not call God to reckoning, as if we had Him in our debt-books; our continual suit to Him is, and must be, to bear with our infirmities, and pardon our offences.'

but doth daily break them
There are three transgressions, say the Talmudists, from which a man can no day ever in this life be free: the thoughts of sin, wanderings in prayer, and an evil tongue.

in thought, word, and deed
See Answer 18. 'All the sins which men commit are reducible to three heads, as being either in thought, in word, or in deed' (Waterland).

'If our hands did never offer violence to our brethren, a bloody thought doth prove us murderers before God: if we had never opened our mouths to utter any scandalous, offensive, or hurtful word, the cry of our secret cogitations is heard in His ears. If we did not commit the evils which we do daily and hourly, either in deeds, words, or thoughts, yet in the good things which we do, how many defects are there intermingled! ...It may seem somewhat extreme which I will speak; therefore let every man judge of it, even as his own heart shall tell him, and no otherwise; I will but only make a demand: If God should yield to us, not as unto Abraham; if fifty, forty, thirty, twenty, yea, if ten good persons could be found in a city, for their sakes that city should not be destroyed; but if God should make us an offer thus large: Search all the generations of man sithever the fall of your father Adam, find one man that hath done any one action, which hath past from him pure, without any stain or blemish at all; and for that man's one only action, neither man nor angel shall feel the torments that are prepared for both; do you think that this ransom, to deliver men and angels, would be found among the sons of men?' (Hooker).

Uses

1. 'I will never forget Thy precepts, for with them Thou hast quickened me.... Through Thy precepts I get understanding; therefore I hate every false way' (Ps. 119:93, 104).

2. 'A true Christian hath ten times more to do with his heart and its corruptions than a hypocrite has. The sins of his heart and life appear to him in their awful blackness; they look dreadful; and it often appears to him a very mysterious thing that any grace can be consistent with such corruption, or should live at all in such a heart' (Edwards).

3. 'The very smallest of our Lord's commandments are to a spiritual mind solemn, arduous, and inexhaustible.... How manifold are the ways of

the Spirit, how various the grace which He imparts; what depth and width is therein that moral truth and virtue for which we are created!' (Newman).

QUESTION 83

Are all transgressions of the law equally heinous?

Answer: Some sins in themselves, and by reason of several aggravations, are more heinous in the sight of God than others.[1]

Some sins in themselves

'The Stoic philosophers, and some few of the less considerate Christians, have pretended that all sins are equal. Their reasons for it are not worth the mentioning; for the conceit is so groundless, and so repugnant to the common sense of mankind, that barely to speak of it is to expose it, and it carries its own confutation with it. For a man must be very weak to imagine that theft, suppose, is as great a sin as murder; or telling a lie as wicked a thing as robbing a house, or plundering a church, or firing a town. Everybody is sensible of a difference between high crimes and trivial trespasses; between sins of the first magnitude and slight offences; our Lord therefore compares some to gnats, while He compares others to camels; some to motes in the eye, others to beams' (Waterland).

and by reason of several aggravations

To aggravate is to add to what is too heavy already. Thus in Bacon: 'The offence was aggravated by the motive.' The Larger Catechism has a most instructive discussion of this subject under these heads: Sins receive their aggravations: (1) From the persons offending. (2) From the parties offended. (3) From the nature and quality of the offence. (4) From circumstances of time and place. Earnest students will master the remarkable analysis and exposition in Answer 151.

---

1. Ezekiel 8:6-15. 1 John 5:16: If any man see his brother sin a sin which is not unto death, he shall ask, and he shall give him life for them that sin not unto death. There is a sin unto death: I do not say that he shall pray for it. Psalm 78:17: And they sinned yet more against him, by provoking the Most High in the wilderness. Verse 32: For all this they sinned still, and believed not for his wondrous works. Verse 56: Yet they tempted and provoked the most high God, and kept not his testimonies.

more heinous
Old Saxon for hateful, odious, atrocious. The word occurs once and once only in Scripture (Job 31:11). 'Actions gross and great for bulk are often less sinful in the eyes of God than smaller actions, because less filled with the evil disposition of the heart. And thus the philosophers themselves acknowledged that an evil action done, *ex prava dispositione*, an act proceeding from a rooted habitual disposition, was worse, and more to be punished than another, though outwardly as bad, if but done out of some sudden passion, as they call it. Witness that sentence of the Athenian judges, who condemned a boy to death but for tearing out in a cruel manner the eyes of a few crows and partridges, as being (though for the act but small) the evidence and indicium of habitual cruel nature' (Goodwin).

Uses

1. 'I would recommend to you, my young friends, as a very profitable employment for an hour on the Lord's day, to go over deliberately this enumeration of the aggravations of sin, contained in your Larger Catechism; to consider each article attentively; to connect it with an intelligent reading of the Scripture proof, to which you will find a reference, and with a serious meditation on the whole' (Ashbel Green).

2. '*Q.* Are heinous and crying sins capable of forgiveness? *A.* Yes; great and heinous sins are capable of forgiveness upon true repentance (Isa. 1:18). *Q.* What is the first inference hence? *A.* Though some sins are more heinous than others, yet no sinner should absolutely despair of mercy; for the vilest have been pardoned (1 Cor. 6:2). *Q.* What is the next inference? *A.* That great sinners when pardoned and received to mercy, should excel all others in love to Christ (Luke 7:42, 43)' (Flavel).

QUESTION 84

What doth every sin deserve?

Answer: Every sin deserveth God's wrath and curse, both in this life, and that which is to come.[1]

---

1. Ephesians 5:6: Because of these things cometh the wrath of God upon the children of disobedience. Galatians 3:10: For as many as are of the works of the law are under the curse: for it is written, Cursed is every one that continueth not in all things which are written in the book

Every sin deserveth

This answer only casts into a form of words fitting its place in the development of catechetical doctrine what is the universal teaching of Scripture on the nature and heinousness of sin. James, the least doctrinal, so to say, and the most entirely ethical of all the apostles, more than sustains the teaching of the text in that famous passage in which he sets forth the solidarity and inviolability of the divine law: 'For whosoever shall keep the whole law, and yet offend in one point, he is guilty of all' (Jas. 2:10). 'What he means is, that God will not be honoured with exceptions, nor will He allow us to cut off from His law what is less pleasing to us' (Calvin).

'For every one vice kills the soul, though every virtue does not make alive. A man is spotted although he have but one stain: he is not clean unless he be all clean. A cup is broken if only the top is broken, but it is not entire unless every part of it is inviolate' (Taylor).

'The favourite notion of many people, that the province of morals recognizes a greater or a smaller number of adiaphora [unimportant and indiffernt matters], is here emphatically denied' (Lange).

'If indeed there be deeper and deeper dyes of guilt: which, though it be a true idea to a creature already in a fallen state, is not so, as I take it, to a creature who hath not fallen, to whom any insurrection of the will, or disobedience of the act, doth constitute the very essence and substance of sin, which may afterwards be varied by particular accidents, but cannot, as I take it, be changed in its essence' (Irving).

'It is well to observe how apparently slight a fault it was for which Moses suffered: for this shows us the infinite difference between the best of a sinful race and Him who was sinless, the least taint of human corruption having in it an unspeakable evil' (Newman)This great writer also preaches the 'inconceivable evil of sensuality'.

God's wrath

See Answer 19. Such words and thoughts as these are to be purged as far as may be of all association with human passion and corruption. We cannot, in the nature of things, escape the limitation and taint of human ideas and attributes when we think or speak of God; but the safest way

---

of the law to do them. Lamentations 3:39: Wherefore doth a living man complain, a man for the punishment of his sins? Matthew 25:41: Then shall he say also unto them on the left hand, Depart from me, ye cursed, into everlasting fire, prepared for the devil and his angels.

is to keep close to scriptural usage and example, and above all to study the revelation of God in His love and in His hatred, in His cursing and in His blessing, as He is revealed to us in the character, and works, and words of His Incarnate Son Jesus Christ.

'The Baptist he began that style in the New Testament – the wrath to come – by way of distinction from all that is executed in this life. And the whole New Testament afterwards much useth this phrase.... I shall but further super-add that noticed saying of Luther, which out of a deep experience of the wrath of God in his soul at his first humiliation and conversion he had learned: The wrath of God is hell, the hell of devils and all damned spirits' (Goodwin).

'By anger, wrath, zeal, fury, the effects of anger are denoted. Anger and wrath are not properly ascribed to God, but metaphorically, denoting partly His vindicatory justice, whence all punishments flow; partly the effects of it in the punishments themselves' (Owen).

'Many schools of religion and ethics are to be found amongst us, and they all profess to magnify, in one shape or other, what they consider the principle of love; but what they lack is a firm maintenance of that characteristic of the Divine Nature, which, in accommodation to our infirmity, is named by St. John and his brethren the wrath of God.... Hence they consider all punishment to be remedial, a means to an end; deny that the woe threatened against sinners is of eternal duration, and explain away the doctrine of the Atonement' (Newman).

'From the notion of wrath, when it is applied to God, we must, of course, remove all that pollutes human wrath, personal resentment and revenge. In God, who is the living good, wrath appears as the holy disapprobation of evil, and the firm resolve to destroy it. But it is false to say, as is often said, that this divine emotion applies only to the evil and not to the evil-doer. The voluntary and determined evil-doer comes under God's wrath and all its consequences' (Godet).

and curse

See Answer 19. What has been said above may all be applied here also. Wrath is not rage: God's curse is not violent language or cruel treatment: the fire that is not quenched is not kindled with wood or coals; as Goodwin says, 'It is a far subtiler fire than culinary or kitchen fire.'

'*Q.* Wherein doth the curse of God consist? *A.* In divers things: first, in the guilt of death, temporal and eternal; secondly, the loss of the grace and favour of God; thirdly, guilt and horror of conscience, despair and anguish here; with, fourthly, eternal damnation hereafter' (Owen's Catechism).

Commenting on the fact that the last word of the Old Testament is 'a curse', Pusey says: 'The Jews, who would be wiser and tenderer than the prophet, repeat the previous verse, because Malachi closes so awfully. The Maker of the heart of man knew better the hearts which He had made, and taught their authors to end the books of Isaiah and Ecclesiastes and Malachi with words of awe, from which man's heart so struggles to escape. To turn to God here, or everlasting destruction from His presence hereafter, is the only choice open to thee.' Compare Bengel's note on the ending of the Sermon on the Mount: 'We see, from the present example, that it is not necessary for all sermons to end in a consolatory strain.'

in this life and that which is to come

'And cannot be expiated but by the blood of Christ' (Larger Catechism).

'The least sin which we commit in deed, or word, or thought, is death, without repentance' (Hooker).

'A consideration of the future sanctions of religion is our only security of persevering in our duty in cases of great temptation' (Butler).

'Wrath and threatening are invariably mingled with the love of God; and in the utmost solitudes of nature, the existence of hell seems to me as legibly declared by a thousand spiritual utterances as that of heaven.... Gerizim and Ebal, birth and death, light and darkness, heaven and hell, divide the existence of man, and his futurity' (Ruskin).

Uses

1. 'Justice reigns in hell, and grace in heaven. Men's merit makes hell, and Christ's merit makes heaven (Rom. 6:23)' (Traill).

2. 'My Lord Cardinal,' said Anne of Austria to Richelieu, 'God does not pay at the end of every week, but at last He pays.'

3. 'No sin which is persisted in is small, no sin great for which forgiveness is sought of God' (Arab proverb).

4. *Q.* What is the fourth instruction here? *A.* It teacheth us what an invaluable mercy the full, free, and final remission of sin is (Ps. 32:1, 2) (Flavel).

QUESTION 85

What doth God require of us, that we may escape his wrath and curse due to us for sin?

Answer: To escape the wrath and curse of God due to us for sin, God requireth of us faith in Jesus Christ, repentance unto life,[1] *with the diligent use of all the outward means whereby Christ communicateth to us the benefits of redemption.*[2]

A new section of the Catechism commences with the Question. The last Answer has stopped every mouth, and made all the world guilty before God, much as the 19th Answer had shut up the human race to 'God's wrath and curse'. And just as Answer 20 immediately began to introduce the covenant of grace, and made mention of a Redeemer, so here Answer 85 sets before the individual sinner what God now requires of him that he may escape the wrath and curse due to him for sin. And it is here pointed out that God requires of us three things: first, faith in Jesus Christ; second, repentance unto life; and third, the diligent use of all the outward means whereby Christ communicateth to us the benefits of redemption. Faith and repentance are then described in Answers 86, 87, and in 88 the 'outward means' are resolved into the word, sacraments, and prayer, which again are successively treated of, after which the Catechism closes.

God requireth of us faith in Jesus Christ, etc.

'And, indeed, that I may speak more plainly, what is faith, and love, and repentance, and all these to salvation? They are salvation itself, they are parts of it. When God requires of you that you should believe, and repent, and mortify sin, and walk holily, doth He require these as conditions? No, He requires them as parts of salvation itself, as essentials to salvation. When God bids us believe, what is it? It is to bid us be saved, it is to bid us have eternal life, and the comforts of eternal life in our hearts' (Goodwin).

---

1. Acts 20:21: Testifying both to the Jews, and also to the Greeks, repentance toward God, and faith toward our Lord Jesus Christ.

2. Proverbs 2:1-5, 8:33-36. Isaiah 55:3: Incline your ear, and come unto me: hear, and your soul shall live; and I will make an everlasting covenant with you, even the sure mercies of David.

QUESTION 86

What is faith in Jesus Christ?

Answer: Faith in Jesus Christ is a saving grace,[1] *whereby we receive and rest upon him alone for salvation, as he is offered to us in the gospel.*[2]

Faith in Jesus Christ

Faith in its first and most elementary sense is simply the reliance that is placed by one man on the truthfulness and integrity of another. Nor is this foundation and initial sense of the work unknown in the Holy Scriptures. And thus it is that Luther, who would be the last man to secularize or impoverish any Pauline or Scriptural word, says: 'The apostle sometimes useth faith of the fidelity and humanity of one man towards another. Faith sometimes in the Scriptures means the credit one man giveth to another in things pertaining to this present life; for what manner of life should we live in this world, if one man should not credit another?'

But it is with the highest, most sacred, and most fruitful sense of the word we have here to do. And a better definition of faith, in its scriptural, Pauline and evangelical sense, is nowhere to be found than in the fourteenth chapter of the Westminster Confession of Faith. In the second section of that chapter we read: 'By saving faith a Christian believeth to be true whatsoever is revealed in the word of God; for the authority of God Himself speaking therein; and it acteth differently upon that which each particular passage thereof containeth: yielding obedience to the commands; trembling at the threatenings; and embracing the promises of God for this life and that which is to come. But the principal acts of saving faith are accepting, receiving, and resting upon Christ alone for justification, sanctification, and eternal life, by virtue of the covenant of grace.' Now it is with one of the principal acts of saving faith, if not with its very principal act, that we have here to do.

---

1. Hebrews 10:39: But we are ...of them that believe to the saving of the soul.

2. John 1:12: But as many as received him, to them gave he power to become the sons of God, even to them that believe on his name. Isaiah 26:3, 4: Thou wilt keep him in perfect peace, whose mind is stayed on thee; because he trusteth in thee. Trust ye in the Lord for ever: for in the Lord JEHOVAH is everlasting strength. Philippians 3:9: And be found in him, not having mine own righteousness, which is of the law, but that which is through the faith of Christ, the righteousness which is of God by faith. Galatians 2:16: Knowing that a man is not justified by the works of the law, but by the faith of Jesus Christ, even we have believed in Jesus Christ, that we might be justified by the faith of Christ.

'The import of the word faith is nothing recondite; otherwise it would be a term altogether unsuitable for being used in an exhibition of the duty of universal man, uncultured as well as cultured. Faith is such a persuasion or conviction of the mind in reference to things unseen, and, so far as direct intuition is concerned, unknown, as supplies the place of vision. Its moral power, in its relation to the gospel of Jesus Christ, is resolvable into the peculiarity of its object, and not into any peculiarity in the act.... It is apparently in virtue of this mighty moral power of faith in Jesus that it has been divinely invested with what is called its justifying function' (Morison).

'So that they who know what is meant by faith in a promise, know what is meant by faith in the gospel; they who know what is meant by faith in a remedy, know what is meant by faith in the blood of the Redeemer; they who know what is meant by faith in a physician, faith in an advocate, faith in a friend, know, too, what the Scriptures mean to express when they speak of faith in the Lord Jesus Christ' (O'Brien).

a saving grace

Grace as it is used and described in Answers 33, 34, 35, is a divine disposition toward us; grace in this and the following Answer is a divine gift in us, and especially a disposition or inclination wrought in the soul by the Holy Ghost. Thus the fruits or graces of the Spirit are love, long-suffering, gentleness, meekness, temperance, and such like. Now faith is such a divine gift or disposition, that when it turns to and rests on Jesus Christ it saves the soul; that is to say, He saves the soul which inclines to Him, receives Him, and reposes on Him.

receive and rest upon him

We receive what is offered us; we rest on one who is able and willing to help us. Now the text says that Christ is offered to us in the gospel, and consequently to believe the gospel and to accept Christ are one and the same thing. Receiving needs no explanation; and when God offers Christ to the sinner who has faith wrought in his heart by the Holy Ghost, the sinner opens his heart and receives Christ for salvation.

'I believe that the root of almost every schism and heresy from which the Christian Church has ever suffered, has been the effort of man to earn, rather than to receive his salvation; and that the reason that preaching is commonly so ineffectual is, that it calls on men oftener to work for God, than to behold God working for them' (Ruskin).

alone for salvation

See on Question 33. Everyone has heard of that watchword of the Reformers, *sola fide*, by faith alone. And that doctrine was not more the doctrine of Luther and Knox in the sixteenth century than it was the doctrine of Paul and John in the first century. This doctrine, namely, is that forgiveness of sins and eternal life have been purchased for us by Jesus Christ, and that faith in Christ, and faith alone, 'putteth on Christ to justification.' And this is still the peculiar and characteristic message of the evangelical pulpit, the all-sufficiency and aloneness of Christ's obedience and death for the taking away of sin, and the corresponding aloneness of faith in the matter of justification.

Dr. Donne, a standard divine of the Church of England, and originally a convert from Romanism, thus states the Calvinistic and evangelical doctrine on this point: '*Deus solus justificat*, God only justifies us; *efficienter*, nothing can work towards it but only the mere goodness of God. But it is also truly said of Christ, *Christus solus justificat*, Christ only justifies us; *materialiter*, nothing enters into the body and substance of the ransom of our sins but the obedience of Christ. It is also truly said, *sola fides justificat*, only faith justifies us; *instrumentaliter*, nothing apprehends, nothing applies the merit of Christ to thee, but thy faith. And lastly, it is as truly said, *sola opera justificat*, only our works justify us; *declaratorie*, only thy good life can assure thy conscience and the world that thou art justified.'

'And I, my loving Brentius,' writes Luther, 'do use to think as if in my heart were no quality or virtue at all which is called faith or love, but I set all on Christ, and say, my formalis justitia, that is, my sure, my constant and complete righteousnes, in which there is no want or failing, is Christ my Lord and Saviour.'

as he is offered to us in the gospel

'Freely offered to us in the gospel' (Answer 31). Now when any offer is made to us, by the mere fact of that offer we are placed in a new, and peculiar, and responsible position. We are not after the offer just as we were before it. The offerer has put a constraint, and an obligation, and a responsibility upon us. For we must either accept the offer or refuse it. And, indeed, not to accept is to refuse. Not to say we refuse and yet not to accept, is to do worse than refuse, it is to despise. Proverbs 1:29-33.

'I have despised His Person, I have despised His righteousness, I have counted His blood an unholy thing, I have done despite to His spirit of grace: therefore I have shut myself out of all His promises; and there now remains to me nothing but threatenings, dreadful threatenings, faithful threatenings of certain judgment, which shall devour me as an adversary' (The Man in the Iron Cage in *Pilgrim's Progress*).

'There is all reason to suppose that God deals with particular believers as He dealt with His Church, which he first made to hear His voice in the law, with terrible thunders and lightnings, and kept her under a schoolmaster to lead her to Christ; and then comforted her with the joyful sound of the gospel from Mount Zion. And it seems to be the natural import of the word gospel, glad tidings, that it is news of a deliverance and salvation after great fear and distress' (Edwards).

Uses

1. 'Truly, I am persuaded, if it were possible all men could agree in what signification those three words, faith, grace, and spirit, were to be understood in each place where any of them are found, three full parts, at least, of four of those unhappy controversies that have been held up in the Christian Church would vanish' (Sanderson).

2. The Confession says that faith acteth differently upon that which each particular passage in Scripture containeth. And so it is with faith in Christ. Faith acts differently on the Lord Jesus, according as He is set forth in the gospel before the believing soul. Faith answers to all Christ's fulness. There is nothing in God, as He is the God of all grace; there is nothing in Christ as containing the fulness of the Godhead bodily, nothing that faith is not fitted and intended to appropriate. As a believer contemplates and considers Christ in His one Person, in His two Natures, and in His three Offices, he receives Him in all, and still says, as he sees so much he cannot appropriate, Lord, increase my faith!

3. 'Why did He choose faith of all graces to save a man by? Because the poorest in the world, the weakest understanding, can believe and trust. When he heareth that God will save sinners, he is able to trust God, as strongly and as firmly as the wisest understanding man in the world. Nay, your weak men, they are aptest to believe, they are more suited for faith' (Goodwin).

4. Bellarmine, the great Romish controversialist, after all his disputes about works and relying on saints and angels, says, 'After all, it is safest to place our trust in the mercy of God alone.'

QUESTION 87

What is repentance unto life?

Answer: Repentance unto life is a saving grace,[1] whereby a sinner, out of a true sense of his sin,[2] and apprehension of the mercy of God in Christ,[3] doth, with grief and hatred of his sin, turn from it unto God,[4] with full purpose of, and endeavour after, new obedience.[5]

Repentance

This word originally merely an afterthought, a second thought. Before it had any moral or religious sense attached to it, the word signified the sight we get of an action when we look at it after it is past. But words grow, and they grow with the growth of the mind that uses them; sometimes they grow better, and sometimes they grow worse: they are like the dyer's hand, their nature is subdued to what they work in. And thus it is that with us the pure intellectual act of memory becomes entangled, embarrassed and burdened with the past it is continually revisiting. So full is our past of matter that causes regret and remorse, shame and sorrow, that memory in us has almost lost its pure and natural operation, and become transformed into an evil conscience. The return of a man's mind upon his past is almost equivalent to a condemnation of his past. And thus here, as so often elsewhere, the grammarian, before he is aware, is

---

1. Acts 11:18: Then hath God also to the Gentiles granted repentance unto life.

2. Acts 2:37, 38: Now when they heard this, they were pricked in their heart, and said unto Peter, and to the rest of the apostles, Men and brethren, what shall we do? Then Peter said unto them, Repent, and be baptized every one of you in the name of Jesus Christ for the remission of sins, and ye shall receive the gift of the Holy Ghost.

3. Joel 2:12: Therefore also now, saith the Lord, Turn ye even to me with all your heart, and with fasting, and with weeping, and with mourning. Jeremiah 3:22: Return, ye backsliding children, and I will heal your backslidings. Behold, we come unto thee; for thou art the Lord our God.

4. Jeremiah 31:18, 19. Ezekiel 36:31: Then shall ye remember your own evil ways, and your doings that were not good, and shall loathe yourselves in your own sight, for your iniquities, and for your abominations.

5. 2 Corinthians 7:11: For, behold, this selfsame thing, that ye sorrowed after a godly sort, what carefulness it wrought in you, yea, what clearing of yourselves, yea, what indignation, yea, what fear, what vehement desire, yea, what zeal, yea, what revenge! In all things ye have approved yourselves to be clear in this matter. Isaiah 1:16, 17: Wash you, make you clean; put away the evil of your doings from before mine eyes; cease to do evil; Learn to do well; seek judgment; relieve the oppressed; judge the fatherless; plead for the widow.

already within the sphere of the moralist, and etymology has, all unwittingly to itself, become the forerunner of experimental religion. The study of words is often saddening, and this is an example of it.

unto life

To distinguish repentance from remorse and despair, see 2 Corinthians 7:9-11. For repentance unto life is not to be confounded with the sorrow that worketh death. The name of remorse is given to that relentless gnawing pain which is sometimes awakened in a wrong-doer's mind. Remorse is the piercing recollection of having done evil when there is no tenderness or contrition mingled with the inward pain. Remorse crushes rather than breaks the miserable heart. The pains of hell take hold of the remorseful man. He is filled full with self-contempt, 'bitterer to drink than blood.' Saul and Judas are notorious examples of remorse, of sorrow that worketh death. But repentance unto life, on the other hand, is full of a melting, humble, pliable, patient, and affectionate spirit. The tears of repentance are not bitter; they do not burn where they fall; they are sweetened by meekness, and humility, and love. Repentance has sometimes sorrow even to anguish, but it has not bitterness, or cruelty, or impatience mingled with its anguish. Remorse rushes on death, but true repentance has no desire to die, unless indeed it be to die for others. Repentance is unto life.

a saving grace

See under Question 86. Calvin, remarking on John's preaching, says that repentance is not placed first, as some ignorantly suppose, as if it were the ground of the forgiveness of sins, or as if it induced God to begin to be gracious to us; but men are commanded to repent that they may receive the reconciliation that is offered to them. Though John, when he introduces the mention of the grace of God, exhorts men to repentance, yet it must not be forgotten that repentance, not less than the inheritance of the heavenly kingdom, is the gift of God. It is a remark of Bengel's that repentance is a joyful gift, and not a matter of sorrow. And he refers to Acts 5:31, 11:18; 2 Timothy 2:25.

a true sense of sin

See Answers 14, 31, 84. A true sense of sin is to see it and feel it as committed against God, and against God as He is revealed in the Scriptures and in Jesus Christ. A true sense of sin is felt when a penitent, keeping ever before him the injuries he has done to himself and to his neighbour, and doing all that in him lies to make reparation for these, yet cries continually, 'Against Thee, Thee only, have I sinned' (Ps. 51:4). A true sense of sin is to see its sinfulness, and its aggravations. All the experimental scriptures are full of a true sense of sin, and no other writing in the world is, unless such writings as draw their spiritual insight and sensitiveness from Scripture. And of all the Scriptures the fifty-first Psalm is perhaps the best, as it is the fullest, expression of a true repentance under a true sense of sin.

apprehension of the mercy of God in Christ
To apprehend means originally to lay hold of by the hand. In the text the word takes the secondary sense of taking hold of with the understanding. To apprehend the mercy of God is to receive the assurance of it into the mind, and to hold by it (Phil. 3:12).

The mercy of God is His feeling of pity toward our misery. 'Mercy (misericordia) hath but its name from misery, and is no other thing than laying another's misery to heart.' In Christ, because He was the Person, and His was the work in which God's mercy to sinners was and is revealed and offered. God was in Christ reconciling sinners to Himself.

grief and hatred of his sin
'Without hatred of sin, and remorse for transgressions, no man will taste the grace of God' (Calvin).

'Penitents have felt that they deserve no more that the sun should shine upon them, or the earth sustain them, or the air support them, or wine refresh them, or food nourish them, since all these are the creatures and the servants of the God whom themselves have offended' (Pusey).

turn from it unto God
Conversion, in the scriptural and religious sense of that word, is just turning from sin unto God. Matthew Henry says it is not sinning that ruins men, but sinning and not repenting.

full purpose of, and endeavour after, new obedience
'Pharnaces sent a crown to Cæsar at the same time that he rebelled against him; but Cæsar returned the crown, and sent this message back, Let him return to his obedience first' (Plutarch).

'*Christian*. And did you endeavour to mend? *Hopeful*. Yes; and fled not only from my sins, but sinful company too; and betook me to religious duties, as prayer, reading, weeping for sin, speaking truth to my neighbours, etc. These things did I, with many others, too much here to relate.'

All obedience is not 'new obedience'. For there may be reformation when there is not repentance unto life and its new fruits. Outward reformation is not evangelical repentance. Reformation of life and habits need not extend to, and as a matter of fact and experience it often does not extend to, true repentance. Before the reformed man can take rank with the penitent, he must first feel both grief and hatred of his sin; the more other men forgive him, and forget his past, the more keenly and bitterly must he remember it. Instead of excusing and condoning and forgetting his sin, he must take up the language of the Psalmist continually, 'He hath not dealt with us after our sins, nor rewarded us according to our iniquity' (Ps. 103:10).

Ezra is the scriptural type of a true penitent. 'After all that is come upon us for our evil deeds, and for our great trespass,... Thou our God hast punished us less than our iniquities deserve' (Ezra 9:13). It is the reformation and amendment that spring from a soil and a root like this that is denominated new obedience in the text.

'A really obedient mind is necessarily dissatisfied with itself, and looks out of itself for help, from understanding the greatness of its task; in other words, in proportion as a man obeys is he driven to faith, in order to learn the remedy of the imperfections of his obedience' (Newman).

Uses

1. In the fifteenth chapter of the Confession of Faith, which treats of Repentance unto Life, we read: 'Men ought not to content themselves with a general repentance; but it is every man's duty to endeavour to repent of his particular sins particularly.'

And Hooker and Taylor, standard divines in a somewhat different ecclesiastical school, agree with the Confession in this. For Hooker says: 'A general persuasion that thou art a sinner will neither so humble and bridle thy soul as if the catalogue of thy sins examined severally be kept continually in mind.' And Jeremy Taylor, in his *Unum Necessarium*, says: 'Every single act of vice may and must be repented of particularly, if it be a wilful, deliberate, and observed action. A general repentance will not serve thy turn in those cases.'

'I was a blasphemer,' particularizes the apostle, 'and a persecutor, and injurious.' Let no man, then, who would truly repent of his sins content and deceive himself with the easy and unprofitable impeachment, I am a sinner. Let no man suppose that he has perfected his repentance before God by uttering the penitential words, 'Pardon mine iniquity, for it is great.' But let him with a noble self-accusation take hold of his sins, and lead them out of the darkness, and tell out before God and his own conscience their particulars and their aggravations. Let him be beforehand with the great day. Let him relieve the Judge of His strange work.

2. It is only an extension of the same great principle of true repentance to apply it to particular persons with whom we have had to do, and against whom we have sinned. On this point the Confession takes up this position: 'As every man is bound to make private confession of his sins to God,... so he that scandalizeth his brother, or the Church of Christ, ought to be willing, by a private or public confession of his sin, to declare his repentance to those that are offended; who are thereupon to be reconciled to him, and in love to receive him.'

3. But we must not only repent continually of what we have done, we must still more repent of what we are. The most perfect penitents aim at this, and in measure attain to it. It is not so much for the sins that have come out of their hearts that they are humbled, as for the bottomless sinfulness out of which the sins sprang.

4. 'No true penitent forgets or forgives himself; an unforgiving spirit toward himself is the very price of God's forgiving him. Still let this comfort and encourage all penitents; they may be high, they may be highest, in the kingdom of heaven; they may be, like St. Paul, not a whit behind the chiefest' (Newman).

5. 'But we profess that as ravishing joy is not necessary and essential to faith, so nor deep vexing gashes and impressions of wrath are necessary to humiliation, though they often accompany it; as the one is the overflow of faith, and the other of humiliation' (Goodwin).

QUESTION 88

What are the outward means whereby Christ communicateth to us the benefits of redemption?

Answer: The outward and ordinary means whereby Christ communicateth to us the benefits of redemption, are his ordinances, especially the word, sacraments, and prayer; all which are made effectual to the elect for salvation.[1]

The outward and ordinary means
See Answer 85. The inward means whereby Christ communicateth to us the benefits of redemption, faith and repentance, having already been discussed, we come now to the outward means, and they are here enumerated as the word, sacraments, and prayer. And what remains of the Catechism is taken up with the successive discussion of these three means of grace and salvation.

'By means of grace are not meant every instrumentality which God may please to make the means of spiritual edification to His children. The phrase is intended to indicate those institutions which God has ordained to be the ordinary channels of grace, i.e. of the supernatural influence of the Holy Spirit, to the souls of men. The means of grace, according to the standards of our Church, are the word, sacraments, and prayer.... The Reformed teach that the operations of the Holy Ghost are absolutely confined neither to the word not to the sacraments. He works when and where He sees fit; as in the times of the Old Testament and during the Apostolic Age His extraordinary gifts were not conveyed through the medium of the truth, so neither now are the gifts for ecclesiastical office, nor is the regeneration of infants, effected by any such instrumentality' (Hodge).

1. Matthew 28:19, 20: Go ye therefore, and teach all nations, baptizing them in the name of the Father, and of the Son, and of the Holy Ghost; teaching them to observe all things whatsoever I have commanded you: and, lo, I am with you alway, even unto the end of the world. Amen. Acts 2:42: And they continued stedfastly in the apostles' doctrine and fellowship, and in breaking of bread, and in prayers. Verses 46, 47: And they, continuing daily with one accord in the temple, and breaking bread from house to house, did eat their meat with gladness and singleness of heart, praising God, and having favour with all the people. And the Lord added to the church daily such as should be saved.

QUESTION 89

How is the word made effectual to salvation?

Answer: The Spirit of God maketh the reading, but especially the preaching of the word, an effectual means of convincing and converting sinners, and of building them up in holiness and comfort, through faith, unto salvation.[1]

The Spirit of God maketh the reading

'God's own words will not obtain full credit in the hearts of men, until they are sealed by the inward testimony of the Spirit. The same Spirit therefore who spoke by the mouth of the prophets, must penetrate our hearts, in order to convince us that they faithfully delivered the message with which they were divinely entrusted.... Let it therefore be held as fixed, that those who are inwardly taught by the Holy Ghost acquiesce implicitly in Scripture; that Scripture, carrying its own evidence along with it, deigns not to submit to proofs and arguments, but owes the full conviction with which we ought to receive it to the testimony of the Spirit' (Calvin).

---

1. Nehemiah 8:8: So they read in the book, in the law of God distinctly, and gave the sense, and caused them to understand the reading. 1 Corinthians 14:25: And thus are the secrets of his heart made manifest; and so, falling down on his face, he will worship God, and report that God is in you of a truth. Acts 26:18: To open their eyes, and to turn them from darkness to light, and from the power of Satan unto God, that they may receive forgiveness of sins, and inheritance among them which are sanctified by faith that is in me. Psalm 19:8: The statutes of the Lord are right, rejoicing the heart: the commandment of the Lord is pure, enlightening the eyes. Acts 20:32: And now, brethren, I commend you to God, and to the word of his grace, which is able to build you up and to give you an inheritance among all them which are sanctified. Romans 15:4: For whatsoever things were written aforetime were written for our learning; that we, through patience and comfort of the scriptures, might have hope. 2 Timothy 3:15-17: And that from a child thou hast known the holy scriptures, which are able to make thee wise unto salvation through faith which is in Christ Jesus. All scripture is given by inspiration of God, and is profitable for doctrine, for reproof, for correction, for instruction in righteousness; That the man of God may be perfect, thoroughly furnished unto all good works. Romans 10:14: How then shall they call on him in whom they have not believed? and how shall they believe in him of whom they have not heard? and how shall they hear without a preacher? Verse 17: So then faith cometh by hearing, and hearing by the word of God. Romans 1:16: For I am not ashamed of the gospel of Christ: for it is the power of God unto salvation to every one that believeth; to the Jew first, and also to the Greek.

'But there is a thing ye man ever remember; there is na doctrine, nather of the simple word, nor yet of the sacraments, gif Christ abstract His Haly Spirit, that is able to move. Therefore, quhen ever ye come to hear the doctrine, quhider it be of the sacraments or of the simple word, crave of God that He wald be present by His Haly Spirit, or utherwise al the doctrine in the earth will not availe you' (Robert Bruce).

but especially the preaching of his word
'It does not answer the end which God had in instituting the office of preaching, merely for men to have good commentaries and expositions on the Scripture, and other good books of divinity; because, though these may tend, as well as preaching, to give a good doctrinal or speculative understanding of the word of God, yet they have not an equal tendency to impress them on men's hearts and affections' (Jonathan Edwards).

'The sermon has ever been the great central feature of primitive and Protestant worship, and still serves to distinguish the evangelical from the ritualistic type of Christianity' (Shields' *Liturgia Expurgata*).

'It is mainly by the institution of preaching that religion is kept a conspicuous thing, a public acknowledged reality.... If we are told that we ought rather to say that it is public worship that has this effect, we have to answer, that public worship, separately from preaching, has a very small effect in favour of religion, as far as instruction is concerned. It is quite certain that when the conductors of that worship have not knowledge and religion enough to preach, that worship will be little more than a ceremonial routine of forms' (John Foster).

convincing and converting sinners
See Answer 31. Savonarola, in his *Triumph of the Cross*, tells us that when he neglected the preaching of the word, and applied himself to discourses of philosophy, he gained little upon the hearts of the people; but when he came to illustrate and explain the Scriptures, the minds of the people were wonderfully inflamed and excited to a serious frame; and that when he discoursed in a philosophical manner, there was a non-attention, not only of the more ignorant, but of the more learned sort too; but when he preached Scripture truths, he found the minds of men mightily delighted, stunned with divine truth, brought to compunction, and a reformation of their lives, which shows, he says, the power of the word, acting more vigorously than all human reason in the world.

'When the word of God came into Paul's conscience, then he died. As some metals will not melt till some other metal be put to them, so nor will sins melt or dissolve in the conscience till the word comes as fire and mingles with them; but when God sets it on work, it runs through the soul like hail-shot or like quicksilver. Have you seen hurricane winds or tempests that overthrew towers to their very foundation, tear up hills by the roots and cast them into the sea, toss up ships riding at anchor like tennis balls, and hurl them upon the dry land? Such and so great, though not so visible to the outward sense, is the power of the word. It tears men's hearts, rooted in evil, from their dearest lusts; it makes their consciences to boil like a pot, and the waves thereof to roar, and with one word it stills them, and calms the winds and the waves, and they obey it, and the heart is pacified.... Such is the word, and every portion of it. Therefore take heed how ye hear. Men feel not this now, nor do they imagine what a design God hath upon men in this dispensation of hearing and preaching. He prepares and lays a train for the other world; yea, and this instrumentality serves to all His designs upon the ungodly that obey not His word' (Goodwin).

Use

'You read your Bible regularly, of course; but do try to understand it, and still more to feel it. Read more parts than one at a time. For example, if you are reading Genesis, read a Psalm also; or if you are reading Matthew, read a small bit of an Epistle also. Turn the Bible into prayer' (McCheyne).

QUESTION 90

How is the word to be read and heard, that it may become effectual to salvation?

Answer: That the word may become effectual to salvation, we must attend thereunto with diligence,[1] preparation,[2] and prayer;[3] receive it with faith and love,[4] lay it up in our hearts,[5] and practise it in our lives.[6]

---

1. Proverbs 8:34: Blessed is the man that heareth me, watching daily at my gates, waiting at the posts of my doors.

2. 1 Peter 2:1, 2: Wherefore, laying aside all malice, and all guile, and hypocrisies, and envies, and all evil speakings, as new-born babies, desire the sincere milk of the word, that ye may grow thereby.

We must attend with diligence

Trench, in his seventh lecture on The Study of Words, as if he had had this very answer in his eye, says: 'But "attentive" and "assiduous" are words which it is worth our while to realize what they mean. He then is "assiduous" who sits close to his work; he is "attentive" who stretches out his neck so that he may bring the organ of his hearing nearer to the speaker, and lose none of his words. And then what a lesson the word "diligence" contains! How good for all of us to be reminded, as we are reminded when we make ourselves aware of its derivation from *diligo*, to love, that the only secret of true industry in our work is love of that work!' And what is true of work is true of hearing and reading. Luke tells us that the Lord opened Lydia's heart so that she attended to the things which Paul spoke. And in the same way Luther recommends us to pause at every verse of Scripture, and shake it as we shake the boughs of a tree when we wish to enjoy the fruit.

'The name familiarly given by the people of New England to revivals of religion – "a religious attention," "a general attention to religion" – indicates their nature.... A revival of religion is nothing but the immediate result of an uncommon attention' (Edwards).

preparation, and prayer

The Jews had such reverence for their holy Sabbath that they held the Friday afternoon sacred for its sake, and called the Friday afternoon the Preparation. Josephus tells us in his *Antiquities* that his fellow-countrymen refused to do any business after the ninth hour, three o'clock on Friday. To this day in many parts of the East the Friday bears the additional designation of the Preparation. And in many well-ordered households among ourselves, the Saturday evening has a special quietness and repose in preparation for the approaching Lord's day. And the Catechism here teaches that before reading the word of God, and especially before

3. Psalm 119:18: Open thou mine eyes, that I may behold wondrous things out of thy law.

4. Hebrews 4:2: The word preached did not profit them, not being mixed with faith in them that heard it. 2 Thessalonians 2:10: And with all deceivableness of unrighteousness in them that perish; because they received not the love of the truth, that they might be saved.

5. Psalm 119:11: Thy word have I hid in mine heart, that I might not sin against thee.

6. Luke 8:15: But that on the good ground are they, which in an honest and good heart, having heard the word, keep it, and bring forth fruit with patience. James 1:25: But whoso looketh into the perfect law of liberty, and continueth therein, he being not a forgetful hearer, but a doer of the work, this man shall be blessed in his deed.

going to the house of God to hear His word preached, the mind should be studiously and habitually put into a state of preparation befitting the solemnity and importance of the occasion. '*Q.* Must a man neglect his duty, if his heart be not duly prepared for it? *A.* No; for that would be to add a new sin to the former, and aggravate it the more. *Q.* Doth unpreparedness for the word always hinder its efficacy on the heart? *A.* No; God sometimes is found of them that seek Him not. But it is a sin to neglect it, and needs pardon of God (Flavel).

receive it with faith and love
'The heritage of Scepticism is rather the settled spirit of doubt than the accumulated store of arguments' (Westcott).

lay it up in our hearts
'According to a man's thoughts so are his affections inflamed. Multiplied thoughts inflame affections, and inflamed affections increase the number of thoughts concerning them' (Owen).

practise it in our lives
From the heart are the issues of life, and unless the truth be lodged in the heart, it is impossible it can be practised in the life. Practice is the end of all reading and preaching (Matt. 7:24-27).

Use
'A wise man will make better use of an idle pamphlet than a fool will do of Sacred Scripture' (Milton).

QUESTION 91

How do the sacraments become effectual means of salvation?

Answer: The sacraments become effectual means of salvation, not from any virtue in them, or in him that doth administer them; but only by the blessing of Christ,[1] and the working of his Spirit in them that by faith receive them.[2]

effectual means of salvation
For effectual, see Answer 31. What is a *mean* of salvation? A mean of salvation signifies any appointment of God, whereby He promotes and accomplishes His design of saving our souls; so the word is a mean, Romans 1:16. What is meant by an effectual mean of salvation? By an *effectual* mean is meant such a mean as fully obtains and accomplishes the end it was appointed for, 1 Thessalonians 2:13 (Flavel).

not from any virtue in them
'Not from any power in themselves' (Larger Catechism).

'We must not suppose that there is some latent virtue inherent in the sacraments by which they, in themselves, confer the gifts of the Holy Spirit upon us, since the only office divinely assigned them is to attest and ratify the benevolence of the Lord toward us' (Calvin).

'The Romish doctrine upon this subject is, that the sacraments contain the grace which they signify; that they confer grace always and certainly, where men do not put an obstacle in the way; and that they do this *ex opere operato*, or by some sort of physical or intrinsic power bestowed upon them, apart from the state of mind of the recipients; that baptism is the instrumental cause of justification as including both remission of sins and regeneration; and that the Lord's Supper invariably conveys spiritual nourishment' (Cunningham).

The student will see from the above extracts why this Answer is constructed on the polemical form in which it stands; first negative and then positive.

or in him that doth administer them
'Or any virtue derived from the piety or intention of him by whom they are administered' (Larger Catechism). 'A sacrament is not to be estimated by the hand of him by whom it is administered, but is to be received as from the hand of God Himself, from whom it undoubtedly proceeded; its dignity neither gains nor loses by the administrator.'

---

1. 1 Peter 3:21: The like figure whereunto even baptism doth also now save us, (not the putting away of the filth of the flesh, but the answer of a good conscience toward God,) by the resurrection of Jesus Christ. Matthew 3:11: I indeed baptize you with water unto repentance: but he that cometh after me is mightier than I whose shoes I am not worthy to bear: he shall baptize you with the Holy Ghost, and with fire. 1 Corinthians 3:6, 7: I have planted, Apollos watered; but God gave the increase. So then neither is he that planteth any thing, neither he that watereth; but God that giveth the increase.

2. 1 Corinthians 12:13: For by one Spirit are we all baptized into one body, whether we be Jews or Gentiles, whether we be bond or free; and have been all made to drink into one Spirit.

only by the blessing of Christ, and the working of his Spirit
'The sacraments duly perform their office only when accompanied by the Spirit, the internal Master, whose energy alone penetrates the heart, stirs up the affections, and procures access for the sacraments into our souls. If He is wanting, the sacraments can avail us no more than the sun shining on the eyeballs of the blind, or sounds uttered in the ears of the deaf' (Calvin).

'All the seales in the warld will not worke, except the Spirit of God concurre, and seale the same truth in your hearts quhilk the sacrament seales outwardlie. Except He mak cleare the sight of thy mind inwardlie, and worke a feeling in thy hart, baith word and sacrament sal tine their fruit and effect quhilk they suld have. All the Scriptures are full of this' (Robert Bruce).

QUESTION 92

What is a sacrament?

> *Answer: A sacrament is an holy ordinance instituted by Christ; wherein, by sensible signs, Christ, and the benefits of the new covenant, are represented, sealed, and applied to believers.*[1]

A sacrament
This is a theological and ecclesiastical and not a biblical word. The term 'sacrament' is not found in Holy Scripture. In this respect it stands on the same footing as Trinity, incarnation, consubstantial, and suchlike scientific terms. The word 'sacrament' has a very interesting and instructive history. In seeking out the origin and original use of this word which we have appropriated to a religious use, we must not only pass beyond Scripture, but beyond the Church and Church life altogether, and seek it among the usages of the judicial and military life of ancient Rome. The word sacrament, *sacramentum*, a sacred, a dedicated thing, originally signified that sum of money which was deposited by parties who entered on a lawsuit before a Roman tribunal: it was a kind

---

1. Genesis 17:7: And I will establish my covenant between me and thee, and thy seed after thee, in their generations, for an everlasting covenant, to be a God unto thee, and to thy seed after thee. Verse 10: This is my covenant, which ye shall keep, between me and you, and thy seed after thee; Every man-child among you shall be circumcised. Exodus 12. throughout. 1 Corinthians 11:23: For I have received of the Lord that which also I delivered unto you, That the Lord Jesus, the same night in which he was betrayed, took bread. Verse 26: For as often as ye eat this bread, and drink this cup, ye do shew the Lord's death till he come.

of wager as to the right, and it took this name because when forfeited it was handed over to the treasury of some temple, or other sacred institution, much as contending parties among ourselves sometimes agree to hand over forfeited sums to hospitals or other public charities. The word next came to signify the military oath that the Roman recruit took to his general or to the emperor. From these senses the term became extended to any solemn promise or undertaking. And when the Church took over the term into her vocabulary, she applied it to designate certain religious doctrines and ordinances, especially such as contained an element of mystery, and inwardness, and depth. Thus the word 'sacramentum' was employed in the Vulgate to translate the Greek word 'mystery', wherever that work occurred in the New Testament: thus we find Jerome, in speaking of the book of Revelation, saying *tot verba, quot sacramenta*, every word in this book contains a mystery. And thus through a long and instructive history it has come about that baptism and the Lord's Supper are known among ourselves as the sacraments; and that because they, by Christ's appointment, mystically represent, seal and apply Christ and the benefits of the new covenant.

instituted by Christ

'Instituted by Christ in His Church' (Larger Catechism): 'immediately instituted by God' (Confession). To institute is to set up, appoint, originate. The accounts of the institution of the two sacraments are given repeatedly in the Gospels. In the First Epistle to the Corinthians, Paul also gives us an authoritative account of the institution of the Supper, which, he says, he received of the Lord Himself. In instituting the ordinance of the Supper, Christ Himself knit the sacramental bond between the sign and the things signified: and that bond holds and operates wherever and whenever the Supper is rightly dispensed and received.

Calvin says that the term sacrament, taken generally, includes all the signs which God ever commanded men to use, that He might make them sure and confident of the truth of His promises. Sometimes God took a natural object and attached to it a sacramental significance and value. The tree of life was such a sacrament to Adam: as again the rainbow was to Noah. The tree was previously a tree, and the bow a bow: but when they were, so to say, inscribed with the word of God, a new use was attached to them: they became signs and seals of God's covenants: they became sacraments. Miracles were sometimes wrought, on the other hand, to seal and confirm the bare word of God, as in the case of the burning furnace that Abraham saw, and the fleece now dry and now wet which fortified Gideon's faith, and the backgoing shadow on Hezekiah's sun-dial. All these things were of the nature of sacraments.

On this subject Flavel says: 'Of sacraments there are two sorts, some extraordinary and transient, as the fiery pillar, the manna, and the water out of the rock; and some ordinary and standing, as circumcision and the Passover before Christ, and baptism and the Lord's Supper since Christ's death.'

But Calvin's instances agree better with the correct definition and true nature of a sacrament than some of Flavel's. The manna and the water were miracles of grace, and no doubt, over and above their immediate use, they supported the faith of Israel in God and in His promises. But these things were not directly and immediately given to Israel as signs and seals of the word of God.

'But leving the ambiguitie of the word, I take the worde sacrament, as it is tane and used in the Kirk of God, for a haly signe and seal that is annexed to the preached word of God, to seal up and confirme the truth contained in the same word, in sick sort, that I call not the seal separated fra the word a sacrament.... Therefore the word only cannot be a sacrament; nor the element only cannot be a sacrament: bot word and element conjunctly man make a sacrament: and so Augustine said weill, Let the word come to the element and ye sal have a sacrament: then I call a sacrament the word and seal conjunctlie, the ane hung to the uther' (Robert Bruce).

by sensible signs

Sensible: the senses are those faculties by which man, and in their measure the lower animals also, perceive external objects by means of impressions made on certain organs of the body. The senses are usually spoken of as being five in number, namely, sight, hearing, taste, smell and touch. And that is called sensible which possesses properties or attributes that affect the senses. Thus water in the one sacrament, and bread and wine in the other, are sensible, that is, they are capable of being perceived and apprehended through the senses and organs of the body.

Signs: a sign is that by which anything is represented, a token, an indication. The student who takes the trouble will easily discover the leading uses of this word in Scripture.

'I call the signs in the sacrament quhatsoever I perceive and takis up be my outwarde senses, by myne eye especially.... The reasoun quherfore

I call them signes is this: I call them not signes, because they signifie only, as the bread signifies the body of Christ, and the wine signifies the blood of Christ. I call them not signes, because they represent only, but I call them signes because they have the body and blood of Christ conjoyned with them.... They are instruments to deliver and exhibite the thing that they signifie, and not in respect onely of their representation, they are called signes. For if they did nathing bot represented or signified a thing absent, then ony picture or dead image suld be a sacrament.... There is na picture of the king that will deliver the king unto you; therefore na picture can be a sacrament.... Then, I say, I call the sacraments signs, because God has maid them potent instrumentis to deliver that same thing quhilk they signifie' (Robert Bruce).

Christ, and the benefits of the new covenant

For the old covenant, the covenant of works and resulting life, see Answer 12. And for new covenant, the covenant of grace, see Answer 20, and for 'Christ and the benefits of the new covenant' see Answers 20 to 38 inclusive.

'Nowe, I ga to the thing signified, and I call the thing signified be the signes in the sacrament, that quhilk Ireanæus, that auld writer, callis the heavenly and spiritual thing, to wit, hail Christ, with His hail figts, benefits, and graces, applied and given to my saul.... Sa I call not the thing signified the grace and virtue that flowes fra Christ onelie, nor Christ Himself and His substance, without the vertue and grace onelie: but jointly the substance with the graces, hail Christ, God and man, without separation of His natures, without discretion of His substance fra His graces' (Robert Bruce).

'The sacraments are auxiliary or instrumental in conveying to believing men the spiritual blessings of the forgiveness of the sins which they continue to commit, a growing sense of God's pardoning mercy, and grace and strength to resist temptation and discharge duty, and improve privilege, and to be ever advancing in holiness: or, to adopt the language of the Shorter Catechism, the sacraments instrumentally convey assurance of God's love, peace of conscience, joy in the Holy Ghost, increase of grace, and perseverance therein to the end' (Cunningham).

represented

Re-presented, presented over again: as before in the word, so now in the sacramental elements and actions. In addition to the expository use of the word here, there may also be a certain polemical reference to the Popish position that the sacraments 'contain the grace which they signify and represent'.

'God, considering our frame, hath not only appointed that we should be told of the great things of the gospel and the redemption of Christ, and be instructed in them by His word: but also that they should be, as it were, exhibited to our view by sensible representations, the more to affect us with them' (Edwards).

sealed

'A metaphor from contracts' (Bengel); a securing and authenticating mark or stamp. Hence that which confirms and ratifies a promise or an engagement; as in many Scripture passages.

The classical Scripture passage for the sacramental use of sign and seal is of course Romans 4:2, on which Schaff, supplementing Lange, remarks: 'We have here an intimation of the true idea of sacraments: they are signs, seals, and means of grace, but not the grace itself. Circumcision is not the covenant, neither is baptism regeneration. A sign and seal can never be the substitute for the thing signed and sealed, nor should it be made a ground of confidence or hope; but it is all-important as a divine ratification, and gives, so to say, legal validity to our claims, as the governmental seal to a written instrument.'

And Bruce is here, as always, as true as he is racy: 'Sacraments serve to this end also, to seal up and confirm the truth that is in the word: for as the office of the seale hung to the evident is not to confirme ane uther truth nor that quhilk is in the evident; and suppose ye believed the evident of before, yet be the seales ye beleeve it the better; even sa, the sacrament assures me of na uther truth nor is conteined within the word: yit because it is a seale annexed to the word, it persuades me the better of the same: for as the mair that the outward senses be walkned, the mair is the inward hart and mind persuaded to belief. Now, the sacrament walknes all the outward senses, sick as the eye, the hand, and all the rest: and the outward senses being moved, na question, the Spirit of God concurring therewith, moves the hart the mair.'

and applied

The Larger Catechism has 'signify, seal, and exhibit'. At first sight 'exhibit' seems a repetition of 'signify', but when we carefully examine the word we find that apply was a once well-known though now obsolete sense of exhibit. In its modern sense 'exhibit' means much the same as 'represent' or 'signify', but in old Scotch and English it meant, as it still means in the technical language of medicine, and as in the text of the Larger Catechism, to deliver over, to administer, to make application of. Thus Bruce: 'The sacrament exhibits and delivers the thing that it signifies to the soul and hart. Then in respect the Lord hes appointed the sacrament as hand to deliver and exhibit the thing signified.' And Bishop Gardner: 'But in this sacrament, we be made participaunt of His Godhode, by His humanite exhibite vnto vs for fode.' And George Gillespie, explaining what 'exhibitive signs' means in Protestant writers, says: 'I answer, that exhibition is a real, effectual, lively application of Christ, and of all His benefits, to every one that believeth, for the staying, strengthening, confirming, and comforting of the soul.'

to believers

This is a scriptural name and description of those who are true disciples of Christ and genuine children of God. See Acts 5:14; 1 Timothy 4:12. This name is borne by those who by faith receive, depend and rely upon Jesus Christ for salvation and eternal life. And the doctrine of the Catechism is that the sacraments are appointed for such, and for such alone.[1]

Uses

1. 'It wald be speered, Quherefore are sacraments annexed, seeing we gat na mair in the sacrament nor we get in the word? Thy hart cannot wist nor imagine a greater figt nor to have the Sonne of God, quha is King of heaven and earth. And therefore, I say, quhat new thing walk thou have? The sacrament is appointed that we may get a better grip of Christ nor we get in the simple word. The sacraments are appointed that I might have Him mair fullie in my saul; that He might make the better risidence in me. This, na doubt, is the cause quherefore thir seales are annexed to the evident of the simple word' (Bruce).

---

1. A full discussion of the question as to whether the sacraments are regenerating and converting ordinances will be found in the fourth book of George Gillespie's Aaron's Rod Blossoming. Jonathan Edwards also, with all his matchless strength and insight, fully discusses this matter. Dr. Cunningham epitomizes Gillespie's arguments in his essay on 'Zwingle and the Doctrine of the Sacraments', an essay that all students who would understand the Reformed doctrine as to the sacraments should carefully read. Divinity students are earnestly urged to master Robert Bruce's 'Five Sermons on the Sacraments'. They who do so will carry clear and fruitful views with them into their expositions and exhortations in connection with this important subject. Professor James Candlish's beautiful Handbook is accessible to all.

2. 'Therefore let it be a fixed point, that the office of the sacrament differs not from that of the word of God; and this is to hold forth and offer Christ to us, and in Him the treasure of heavenly grace' (Calvin).

QUESTION 93

Which are the sacraments of the New Testament?

Answer: The sacraments of the New Testament are, Baptism,[1] *and the Lord's Supper.*[2]

The Church of Rome having departed from apostolic teaching and practice in regard to the sacraments, has added to Baptism and the Supper these five, namely, Confirmation, Penance, Ordination, marriage, and Extreme Unction. The careful study of the scriptural teaching set forth under Question 92 will enable the student to see how and where these ordinances and institutions and practices fall short of the true nature and function of sacraments.

QUESTION 94

What is baptism?

Answer: Baptism is a sacrament, wherein the washing with water in the name of the Father, and of the Son, and of the Holy Ghost,[3] *doth signify and seal our ingrafting into Christ, and partaking of the benefits of the covenant of grace, and our engagement to be the Lord's.*[4]

---

1. Matthew 28:19: Go ye therefore, and teach all nations, baptizing them in the name of the Father, and of the Son, and of the Holy Ghost.

2. Matthew 26:26-28: And as they were eating, Jesus took bread, and blessed it, and brake it, and gave it to the disciples, and said, Take, eat; this is my body. And he took the cup, and gave thanks, and gave it to them, saying, Drink ye all of it: For this is my blood of the new testament, which is shed for many for the remission of sins.

3. Matthew 28:19: Go ye therefore, and teach all nations, baptizing them in the name of the Father, and of the Son, and of the Holy Ghost.

4. Romans 6:4: Therefore we are buried with him by baptism into death; that like as Christ was raised up from the dead by the glory of the Father, even so we also should walk in newness of life. Galatians 3:27: For as many of you as have been baptized into Christ have put on Christ.

Liddell and Scott in their Greek Lexicon give only the classical senses of the word 'baptism'. The example, taken from Homer, is that of a smith tempering the red-hot steel by plunging it in water. The word was used of the dyer also who steeped his fabrics in a vat; of a vessel also when let down to draw up water; and of a ship dipping when launched or loaded. These are the original and root ideas in the word baptism.

The scriptural and ecclesiastical use of the word is familiar to all through John's ministry as the forerunner of our Lord. The epithet of 'The Baptist' was given to him because of the prominence he gave to that ceremony. In his ministry baptism symbolized the purifying of the unclean heart and character of the penitent, and his entrance on a purer and holier life. And this Johannine idea is at the root of all those Pauline passages where Christian baptism is alluded to and enforced. New ideas are added; more evangelical and more sacramental ideas were added to the original idea and doctrine of baptism after Christ's mission and work were fully understood in the Church. But the Catechism here gives both the original and the fuller contents of the word with admirable clearness and completeness.

The washing with water

'Whether the person baptized is to be wholly immersed, and that once or thrice, or whether he is only to be sprinkled with water, is not of the least consequence. Churches should be at liberty to adopt either, acording to the diversity of climates, although it is evident that the term baptize means to immerse, and that this was the form used by the primitive Church' (Calvin).

'Dipping of the person into the water is not necessary; but baptism is rightly administered by pouring or sprinkling water upon the person' (Confession).

in the name of the Father, and of the Son, and of the Holy Ghost

In or unto the name. That is, the washing, dipping, or sprinkling, symbolizes the separation of the baptized person from all his evil past, and his entrance on a new life in and unto the Father, and the Son, and the Holy Ghost. Their names are themselves; as Candlish points out, their names are all 'that whereby they make themselves known.' Unto all that the baptized person is delivered over. Butler points out how, as the dispensations of Revelation are developed, new obligations of duty, unknown before, are revealed; and he instances baptism into the names of Father, Son, and Holy Ghost as an illustration. But in the evangelical system, baptism is less an entrance on new duties than an admission into new privileges and blessings out of which both duty and ability arise.

doth signify and seal
On the true meaning of these terms in the sacramental system, see Answer 92, and the works there recommeded. Those who have read Church history, and who are observers of contemporary Church life, and who have been taught the truth about the sacraments, as it is drawn from the Scriptures and embodied in the best Reformed and Puritan symbols, will not think Dr. Cunningham's words one whit too strong, when he says, 'The doctrine of baptismal regeneration has been perhaps as powerful and extensive a cause of deadly error as any doctrine that Satan ever invented.'

our grafting
The classical passages in the Scriptures for the use of this metaphor are of course John 15 and Romans 11:16-24. And Paul connects the figure of ingrafting with the ordinance of baptism in Romans 6:1-6. Baptism does not effect our ingrafting into Christ; it only signifies and seals it. The ingrafting is performed in regeneration, which is union to Christ as our Life, our Head, and our Root.

'He who is baptized puts on Christ, the Second Adam; he is baptized, I say, into a whole Christ, and so also into His death, and it is the same thing as if, at that moment, Christ suffered, died, and was buried for such a man, and as if such a man suffered, died, and was buried with Christ' (Bengel).

and our engagement to be the Lord's
'An open and professed engagement to be wholly and only the Lord's' (Larger Catechism).

'His giving himself up unto God through Jesus Christ to walk in newness of life' (Confession).

'Who is this that engaged his heart to approach unto me, saith the LORD? (Jer. 30:21).'

'On our part, baptism is a badge and a bond to oblige us to the duties of the covenant: a badge of the profession, and a bond to engage us to the duties which that profession calls for' (Manton).

QUESTION 95

To whom is baptism to be administered?

Answer: Baptism is not to be administered to any that are out of the visible church, till they profess their faith in Christ, and obedience to him;[1] but the infants of such as are members of the visible church are to be baptized.[2]

Baptism is not to be administered

This Answer consists of two parts: the first part takes up the case of adults, and the second touches on the case of infants. That the teaching of the Catechism as to the admission of adults is in accordance with the mind of Christ, is evident from the terms of the baptismal commission our Lord issued to His disciples, and from the invariable practice of His apostles. On a profession of faith in Christ, men were to be baptized and thus admitted into the visible Church.

the visible church

The Confession thus defines and describes the Church invisible and visible: 'The Catholic universal Church, which is invisible, consists of the whole number of the elect, that have been, are, or shall be gathered into one, under Christ the Head thereof; and is the spouse, the body, the fulness of Him that filleth all in all. The visible Church consists of all those throughout the world that profess the true religion, together with their children.'

'I have observed,' says Calvin, 'that the Scriptures speak of the Church in two ways. Sometimes when they speak of the Church, they mean the Church as it is before God: the Church into which none are admitted but

---

1. Acts 8:36, 37: And as they went on their way, they came unto a certain water: and the eunuch said, See, here is water; what doth hinder me to be baptized? And Philip said, If thou believest with all thine heart, thou mayest. And he answered and said, I believe that Jesus Christ is the Son of God. Acts 2:38: Then Peter said unto them, Repent, and be baptized every one of you in the name of Jesus Christ for the remission of sins, and ye shall receive the gift of the Holy Ghost.

2. Acts 2:38, 39: Then Peter said unto them, Repent, and be baptized every one of you in the name of Jesus Christ for the remission of sins, and ye shall receive the gift of the Holy Ghost. For the promise is unto you, and to your children. Genesis 17:10 compared with Colossians 2:11, 12. 1 Corinthians 7:14: Else were your children unclean; but now are they holy.

those who by the gift of adoption are sons of God, and by the sanctification of the Spirit are true members of Christ. Often, too, by the name of Church is designated the whole body of mankind scattered throughout the world, who profess to worship one God and Christ, who by baptism are initiated into the faith.'

Accordingly, when the apostles preached Christ, they always demanded a profession of faith in Him before they administered baptism in His name; and our missionaries, who are in this respect incontestably the true successors of the apostles, invariably act on this principle.

but the infants

Infant baptism is sometimes called pædo-baptism from the Greek word *paides*. The Directory for Public Worship says that children of professing parents are Christians, and federally holy before baptism, and therefore are they baptized; for their baptism supposeth them to be Church members, and doth not make or constitute them such. And in Jonathan Edwards' *Qualifications for Communion*, it is set forth as the general opinion of Protestant divines that the same qualifications are required in a parent bringing his child to baptism as in an adult person for his own admission to this ordinance.

This is not the place to set forth the scriptural arguments and considerations that have led the vast majority of Christian parents in all ages to seek baptism for their children. There exists a large literature that has sprung up in connection with this observance. And the reader may be referred to Calvin, Cunningham, Hodge, M'Crie, and Edwards for the arguments that support the practice of Christendom and the doctrines of the Catechism.

As to the connection between the naming of children and their baptism, Alford said: 'The names of children were given at circumcision, because, at the institution of that rite, the names of Abram and Sarai were changed to Abraham and Sarah.' A not less historical, if less remote origin of this practice was the giving of a new name to heathen converts, on their public reception into the Church by baptism. 'The giving of a child its name, was no more a part of the original intent of circumcision than of baptism; it was an incidental circumstance that custom had added. And I cannot forbear saying, that, in administering baptism, I think care should be taken so to order the voice that it may plainly appear that we then only speak to the child by the name that hath been already given to it' (Doddridge).

Uses

1. 'It is no slight stimulus to bring up our children in the fear of God, and the observance of His law, when we reflect that from their birth they have been considered and acknowledged by Him as His children' (Calvin).

2. But we have no express command in the New Testament to baptize infants. There needed no new command; their privilege had been settled many years before on them, and never reversed by Christ or His apostles, but their former right declared to continue to them still. For the promise is to you and to your children (Acts 2:39).

3. But many baptized infants prove naught. And so do many baptized at age too. Duties are not to be measured by events (Flavel).

QUESTION 96

What is the Lord's supper?

Answer: The Lord's supper is a sacrament, wherein, by giving and receiving bread and wine, according to Christ's appointment, his death is showed forth; and the worthy receivers are, not after a corporal and carnal manner, but by faith, made partakers of his body and blood, with all his benefits, to their spiritual nourishment, and growth in grace.[1]

The Lord's Supper

The second sacrament of the New Testament has several names given to it in Scripture according to the way it is looked at, and according to the feature in this ordinance that is specially pointed at:

---

1. 1 Corinthians 11:23-26: For I have received of the Lord that which also I delivered unto you, That the Lord Jesus, the same night in which he was betrayed, took bread: And, when he had given thanks, he brake it, and said, Take, eat; this is my body, which is broken for you: this do in remembrance of me. After the same manner also he took the cup, when he had supped, saying, This cup is the new testament in my blood: this do ye, as oft as ye drink it, in remembrance of me. For as often as ye eat this bread, and drink this cup, ye do shew the Lord's death till he come. 1 Corinthians 10:16: The cup of blessing which we bless, is it not the communion of the blood of Christ? the bread which we break, is it not the communion of the body of Christ?

(1) Luke's favourite name for the Supper is 'the breaking of bread' (see Luke 24:30; Acts 2:42, 20:7).

(2) The second scriptural name given to this sacrament is 'the communion of the body and blood of Christ' (1 Cor. 10:16). This name brings out that idea of spiritual community and believing and loving fellowship which is an essential element in this ordinance.

(3) The third scriptural designation is the Eucharist, or the thanksgiving, referring to Matthew 26:26, 27; 1 Corinthians 11:24, and 14:16. The Western Church translated the Greek Eucharist into the Latin *actio gratiarum*; and it is from this latter phrase we still retain the name of action sermon, the sermon before the action.

(4) The fourth, and perhaps the most universal and familiar name, is the Lord's Supper or the Lord's Table. It is called a Supper because it takes the place in the new Testament Church of the Passover Supper in the Old Economy. And it bears the name of the Lord's Supper because our Lord instituted it, and because in it Christ and all His benefits are represented, sealed, and applied to believers.

'It is called also "the Supper of the Lorde," to put a difference betwixt it and ane prophane supper; for this is the Lord's Supper, a halie supper, not a prophane nor common supper; a supper appointed for the increase of haliness, for the foode of the saule in haliness, to feede the soule to life everlasting. It is called also in the Bible the "Table of the Lord," it is not called the Altar of the Lord; but the apostle calls it a table to sit at, and not ane altar to stand at; a table to take and receave, and not an altar to offer and propine' (Bruce).

by giving and receiving bread and wine

'Communicating.' 'Take this, and divide it among yourselves.' 'For we being many are one bread, and one body; for we are all partakers of that one bread' (1 Cor. 10:17).

'Are not bread and wine too small and common things to represent the body and blood of Christ? Though a bit of bread and a draught of wine be of small value in themselves, yet they are great in respect of their use and end. A pennyworth of wax is a small thing in itself, but being applied to the label of a deed, may be advanced to the value of thousands of pounds, as it receives the seal of a great inheritance' (Flavel).

according to Christ's appointment
(See the accounts of the institution of the Supper in the Gospels and in First Corinthians.)

On John 6 Bengel says: 'Jesus framed His words so skilfully, that immediately at the time, and at all times subsequently, they would indeed apply in their strict literal sense to the spiritual enjoyment of Himself; and yet that afterwards, the same words should by consequence be appropriate to express the most august mystery of the Holy Supper, when that should be instituted.... The whole of those words concerning His flesh and blood have in view the Passion of Jesus, and along with it the Holy Supper.'

But some able and evangelical Protestant divines have denied that our Lord had any reference at all to the Supper in His great discourse in the sixth chapter of John. And when we reflect on the disastrous effects the Popish and High Church interpretation of that discourse has had on the Church of Christ, we would gladly believe that Bengel's first explanation is the true and exclusive one.

his death is showed forth
Represented. See Answer 92; Galatians 3:1.

the worthy receivers
No man properly speaking is worthy. But worth is one thing when a communicant is viewed in himself, and it is another thing when he is looked at as in Christ, and invited by Him. Worth is one thing in the covenant of works, when worth is measured by personal merit, and it is an altogether different thing in the covenant of grace, when worth is measured according to the work and merit of Christ, and the reality of a believer's union with Him. He who esteems himself to be worthy is clearly debarred from the table: a sense of utter unworthiness is one mark of worth in a communicant.

'Are morally honest and sober persons qualified for this sacrament? No; civility and morality do not qualify persons: they are not the wedding-garment, but regenerating grace and faith in the smallest measure are' (Flavel).

Morality does not qualify, though immorality absolutely, and in all men, disqualifies and shuts out. On this whole subject, see the able and scriptural discussion in the Larger Catechism.

not after a corporal or carnal manner, but by faith made partakers of his body and blood

This is directed against the Popish doctrine of transubstantiation. According to this doctrine, 'the substance of the bread and wine is converted into the substance of the very flesh and blood of Christ, so that all communicants literally and substantially partake of His flesh and blood.' But the Catechism, in common with all the Reformed and Evangelical symbols, teaches the scriptural and sacramental doctrines of the Supper. It is the soul that sups here, and not the body. The communicant looks not on the things which are seen, but on the things which are not seen. Only, as the soul resides in the body, and is ministered to in intellectual and spritual things by means of the body, so is it at the supper-table. There is nothing on this table worth speaking of for the needs of the body; all that is here is for the soul; and it is here offered and received in a bodily way, only because thus the true supper of the soul is more vividly and impressively brought before it. 'It is the Spirit that quickeneth; the flesh profiteth nothing; the words that I speak unto you, they are spirit, and they are life' (John 6:63).

with all his benefits

See under Question 92. (Cf. Psalms 68:19, 103:2-5, 116:12.)

to their spirtual nourishment

Spiritual because administered to the spiritual man, and because administered to him by the Spirit of God. The meaning is not exhausted by the antithesis between carnal and spiritual taken in the sense of bodily and mental. Spiritual here is opposed both to the corporal participation of the Papist, and the merely carnal participation of the unspiritual man.

'Now in respect this flesh is a spirituall food, serving me to a spirituall life, for this cause it is called a spirituall thing. It is called spirituall, in respect to the spirituall ende quhareunto it servis to my body and soul: because the flesh and blood of Christ servis to nurish mee, not to a temporal life, but to a spirituall and heavenly life' (Bruce).

growth in grace

Neither Baptism nor the Supper is for the beginning or implanting of grace in the soul: grace must be in the soul already before the sacraments are partaken of with any right meaning or good result. George Gillespie argues at great length, following Calvin and other Reformers, that the Supper is not a converting ordinance, but that it is given to nourish and increase the life of grace when it has been already begun; and he adds that the sacraments are just another example of the rule, 'Unto every one that hath shall be given, and he shall have abundance: but from him that hath not shall be taken away even that which he hath.'

Uses

1. Flavel points out to those who study this subject that the remembrance of Christ here intended is not a mere speculative or historical, but an affectionate and appropriating remembrance.

2. 'Pious souls may derive great confidence and delight from this sacrament, as being a testimony that they form one body with Christ, so that anything which is His they may call their own' (Calvin).

3. 'Speers thou quhat new thing we get in the sacrament? I say, we get Christ better nor we did before: we get a better grip of Christ now. That same thing quhilk thou possessed be the hearing of the word, thou possesses now more largely. For be the sacrament my faith is nurished, the bounds of my soull are enlarged, and sa, quhen I had but a little grip of Christ before, as it were betwixt my finger and my thumb, now I get Him in my haill hand: for aye the mair my faith growes, the better grip I get of Christ Jesus' (Robert Bruce).

QUESTION 97

What is required to the worthy receiving of the Lord's supper?

Answer: It is required of them that would worthily partake of the Lord's supper, that they examine themselves of their knowledge to discern the Lord's body,[1] of their faith to feed upon him,[2] of their repentance,[3] love,[4] and new obedience;[5] lest coming unworthily, they eat and drink judgment to themselves.[6]

---

1. 1 Corinthians 11:28, 29. But let a man examine himself, and so let him eat of that bread, and drink of that cup. For he that eateth and drinketh unworthily, eateth and drinketh damnation to himself, not discerning the Lord's body.

2. 2 Corinthians 13:5: Examine yourselves, whether ye be in the faith: prove your own selves. Know ye not your own selves, how that Jesus Christ is in you, except ye be reprobates?

It is required
By Christ and by His Church.

that they examine themselves
'Look and behold in quhat estate your hart is in with God, and in what estate your conscience is with your neighbour. Others can nocht try you so narrowlie as ye yourself can; na man can be certain of the estate of your heart and condition of your conscience, and yit ye yourself may be certain of it.... Revolve in your memories and remember gif at ony time it pleased the Lord, in His mercy, to turn the darkness of your mind unto light, to make that darkness quhilk was in you to depart. Examine, I say, quhither gif this darkness of the naturale understanding be turned to light, be the working of the Spirit or not: gif thou art become a child of the light, of the day; gif thou art become, as the apostles say, light in the Lord: gif the Lord has at ony time enlightened the eye of the mind, and made thee be thine owin miserie to see the ugliness of thine owin nature, to see the hainous sins in the quhilk be natuer thou lyes: fit He has granted thee ane insight of thyself in some measure: And, upon the uther side, if He has granted ane outgett, and has given thee ane insight of the grace of God in Christ Jesus; gif thou have gotten ane insight of the riches of the grace of Christ: Na doubt, the Halie Spirit has begun a good work in thee!' (Robert Bruce).

'Again, being so prone as we are to fawn upon ourselves, and to be ignorant as much as may be of our own deformities, without the feeling sense whereof we are most wretched; even so much the more, because not knowing them we cannot so much as desire to have them taken away: how should our festered sores be cured, but that God hath delivered a law as sharp as a two-edged sword, piercing the closest and most searchable corners of the heart, which the law of nature can hardly, human laws by no means possibly, reach unto? Hereby we know even

3. 1 Corinthians 11:31: For if we would judge ourselves, we should not be judged.

4. 1 Corinthians 10:16, 17: The communion of the blood of Christ ...the communion of the body of Christ. For we, being many, are one bread, and one body: for we are all partakers of that one bread.

5. 1 Corinthians 5:7, 8: Purge out therefore the old leaven, that ye may be a new lump, as ye are unleavened. Therefore let us keep the feast, not with old leaven, neither with the leaven of malice and wickedness; but with the unleavened bread of sincerity and truth.

6. 1 Corinthians 11:28, 29. [See in number 1.]

secret concupiscence to be sin: and are made fearful to offend, though it be but in a wandering cogitation' (Hooker).

'Search others for their virtues, and thyself for thy vices' (Thomas Fuller).

'No man is fit to communicate, who is not fit to die' (Jeremy Taylor).

knowledge to discern the Lord's body
Discern is a scriptural word, and means in this connection, as always, to understand aright, to discriminate, to distinguish. Now to discern the body of the Lord is to put that distinction and esteem upon it that He and it deserve at our hands. He discerns the body of his Lord who asks himself and answers aright: Whose body is that on the middle cross on Calvary? and why is it there? Of what did its Divine Owner speak when He said, My body is broken for you? In what sense and to what result is that body present in the Supper? and how am I aright to become incorporate with it? To look at our Lord's body in these and suchlike ways is aright to discern it.

of their faith to feed upon him
See under 'eat and drink judgment'. 'No faith, no covenant; no covenant, no seal; no seal, no sacrament' (Dr. Reynolds). Faith is sometimes spoken of as an eye, sometimes as a foot, and sometimes as a hand. Here its action is set forth as that of the mouth of the soul. This metaphor of eating is frequent in the Old Testament, and the great discourse in the sixth chapter of John, taken along with the ordinance of the Supper, has made this figure very familiar to the Christian mind and heart. Faith is there a feeding, assimilating, and nourishing faculty, and Christ, with His word, and work, and grace, is the proper and peculiar food of faith. They who worthily communicate feed spiritually on Christ, and if they examine themselves aright they will see that they do.

of their repentance
See Answer 87.

love
See Answer 42.

new obedience
See Answer 87.

lest they eat and drink judgment
Professor James Candlish points out that the Shorter Catechism is here more correct that the Authorized Version of the New Testament, in that it renders the original by 'judgment' rather than by 'damnation'. The Revised Version follows the Catechism in translating 'judgment'. Dr. Maclear, commenting on Mark 12:40, points out that the words in 1 Corinthians 11:29-32 rendered damnation, discerning, judged, condemnation, are all, in the Greek, parts or derivatives of one and the same original word; and refers to Wycliffe, who imitated the uniformity of the Greek in rendering all these words into forms of the same English word, thus: 'He that etith and drinketh vnworthili, etith and drinkith doom to him, not wisely demyng the bodi of the Lord.... And if we demyden wiseli us silf we schulden not be dampnyd with this world.' The richer the grace that is despised, the greater the sin: and the deeper will be the punishment of those despisers who perish with the sin of unworthy communicating added to all their other sins. The greater the benefits to worthy communicating, the greater the guilt to those who despise and profane both word and sacrament.

And to part with Robert Bruce's powerful and savoury sermons: 'Now come on: this may be maid mair clear be a similitude. Ye see amonge worldly princes their custome is, they will not suffer their majesty to be interest in the smallest thing that they love. Quhere can be a smaller thing that concerns the majestie of a prince nor a seall, for the substance of it is but wax? Yit, gif thou disdanfully use that seall, and contemn it, and stampe it under thy feet, thou art counted as if thou didst put hands on the king, and thou wilt be handled aefter sic way. Meikle mair, gif thou come as a sow or a dog to handle the seals of the body and blood of Christ, meikle mair may thou be compted to be guiltie of the body and blood.... Take up, therefor, yourselves in time; take your pennieworths of it, for ye wott not how lang it lasts. Crave a mouth to receive, and take this food while ye may have it, or assuredly the time will come quhen ye sall cry for it, and sall not get it: but in place of grace and mercie sall come judgment, vengeance, and the dispensation of wrath.'

Use

By far the best book on self-examination accessible to the English reader is Jonathan Edwards' *Treatise Concerning Religious Affections*. The Third Part, showing what are distinguishing signs of truly gracious and holy affections, is one of the best pieces of practical divinity ever written. Discoursing generally of assurance in his introductory remarks, Edwards says: 'It is not God's design that men should obtain assurance in any other way than by mortifying corruption, increasing in grace, and obtaining the lively exercises of it. And although self-examination be a duty of great use and importance, and by no means to be neglected; yet it is not the principal means by which the saints do get satisfaction of their good estate. Assurance is not to be obtained so much by self-examination as by action.... Paul obtained assurance of winning the prize more by running than by considering. The swiftness of his pace did more toward his assurance of a conquest than the strictness of his examination.'

QUESTION 98

What is prayer?

> *Answer: Prayer is an offering up of our desires unto God,*[1] *for things agreeable to his will,*[2] *in the name of Christ,*[3] *with confession of our sins,*[4] *and thankful acknowledgment of his mercies.*[5]

We come now to the subject of Prayer, the third and last of the three great Christian ordinances enumerated in Answer 88. As will be seen on examination, the structure of the Catechism takes a new departure with that Question and Answer. And in it we are taught that the word, sacraments and prayer are Christ's 'ordinary means whereby He communicateth to us the benefits of redemption'. We have already studied the Questions connected with the word read and preached, and we have

1. Psalm 62:8: Trust in him at all times; ye people, pour out your heart before him: God is a refuge for us. Selah.

2. 1 John 5:14: And this is the confidence that we have in him, that, if we ask any thing according to his will, he heareth us.

3 John 16:23: Verily, verily, I say unto you, Whatsoever ye shall ask the Father in my name, he will give it you.

4. Psalm 32:5: I acknowledged my sin unto thee, and mine iniquity have I not hid. I said, I will confess my transgressions unto the Lord; and thou forgavest the iniquity of my sin. Selah. Daniel 9:4: And I prayed unto the Lord my God, and made my confession, and said, O Lord, the great and dreadful God, keeping the covenant and mercy to them that love him, and to them that keep his commandments.

5. Philippians 4:6: In every thing by prayer and supplication, with thanksgiving, let your requests be made known unto God.

just finished the doctrine of the sacraments, and now we enter on the last of the three means of grace above enumerated. And according to the uniform and careful method of the Catechism, a definition or description of prayer is asked for and supplied.

Prayer is an offering up of our desires unto God

All prayer presupposes need, and a desire to possess the things needed. Such desire is altogether indispensable to true prayer. And in many passages of Scripture a true desire is presented as all that is needed to make prayer acceptable and effectual. And on the other hand, where earnest desire is absent, nothing will make up for the want of it. God answers no man's prayer when his heart is not engaged in his supplication.

'Every good and holy desire, though it lack the form, hath nowithstanding in itself the substance, and with Him the force of a prayer, who regardeth the very moanings, groans, and sighs of the heart of man. Petitionary prayer presupposeth in us first the want of that which we pray for; secondly, a feeling of that want; thirdly, an earnest willingness of mind to be eased therein; and fourthly, a declaration of our desire in the sight of God' (Hooker).

for things agreeable to his will

We ought to ask nothing in prayer that we know not to be agreeable to the will of God, and we ought to use every endeavour to find out what is agreeable to His will; for assuredly, neither by prayer, nor by any other effort of ours, shall we get anything that is not so agreeable. Before we pray, we must, so far as we can, learn His will about the things we desire, and restrain or put forward our prayer accordingly. And we have God's will revealed so as to be our guide in prayer as in all other matters of faith and duty.

'The first step toward prayer, therefore, is the knowledge of the promises of God, which are, as it were, the charter to go by. Further than these revealed purposes, His will is an impenetrable mystery' (Irving). (See Answers 2, 39, and 99.)

Writers on practical religion teach us that there are some things we may and ought to ask for absolutely, and other things we must ask for only conditionally, and they are able to illustrate this distinction at great fulness from the Scriptures.

in the name of Christ

(See Larger Catechism, Answers 180, 181.) Mediation was a fundamental principle of the Mosaic economy, and as soon as that economy 'decayed and waxed old', and the One Mediator between God and man appeared, that divine principle began to display itself in Him. Even before He had entered into the Holiest with His own blood, and while as yet His best disciples were scarcely able to hear it, He declared plainly His own unique position between God and man as the Son in the house, the way, the door, the alone access. And in our day, and in our case, prayer in His name, when offered with the enlightened understanding and the believing heart, is just the believer's recognition and acceptance of Christ as his alone sacrifice and intercessor before God. This is far from a 'bare mentioning of His name', for it is our 'drawing of our encouragement to pray, and our boldness, strength, and hope of acceptance in prayer from Christ and His mediation'. The 'name of Christ' in a true believer's prayer is not a written word or an uttered sound; it is rather our richest conception and utterance of all that Scripture teaches us of the divinity, incarnation, sacrifice and intercession of Him we call Christ. 'What is His name, and what is His Son's name if thou canst tell?' Who is the Redeemer of God's elect? (See Answers 21-28.)

To the clause, 'in the name of Christ', the Larger Catechism adds, 'by the help of His Spirit,' which comfortable addition is true both to many scriptures and to manifold Christian experience. The Larger Catechism is the best commentary on itself, and on the Shorter Catechism also, and it expands and illustrate this clause in its own admirable and scriptural way.

'The Holy Ghost, who is the intercessor in us, and who searcheth the deep things of God, doth offer, prompt, and suggest to us in our prayer those very motives that are in God's heart, to grant the thing we desire of Him, so as it often comes to pass, that a poor creature is carried on to speak God's very heart to Himself, and then God cannot, nor doth not deny' (Goodwin).

For our dependence on His Holy Spirit's working in other things, see Answers 22, 24, 30, 31, 89, 91.

with confession of our sins

It is impossible that a sinner should truly draw near to God in the name of Christ without such a sense of his corruption and guilt being awakened within him as to make him introduce and intersperse his prayer with confession of sin and lamentation on account of it. Let the student pass his mind over the record of Scripture, and mark how universal and how acceptable this state of mind was in God's people. There is nothing more becoming sinful men than confession and contrition. It is the very 'spot' of His children.

and thankful acknowledgement of his mercies
'We are to pray with an awful apprehension of the majesty of God, and a deep sense of our own unworthiness, necessities, and sins; with penitent, thankful, and enlarged hearts; with understanding, faith, sincerity, fervency, love, and perseverance waiting upon Him with humble submission to His will.' 'Prayer and thanks are like the double motion of the lungs; the air that is sucked in by prayer is breathed out again by thanks' (Old writer).

Uses
1. Desire aright, and then seek inflamed desires.

2. 'It is best to be careful in prayer not to put up those petitions of which I do not feel a sincere desire; for thereby my prayer is rendered less sincere, less acceptable to God, and less useful to myself' (Edwards).

3. 'Is it enough to make prayer acceptable that the matter is agreeable to God's will? No, it is not; for the manner as well as the matter must be so too. If I regard iniquity in my heart, the Lord will not hear me' (Flavel's Catechism).

4. Never let Christ's name pass in a prayer with a 'bare mention', but seize on some aspect of His Person or work suitable to the matter in hand. Be sure there is something somewhere in Christ's fulness to support and carry with God every right petition. Seeking it out will in course of time make you wiser than all your teachers.

QUESTION 99

What rule hath God given for our direction in prayer?

Answer: The whole word of God is of use to direct us in prayer;[1] *but the special rule of direction is that form of prayer which Christ taught his disciples, commonly called The Lord's Prayer.*[2]

The whole word of God

It is a most interesting and instructive study to trace how one psalm or prayer is incorporated with another, and how the matter and language of prayer thus grow as Scripture and the life of the Church grow. Our Lord Himself, in this lesson He taught His disciples, only gathers into a short and memorable form certain petitions that are scattered up and down the whole of the Old Testament. The whole word of God is of use to direct us in prayer, and the better that any man knows the word of God, the less will be needed to depend on any special rule of direction. 'Let the word of Christ dwell in you richly' (Col. 3:16).

the special rule of direction

'How is the Lord's Prayer to be used? The Lord's Prayer is not only for direction, as a pattern, according to which we are to make other prayers; but may also be used as a prayer, so that it be done with understanding, faith, reverence, and other graces necessary to the right performance of the duty of prayer.' The student of Church history will trace in this statement an echo of the Puritan contendings against the abuse of liturgical forms of public worship.

which Christ taught his disciples

'One of His disciples said unto Him, Lord, teach us to pray, as John also taught his disciples. And He said unto them, When ye pray, say, Our Father ...' (Luke 11:1-4). 'The disciples of John the Baptist, and the disciples of Christ, waited on their respective masters for instructions how to pray. It was in vain that the duty of repentance was preached to the one, and of faith to the other; they knew the truth, but they could not use it. So different a thing is it to be instructed in religion, and to have so mastered it in practice that it is altogether our own' (Newman, i. 257).

commonly called The Lord's Prayer

Commonly, but somewhat improperly. This is properly the disciples' prayer. The prayer recorded in the seventeenth chapter of John is with more propriety called 'The Lord's Prayer'.

---

1. 1 John 5:14: And this is the confidence that we have in him, that, if we ask anything according to his will, he heareth us.

2. Matthew 6:9-13: After this manner therefore pray ye: Our Father, etc. Compared with Luke 11:2-4: And he said unto them, When ye pray, say, Our Father, etc.

Uses

1. 'What is it then? I will pray with the spirit, and I will pray with the understanding also' (1 Cor. 14:15).

2. 'Its end is answered, not when we repeat it once or often, but when we conform the feeling and expression of our prayer to its model; when they have the same fulness of meaning; the same sobriety of utterance, the same distinction of conceptions, the same conformity to the spirit of the Divine revelations' (Edward Irving).

3. 'It is a lesson for children, for spiritual minors, for Christians in the crude stage of the divine life, afflicted with confusion of mind, dumbness, dejection, unable to pray for want of clear thought, apt words, and above all faith' (A. B. Bruce).

QUESTION 100

What doth the preface of the Lord's prayer teach us?

Answer: The preface of the Lord's prayer (which is, Our Father which art in heaven[1]) teacheth us to draw near to God with all holy reverence and confidence, as children to a father, able and ready to help us;[2] and that we should pray with and for others.[3]

The preface

The Lord's Prayer consists of three parts: a preface, certain petitions, and a conclusion. And the preface is:

Our Father which art in heaven

'God lovingly inviteth us, in this little preface, truly to believe in Him, that He is our true Father, and that we are truly His children, so that full of confidence we may more boldly call upon His name, even as we see children with a kind of confidence ask anything of their parents' (Luther).

---

1. Matthew 6:9: After this manner therefore pray ye: Our Father which art in heaven.

2. Romans 8:15: For ye have not received the spirit of bondage again to fear, but ye have received the Spirit of adoption, whereby we cry, Abba, Father. Luke 11:13: If ye then, being evil, know how to give good gifts unto your children; how much more shall your heavenly Father give the Holy Spirit to them that ask him?

3. Acts 12:5: Peter therefore was kept in prison; but prayer was made without ceasing of the church unto God for him. 1 Timothy 2:1, 2: I exhort therefore, that, first of all, supplications, prayers, intercessions, and giving of thanks, be made for all men; for kings, and for all that are in authority: that we may lead a quiet and peaceable life in all godliness and honesty.

'God hath not taken the name of a Father, nor Christ of an Elder Brother for nought, but because these names import more nearly than any other the nature of the affection which they bear us' (Irving).

'Our Father which art in heaven' is the Christian child's first prayer, just as 'The Lord's my Shepherd' is his first psalm. From the very beginning of the Christian Church this prayer has been in constant use. It has been offered daily among the disciples of Jesus Christ ever since that fruitful day when one of the twelve came to Him, saying, "Lord, teach me to pray." But though it was first taught in the childhood of the Church, and is still taught to the children of every Christian home, it is not for all that to be taken as only a child's prayer. It is true the shortest memory may retain it, and the busiest life may utter it; the weakest understanding may sufficiently grasp it, and the most childlike faith may feel at home in it; but while all that is true, yet men of God who have their senses best exercised among divine things will feel that this prayer grows with their growing experience, and gradually gathers unto itself the whole fulness of the Word of God and the need of man.

God is named Father in several senses in the Bible. He is sometimes called Father simply as the Creator of all things. Again, He is called the Father of mankind, because they were made in His Image, and made to be His spiritual children. But in a sense still He is called the Father of regenerate sons, because by their new birth, union to Christ, and adoption into His family, they have become in more than a metaphorical sense the sons of God, and He their Father. 'They have been received into the number, and have a right to all the privileges, of the sons of God.' (See Answer 34.) But all this leaves unmentioned the real and true sense, the eternal and divine sense, in which God is the Father of His Only Begotten Son. (For this see Answers 6 and 21.)

At every step of our exposition we shall have occasion to remark on the mistake of calling this series of petitions the Lord's Prayer. The very preface compels us to distinguish betwen the Paternity of the Father toward Jesus Christ and toward us. And all our Lord's utterances in this direction observe this distinction. He never once says, 'Our Father,' including Himself with us as a son. He says, 'Father,' 'Holy Father,' 'Righteous Father,' and 'My Father;' but never Our Father. Once He says, 'My Father and your Father,' but He distinguishes in so saying. 'God is the Father of Him and of us, but not of us as of Him' (Pearson).

Heaven is the dwelling-place of God; it is our Father's house. And though it is not to be limited and localized as a place in our most spiritual conceptions, yet it is right and necessary for us to think of heaven as above us. Thus we read that Jesus Himself, when He prayed, 'lifted up His eyes to heaven.' Heaven is not among or above the stars; it is high above us as God is high above man; and as good is above evil, and as blessedness is above condemnation and misery. There is a spiritual world as well as a material; and there is a spiritual geometry, with its various directions, as well as a material. 'But as it is only half of our reliance that is founded on the goodness of God, in the next clause, which are in heaven, He gives us a lofty idea of the power of God' (Calvin).

teacheth us to draw near to God
Before we begin to pray we are to think of ourselves as at a greater distance from God than we ought to be, need be, and now desire to be. Prayer is a drawing near to God. No utterance of Augustine's has been oftener quoted by commentators and devotional writers than this: 'Oh for a mountain to pray on, thou criest, high and inaccessible, that I may be nearer to God, and God may hear me better, for He dwelleth on high. Yes, God dwelleth on high, but He hath respect unto the humble! …Wouldst thou pray in His temple, pray in thyself; but first do thou become the temple of God.'

with all holy reverence
Reverence is a filial affection; it is composed of equal parts of love and fear. 'Holy and reverend is His name…. let us have grace whereby we may serve God acceptably with reverence and godly fear.'

'Let the holiest and best thing we do be considered. We are never better affected unto God than when we pray; yet, when we pray, how are our affections many times distracted! How little remorse of our own miseries! How little taste of the sweet influence of His tender mercy do we feel!' (Hooker).

and confidence
Confidence is just another form of the word faith: confidence is childlike trust. The Larger Catechism, Answer 189, translates it 'childlike dispositions'. 'The LORD shall be thy confidence, and shall keep thy foot from being taken' (Prov. 3:26).

'Without the constant exercise of faith there is no life in worship, nor satisfaction to be obtained by it. Men must therefore have something in it, or accompanying it, which may entertain their minds, and engage their affections unto it. Hereon were invented forms of prayer in great diversity, with continual diversions and avocations of the mind, because it cannot abide in the pursuit of anything spiritual without the exercise of faith. Hereunto are added outward ceremonies of vestures, postures, and gestures of veneration unto the same end. There is no other design in them all but to entertain the mind and affections with some complacency and satisfaction in outward worship upon the loss or want of that exercise of faith which is the soul and life of it in believers' (Owen).

able and ready to help us
Able, because ALL-Mighty; ready, because waiting to be gracious. 'All things are ready' (Matt. 22:4). 'Thou art a God ready to pardon' (Neh. 9:17). 'Thou, Lord, art good, and ready to forgive' (Ps. 86:5). 'The waterman in the boat, who with his hook takes hold of the shore. So in prayer we do not draw the mercy to ourselves, but ourselves to the mercy' (Matthew Henry). The shore is ready for the boatman's hook.

and that we should pray with and for others
'Great stress is laid on the injunction of united prayer. Private devotion is essential to the spiritual life – without it there is no life. But it cannot replace united prayer. Solitary prayer is feeble in comparison with that which rises before the throne, echoed by the hearts of hundreds, and strengthened by the feeling that other aspirations are mingling with our own.... The value and power of public prayer seems chiefly to depend on that mysterious affection of our nature-sympathy' (Robertson).

And for others. 'For whom are we to pray? We are to pray for the whole Church of Christ upon earth; for magistrates and ministers; for ourselves, our brethren, yea, our enemies; and for all sorts of men living, or that shall live hereafter' (Larger Catechism).

'The two blind men did not each of them say for himself, "Have mercy on me;" but both for one another, "Have mercy on us" ' (Matthew Henry).

Uses

1. 'As to the Lord's Prayer, although it be an easy thing to say "Our Father" with the mouth, yet there are very few that can, in the spirit, say

the two first words in that prayer; that is, can call God their Father, as knowing what it is to be born again, and as having experienced that they are begotten of the Spirit of God' (Bunyan).

2. 'with all holy reverence.' 'So it was concluded, since Christiana was the eldest, that she should knock for entrance, and that she should speak to him that did open for the rest.'

3. Calvin commenting on Hezekiah turning his face to the wall in prayer, says: 'The mere attitude, indeed, is immaterial; but it is of very great importance to us, that nothing should be presented to our eyes or senses that would drag us away from prayer, that we may pour out our desires more freely before God. We are naturally unsteady, and easily drawn aside, and therefore we cannot be too diligent in fixing our attention.' This is the rationale of the universal practice of shutting the eyes in prayer. We do so that 'nothing may be presented to our eyes that would drag us away from prayer.'

4. 'What is the last inference from hence? That seeing believers have a Father in heaven, they should never fear wants while they live, nor be afraid to die, since death brings them to heaven, their Father's house' (Flavel).

QUESTION 101

What do we pray for in the first petition?

Answer: In the first petition (which is, Hallowed be thy name[1]) we pray, That God would enable us and others to glorify him in all that whereby he maketh himself known;[2] and that he would dispose all things to his own glory.

Hallowed be thy name

We have already had this word 'hallow' before us in the Fourth Commandment. And it bears the same meaning when it is applied to the name of God as when it is attached to the day of God. In this petition we pray that the name of God may be reverenced and sanctified, praised and glorified by all men, and especially by those who are His children in Christ. In his excellent little article on Sanctification, Cruden says that we may the

1. Matthew 6:9.

2. Psalm 67:2, 3: That thy way may be known upon earth, thy saving health among all nations. Let the people praise thee, O God; let all the people praise thee.

better see what is meant by hallowing God's name, by looking at what is opposite to it; by considering what irreverence and profanity, vain swearing and blasphemy are. We hallow God's name when we feel a holy fear, reverence, and adoration toward Him, and toward it when we read it, or hear it, or ourselves speak it. 'Holy and reverend is His name.'

Cruden's method of seeking a clearer sense of 'hallowed' by considering its opposite is admirably illustrated in what Frederick Robertson says about France: 'A nation may reach the state in which the Eternal Name can be used to point a sentence, or adorn a familiar conversation, and no longer shock the ear with the sound of blasphemy.... For example, in a foreign language, the language of a light and irreligious people, the Eternal Name can be used as a light expletive and conversational ejaculation, and not shock any religious sensibility. You could not do that in English. It would sound like blasphemy to say, in light talk, My God! or, Good God! Your flesh would creep at hearing it.... No marvel we are taught to pray, "Hallowed be Thy name." '

thy name ... all that whereby he maketh himself known

See under the Third Commandment. A name is that word, that written sign or spoken sound, by which any person or thing is know. But from this elementary sense of the word, it rises to mean, as in the text, all whereby God maketh Himself known. As Calvin says: 'God's name is not made up of letters and syllables.' And indeed, our own names are more than a matter of letters and syllables, spoken sounds, or written signs. Our name is ourself, our fame, our worth, our character. We have a good or an evil name. And this principle or nomenclature applies not less but more to the name of God. His name is all that whereby He maketh Himself known. The name of God, accordingly, in this petition, embraces not His Bible names and attributes only, but also every person, providence, ordinance, institution, rite, observance – everything in nature and in grace whereby God speaketh to us and manifesteth Himself. And in offering the petition 'Hallowed be Thy name,' the petitioner asks that the grace of reverence and godly fear should be implanted in all men's hearts and his own. He asks to be protected from a profane and irreverent mind. For a profane mind is the mind of a man who sees God in nothing. It is a mind without reverence, without fear, without humility, without a sense of sin and guilt, and consequently, without any sense of God's existence or nearness either in grace or judgment. A profane mind is a hard, secular, indevout, irreligious mind; and in this prayer, he who offers it aright asks to be saved from the dominion of such an unblest state of mind.

and that he would dispose all things to his own glory
'But though the universal cause made all things for the benefit of some creatures framed by Him, yet hath He made them ultimately for Himself, and God is as universally the final as the efficient cause of His own operation' (Pearson).

' "Hallowed be Thy name" is the top petition in that gospel prayer which Christ taught us.... In "Hallowed by Thy name" the soul desires that itself and all others may give glory to God for all that is due to His name every way, and principally for what His name is.... Some strains of these are attainable in this world' (Goodwin). (See under Question 1.)

Uses

1. 'The necessity of presenting this first petition bespeaks our great disgrace' (Calvin). 'It ought to be noted, that when we pray that God would enable us and others to glorify Him, we impliedly confess that we are unable to do it without His gracious assistance. The utter impotence of fallen man, if left to himself, for any good thought, word, or work, is a truth most clearly taught in the oracles of inspiration' (Green).

2. When we pray that God's name may be hallowed, we thereby promise that we shall, by God's help, so hallow it ourselves. Let us with a purpose set this great duty before ourselves, especially in all acts of worship, public or private. Worship has been largely instituted to create and develop and discipline this grace among God's children. Let us therefore educate ourselves into the habit of never hearing the Divine Name uttered in Scripture or psalm or prayer without lifting up our hearts to Him whose name it is. Let us set the Lord always before us.

QUESTION 102

What do we pray for in the second petition?

Answer: In the second petition (which is, Thy kingdom come[1]) we pray, That Satan's kingdom may be destroyed;[2] and that the kingdom of grace may be advanced,[3] ourselves and others brought into it, and kept in it;[4] and that the kingdom of glory may be hastened.[5]

Thy kingdom come

It is a common saying that experience is the best schoolmaster. And that proverb is proved true even in the present instance, where the scholars are inquiring disciples, and the schoolmaster is the Truth Himself. For there was no lesson among all the lessons that were set the disciples to learn that they approached with a slower heart and a more shut understanding than just this very matter of the coming of the kingdom of God. The kingdom of David was the first stage in the development and manifestation of the kingdom of God on the earth. And in spite of all their Master could say and do, this exhausted and abolished sense was still the sense in which the disciples insisted in offering their daily prayer: 'Our Father which art in heaven...Let the domination of Cæsar be broken, and let the ruined kingdom of David be restored.' But experience taught even those slow-hearted disciples how great a prayer they had all unknown to themselves been uttering when they said, 'Thy kingdom come' (Rom. 8:26, 27).

'No idea comes so markedly into the foreground in the teaching of our Lord, according to the first three Gospels, as that of the kingdom of God or kingdom of heaven, which had been of old foretold by the prophets, and was expected by the contemporaries of Jesus. The gospel which He proclaims is the gospel of the kingdom, and the kingdom itself is a religious-moral institution, which – boundless in extent, and everlasting in duration, in its design to unite, sanctify, and save humanity – embraces heaven and earth' (Oosterzee).

'The kingdom of God among men is nothing else than a restoration to a happy life; or, in other words, it is true and everlasting happiness' (Calvin).

---

1. Matthew 6:10.

2. Psalm 68:1: Let God arise, let his enemies be scattered: let them also that hate him flee before him. Verse 18: Thou hast ascended on high, thou hast led captivity captive.

3. Revelation 12:10, 11: And I heard a loud voice saying in heaven, Now is come salvation, and strength, and the kingdom of our God, and the power of his Christ: for the accuser of our brethren is cast down, which accused them before our God day and night. And they overcame him by the blood of the Lamb, and by the word of their testimony; and they loved not their lives unto the death.

4. 2 Thessalonians 3:1: Finally, brethren, pray for us, that the word of the Lord may have free course, and be glorified, even as it is with you. Romans 10:1: Brethren, my heart's desire and prayer to God for Israel is, that they might be saved. John 17:9: I pray for them: I pray not for the world, but for them which thou hast given me; for they are thine. Verse 20: Neither pray I for these alone, but for them also which shall believe on me through their word.

5. Revelation 22:20: He which testifieth these things saith, Surely I come quickly: Amen. Even so, come, Lord Jesus.

we pray that Satan's kingdom may be destroyed
'His great competitor, Christ, acknowledgeth Satan to have a kingdom (Matt. 12:26). Yea, and he had the start with his kingdom in this world before Christ came into it' (Goodwin).

'But, methinks, I see by this, that Satan will use any means to keep the soul from Christ; he loveth not an awakened frame of spirit: security, blindness, darkness, and error is the very kingdom and habitation of the wicked one' (Bunyan).

The various steps in the destruction of Satan's kingdom in the soul are excellently set forth in Answers 31, 35, and 36.

The kingdom of grace advanced
Paul speaks of the kingdom of God as a reign of grace, and the Catechism here follows his example. The kingdom of grace is advanced with the conversion of every sinner and the sanctification of every believer, and with the spread of the gospel in heathen lands. This clause is fully expanded in the Larger Catechism.

ourselves and others brought into it
We are brought into this kingdom by being born again and effectually called. That was a most startling utterance that Nicodemus, a ruler of the Jews, a prince of the house of David, heard from the lips of David's Son: 'Except a man be born again, he cannot see the kingdom of God' (John 3:3). For this is as much as to say, no antiquity or nobility of descent, no amount of personal worth, no sacramental sealing, no ecclesiastical rank or office, no attainments in sacred learning, and no fulfilment of sacred service – nothing that any man can of himself be or do will admit him into the kingdom of heaven. It is only what God does for him, and in him, that capacitates and enfranchises any man as a citizen of the kingdom of heaven. Art thou a master of Israel, and knowest not these things?

and kept in it
'Holy Father, keep through Thine own name those whom Thou hast given me.... While I was with them in the world, I kept them in Thy name, and none of them is lost.... I pray not that Thou shouldest take them out of the world, but that Thou shouldest keep them from the evil' (John 17:11,12,15).

'Who are kept by the power of God through faith unto salvation, ready to be revealed in the last time' (1 Pet. 1:5).

'I know whom I have believed, and am persuaded that He is able to keep that which I have committed unto Him against that day' (2 Tim. 1:12).

and that the kingdom of glory may be hastened
This is the prayer of those who 'look for that blessed hope, and the glorious appearing of the great God and our Saviour Jesus Christ' (Tit 2:13). They who offer this prayer with the spirit and with the understanding also know as they offer it that God hath appointed the day when that glory shall dawn, and they know that neither prayer nor effort will literally hasten it. But they pray in holy impatience because they are 'looking for and hasting unto the coming of the day of God' (2 Pet. 3:12). 'He which testifieth these things saith, Surely I come quickly. Amen. Even so, come, Lord Jesus' (Rev. 22:20).

Uses
1. There must be many things in the constitution and administration of such a kingdom that the subjects of it cannot comprehend. There must be many counsels between the Father and the Son that we cannot fathom. But it is our loyalty and no small part of our obedience to believe that what we know not now we shall know hereafter. And in every dispensation of His rule the disciples and subjects of Jesus Christ can quiet and comfort their hearts, saying, He is our Lawgiver, He is our King, and He will save us.

2. 'Every man falls either under the kingdom of Christ or under the kingdom of Satan; and we ourselves do this hour, this moment, actually stand members either of the one or of the other; there is not a third kingdom, as there is not a third place to go' (Goodwin).

3. It is the King's command, 'Seek ye first the kingdom of God' (Matt. 6:33). Let then the young seek it first, as Solomon sought first, and before all else, a wise and an understanding heart. Let all, old and young, seek the kingdom of heaven, as the five virgins in the parable of the kingdom sought for the oil; only, let us seek it more wisely and earlier than they. And lest we awake to seek it too late, let us arise and seek it now. Now, while as yet it is said by the King Himself, Knock, and it shall be opened unto you.

4. 'I had great longings for the advancement of Christ's kingdom in the world; and my secret prayers used to be in great part taken up with it. If I heard the least hint of anything that happened in any part of the world, that appeared, in some respect or other, to have a favourable aspect on the interests of Christ's kingdom, my soul eagerly catched at it, and it would much animate and refresh me. I used to be eager to read public news-letters mainly for that end, to see if I could not find some news favourable to the interest of religion in the world' (Edwards).

QUESTION 103

What do we pray for in the third petition?

Answer: In the third petition (which is, Thy will be done in earth, as it is in heaven[1]) we pray, That God, by his grace, would make us able and willing to know, obey, and submit to his will in all things,[2] as the angels do in heaven.[3]

Thy will be done

Connecting the previous Question with the present, Calvin says, 'The most important part of God's kingdom lies in His will being done.' Divines have drawn out the Scripture doctrine of the Divine Will under such heads as His decretive and preceptive, absolute and conditional will. The text deals with God's preceptive will, or, as it has already been termed in the Catechism, His 'revealed will'.

---

1. Matthew 6:10.

2. Psalm 67 throughout. Psalm 119:36: Incline my heart unto thy testimonies, and not to covetousness. Matthew 26:39: And he went a little farther, and fell on his face, and prayed, saying, O my Father, if it be possible, let this cup pass from me: nevertheless, not as I will, but as thou wilt. 2 Samuel 15:25: And the king said unto Zadok, Carry back the ark of God into the city; if I shall find favour in the eyes of the Lord, he will bring me again, and shew me both it and his habitation. Job 1:21: And (Job) said, Naked came I out of my mother's womb, and naked shall I return thither: the Lord gave, and the Lord hath taken away; blessed be the name of the Lord.

3. Psalm 103:20, 21: Bless the Lord, ye his angels, that excel in strength, that do his commandments, hearkening unto the voice of his word. Bless ye the Lord, all ye his hosts; ye ministers of his, that do his pleasure.

by his grace
Larger Catechism, 'by His Spirit.' (See also Answer 20, Shorter Catechism.)

would make us able and willing to know, obey, and submit to his will
God's will is good as God Himself is good, and He desires and commands us to imitate Him in our volitions as well as our actions. But a corruption and curse have fallen upon us, such that we naturally and necessarily will and wish that which is evil. We cannot help it. We may struggle against it, but we struggle in vain. It is the cross of our inner life that our will is so naturally, spontaneously, and unconquerably selfish and proud, inhumane and ungodly. It fills us with guilt and bondage; it wrings from our hearts groanings that cannot be uttered. It is not that we cannot see to the depth of things and to the issue of events. That sometimes causes division of mind and disharmony of will between man and man, and between man and God. But after all allowance is made for limitation of understanding and imperfection of judgment, there remains a terrible mystery of iniquity, an insoluble and inexpugnable mystery of evil in our heart. And it is into our mouth who are thus sin-mastered and sin-tormented that our Lord has put this penitential and submissive prayer.

But apart from this evil opposition to the will of God there is another manner of occasional opposition which gives opportunity for the offering of this filial prayer. Every human will has two kinds of operation, one instinctive and spontaneous, and another instructed and deliberate. Now, the instinctive operations of my will may, without any vice in it or any blame to me, be opposed to the will and purpose of God concerning me. It may be so opposed for a season, yet without sin. It may be so opposed till my better will, my spiritually reinforced and instructed will comes forward to reduce and silence all opposition, and to choose and cause immediate and entire submission. We see all this finely illustrated in our Lord Himself, as the conflicting operations of His will are set before us in the gospel history. His will, acting naturally and instinctively, turned away with deep horror and strong recoil from His coming death, and especially from the curse that in His case accompanied death. But the next moment His nobler will, His will instructed and deliberate, resolved and devoted, put itself with all its weaknesses and fears into His Father's hand. If I may say so, our Lord made a kind of correction and retractation of His first prayer of agony. Nature, oppressed and overwhelmed nature, had the first alarmed and astonied word, but grace and the Sonship soon had the second. The God of grace is first the God of nature, and nature has her dues before Him, her dues which He will not deny. And one of the dearest and most necessary of her dues is just her permission to recoil from and appeal against grace. Let us be ready to imitate and follow Him in both; and if in the recoil appeal of nature, then also in the surrender and victory of faith when our Gethsemane receives us, and our full cup approaches us.

in all things
'We pretend,' says a Puritan preacher, 'to do God's will in the general, but when we come to particulars we stick at it.' It is an excellent and profitable exercise to learn to reduce this large and general petition into its parts and particulars; into the particular drops that fill our cup, and the particular pains produced by our cross.

as the angels do in heaven
'The angels,' says the hundred and third Psalm, 'that excel in strength, do His commandments, hearkening to the voice of His word.' And Dante, who was caught up into the heavenly places, reports to us that he heard the mighty ranks of the angelic and glorified hosts singing,

> As we from step to step
> Are placed throughout this kingdom, pleases all,
> E'en as our King, who in us plants his will;
> And in his will is our tranquillity.

That is to say, there is no rebellion, no disappointment, no discontent, no envy among the angelic hosts. Gabriel and Michael may be summoned into their Sovereign's presence, and taken into His counsels, and sent down to earth on the most glorious of errands, and those who are not so summoned, and trusted, and rewarded, feel no bitterness, and entertain no malice toward their more honoured and promoted brethren. And as God's holy angels are, such are His glorified saints. He in them also plants His will, and in His will is their tranquillity. Each saint occupies and fills, and is occupied and filled with the place prepared for him in his Father's house. They aspire to no higher place than that He appoints them, and they humble themselves to no lower. And it is amid the ambitions, contentions, envies, jealousies, and detractions of this life that we are permitted and enabled to offer our submissive supplic-ations, and say, 'Thy will be done on earth, as it is in heaven.'

'Touching angels which are spirits immaterial and intellectual, the glorious inhabitants of those sacred palaces, where nothing but light and blessed immortality, no shadow of matter for tears, discontentments, griefs, and uncomfortable passions to work upon, but all joy, tranquillity, and peace, even for ever and ever doth dwell: as in number and order they are huge, mighty, and royal armies, so likewise in perfection of obedience unto that law, which the Highest, whom they adore, love, and imitate, hath imposed upon them. Such observants are they thereof, that our Saviour Himself, being to set down the perfect ideal of that which we are to wish and pray for on earth, did not teach to pray or wish for more than only that here it might be with us as with them it is in heaven' (Hooker).

Isaac Walton tells us that when this great divine was on his deathbed, 'Dr. Saravia visited him, and found him deep in contemplation, and not inclined to discourse, which gave the doctor occasion to inquire his present thoughts, to which Hooker replied "that he was meditating the nature and number of angels, and their blessed obedience and order, without which peace could not be in heaven; and oh that it might be so on earth!" '

Uses

1. Robert Traill says, 'Learn to pray moderately and modestly;' and Jeremy Taylor, writing on the same subject, says, 'For spiritual blessings let our prayers be particularly importunate, perpetual, and persevering; for temporal blessings let them be generally short, conditional, and modest.'

2. 'Give up thy ways to God. It is not in man to direct his own steps. It is God that must direct them for thee, for He works all things according to His will. If any man in the world, if his understanding and will were a rule to mine, and I knew he were infallible, I would certainly go give up all my ways to what he saith. As you say you must be ruled by him that bears the purse, so must you be ruled by him that bears the understanding' (Goodwin).

3. 'The firmest hold of theological truth is gained by habits of personal religion. When men begin all their works with the thought of God,

acting for His sake and to fulfil His will, when they ask His blessing on themselves and their life, pray to Him for the objects they desire, and see Him in the event, whether it be according to their prayers or not, they will find that everything that happens tends to confirm them in the truths about Him which live in their imagination, varied and unearthly as those truths may be' (*Grammar of Assent*).

QUESTION 104

What do we pray for in the fourth petition?

Answer: In the fourth (which is, Give us this day our daily bread[1]) we pray, That of God's free gift we may receive a competent portion of the good things in this life, and enjoy his blessing with them.[2]

The fourth petition – 'It is known,' says Archbishop Leighton, 'to be the ordinary course of skilful orators to place the meanest part of their speech in the middle; and in this let the ear of any understanding mind be judge whether it sounds not much better that this request pass in the middle than if the prayer should have ended with it, whereas now it begins spiritually and closes so.'

Give us this day our daily bread

The first step to be taken toward the full understanding of this petition is to ask what exactly it meant in the mouths of the first disciples who offered it. Now, to answer that question we have only to recall the new and peculiar circumstances into which their Master had brought them by the call He had addressed to them, and then to reflect on the extraordinary 'ordination charge' He had subsequently given them. For what is expressly stated of some of the disciples may be assumed concerning every one of the twelve: they had left all and followed Him. And it was to men in that

---

1. Matthew 6:11.

2. Proverbs 30:8, 9: Remove far from me vanity and lies; give me neither poverty nor riches; feed me with food convenient for me: lest I be full, and deny thee, and say, Who is the Lord? or lest I be poor, and steal, and take the name of my God in vain. Genesis 28:20: And Jacob vowed a vow, saying, If God will be with me, and will keep me in this way that I go, and will give me bread to eat, and raiment to put on. 1 Timothy 4:4, 5: For every creature of God is good, and nothing to be refused, if it be received with thanksgiving: For it is sanctified by the word of God and prayer.

impoverished condition that their Master issued this injunction, Provide neither gold, nor silver, nor brass in your purses, but offer this as your daily prayer, Give us this day our daily bread. At His call they had cut themselves off for ever from their wonted means of livelihood, and, as they enter on their new occupation for life – that of preaching the gospel of the kingdom – their Master commands them to cast themselves on this new means of subsistence, on daily and special prayer, and on the fruit of their Messianic labours in the land. But prayer for daily bread does not supersede provident habits. Nothing, indeed, could better bring out the spiritual, and, so to say, elastic nature of our Lord's injunction than the fact that before long we find the little company possessed of a common purse, held in the hand of a recognised purse-bearer, whose duty it was to receive such gifts as were offered to him, to lay them out on buying what was needed by his colleagues, and in relieving such deserving poor as they came across.

a competent portion of the good things of this life

A competent portion is a comparative expression. It varies with the varying circumstances and characters of men. 'Cedars,' said old Ezekiel Hopkins, 'require more sap then shrubs.' By that metaphor he means that what would be straitness and want to one man would be abundance and richness to another. Men of birth, and position, and employment, and opportunity, when they are also men of piety, and offer this prayer, they offer it for far other and far nobler things than wheaten or barley bread. They offer it for all things that are needed to support them in, and equip them for, the eminent life into which God hath lifted them. For deprived of the means of doing their work and fulfilling the duties and opportunities of their office would be to them the taking away of life itself. A cedar may thus stretch forth its branches, seeking showers that would drown and destroy a less noble and less stately tree.

Matthew Henry says that 'Nature is content with little, grace with less, but lust with nothing.' And in another place, 'If you seek first the kingdom of heaven, you shall have food and raiment by way of overplus, as he that buys goods hath paper and packthred given him over and above into the bargain.'

his blessing with them

'The Christian custom of saying grace at meals, after the example of Christ (Matt. 14:19, 15:36), and which prevailed also generally in the ancient Church (Acts 27:35), has a high moral significancy; it rescues the natural enjoyments from the stage of mere sensuousness, and elevates it into the sphere of the moral' (Wuttke).

Note

The original word here rendered daily is a remarkable word. Remarkable in this respect, that it occurs but once in all the New Testament, and the most careful search has failed to discover it in any other Greek writing. How then can we be sure what it means? For we usually arrive at the meaning of a word in one passage by studying its use in other passages. But how are we to know what a particular word means when it is used but once in all the language in which it is found? There is, indeed, another way of coming at the meaing of a word, and that way is by searching out its etymology, and interrogating the root from which it springs. But here, too, our best scholarship is at fault; for learned men are not agreed as to the parentage of this singular and isolated word. At the same time, from the context, from the analogy of Scripture, and other things, the vast majority of translators and commentators have come to render this unique term by the familiar word 'daily'. They believe that our Lord meant simply, in the first intention at any rate, daily bread for the bodily life of His detached and itinerant disciples. At the same time, no man with much of the mind and spirit of Christ in him will be content, in offering this prayer, to limit himself to bread baked in any earthly oven. No spiritual man, however scrupulously and jealously grammatical he may be in his interpretation of the written word, could read this petition in Scripture or offer it in public or private prayer without far other bread coming up before his mind than simply the bread needful for the body. Jerome, the great translator of the Bible, was so impressed with the spiritual bearing of this petition, that he rendered it super-substantial or transcendental bread. And with such passages before him as Deuteronomy 8:3, Job 23:12, Jeremiah 15:16, Matthew 4:4, John 4:8, 31-34, 6:35, 51, he is not to be blamed for leaning in his version to the mystical and spiritual interpretation.

Uses

1. What is the first inference? That we seek not great matters for ourselves, neither make them the matter of prayer to God, nor the end and design of our labours and callings among men.

2. What is the second inference from hence? That having food and raiment, we must therewith be content and be thankful.

3. What is the third inference? That we ascribe not our success in the world to our own skill and industry – for the wisest and most industrious do sometimes labour in the fire, and put their gains in a bag of holes – but to God's free donation to us, and to His blessing upon our endeavours (Flavel).

QUESTION 105

What do we pray for in the fifth petition?

Answer: In the fifth petition (which is, And forgive us our debts, as we forgive our debtors[1]) we pray, That God, for Christ's sake, would freely pardon all our sins;[2] which we are the rather encouraged to ask, because by his grace we are enabled from the heart to forgive others.[3]

Forgive us our debts, as we forgive our debtors

'We have now done with the supplications of this prayer, and are come to the deprecations. The supplications are those petitions which we make to God for obtaining of that which is good. The deprecations are those petitions we make to God for removing of that which is evil' (Manton).

Debt is one of a 'mournfully numerous group' of names that are applied to human sin and guilt in the word of God. This is one of the least odious and loathsome of those evil names, but it has a sufficiently solemn sense of its own. Debt is that which we owe; it is that which is due; it is that which lays one man under obligation and liability to another. A debt may be expressed and described in terms of money, or service, or suffering, but its ruling idea is always that of obligation and liability. Only, in the

1. Matthew 6:12.

2. Psalm 51:1, 2: Have mercy upon me, O God, according to thy loving-kindness; according unto the multitude of thy tender mercies blot out my transgressions. Wash me throughly from mine iniquity, and cleanse me from my sin. Verse 7: Purge me with hyssop, and I shall be clean; wash me, and I shall be whiter than snow. Verse 9: Hide thy face from my sins, and blot out all mine iniquities. Daniel 9:17-19.

3. Luke 11:4: And forgive us our sins; for we also forgive every one that is indebted to us. Matthew 18:35: So likewise shall my heavenly Father do also unto you, if ye from your hearts forgive not every one his brother their trespasses.

present case, we must exclude from our definition of debt all associations connected with monetary or commercial transaction. The liability here is of a far other and more awful kind than that which is connected with any earthly merchandise or exchange. The debts we have to do with here are those we all owe to the divine law and justice.

'The faults or sins we are guilty of oblige us and bind us to punishment; and therefore sins are called debts. The original debt we owe is obedience; and, in case of default, the next debt we owe is punishment' (Manton).

'*Q.* Wherefore are sins called debts? *A.* Because they are a non-payment of God's dues, a non-performance of our duty, which makes us liable to the arrest of death, and to the prison of hell' (Flavel's Catechism).

we pray that God, for Christ's sake

It will be seen that the Catechism borrows from later and fuller Scriptures, and imports into its text a clause that is not found in either of the original versions of the Lord's Prayer. 'For Christ's sake' is a scriptural and necessary addition to all our prayers, but it had not as yet taken its place in any prayer offered during our Lord's earthly lifetime.

'The Lord's Prayer does not end, as our prayers now commonly do, with the formula, "for Christ's sake;" nor could it. No prayer given by Him for the present use of His disciples before His death could have such an ending, because the plea it contains was not intelligible to them previous to that event. The disciples did not yet know what Christ's sake meant, nor would they till after their Lord had ascended, and the Spirit had descended and revealed to them the true meaning of the facts of Christ's earthly history' (A. B. Bruce). (See John 16:24, 14:6; Rom. 5:2; Eph. 4:32.)

On 2 Corinthians 13:14, Bengel says, 'Christ is mentioned in the first place, because it is by the grace of Christ we come to the Father.'

freely pardon all our sins

See Answer 33 and notes. In considering God's promises to forgive sins, Donne asks, 'Does He mean all my sins? He knows what original sin is, and I do not; and will He forgive me sins in that root, and sin in the branches too? He knows my secret sins, and I do not; will He forgive my manifest sins and those too? He knows my relapses into sins repented of; and will He forgive my faint relapses, and my rebellious relapses after them? Will His mercy dive into my heart, and forgive my sinful thoughts there, and shed itself upon my lips, and forgive my blasphemous words there, and bathe the members of my body, and forgive my unclean actions there? Will He forgive that dim sight which I have of sins now, when sins scarce appear to be sins unto me; and will He forgive that overquick sight when I shall see my sins through Satan's multiplying glass of desperation, when I shall see them greater than His mercy on my death-bed?'

'The forgiveness that there is with God is not like that narrow, difficult, halving, and manacled forgiveness that is found among men; but it is full, free, bottomless, boundless, absolute, such as becomes His nature and His excellencies' (Owen).

which we are the rather encouraged to ask

If pardon is impossible to the implacable man (Matt. 6:15, 18:35; Jas. 2:13), on the other hand this 'terrible petition' becomes a positive ground of assurance to the meek and loving and forgiving heart. The forgiveness of our enemies is nowhere set forth as the ground of any sinner's acceptance before God, but it is often set forth, and may be relied on as a most valid ground of assurance of acceptance. The cross of Jesus Christ is the only door open to us out of our estate of guilt and alienation; but if something of that mind that was found in Christ on the cross when He prayed for His murderers is found in us, then that mind is a little wicket-gate that opens under the great gate of the cross through which a too diffident mind may find some little liberty of access. Calvin says that the consciousness of possessing a forgiving spirit is a sort of seal that God sets to our own hope of forgiveness. 'The Spirit itself beareth witness with our spirit that we are the children of God.'

from the heart to forgive others

Augustine somewhere calls this a 'terrible petition', and when we sufficiently think of it we feel that he is right. For do I not ask a terrible thing when I ask God to do to me as I do to my most evil neighbour and most hurtful enemy? Augustus Hare, in his *Sermons to a Country Congregation*, has expanded this idea of Augustine's into what he calls 'The Revengeful Man's Prayer.' Those who possess the book will do well to read that prayer and try to offer it, and those who cannot read it may not less profitably imagine it for themselves.

'This condition is added, that no one may presume to approach God and ask forgiveness, who is not pure and free from all resentment.... And certainly, if the Spirit of God reigns in our hearts, every description of revenge and ill-will ought to be banished. The Spirit is the witness of our adoption, and therefore this is simply put down as a mark to distinguish the children of God from strangers' (Calvin).

'Shall I send you to the old saying which contains as much mercy and as much wisdom as was ever put by man into three words? – the saying, Forgive and forget. Forgiving and forgetting is the pardon which we desire from God; therefore, forgiving and forgetting is the pardon which we are to grant to man' (Hare).

Uses

1. 'This injunction has ever been a stumbling-block in the way of the advocates of perfection, from Pelagius to the present day. For not only do the holy men of God throughout the Scriptures, in coming into His presence, come always with the confession of sin and imperfections, praying for mercy, but our Lord has taught all His disciples, whenever they address their Father in heaven, to say, Forgive us our trespasses' (Hodge).

2. 'Here is a ground of trial whether we are pardoned or no: Is our revengeful disposition, that is so natural and so pleasing to us, mortified? That is one trial or evidence whether we are forgiven of God; can we freely, from the heart, forgive others?' (Manton).

3. We must be very watchful and scrupulous to cleanse our hearts of all anger and hatred and malice and desire for revenge. We must cast all men's insults and injuries into the depths of the sea. We must be not less anxious to wash out of our hearts every stain that our enemies have left there, than we are that our sins may be blotted out of God's remembrance book. Nor must we be content with freely and fully forgiving our enemies; we must wish them well, and befriend them when we have opportunity. And when we have no opportunity, we must make it, if we would do to our enemies as God did to His. For God made opportunities to forgive and favour and befriend us. He saw there was no man, and He wondered there was no intercessor; therefore His arm brought salvation, and His righteousness it sustained Him.

QUESTION 106

What do we pray for in the sixth petition?

> *Answer: In the sixth petition (which is, And lead us not into temptation, but deliver us from evil*[1]*) we pray, That God would either keep us from being tempted to sin,*[2] *or support and deliver us when we are tempted.*[3]

Lead us not into temptation

The familiar word 'temptation' is used in two very different senses in Holy Scripture. For example, in the twenty-second chapter of the Book of Genesis we read that 'God did tempt Abraham' (Gen. 22:1); and again, in the Epistle of James we find it written, 'My brethren, count it all joy when ye fall into divers temptations' (Jas. 1:2). In both these passages the word temptation is employed in what may be called its good sense. Temptation in this sense has for its end and object the testing and manifestation of spiritual strength and moral integrity, that but for the temptation would neither be exercised nor exhibited. The furnace tests or tempts the true gold. The storm tests or tempts the rooted tree. And 'divers temptations' test and strengthen the faithful and patient soul, making it perfect and entire, wanting nothing.

But the evil sense of temptation is the more familiar sense in the word of God. And this is the sense of the word in the text. Dr. John Owen, in his treatise *Of Temptation*, thus defines temptation in its evil sense: 'Temptation is any thing, state, way, or condition that, upon any account whatever, hath a force or efficacy to seduce or draw the mind and heart of a man from its obedience, which God requires of him, into any sin, in any degree of it whatever.'

A temptation, then, may be good or evil, may be for salvation or destruction, according to circumstances, according to the intention with which it is sent, and according to the spirit in which it is met. A temptation may lead the unwary soul into the chambers of death, or it may put a man in the way of gaining for himself the crown of eternal life. A tempted man may come out of his temptations a stronger, holier, hap-

---

1. Matthew 6:13.

2. Matthew 26:41: Watch and pray, that ye enter not into temptation: the spirit indeed is willing, but the flesh is weak.

3. 2 Corinthians 12:8: For this thing I besought the Lord thrice, that it might depart from me.

pier man; in Job's words, when he is tried he may come forth like gold; or, on the other hand, he may 'crumble to dust beneath the tempter's dart'; he may come forth of the refiner's fire like reprobate silver. And it is just because weak and corrupt men come, for the most part, so ill out of their temptations, that they are taught to make it their daily prayer, 'lead us not into temptation' (Matt. 6:13).

but deliver us from evil

'The last words are, as it were, exegetical.' There are two exegetical questions that have been debated from the beginning about this clause in the Lord's Prayer. Is this clause to be taken as a separate and additional petition? Is this a seventh and different petition? or is it only another way of repeating the sixth – an antithetical way of repeating what has already been said, 'lead us not into temptation, but deliver us from evil'? That is the first question raised about this clause, and the second is this: Ought the original to be translated from evil, or from the Evil One? This question has of late been brought into great prominence by the publication of the Revised Version, and among the learned productions that the late revision of the New Testament has called forth, this proposed reading has been fully dealt with.

keep us from being tempted to sin, or support and deliver us when we are tempted

Every temptation has its times, and runs its course. There is a season, short or long, when the trangression is still a temptation. There is a time when, if it is not exactly easy to resist the temptation, it is at least possible to do so. For as Thomas à Kempis, a great master in the things of the soul, says, 'There first cometh to the mind a bare thought of evil, then a strong imagination thereof, afterwards delight and an evil motion, and then consent.' He, then, who offers this prayer must keep a sleepless watch over his thoughts. He must beware of those times, and places, and states of mind in which evil thoughts intrude themselves. And he will soon learn by experience that a vacant mind and an idle life is a very door of temptation. A busy life, by God's blessing, is a safe life. Curiosity concerning evil and forbidden things is a cause of many temptations assailing the soul. It is impossible to quench such sinful curiosity in a human heart; and unhappily, once learned, the knowledge of sin is a knowledge that is never forgotten. Times of reaction also, times of isolation and mental depression, are often times when it is most difficult to keep temptation out of the heart. Loneliness, also, supplies a vantage ground to temptation.

Now it is just at such times as these that our Lord encourages us to look up and offer the prayer, Lead us not into temptation, or, Support and deliver us when we are tempted. And this God sometimes does by means of providential interpositions, of which every gracious heart has many records. Sometimes, again, He suddenly chills the heart against the offered evil, or draws the soul into the secret of His pavilion till the storm of temptation is wholly overpast.

Uses

1. 'Temptations, when we meet them first, are as the lion that roared upon Samson; but if we overcome them, the next time we see them we shall find a nest of honey within them' (Bunyan).

2. 'What is meant by evil? Some understand it of the devil, but the best meaning is sin, which is the worst of evils, and makes the devil evil, and is the worst of evils the devil can bring upon us, and is usually so understood in Scripture' (Flavel).

3. 'When you have conceived sin, hath God weakened your power for sin, or denied you opportunity, or taken away the object of your lusts, or diverted your thoughts by new providences? Know assuredly that you have received grace thereby.... Had not God thus dealt with you, it may be this day you had been a terror to yourselves, a shame to your relations, and under the punishment due to notorious sins' (Owen).

QUESTION 107

What doth the conclusion of the Lord's prayer teach us?

Answer: The conclusion of the Lord's prayer (which is, For thine is the kingdom, and the power, and the glory, for ever, Amen[1]*) teacheth us to take our encouragement in prayer from God only,*[2] *and in our prayers to praise him, ascribing kingdom, power, and glory to him,*[3] *And, in testimony of our desire, and assurance to be heard, we say, Amen.*[4]

---

1. Matthew 6:13.

For thine is the kingdom

The conjunction *for* grounds the whole prayer on the fact that the kingdom prayed for in the second petition is God's kingdom, and the power put forth in it, and petitioned to be put forth in this prayer is God's power, and is and will be all the glory. All this is put forward as a sufficient and final reason why the petitioner should be heard. The full and final New Testament ground of a Christian prayer is the name and merits and mediation of Jesus Christ; but this prayer was taught by our Lord before the time had come to ask in His name. But no Christian can now offer this or any prayer without putting forward the Lord Jesus as his alone ground an argument with the Father.

to take our encouragement in prayer from God only

'The knowledge of our own unworthiness is not without belief in the merits of Christ. With that true fear which the one causeth there is coupled true boldness, and encouragement drawn from the other. The very silence that our unworthiness putteth us into, doth itself make request for us, and that in the confidence of His grace. Looking inward we are stricken dumb; looking upward we speak and prevail' (Hooker).

in our prayers to praise him

'Faith, self-denial, a holy life, patient endurance of the cross, are all sacrifices which please God. But as prayer is the offering of faith, and uniformly accompanied with patience and mortification of sin, while praise, where it is genuine, indicates holiness of heart, we need not wonder that these two points of worship should here be employed to represent the whole' (Calvin).

'Thanksgiving is a nobler and more divinely generous duty than prayer, for self-love puts us upon praying for benefits; but thanks is a more free and pure act' (Goodwin).

---

2. Daniel 9:4-19.

3. 1 Chronicles 29:10-13: Thine, O Lord, is the greatness, and the power, and the glory, and the victory, and the majesty: for all that is in the heaven and in the earth is thine; thine is the kingdom, O Lord, and thou art exalted as head above all.

4. 1 Corinthians 14:16: Else, when thou shalt bless with the spirit, how shall he that occupieth the room of the unlearned say Amen at thy giving of thanks, seeing he understandeth not what thou sayest? Revelation 22:20, 21: He which testifieth these things saith, Surely I come quickly. Amen. Even so, come, Lord Jesus. The grace of our Lord Jesus Christ be with you all. Amen.

There was a rabbinical saying to the effect that in the days of the Messiah all prayer shall cease, but thanksgiving shall not cease; all oblations shall cease, but the eucharistical oblation shall not cease.

in testimony of our desire, and assurance to be heard, we say, Amen
The Hebrew idiom rendered literally in the margin of James 5:17, brings out finely the force of the prophet's desire. And it suggests to us to inquire whether we pray in our prayers. Desire is the life and power of prayer. The assurance of this passage is not the assurance of Answer 36. There it is the assurance of our personal acceptance and adoption, here it is the assurance that what we ask we shall receive, because God has so promised. This is 'the full assurance of faith' set forth in Hebrews 10:22. And Amen correctly understood and rightly used, expresses, as the text teaches, both our desire to be heard, and our assurance that we shall be heard.

'The short word with which the person spoken to answered all adjurations, was the familiar amén, a little word which properly corresponds only to our yes! and which subsequently found the most diverse applications, but which, in the use here explained, goes back to the earliest times of the community' (Ewald).

Amen is a Hebrew word transliterated and naturalized into English, which when translated means true, faithful, trustworthy. It was transliterated also into the language spoken by our Lord, and we find Him constantly using the word as a formula for introducing His more weighty and solemn utterances. Amen, Amen; verily, verily, I say unto you. In the Epistle to Laodicea, our Lord takes to Himself the name of Amen, the faithful and true Witness; and in the Second Epistle to the Corinthians, the apostle says that all the promises of God are in His Son Jesus Christ, Yea, and Amen. Augustine says that when this word is found on the lips of the faithful, it is their seal and consent to all that has been spoken. And Jerome says, 'It is the seal of our consent.' 'Faith has its silence to lend an ear to the word of God. It has afterwards its turn to speak and answer Amen, according to that passage, Hosea 2:23' (Calvin). Sometimes the word is used among ourselves in a secondary and conventional sense, as if it meant a conclusion, but this is a loose use of the word, which is never so employed in Scripture.

The Westminster Confession of Faith

CHAPTER I. ***Of the Holy Scripture.***

I. Although the light of nature, and the works of creation and providence, do so far manifest the goodness, wisdom, and power of God, as to leave men inexcusable; yet are they not sufficient to give that knowledge of God, and of his will, which is necessary unto salvation; therefore it pleased the Lord, at sundry times, and in divers manners, to reveal himself, and to declare that his will unto his Church; and afterwards for the better preserving and propagating of the truth, and for the more sure establishment and comfort of the Church against the corruption of the flesh, and the malice of Satan and of the world, to commit the same wholly unto writing; which maketh the holy Scripture to be most necessary; those former ways of God's revealing his will unto his people being now ceased.

II. Under the name of holy Scripture, or the Word of God written, are now contained all the Books of the Old and New Testament, which are these:

Of the Old Testament: Genesis, Exodus, Leviticus, Numbers, Deuteronomy, Joshua, Judges, Ruth, 1 Samuel, 2 Samuel, 1 Kings, 2 Kings, 1 Chronicles, 2 Chronicles, Ezra, Nehemiah, Esther, Job, Psalms, Proverbs, Ecclesiastes, The Song of Songs, Isaiah, Jeremiah, Lamentations, Ezekiel, Daniel, Hosea, Joel, Amos, Obadiah, Jonah, Micah, Nahum, Habakkuk, Zephaniah, Haggai, Zechariah, Malachi.

Of the New Testament: The Gospels according to Matthew, Mark, Luke, John; The Acts of the Apostles, Paul's Epistles to the Romans, 1 Corinthians, 2 Corinthians, Galatians, Ephesians, Philippians, Colossians, Philemon, 1 Thessalonians, 2 Thessalonians, 1 Timothy, 2 Timothy, Titus, Philemon, The Epistle to the Hebrews, The Epistle of James, The First and Second Epistles of Peter, The First, Second, and Third Epistles of John, The Epistle of Jude, The Revelation.

All which are given by inspiration of God, to be the rule of faith and life.

III. The books commonly called Apocrypha, not being of divine inspiration, are no part of the canon of the Scripture; and therefore are of no authority in the Church of God, nor to be any otherwise approved, or made use of, than other human writings.

IV. The authority of the holy Scripture, for which it ought to be believed and obeyed, dependeth not upon the testimony of any man or Church, but wholly upon God (who is truth itself), the Author thereof; and therefore it is to be received, because it is the Word of God.

V. We may be moved and induced by the testimony of the Church to an high and reverent esteem of the holy Scripture; and the heavenliness of the matter, the efficacy of the doctrine, the majesty of the style, the consent of all the parts, the scope of the whole (which is to give all glory to God), the full discovery it makes of the only way of man's salvation, the many other incomparable excellencies, and the entire perfection thereof, are arguments whereby it doth abundantly evidence itself to be the Word of God; yet, notwithstanding, our full persuasion and assurance of the infallible truth and divine authority thereof, is from the inward work of the Holy Spirit, bearing witness by and with the Word in our hearts.

VI. The whole counsel of God, concerning all things necessary for his own glory, man's salvation, faith, and life, is either expressly set down in Scripture, or by good and necessary consequence may be deduced from Scripture: unto which nothing at any time is to be added, whether by new revelations of the Spirit, or traditions of men. Nevertheless we acknowledge the inward illumination of the Spirit of God to be necessary for the saving understanding of such things as are revealed in the Word; and that there are some circumstances concerning the worship of God, and the government of the Church, common to human actions and societies, which are to be ordered by the light of nature and Christian prudence, according to the general rules of the Word, which are always to be observed.

VII. All things in Scripture are not alike plain in themselves, nor alike clear unto all; yet those things which are necessary to be known, believed, and observed, for salvation, are so clearly propounded and opened in some place of Scripture or other, that not only the learned, but the unlearned, in a due use of the ordinary means, may attain unto a sufficient understanding of them.

VIII. The Old Testament in Hebrew (which was the native language of the people of God of old), and the New Testament in Greek (which at the time of the writing of it was most generally known to the nations), being immediately inspired by God, and by his singular care and providence kept pure in all ages, are therefore authentical; so as in all controversies of religion the Church is finally to appeal unto them. But because these original tongues are not known to all the people of God who have right unto, and interest in, the Scriptures, and are commanded, in the fear of God, to read and search them, therefore they are to be translated into the language of every people unto which they come, that the Word of God dwelling plentifully in all, they may worship him in an acceptable manner, and, through patience and comfort of the Scriptures, may have hope.

IX. The infallible rule of interpretation of Scripture, is the Scripture itself; and therefore, when there is a question about the true and full sense of any scripture (which is not manifold, but one), it must be searched and known by other places that speak more clearly.

X. The Supreme Judge, by which all controversies of religion are to be determined, and all decrees of councils, opinions of ancient writers, doctrines of men, and private spirits, are to be examined, and in whose sentence we are to rest, can be no other but the Holy Spirit speaking in the Scripture.

CHAPTER II. ***Of God, and of the Holy Trinity.***

I. There is but one only living and true God, who is infinite in being and perfection, a most pure spirit, invisible, without body, parts, or passions, immutable, immense, eternal, incomprehensible, almighty, most wise, most holy, most free, most absolute, working all things according to the counsel of his own immutable and most righteous will, for his own glory, most loving, gracious, merciful, long-suffering, abundant in goodness and truth, forgiving iniquity, transgression, and sin; the rewarder of them that diligently seek him; and withal most just and terrible in his judgments; hating all sin; and who will by no means clear the guilty.

II. God hath all life, glory, goodness, blessedness, in and of himself; and is alone in and unto himself all-sufficient, not standing in need of any creatures which he hath made, nor deriving any glory from them, but only manifesting his own glory in, by, unto, and upon them; he is the alone foundation of all being, of whom, through whom, and to whom, are all things; and hath most sovereign dominion over them, to do by them, for them, or upon them, whatsoever himself pleaseth. In his sight all things are open and manifest; his knowledge is infinite, infallible, and independent upon the creature; so as nothing is to him contingent or uncertain. He is most holy in all his counsels, in all his works, and in all his commands. To him is due from angels and men, and every other creature, whatsoever worship, service, or obedience he is pleased to require of them.

III. In the unity of the Godhead there be three Persons of one substance, power, and eternity: God the Father, God the Son, and God the Holy Ghost. The Father is of none, neither begotten nor proceeding; the Son is eternally begotten of the Father; the Holy Ghost eternally proceeding from the Father and the Son.

CHAPTER III. ***Of God's Eternal Decree.***

I. God from all eternity did by the most wise and holy counsel of his own will, freely and unchangeably ordain whatsoever comes to pass; yet so as thereby neither is God the author of sin; nor is violence offered to the will of the creatures, nor is the liberty or contingency of second causes taken away, but rather established.

II. Although God knows whatsoever may or can come to pass, upon all supposed conditions; yet hath he not decreed any thing because he foresaw it as future, or as that which would come to pass, upon such conditions.

III. By the decree of God, for the manifestation of his glory, some men and angels are predestinated unto everlasting life, and others foreordained to everlasting death.

IV. These angels and men, thus predestinated and foreordained, are particularly and unchangeably designed; and their number is so certain and definite that it cannot be either increased or diminished.

V. Those of mankind that are predestinated unto life, God, before the foundation of the world was laid, according to his eternal and immutable purpose, and the secret counsel and good pleasure of his will, hath chosen in Christ, unto everlasting glory, out of his free grace and love alone, without any foresight of faith or good works, or perseverance in either of them, or any other thing in the creature, as conditions, or causes moving him thereunto; and all to the praise of his glorious grace.

VI. As God hath appointed the elect unto glory, so hath he, by the eternal and most free purpose of his will, foreordained all the means thereunto. Wherefore they who are elected being fallen in Adam are redeemed by Christ, are effectually called unto faith in Christ by his Spirit working in due season; are justified, adopted, sanctified, and kept by his power through faith unto salvation. Neither are any other redeemed by Christ, effectually called, justified, adopted, sanctified, and saved, but the elect only.

VII. The rest of mankind, God was pleased, according to the unsearchable counsel of his own will, whereby he extendeth or withholdeth mercy as he pleaseth, for the glory of his sovereign power over his creatures, to pass by, and to ordain them to dishonour and wrath for their sin, to the praise of his glorious justice.

VIII. The doctrine of this high mystery of predestination is to be handled with special prudence and care, that men attending the will of God revealed in his Word, and yielding obedience thereunto, may, from the certainty of their effectual vocation, be assured of their eternal election. So shall this doctrine afford matter of praise, reverence, and admiration of God; and of humility, diligence, and abundant consolation to all that sincerely obey the gospel.

CHAPTER IV. ***Of Creation.***

I. It pleased God the Father, Son, and Holy Ghost, for the manifestation of the glory of his eternal power, wisdom, and goodness, in the beginning, to create or make of nothing the world, and all things therein, whether visible or invisible, in the space of six days, and all very good.

II. After God had made all other creatures, he created man, male and female, with reasonable and immortal souls, endued with knowledge, righteousness, and true holiness after his own image, having the law of God written in their hearts, and power to fulfil it; and yet under a possibility of transgressing, being left to the liberty of their own will, which was subject unto change. Beside this law written in their hearts, they received a command not to eat of the tree of the knowledge of good and evil; which while they kept were happy in their communion with God, and had dominion over the creatures.

CHAPTER V. **Of Providence.**

I. God, the great Creator of all things, doth uphold, direct, dispose, and govern all creatures, actions, and things, from the greatest even to the least, by his most wise and holy providence, according to his infallible foreknowledge, and the free and immutable counsel of his own will, to the praise of the glory of his wisdom, power, justice, goodness, and mercy.

II. Although in relation to the foreknowledge and decree of God, the first cause, all things come to pass immutably and infallibly, yet, by the same providence, he ordereth them to fall out according to the nature of second causes, either necessarily, freely, or contingently.

III. God, in his ordinary providence, maketh use of means, yet is free to work without, above, and against them, at his pleasure.

IV. The almighty power, unsearchable wisdom, and infinite goodness of God, so far manifest themselves in his providence, that it extendeth itself even to the first Fall, and all other sins of angels and men, and that not by a bare permission, but such as hath joined with it a most wise and powerful bounding, and otherwise ordering and governing of them, in a manifold dispensation, to his own holy ends; yet so, as the sinfulness thereof proceedeth only from the creature, and not from God; who being most holy and righteous, neither is nor can be the author or approver of sin.

V. The most wise, righteous, and gracious God, doth oftentimes leave for a season his own children to manifold temptations and the corruption of their own hearts, to chastise them for their former sins, or to discover unto them the hidden strength of corruption and deceitfulness of their hearts, that they may be humbled; and to raise them to a more close and constant dependence for their support upon himself, and to make them more watchful against all future occasions of sin, and for sundry other just and holy ends.

VI. As for those wicked and ungodly men whom God, as a righteous judge, for former sins, doth blind and harden; from them he not only withholdeth his grace, whereby they might have been enlightened in their understandings, and wrought upon their hearts; but sometimes also withdraweth the gifts which they had; and exposeth them to such objects as their corruption makes occasion of sin; and withal, gives them over to their own lusts, the temptations of the world, and the power of Satan; whereby it comes to pass that they harden themselves, even under those means which God useth for the softening of others.

VII. As the providence of God doth, in general, reach to all creatures, so, after a most special manner, it taketh care of his church, and disposeth all things to the good thereof.

CHAPTER VI. ***Of the Fall of Man, of Sin, and of the Punishment thereof.***

I. Our first parents, begin seduced by the subtilty and temptation of Satan, sinned in eating the forbidden fruit. This their sin God was pleased, according to his wise and holy counsel, to permit, having purposed to order it to his own glory.

II. By this sin they fell from their original righteousness and communion with God, and so became dead in sin, and wholly defiled in all the faculties and parts of soul and body.

III. They being the root of mankind, the guilt of this sin was imputed, and the same death in sin and corrupted nature conveyed to all their posterity, descending from them by original generation.

IV. From this original corruption, whereby we are utterly indisposed, disabled, and made opposite to all good, and wholly inclined to all evil, do proceed all actual transgressions.

V. This corruption of nature, during this life, doth remain in those that are regenerated; and although it be through Christ pardoned and mortified, yet both itself, and all the motions thereof, are truly and properly sin.

VI. Every sin, both original and actual, being a transgression of the righteous law of God, and contrary thereunto, doth, in its own nature, bring guilt upon the sinner, whereby he is bound over to the wrath of God, and curse of the law, and so made subject to death, with all miseries spiritual, temporal, and eternal.

CHAPTER VII ***Of God's Covenant with Man.***

I. The distance between God and the creature is so great, that although reasonable creatures do owe obedience unto him as their Creator, yet they could never have any fruition of him, as their blessedness and reward, but by some voluntary condescension on God's part, which he hath been pleased to express by way of covenant.

II. The first covenant made with man was a covenant of works, wherein life was promised to Adam, and in him to his posterity, upon condition of perfect and personal obedience.

III. Man by his fall having made himself incapable of life by that covenant, the Lord was pleased to make a second, commonly called the covenant of grace: wherein he freely offered unto sinners life and salvation by Jesus Christ, requiring of them faith in him, that they may be saved, and promising to give unto all those that are ordained unto life, his Holy Spirit, to make them willing and able to believe.

IV. This covenant of grace is frequently set forth in the Scripture by the name of a testament, in reference to the death of Jesus Christ, the testator, and to the everlasting inheritance, with all things belonging to it, therein bequeathed.

V. This covenant was differently administered in the time of the law, and in the time of the gospel: under the law it was administered by promises, prophecies, sacrifices, circumcision, the paschal lamb, and other types and ordinances delivered to the people of the Jews, all fore-signifying Christ to come, which were for that time sufficient and efficacious, through the operation of the Spirit, to instruct and build up the elect in faith in the promised Messiah, by whom they had full remission of sins, and eternal salvation, and is called the Old Testament.

VI. Under the gospel, when Christ the substance was exhibited, the ordinances in which this covenant is dispensed, are the preaching of the Word, and the administration of the sacraments of Baptism and the Lord's Supper; which, though fewer in number, and administered with more simplicity and less outward glory, yet in them it is held forth in more fulness, evidence, and spiritual efficacy, to all nations, both Jews and Gentiles; and is called the New Testament. There are not, therefore, two covenants of grace differing in substance, but one and the same under various dispensations.

CHAPTER VIII. ***Of Christ the Mediator.***

I. It pleased God, in his eternal purpose, to choose and ordain the Lord Jesus, his only-begotten Son, to be the Mediator between God and men, the Prophet, Priest, and King; the Head and Saviour of his church, the Heir of all things, and Judge of the world; unto whom he did, from all eternity, give a people to be his seed, and to be by him in time redeemed, called, justified, sanctified, and glorified.

II. The Son of God, the second Person in the Trinity, being very and eternal God, of one substance, and equal with the Father, did, when the fulness of time was come, take upon him man's nature, with all the essential properties and common infirmities thereof; yet without sin: being conceived by the power of the Holy Ghost, in the womb of the Virgin Mary, of her substance. So that two whole, perfect, and distinct natures, the Godhead and the manhood, were inseparably joined together in one person, without conversion, composition, or confusion. Which person is very God and very man, yet one Christ, the only Mediator between God and man.

III. The Lord Jesus in his human nature thus united to the divine, was sanctified and anointed with the Holy Spirit above measure; having in him all the treasures of wisdom and knowledge, in whom it pleased the Father that all fulness should dwell: to the end that being holy, harmless, undefiled, and full of grace and truth, he might be thoroughly furnished to execute the office of a Mediator and Surety. Which office he took not unto himself, but was thereunto called by his Father; who put all power and judgment into his hand, and gave him commandment to execute the same.

IV. This office the Lord Jesus did most willingly undertake, which that he might discharge, he was made under the law, and did perfectly fulfil it; endured most grievous torments immediately in his soul, and most painful sufferings in his body; was crucified and died; was buried, and remained under the power of death, yet saw no corruption. On the third day he arose from the dead, with the same body in which he suffered; with which also he ascended into heaven, and there sitteth at the right hand of his Father, making intercession; and shall return to judge men and angels, at the end of the world.

V. The Lord Jesus, by his perfect obedience and sacrifice of himself, which he through the eternal Spirit once offered up unto God, hath fully satisfied the justice of his Father; and purchased not only reconciliation, but an everlasting inheritance in the kingdom of heaven, for all those whom the Father hath given unto him.

VI. Although the work of redemption was not actually wrought by Christ till after his incarnation, yet the virtue, efficacy, and benefits thereof were communicated unto the elect, in all ages successively from the beginning of the world, in and by those promises, types, and sacrifices, wherein he was revealed, and signified to be the seed of the woman which should bruise the serpent's head; and the Lamb slain from the beginning of the world, being yesterday and today the same, and for ever.

VII. Christ, in the work of mediation, acteth according to both natures; by each nature doing that which is proper to itself; yet by reason of the unity of the person, that which is proper to one nature is sometimes, in Scripture, attributed to the person denominated by the other nature.

VIII. To all those for whom Christ hath purchased redemption, he doth certainly and effectually apply and communicate the same; making intercession for them, and revealing unto them, in and by the Word, the mysteries of salvation; effectually persuading them by his Spirit to believe and obey; and governing their hearts by his Word and Spirit; overcoming all their enemies by his almighty power and wisdom, in such manner and ways as are most consonant to his wonderful and unsearchable dispensation.

CHAPTER IX. ***Of Free Will.***

I. God hath endued the will of man with that natural liberty, that is neither forced, nor by any absolute necessity of nature determined to good or evil.

II. Man, in his state of innocency, had freedom and power to will and to do that which is good and well-pleasing to God; but yet mutably, so that he might fall from it.

III. Man, by his fall into a state of sin, hath wholly lost all ability of will to any spiritual good accompanying salvation; so as a natural man, being altogether averse from that good, and dead in sin, is not able, by his own strength, to convert himself, or to prepare himself thereunto.

IV. When God converts a sinner and translates him into the state of grace, he freeth him from his natural bondage under sin, and, by his grace alone, enables him freely to will and to do that which is spiritually good; yet so as that, by reason of his remaining corruption, he doth not perfectly, nor only, will that which is good, but doth also will that which is evil.

V. The will of man is made perfectly and immutable free to good alone, in the state of glory only.

CHAPTER X. ***Of Effectual Calling.***

I. All those whom God hath predestinated unto life, and those only, he is pleased, in his appointed and accepted time, effectually to call, by his Word and Spirit, out of that state of sin and death in which they are by nature, to grace and salvation by Jesus Christ: enlightening their minds, spiritually and savingly, to understand the things of God, taking away their heart of stone, and giving unto them an heart of flesh; renewing their wills, and by his almighty power determining them to that which is good; and effectually drawing them to Jesus Christ; yet so as they come most freely, being made willing by his grace.

II. This effectual call is of God's free and special grace alone, not from any thing at all foreseen in man, who is altogether passive therein, until, being quickened and renewed by the Holy Spirit, he is thereby enabled to answer this call, and to embrace the grace offered and conveyed in it.

III. Elect infants, dying in infancy, are regenerated and saved by Christ through the Spirit, who worketh when, and where, and how he pleaseth. So also are all other elect persons who are incapable of being outwardly called by the ministry of the Word.

IV. Others, not elected, although they may be called by the ministry of the Word, and may have some common operations of the Spirit, yet they never truly come to Christ, and therefore cannot be saved: much less can men not professing the Christian religion, be saved in any other way whatsoever, be they ever so diligent to frame their lives according to the light of nature, and the law of that religion they do profess; and to assert and maintain that they may, is very pernicious, and to be detested.

CHAPTER XI. ***Of Justification.***

I. Those whom God effectually calleth, he also freely justifieth: not by infusing righteousness into them, but by pardoning their sins, and by accounting and accepting their persons as righteous; not for any thing wrought in them, or done by them, but for Christ's sake alone; not by imputing faith itself, the act of believing, or any other evangelical obedience, to them as their righteousness; but by imputing the obedience and satisfaction of Christ unto them, they receiving and resting on him and his righteousness by faith: which faith they have not of themselves; it is the gift of God.

II. Faith, thus receiving and resting on Christ and his righteousness, is the alone instrument of justification; yet is it not alone in the person justified, but is ever accompanied with all other saving graces, and is no dead faith, but worketh by love.

III. Christ, by his obedience and death, did fully discharge the debt of all those that are thus justified, and did make a proper, real, and full satisfaction to his Father's justice in their behalf. Yet inasmuch as he was given by the Father for them, and his obedience and satisfaction accepted in their stead, and both freely, not for any thing in them, their justification is only of free grace, that both the exact justice and rich grace of God might be glorified in the justification of sinners.

IV. God did, from all eternity, decree to justify all the elect; and Christ did, in the fulness of time, die for their sins and rise again for their justification; nevertheless they are not justified until the Holy Spirit doth, in due time, actually apply Christ unto them.

V. God doth continue to forgive the sins of those that are justified; and although they can never fall from the state of justification, yet they may by their sins fall under God's fatherly displeasure, and not have the light of his countenance restored unto them, until they humble themselves, confess their sins, beg pardon, and renew their faith and repentance.

VI. The justification of believers under the Old Testament was, in all these respects, one and the same with the justification of believers under the New Testament.

CHAPTER XII. ***Of Adoption.***

All those that are justified, God vouchsafeth, in and for his only Son Jesus Christ, to make partakers of the grace of adoption: by which they are taken into the number, and enjoy the liberties and privileges of the children of God; have his name put upon them; receive the Spirit of adoption; have access to the throne of grace with boldness; are enabled to cry, Abba, Father; are pitied, protected, provided for, and chastened by him as by a father; yet never cast off, but sealed to the day of redemption, and inherit the promises, as heirs of everlasting salvation.

CHAPTER XIII. Of Sanctification.

I. They who are effectually called and regenerated, having a new heart and a new spirit created in them, are further sanctified, really and personally, through the virtue of Christ's death and resurrection, by his Word and Spirit dwelling in them; the dominion of the whole body of sin is destroyed, and the several lusts thereof are more and more weakened and mortified, and they more and more quickened and strengthened, in all saving graces, to the practice of true holiness, without which no man shall see the Lord.

II. This sanctification is throughout in the whole man, yet imperfect in this life: there abideth still some remnants of corruption in every part, whence ariseth a continual and irreconcilable war, the flesh lusting against the Spirit, and the Spirit against the flesh.

III. In which war, although the remaining corruption for a time may much prevail, yet, through the continual supply of strength from the sanctifying Spirit of Christ, the regenerate part doth overcome: and so the saints grow in grace, perfecting holiness in the fear of God.

CHAPTER XIV. Of Saving Faith.

I. The grace of faith, whereby the elect are enabled to believe to the saving of their souls, is the work of the Spirit of Christ in their hearts; and is ordinarily wrought by the ministry of the Word: by which also, and by the administration of the sacraments, and prayer, it is increased and strengthened.

II. By this faith, a Christian believeth to be true whatsoever is revealed in the Word, for the authority of God himself speaking therein; and acteth differently upon that which each particular passage thereof containeth; yielding obedience to the commands, trembling at the threatenings, and embracing the promises of God for this life, and that which is to come. But the principal acts of saving faith are, accepting, receiving, and resting upon Christ alone for justification, sanctification, and eternal life, by virtue of the covenant of grace.

III. This faith is different in degrees, weak or strong; may be often and many ways assailed and weakened, but gets the victory; growing up in many to the attainment of a full assurance through Christ, who is both the author and finisher of our faith.

CHAPTER XV. ***Of Repentance Unto Life.***

I. Repentance unto life is an evangelical grace, the doctrine whereof is to be preached by every minister of the gospel, as well as that of faith in Christ.

II. By it a sinner, out of the sight and sense, not only of the danger, but also of the filthiness and odiousness of his sins, as contrary to the holy nature and righteous law of God, and upon the apprehension of his mercy in Christ to such as are penitent, so grieves for, and hates his sins, as to turn from them all unto God, purposing and endeavouring to walk with him in all the ways of his commandments.

III. Although repentance be not to be rested in as any satisfaction for sin, or any cause of the pardon thereof, which is the act of God's free grace in Christ; yet is it of such necessity to all sinners, that none may expect pardon without it.

IV. As there is no sin so small but it deserves damnation; so there is no sin so great that it can bring damnation upon those who truly repent.

V. Men ought not to content themselves with a general repentance, but it is every man's duty to endeavour to repent of his particular sins, particularly.

VI. As every man is bound to make private confession of his sins to God, praying for the pardon thereof, upon which, and the forsaking of them, he shall find mercy: so he that scandalizeth his brother, or the Church of Christ, ought to be willing, by a private or public confession and sorrow for his sin, to declare his repentance to those that are offended; who are thereupon to be reconciled to him, and in love to receive him.

CHAPTER XVI. **Of Good Works.**

I. Good works are only such as God hath commanded in his holy Word, and not such as, without the warrant thereof, are devised by men out of blind zeal, or upon any pretence of good intention.

II. These good works, done in obedience to God's commandments, are the fruits and evidences of a true and lively faith: and by them believers manifest their thankfulness, strengthen their assurance, edify their brethren, adorn the profession of the gospel, stop the mouths of the adversaries, and glorify God, whose workmanship they are, created in Christ Jesus thereunto, that, having their fruit unto holiness, they may have the end, eternal life.

III. Their ability to do good works is not at all of themselves, but wholly from the Spirit of Christ. And that they may be enabled thereunto, besides the graces they have already received, there is required an actual influence of the same Holy Spirit to work in them to will and to do of his good pleasure; yet are they not hereupon to grow negligent, as if they were not bound to perform any duty unless upon a special motion of the Spirit; but they ought to be diligent in stirring up the grace of God that is in them.

IV. They, who in their obedience, attain to the greatest height which is possible in this life, are so far from being able to supererogate and to do more than God requires, that they fall short of much which in duty they are bound to do.

V. We cannot, by our best works, merit pardon of sin, or eternal life, at the hand of God, by reason of the great disproportion that is between them and the glory to come, and the infinite distance that is between us and God, whom by them we can neither profit, nor satisfy for the debt of our former sins; but when we have done all we can, we have done but our duty, and are unprofitable servants: and because, as they are good, they proceed from his Spirit; and as they are wrought by us, they are defiled and mixed with so much weakness and imperfection that they cannot endure the severity of God's judgment.

VI. Yet notwithstanding, the persons of believers being accepted through Christ, their good works also are accepted in him, not as though they were in this life wholly unblameable and unreproveable in God's sight; but that he, looking upon them in his Son, is pleased to accept and reward that which is sincere, although accompanied with many weaknesses and imperfections.

VII. Works done by unregenerate men, although for the matter of them they may be things which God commands, and of good use both to themselves and others; yet, because they proceed not from a heart purified by faith; nor are done in a right manner, according to the Word; nor to a right end, the glory of God; they are therefore sinful and cannot please God, or make a man meet to receive grace from God. And yet their neglect of them is more sinful, and displeasing unto God.

CHAPTER XVII. ***Of The Perseverance of the Saints.***

I. They whom God hath accepted in his Beloved, effectually called and sanctified by his Spirit, can neither totally nor finally fall away from the state of grace; but shall certainly persevere therein to the end, and be eternally saved.

II. This perseverance of the saints depends not upon their own free will, but upon the immutability of the decree of election, flowing from the free and unchangeable love of God the Father; upon the efficacy of the merit and intercession of Jesus Christ; the abiding of the Spirit and of the seed of God within them; and the nature of the covenant of grace; from all which ariseth also the certainty and infallibility thereof.

III. Nevertheless they may, through the temptations of Satan and of the world, the prevalency of corruption remaining in them, and the neglect of the means of their perseverance, fall into grievous sins; and for a time continue therein: whereby they incur God's displeasure, and grieve his Holy Spirit; come to be deprived of some measure of their graces and comforts; have their hearts hardened, and their consciences wounded; hurt and scandalize others, and bring temporal judgments upon theselves.

CHAPTER XVIII. ***Of the Assurance of Grace and Salvation.***

I. Although hypocrites, and other unregenerate men, may vainly deceive themselves with false hopes and carnal presumptions of being in the favour of God, and estate of salvation; which hope of theirs shall perish: yet such as truly believe in the Lord Jesus, and love him in sincerity, endeavouring to walk in all good conscience before him, may in this life be certainly assured that they are in a state of grace, and may rejoice in the hope of the glory of God: which hope shall never make them ashamed.

II. This certainty is not a bare conjectural and probable persuasion, grounded upon a fallible hope; but an infallible assurance of faith, founded upon the divine truth of the promises of salvation, the inward evidence of those graces unto which these promises are made, the testimony of the Spirit of adoption witnessing with our spirits that we are the children of God; which Spirit is the earnest of our inheritance, whereby we are sealed to the day of redemption.

III. This infallible assurance doth not so belong to the essence of faith but that a true believer may wait long and conflict with many difficulties before he be partaker of it: yet, being enabled by the Spirit to know the things which are freely given him of God, he may, without extraordinary revelation, in the right use of ordinary means, attain thereunto. And therefore it is the duty of everyone to give all diligence to make his calling and election sure; that thereby his heart may be enlarged in peace and joy in the Holy Ghost, in love and thankfulness to God, and in strength and cheerfulness in the duties of obedience, the proper fruits of this assurance: so far is it from inclining men to looseness.

IV. True believers may have the assurance of their salvation divers ways shaken, diminished, and intermitted; as, by negligence in preserving of it; by falling into some special sin, which woundeth the conscience, and grieveth the Spirit; by some sudden or vehement temptation; by God's withdrawing the light of his countenance and suffering even such as fear him to walk in darkness and to have no light: yet are they never utterly destitute of that seed of God, and life of faith, that love of Christ and the brethren, that sincerity of heart and conscience of duty, out of which, by the operation of the Spirit, this assurance may in due time be revived, and by the which, in the meantime, they are supported from utter despair.

CHAPTER XIX. ***Of the Law of God.***

I. God gave to Adam a law, as a covenant of works, by which he bound him and all his posterity to personal, entire, exact, and perpetual obedience; promised life upon the fulfilling, and threatened death upon the breach of it; and endued him with power and ability to keep it.

II. This law, after his fall, continued to be a perfect rule of righteousness; and, as such, was delivered by God upon mount Sinai in ten commandments, and written in two tables; the first four commandments containing our duty toward God, and the other six our duty to man.

III. Besides this law, commonly called moral, God was pleased to give to the people of Israel, as a Church under age, ceremonial laws, containing several typical ordinances, partly of worship, prefiguring Christ, his graces, actions, sufferings, and benefits; and partly holding forth divers instructions of moral duties. All which ceremonial laws are now abrogated under the New Testament.

IV. To them also, as a body politic, he gave sundry judicial laws, which expired together with the state of that people, not obliging any other, now, further than the general equity thereof may require.

V. The moral law doth forever bind all, as well justified persons as others, to the obedience thereof; and that not only in regard of the matter contained in it, but also in respect of the authority of God the Creator who gave it. Neither doth Christ in the gospel any way dissolve, but much strengthen, this obligation.

VI. Although true believers be not under the law as a covenant of works, to be thereby justified or condemned; yet is it of great use to them, as well as to others; in that, as a rule of life, informing them of the will of God and their duty, it directs and binds them to walk accordingly; discovering also the sinful pollutions of their nature, hearts, and lives; so as, examining themselves thereby, they may come to further conviction of, humiliation for, and hatred against sin; together with a clearer sight of the need they have of Christ, and the perfection of his obedience. It is likewise of use to the regenerate, to restrain their corruptions, in that it forbids sin, and the threatenings of it serve to show what even their sins deserve, and what afflictions in this life they may expect for them, although freed from the curse thereof threatened in the law. The promises of it, in like manner, show them God's approbation of obedience, and what blessings they may expect upon the performance thereof; although not as due to them by the law as a covenant of works: so as a man's doing good, and refraining from evil, because the law encourageth to the one, and deterreth from the other, is no evidence of his being under the law, and not under grace.

VII. Neither are the forementioned uses of the law contrary to the grace of the gospel, but do sweetly comply with it: the Spirit of Christ subduing and enabling the will of man to do that freely and cheerfully, which the will of God, revealed in the law, requireth to be done.

CHAPTER XX. ***Of Christian Liberty, and Liberty of Conscience.***

I. The liberty which Christ hath purchased for believers under the gospel consists in their freedom from the guilt of sin, the condemning wrath of God, the curse of the moral law; and in their being delivered from this present evil world, bondage to Satan, and dominion of sin, from the evil of afflictions, the sting of death, the victory of the grave, and everlasting damnation; as also in their free access to God, and their yielding obedience unto him, not out of slavish fear, but a childlike love, and a willing mind. All which were common also to believers under the law; but under the New Testament the liberty of Christians is further enlarged in their freedom from the yoke of the ceremonial law, to which the Jewish Church was subjected; and in greater boldness of access to the throne of grace, and in fuller communications of the free Spirit of God, than believers under the law did ordinarily partake of.

II. God alone is Lord of the conscience, and hath left it free from the doctrines and commandments of men which are in any thing contrary to his Word, or beside it in matters of faith or worship. So that to believe such doctrines, or to obey such commandments out of conscience, is to betray true liberty of conscience; and the requiring of an implicit faith, and an absolute and blind obedience, is to destroy liberty of conscience, and reason also.

III. They who, upon pretence of Christian liberty, do practise any sin, or cherish any lust, do thereby destroy the end of Christian liberty; which is, that, being delivered out of the hands of our enemies, we might serve the Lord without fear, in holiness and righteousness before him, all the days of our life.

IV. And because the powers which God hath ordained, and the liberty which Christ hath purchased, are not intended by God to destroy, but mutually to uphold and preserve one another; they who, upon pretence of Christian liberty, shall oppose any lawful power, or the lawful exercise of it, whether it be civil or ecclesiastical, resist the ordinance of God. And, for their publishing of such opinions, or maintaining of such practices, as are contrary to the light of nature, or to the known principles of Christianity, whether concerning faith, worship, or conversation; or, to the power of godliness; or, such erroneous opinions or practices, as either in their own nature, or in the manner of publishing or maintaining them, are destructive to the external peace and order which Christ hath established in the Church, they may lawfully be called to account, and proceeded against by the censures of the Church, and by the power of the civil magistrate.

CHAPTER XXI. ***Of Religious Worship and the Sabbath-day.***

I. The light of nature showeth that there is a God, who hath lordship and sovereignty over all; is good, and doeth good unto all; and is therefore to be feared, loved, praised, called upon, trusted in, and served with all the heart, and with all the soul, and with all the might. But the acceptable way of worshipping the true God is instituted by himself, and so limited by his own revealed will, that he may not be worshipped according to the imaginations and devices of men, or the suggestions of Satan, under any visible representation or any other way not prescribed in the holy Scripture.

II. Religious worship is to be given to God, the Father, Son, and Holy Ghost; and to him alone: not to angels, saints, or any other creature: and since the Fall, not without a Mediator; nor in the mediation of any other but of Christ alone.

III. Prayer with thanksgiving, being one special part of religious worship, is by God required of all men; and that it may be accepted, it is to be made in the name of the Son, by the help of his Spirit, according to his will, with understanding, reverence, humility, fervency, faith, love, and perseverance; and, if vocal, in a known tongue.

IV. Prayer is to be made for things lawful, and for all sorts of men living, or that shall live hereafter; but not for the dead, nor for those of whom it may be known that they have sinned the sin unto death.

V. The reading of the Scriptures with godly fear; the sound preaching, and conscionable hearing of the Word, in obedience unto God with understanding, faith, and reverence; singing of psalms with grace in the heart;

as, also, the due administration and worthy receiving of the sacraments instituted by Christ; are all parts of the ordinary religious worship of God: besides religious oaths, vows, solemn fastings, and thanksgivings upon special occasions; which are, in their several times and seasons, to be used in an holy and religious manner.

VI. Neither prayer, nor any other part of religious worship, is, now under the gospel, either tied unto, or made more acceptable by, any place in which it is performed, or towards which it is directed: but God is to be worshipped everywhere in spirit and in truth; as in private families daily, and in secret each one by himself, so more solemnly in the public assemblies, which are not carelessly or wilfully to be neglected or forsaken, when God, by his Word or providence, calleth thereunto.

VII. As it is of the law of nature, that, in general, a due proportion of time be set apart for the worship of God; so, in his Word, by a positive, moral, and perpetual commandment, binding all men in all ages, he hath particularly appointed one day in seven for a Sabbath, to be kept holy unto him: which, from the beginning of the world to the resurrection of Christ, was the last day of the week; and, from the resurrection of Christ, was changed into the first day of the week, which in Scripture is called the Lord's Day, and is to be continued to the end of the world as the Christian Sabbath.

VIII. This Sabbath is to be kept holy unto the Lord when men, after a due preparing of their hearts, and ordering of their common affairs beforehand, do not only observe an holy rest all the day from their own works, words, and thoughts about their wordly employments and recreations; but also are taken up the whole time in the public and private exercises of his worship, and in the duties of necessity and mercy.

CHAPTER XXII. ***Of Lawful Oaths and Vows.***

I. A lawful oath is a part of religious worship, wherein upon just occasion, the person swearing solemnly calleth God to witness what he asserteth or promiseth; and to judge him according to the truth or falsehood of what he sweareth.

II. The name of God only is that by which men ought to swear, and therein it is to be used with all holy fear and reverence; therefore to swear vainly or rashly by that glorious and dreadful name, or to swear at all by any other thing, is sinful, and to be abhorred. Yet, as, in matters of weight and moment, an oath is warranted by the Word of God, under the New Testament, as well as under the Old, so a lawful oath, being imposed by lawful authority, in such matters ought to be taken.

III. Whosoever taketh an oath ought duly to consider the weightiness of so solemn an act, and therein to avouch nothing but what he is fully persuaded is the truth. Neither may any man bind himself by oath to any thing but what is good and just, and what he believeth so to be, and what he is able and resolved to perform. Yet it is a sin to refuse an oath touching any thing that is good and just, being imposed by lawful authority.

IV. An oath is to be taken in the plain and common sense of the words, without equivocation or mental reservation. It cannot oblige to sin; but in anything not sinful, being taken, it binds to performance, although to a man's own hurt: nor is it to be violated, although made to heretics or infidels.

V. A vow is of the like nature with a promissory oath, and ought to be made with the like religious care, and to be performed with the like faithfulness.

VI. It is not to be made to any creature, but to God alone: and that it may be accepted, it is to be made voluntarily, out of faith and conscience of duty, in way of thankfulness for mercy received, or for obtaining of what we want; whereby we more strictly bind ourselves to necessary duties, or to other things, so far and so long as they may fitly conduce thereunto.

VII. No man may vow to do any thing forbidden in the Word of God, or what would hinder any duty therein commanded, or which is not in his own power, and for the performance of which he hath no promise or ability from God. In which respects, popish monastical vows of perpetual single life, professed poverty, and regular obedience, are so far from being degrees of higher perfection, that they are superstitious and sinful snares, in which no Christian may entangle himself.

CHAPTER XXIII. ***Of the Civil Magistrate.***

I. God, the supreme Lord and King of all the world, hath ordained civil magistrates to be under him over the people, for his own glory and the public good; and to this end, hath armed them with the power of the sword, for the defence and encouragement of them that are good, and for the punishment of evil-doers.

II. It is lawful for Christians to accept and execute the office of a magistrate when called thereunto; in the managing whereof, as they ought especially to maintain piety, justice, and peace, according to the wholesome laws of each commonwealth, so, for that end, they may lawfully, now under the New Testament, wage war upon just and necessary occasions.

III. The civil magistrate may not assume to himself the administration of the Word and sacraments, or the power of the keys of the kingdom of heaven: yet he hath authority, and it is his duty, to take order, that unity and peace be preserved in the Church, that the truth of God be kept pure and entire; that all blasphemies and heresies be suppressed; all corruptions and abuses in worship and discipline prevented or reformed; and all the ordinances of God duly settled, administered, and observed. For the better effecting whereof, he hath power to call synods, to be present at them, and to provide that whatsoever is transacted in them be according to the mind of God.

IV. It is the duty of the people to pray for magistrates, to honour their persons, to pay them tribute and other dues, to obey their lawful commands, and to be subject to their authority, for conscience' sake. Infidelity, or difference in religion, doth not make void the magistrate's just and legal authority, nor free the people from their obedience to him: from which ecclesiastical persons are not exempted; much less hath the Pope any power and jurisdiction over them in their dominions, or over any of their people; and least of all to deprive them of their dominions or lives, if he shall judge them to be heretics, or upon any other pretence whatsoever.

CHAPTER XXIV. ***Of Marriage and Divorce.***

I. Marriage is to be between one man and one woman: neither is it lawful for any man to have more than one wife, nor for any woman to have more than one husband at the same time.

II. Marriage was ordained for the mutual help of husband and wife; for the increase of mankind with a legitimate issue, and of the Church with an holy seed; and for preventing of uncleanness.

III. It is lawful for all sorts of people to marry who are able with judgment to give their consent. Yet it is the duty of Christians to marry only in the Lord. And, therefore, such as profess the true reformed religion should not marry with infidels, Papists, or other idolaters: neither should such as are godly be unequally yoked, by marrying with such as are notoriously wicked in their life, or maintain damnable heresies.

IV. Marriage ought not to be within the degrees of consanguinity or affinity forbidden in the Word; nor can such incestuous marriages ever be made lawful by any law of man, or consent of parties, so as those persons may live together as man and wife. The man may not marry any of his wife's kindred nearer in blood than he may of his own, nor the woman of her husband's kindred nearer in blood than of her own.

V. Adultery or fornication, committed after a contract, being detected before marriage, giveth just occasion to the innocent party to dissolve that contract. In the case of adultery after marriage, it is lawful for the innocent party to sue out a divorce, and after the divorce to marry another, as if the offending party were dead.

VI. Although the corruption of man be such as is apt to study arguments, unduly to put asunder those whom God hath joined together in marriage; yet nothing but adultery, or such wilful desertion as can no way be remedied by the Church or civil magistrate, is cause sufficient of dissolving the bond of marriage; wherein a public and orderly course of proceeding is to be observed; and the persons concerned in it, not left to their own wills and discretion in their own case.

CHAPTER XXV. ***Of the Church.***

I. The catholic or universal Church, which is invisible, consists of the whole number of the elect, that have been, are, or shall be gathered into one, under Christ the head thereof; and is the spouse, the body, the fulness of Him that filleth all in all.

II. The visible Church, which is also catholic or universal under the gospel (not confined to one nation, as before under the law), consists of all those throughout the world that profess the true religion, together with their children; and is the kingdom of the Lord Jesus Christ; the house and family of God, out of which there is no ordinary possibility of salvation.

III. Unto this catholic visible Church, Christ hath given the ministry, oracles, and ordinances of God, for the gathering and perfecting of the saints, in this life, to the end of the world; and doth by his own presence and Spirit, according to his promise, make them effectual thereunto.

IV. This catholic Church hath been sometimes more, sometimes less, visible. And particular Churches, which are members thereof, are more or less pure, according as the doctrine of the gospel is taught and embraced, ordinances administered, and public worship performed more or less purely in them.

V. The purest Churches under heaven are subject both to mixture and error: and some have so degenerated as to become apparently no Churches of Christ. Nevertheless, there shall be always a church on earth, to worship God according to his will.

VI. There is no other head of the Church but the Lord Jesus Christ: nor can the Pope of Rome in any sense be head thereof; but is that Antichrist, that man of sin and son of perdition, that exalteth himself in the Church against Christ, and all that is called God.

CHAPTER XXVI. ***Of the Communion of the Saints.***

I. All saints that are united to Jesus Christ their head, by his Spirit and by faith, have fellowship with him in his graces, sufferings, death, resurrection, and glory: and, being united to one another in love, they have communion in each other's gifts and graces, and are obliged to the performance of such duties, public and private, as to conduce to their mutual good, both in the inward and outward man.

II. Saints by profession, are bound to maintain an holy fellowship and communion in the worship of God, and in performing such other spiritual services as tend to their mutual edification; as also in relieving each other in outward things, according to their several abilities and necessities. Which communion, as God offereth opportunity, is to be extended unto all those who, in every place, call upon the name of the Lord Jesus.

III. This communion which the saints have with Christ, doth not make them in any wise partakers of the substance of his Godhead, or to be equal with Christ in any respect: either of which to affirm is impious and blasphemous. Nor doth their communion one with another as saints, take away or infringe the title or property which each man hath in his goods and possessions.

CHAPTER XXVII. **Of the Sacraments.**

I. Sacraments are holy signs and seals of the covenant of grace, immediately instituted by God, to represent Christ and his benefits, and to confirm our interest in him: as also to put a visible difference between those that belong unto the Church, and the rest of the world; and solemnly to engage them to the service of God in Christ, according to his Word.

II. There is in every sacrament a spiritual relation, or sacramental union, between the sign and the thing signified; whence it comes to pass that the names and effects of the one are attributed to the other.

III. The grace which is exhibited in or by the sacraments, rightly used, is not conferred by any power in them; neither doth the efficacy of a sacrament depend upon the piety or intention of him that doth administer it, but upon the work of the Spirit, and the word of institution, which conatins, together with a precept authorizing the use thereof, a promise of benefit to worthy receivers.

IV. There be only two sacraments ordained by Christ our Lord in the gospel, that is to say, Baptism and the Supper of the Lord: neither or which may be dispensed by any but a minister of the Word, lawfully ordained.

V. The sacraments of the Old Testament, in regard of the spiritual things thereby signified and exhibited, were, for substance, the same with those of the New.

CHAPTER XXVIII. **Of Baptism.**

I. Baptism is a sacrament of the New Testament, ordained by Jesus Christ, not only for the solemn admission of the party baptized into the visible Church, but also to be unto him a sign and seal of the covenant of grace, or his ingrafting into Christ, of regeneration, of remission of sins, and of his giving up unto God, through Jesus Christ, to walk in newness of life: which sacrament is, by Christ's own appointment, to be continued in his Church until the end of the world.

II. The outward element to be used in the sacrament is water, wherewith the party is to be baptized in the name of the Father, and of the Son, and of the Holy Ghost, by a minister of the gospel, lawfully called thereunto.

III. Dipping of the person into the water is not necessary; but baptism is rightly administered by pouring or sprinkling water upon the person.

IV. Not only those that do actually profess faith in and obedience unto Christ, but also the infants of one or both believing parents are to be baptized.

V. Although it be a great sin to contemn or neglect this ordinance, yet grace and salvation are not so inseparably annexed unto it as that no person can be regenerated or saved without it, or that all that are baptized are undoubtedly regenerated.

VI. The efficacy of baptism is not tied to that moment of time wherein it is administered; yet, notwithstanding, by the right use of this ordinance the grace promised is not only offered, but really exhibited and conferred by the Holy Ghost, to such (whether of age or infants) as that grace belongeth unto, according to the counsel of God's own will, in his appointed time.

VII. The sacrament of Baptism is but once to be administered to any person.

CHAPTER XXIX. ***Of the Lord's Supper***

I. Our Lord Jesus, in the night wherein he was betrayed, instituted the sacrament of his body and blood, called the Lord's Supper, to be observed in his Church unto the end of the world; for the perpetual remembrance of the sacrifice of himself in his death, the sealing all benefits thereof unto true believers, their spiritual nourishment and growth in him, their further engagement in and to all duties which they owe unto him; and to be a bond and pledge of their communion with him, and with each other, as members of his mystical body.

II. In this sacrament Christ is not offered up to his Father, nor any real sacrifice made at all for remission of sins of the quick or dead, but a commemoration of that one offering up of himself, by himself, upon the cross, once for all, and a spiritual oblation of all possible praise unto God for the same; so that the Popish sacrifice of the mass, as they call it, is most abominably injurious to Christ's one only sacrifice, the alone propitiation for all the sins of the elect.

III. The Lord Jesus hath, in this ordinance, appointed his ministers to declare his word of institution to the people, to pray, and bless the elements of bread and wine, and thereby to set them apart from a common to an holy use; and to take and break the bread, to take the cup, and (they communicating also themselves) to give both to the communicants; but to none who are not then present in the congregation.

IV. Private masses, or receiving this sacrament by a priest, or any other, alone; as likewise the denial of the cup to the people; worshipping the elements, the lifting them up, or carrying them about for adoration, and the reserving them for any pretended religious use, are all contrary to the nature of this sacrament, and to the institution of Christ.

V. The outward elements in this sacrament, duly set apart to the uses ordained by Christ, have such relation to him crucified, as that truly, yet sacramentally only, they are sometimes called by the name of the things they represent, to wit, the body and blood of Christ; albeit, in substance and nature, they still remain truly, and only, bread and wine, as they were before.

VI. That doctrine which maintains a change of the substance of bread and wine, into the substance of Christ's body and blood (commonly called transubstantiation) by consecration of a priest, or by any other way, is repugnant, not to Scripture alone, but even to common sense and reason; overthroweth the nature of the sacrament; and hath been, and is, the cause of manifold superstitions, yea, of gross idolatries.

VII. Worthy receivers, outwardly partaking of the visible elements in this sacrament, do then also inwardly by faith, really and indeed, yet not carnally and corporally, but spiritually, receive and feed upon Christ crucified, and all benefits of his death: the body and blood of Christ being then not corporally or carnally in, with, or under the bread and wine; yet as really, but spiritually, present to the faith of believers in that ordinance, as the elements themselves are to their outward senses.

VIII. Although ignorant and wicked men receive the outward elements in this sacrament, yet they receive not the thing signified thereby; but by their unworthy coming thereunto are guilty of the body and blood of the Lord, to their own damnation. Wherefore all ignorant and ungodly persons, as they are unfit to enjoy communion with him, so are they unworthy of the Lord's table, and can not, without great sin against Christ, while they remain such, partake of these holy mysteries, or be admitted thereunto.

CHAPTER XXX. **Of Church Censures.**

I. The Lord Jesus, as king and head of his Church, hath therein appointed a government in the hand of Church officers, distinct from the civil magistrate.

II. To these officers the keys of the kingdom of heaven are committed, by virtue whereof they have power respectively to retain and remit sins, to shut that kingdom against the impenitent, both by the word and censures; and to open it unto penitent sinners, by the ministry of the gospel, and by absolution from censures, as occasion shall require.

III. Church censures are necessary for the reclaiming and gaining of offending brethren; for deterring of others from like offences; for purging out of that leaven which might infect the whole lump; for vindicating the honour of Christ, and the holy profession of the gospel; and for preventing the wrath of God, which might justly fall upon the Church, if they should suffer his covenant, and the seals thereof, to be profaned by notorious and obstinate offenders.

IV. For the better attaining of these ends, the officers of the Church are to proceed by admonition, suspension from the sacrament of the Lord's Supper for a season, and by excommunication from the Church, according to the nature of the crime, and demerit of the person.

CHAPTER XXXI. **Of Synods and Councils.**

I. For the better government and further edification of the Church, there ought to be such assemblies as are commonly called synods or councils.

II. As magistrates may lawfully call a synod of ministers and other fit persons to consult and advise with about matters of religion; so, if magistrates be open enemies of the Church, the ministers of Christ, of themselves, by virtue of their office, or they, with other fit persons, upon delegation from their churches, may meet together in such assemblies.

III. It belongeth to synods and councils, ministerially, to determine controversies of faith, and cases of conscience; to set down rules and directions for the better ordering of the public worship of God, and government of his Church; to receive complaints in cases of maladministration, and authoritatively to determine the same: which decrees and determinations, if consonant to the Word of God, are to be received with reverence and submission, not only for their agreement with the Word, but also for the power whereby they are made, as being an ordinance of God, appointed thereunto in his Word.

IV. All synods or councils since the apostles' times, whether general or particular, may err, and many have erred; therefore they are not to be made the rule of faith or practice, but to be used as a help in both.

V. Synods and councils are to handle or conclude nothing but that which is ecclesiastical: and are not to intermeddle with civil affairs which concern the commonwealth, unless by way of humble petition in cases extraordinary; or by way of advice for satisfaction of conscience, if they be thereunto required by the civil magistrate.

CHAPTER XXXII. ***Of the State of Man After Death, and of the Resurrection of the Dead.***

I. The bodies of men, after death, return to dust, and see corruption; but their souls (which neither die nor sleep), having an immortal subsistence, immediately return to God who gave them. The souls of the righteous, being then made perfect in holiness, are received into the highest heavens, where they behold the face of God in light and glory, waiting for the full redemption of their bodies; and the souls of the wicked are cast into hell, where they remain in torments and utter darkness, reserved to the judgment of the great day. Besides these two places for souls separated from their bodies, the Scripture acknowledgeth none.

II. At the last day, such as are found alive shall not die, but be changed: and all the dead shall be raised up with the self-same bodies, and none other, although with different qualities, which shall be united again to their souls forever.

III. The bodies of the unjust shall, by the power of Christ, be raised to dishonour; the bodies of the just, by his Spirit, unto honour, and be made conformable to his own glorious body.

CHAPTER XXXIII. ***Of the Last Judgment.***

I. God hath appointed a day, wherein he will judge the world in righteousness by Jesus Christ, to whom all power and judgment is given of the Father. In which day, not only the apostate angels shall be judged; but likewise all persons, that have lived upon earth, shall appear before the tribunal of Christ, to give an account of their thoughts, words, and deeds; and to receive according to what they have done in the body, whether good or evil.

II. The end of God's appointing this day, is for the manifestation of the glory of his mercy in the eternal salvation of the elect; and of his justice in the damnation of the reprobate, who are wicked and disobedient. For then shall the righteous go into everlasting life, and receive that fulness of joy and refreshing which shall come from the presence of the Lord: but the wicked, who know not God, and obey not the gospel of Jesus Christ, shall be cast into eternal torments, and punished with everlasting destruction from the presence of the Lord, and from the glory of his power.

III. As Christ would have us to be certainly persuaded that there shall be a day of judgment, both to deter all men from sin, and for the greater consolation of the godly in their adversity: so will he have that day unknown to men, that they may shake off all carnal security, and be always watchful, because they know not at what hour the Lord will come; and may be ever prepared to say, Come, Lord Jesus, come quickly. Amen.

The Larger Catechism

Q. 1.What is the chief and highest end of man?

A. Man's chief and highest end is to glorify God, and fully to enjoy him forever.

Q. 2. How doth it appear that there is a God?

A. The very light of nature in man, and the works of God, declare plainly that there is a God; but his Word and Spirit only do sufficiently and effectually reveal him unto men for their salvation.

Q. 3.What is the Word of God?

A. The holy Scriptures of the Old and New Testaments are the Word of God, the only rule of faith and obedience.

Q. 4. How doth it appear that the Scriptures are the Word of God?

A. The Scriptures manifest themselves to be the Word of God, by their majesty and purity; by the consent of all the parts, and the scope of the whole, which is to give all glory to God; by their light and power to convince and convert sinners, to comfort and build up believers unto salvation: but the Spirit of God bearing witness by and with the Scriptures in the heart of man, is alone able fully to persuade it that they are the very Word of God.

What Man Ought to Believe Concerning God

Q. 5.What do the Scriptures principally teach?

A. The Scriptures principally teach, what man is to believe concerning God, and what duty God requires of man.

Q. 6.What do the Scriptures make known of God?

A. The Scriptures make known what God is, the persons in the Godhead, his decrees, and the execution of his decrees.

Q. 7.What is God?

A. God is a Spirit, in and of himself infinite in being, glory, blessedness, and perfection; all-sufficient, eternal, unchangeable, incomprehensible, everywhere present, almighty, knowing all things, most wise, most holy, most just, most merciful and gracious, long-suffering, and abundant in goodness and truth.

Q. 8. Are there more Gods than one?

A. There is but one only, the living and true God.

Q. 9. How many persons are there in the Godhead?

A. There be three persons in the Godhead, the Father, the Son, and the Holy Ghost; and these three are one true, eternal God, the same in substance, equal in power and glory; although distinguished by their personal properties.

Q. 10. What are the personal properties of the three persons in the Godhead?

A. It is proper to the Father to beget the Son, and to the Son to be begotten of the Father, and to the Holy Ghost to proceed from the Father and the Son from all eternity.

Q. 11. How doth it appear that the Son and the Holy Ghost are God equal with the Father?

A. The Scriptures manifest that the Son and the Holy Ghost are God equal with the Father, ascribing unto them such names, attributes, works, and worship, as are proper to God only.

Q. 12. What are the decrees of God?

A. God's decrees are the wise, free, and holy acts of the counsel of his will, whereby, from all eternity, he hath, for his own glory, unchangeably foreordained whatsoever comes to pass in time, especially concerning angels and men.

Q. 13. What hath God especially decreed concerning angels and men?

A. God, by an eternal and immutable decree, out of his mere love, for the praise of his glorious grace, to be manifested in due time, hath elected some angels to glory; and in Christ hath chosen some men to eternal life, and the means thereof: and also, according to his sovereign power, and the unsearchable counsel of his own will (whereby he extendeth or withholdeth favour as he pleaseth), hath passed by and foreordained the rest to dishonour and wrath, to be for their sin inflicted, to the praise of the glory of his justice.

Q. 14. How doth God execute his decrees?

A. God executeth his decrees in the works of creation and providence, according to his infallible foreknowledge, and the free and immutable counsel of his own will.

Q. 15.What is the work of creation?

A. The work of creation is that wherein God did in the beginning, by the word of his power, make of nothing the world, and all things therein, for himself, within the space of six days, and all very good.

Q. 16. How did God create angels?

A. God created all the angels spirits, immortal, holy, excelling in knowledge, mighty in power, to execute his commandments, and to praise his name, yet subject to change.

Q. 17. How did God create man?

A. After God had made all other creatures, he created man male and female; formed the body of the man of the dust of the ground, and the woman of the rib of the man, endued them with living, reasonable, and immortal souls; made them after his own image, in knowledge, righteousness, and holiness; having the law of God written in their hearts, and power to fulfil it, and dominion over the creatures; yet subject to fall.

Q. 18.What are God's works of providence?

A. God's works of providence are his most holy, wise, and powerful preserving and governing all his creatures; ordering them, and all their actions, to his own glory.

Q. 19.What is God's providence towards the angels?

A. God by his providence permitted some of the angels, wilfully and irrecoverably, to fall into sin and damnation, limiting and ordering that, and all their sins, to his own glory; and established the rest in holiness and happiness; employing them all, at his pleasure, in the administrations of his power, mercy, and justice.

Q. 20.What was the providence of God toward man in the estate in which he was created?

A. The providence of God toward man in the estate in which he was created, was the placing him in paradise, appointing him to dress it, giving him liberty to eat of the fruit of the earth; putting the creatures under his dominion, and ordaining marriage for his help; affording him communion with himself; instituting the sabbath; entering into a covenant of life with him, upon condition of personal, perfect, and perpetual obedience, of which the tree of life was a pledge; and forbidding to eat of the tree of the knowledge of good and evil, upon the pain of death.

Q. 21. Did man continue in that estate wherein God at first created him?
A. Our first parents being left to the freedom of their own will, through the temptation of Satan, transgressed the commandment of God in eating the forbidden fruit; and thereby fell from the estate of innocency wherein they were created.

Q. 22. Did all mankind fall in that first transgression?
A. The covenant being made with Adam as a public person, not for himself only, but for his posterity, all mankind descending from him by ordinary generation, sinned in him, and fell with him in that first transgression.

Q. 23. Into what estate did the fall bring mankind?
A. The fall brought mankind into an estate of sin and misery.

Q. 24. What is sin?
A. Sin is any want of conformity unto, or transgression of, any law of God, given as a rule to the reasonable creature.

Q. 25. Wherein consisteth the sinfulness of that estate whereinto man fell?
A. The sinfulness of that estate whereinto man fell, consisteth in the guilt of Adam's first sin, the want of that righteousness wherein he was created, and the corruption of his nature, whereby he is utterly indisposed, disabled, and made opposite unto all that is spiritually good, and wholly inclined to all evil, and that continually; which is commonly called original sin, and from which do proceed all actual transgressions.

Q. 26. How is original sin conveyed from our first parents unto their posterity?
A. Original sin is conveyed from our first parents unto their posterity by natural generation, so as all that proceed from them in that way are conceived and born in sin.

Q. 27.What misery did the fall bring upon mankind?

A. The fall brought upon mankind the loss of communion with God, his displeasure and curse; so as we are by nature children of wrath, bond slaves to Satan, and justly liable to all punishments in this world, and that which is to come.

Q. 28.What are the punishments of sin in this world?

A. The punishments of sin in this world are either inward, as blindness of mind, a reprobate sense, strong delusions, hardness of heart, horror of conscience, and vile affections; or outward, as the curse of God upon the creatures for our sakes, and all other evils that befall us in our bodies, names, estates, relations, and employments; together with death itself.

Q. 29.What are the punishments of sin in the world to come?

A. The punishments of sin in the world to come, are everlasting separation from the comfortable presence of God, and most grievous torments in soul and body, without intermission, in hell-fire forever.

Q. 30. Doth God leave all mankind to perish in the estate of sin and misery?

A. God doth not leave all men to perish in the estate of sin and misery, into which they fell by the breach of the first covenant, commonly called the covenant of works; but of his mere love and mercy delivereth his elect out of it, and bringeth them into an estate of salvation by the second covenant, commonly called the covenant of grace.

Q. 31.With whom was the covenant of grace made?

A. The covenant of grace was made with Christ as the second Adam, and in him with all the elect as his seed.

Q. 32. How is the grace of God manifested in the second covenant?

A. The grace of God is manifested in the second covenant, in that he freely provideth and offereth to sinners a Mediator, and life and salvation by him; and requiring faith as the condition to interest them in him, promiseth and giveth his Holy Spirit to all his elect, to work in them that faith, with all other saving graces; and to enable them unto all holy obedience, as the evidence of the truth of their faith and thankfulness to God, and as the way which he hath appointed them to salvation.

Q. 33. Was the covenant of grace always administered after one and the same manner?

A. The covenant of grace was not always administered after the same manner, but the administrations of it under the Old Testament were different from those under the New.

Q. 34. How was the covenant of grace administered under the Old Testament?

A. The covenant of grace was administered under the Old Testament, by promises, prophecies, sacrifices, circumcision, the passover, and other types and ordinances, which did all fore-signify Christ then to come, and were for that time sufficient to build up the elect in faith in the promised Messiah, by whom they then had full remission of sin, and eternal salvation.

Q. 35. How is the covenant of grace administered under the New Testament?

A. Under the New Testament, when Christ the substance was exhibited, the same covenant of grace was and still is to be administered in the preaching of the Word, and the administration of the sacraments of Baptism and the Lord's Supper; in which grace and salvation are held forth in more fulness, evidence, and efficacy, to all nations.

Q. 36. Who is the Mediator of the covenant of grace?

A. The only Mediator of the covenant of grace is the Lord Jesus Christ, who, being the eternal Son of God, of one substance and equal with the Father, in the fulness of time became man, and so was and continues to be God and man, in two entire distinct natures, and one person, forever.

Q. 37. How did Christ, being the Son of God, become man?

A. Christ the Son of God became man, by taking to himself a true body, and a reasonable soul, being conceived by the power of the Holy Ghost in the womb of the virgin Mary, of her substance, and born of her, yet without sin.

Q. 38. Why was it requisite that the Mediator should be God?

A. It was requisite that the Mediator should be God, that he might sustain and keep the human nature from sinking under the infinite wrath of God, and the power of death; give worth and efficacy to his sufferings, obedience, and intercession; and to satisfy God's justice, procure his favour, purchase a peculiar people, give his Spirit to them, conquer all their enemies, and bring them to everlasting salvation.

Q. 39.Why was it requisite that the Mediator should be man?

A. It was requisite that the Mediator should be man, that he might advance our nature, perform obedience to the law, suffer and make intercession for us in our nature, have a fellow-feeling of our infirmities; that we might receive the adoption of sons, and have comfort and access with boldness unto the throne of grace.

Q. 40.Why was it requisite that the Mediator should be God and man in one person?

A. It was requisite that the Mediator, who was to reconcile God and man, should himself be both God and man, and this in one person, that the proper works of each nature might be accepted of God for us, and relied on by us, as the works of the whole person.

Q. 41.Why was our Mediator called Jesus?

A. Our Mediator was called Jesus, because he saveth his people from their sins.

Q. 42.Why was our Mediator called Christ?

A. Our Mediator was called Christ, because he was anointed with the Holy Ghost above measure; and so set apart, and fully furnished with all authority and ability, to execute the offices of prophet, priest, and king of his church, in the estate both of his humiliation and exaltation.

Q. 43. How doth Christ execute the office of a prophet?

A. Christ executeth the office of a prophet, in his revealing to the church, in all ages, by his Spirit and Word, in divers ways of administration, the whole will of God, in all things concerning their edification and salvation.

Q. 44. How doth Christ execute the office of a priest?

A. Christ executeth the office of a priest, in his once offering himself a sacrifice without spot to God, to be a reconciliation for the sins of his people; and in making continual intercession for them.

Q. 45. How doth Christ execute the office of a king?

A. Christ executeth the office of a king, in calling out of the world a people to himself, and giving them officers, laws, and censures, by which he visibly governs them; in bestowing saving grace upon his elect, rewarding their obedience, and correcting them for their sins, preserving and supporting them under all their temptations and sufferings, restraining and overcoming all their enemies, and powerfully ordering all things for his own glory, and their good; and also in taking vengeance on the rest, who know not God, and obey not the gospel.

Q. 46. What was the estate of Christ's humiliation?

A. The estate of Christ's humiliation was that low condition, wherein he for our sakes, emptying himself of his glory, took upon him the form of a servant, in his conception and birth, life, death, and after his death, until his resurrection.

Q. 47. How did Christ humble himself in his conception and birth?

A. Christ humbled himself in his conception and birth, in that, being from all eternity the Son of God, in the bosom of the Father, he was pleased in the fulness of time to become the son of man, made of a woman of low estate, and to be born of her; with divers circumstances of more than ordinary abasement.

Q. 48. How did Christ humble himself in his life?

A. Christ humbled himself in his life, by subjecting himself to the law, which he perfectly fulfilled; and by conflicting with the indignities of the world, temptations of Satan, and infirmities in his flesh, whether common to the nature of man, or particularly accompanying that his low condition.

Q. 49. How did Christ humble himself in his death?

A. Christ humbled himself in his death, in that having been betrayed by Judas, forsaken by his disciples, scorned and rejected by the world, condemned by Pilate, and tormented by his persecutors; having also conflicted with the terrors of death, and the powers of darkness, felt and borne the weight of God's wrath, he laid down his life an offering for sin, enduring the painful, shameful, and cursed death of the cross.

Q. 50.Wherein consisted Christ's humiliation after his death?

A. Christ's humiliation after his death consisted in his being buried, and continuing in the state of the dead, and under the power of death till the third day; which hath been otherwise expressed in these words, He descended into hell.

Q. 51.What was the estate of Christ's exaltation?

A. The estate of Christ's exaltation comprehendeth his resurrection, ascension, sitting at the right hand of the Father, and his coming again to judge the world.

Q. 52. How was Christ exalted in his resurrection?

A. Christ was exalted in his resurrection, in that, not having seen corruption in death (of which it was not possible for him to be held), and having the very same body in which he suffered, with the essential properties thereof (but without mortality, and other common infirmities belonging to this life), really united to his soul, he rose again from the dead the third day by his own power; whereby he declared himself to be the Son of God, to have satisfied divine justice, to have vanquished death, and him that had the power of it, and to be Lord of quick and dead: all which he did as a public person, the head of his church, for their justification, quickening in grace, support against enemies, and to assure them of their resurrection from the dead at the last day.

Q. 53. How was Christ exalted in his ascension?

A. Christ was exalted in his ascension, in that having after his resurrection often appeared unto and conversed with his apostles, speaking to them of the things pertaining to the kingdom of God, and giving them commission to preach the gospel to all nations, forty days after his resurrection, he, in our nature, and as our head, triumphing over enemies, visibly went up into the highest heavens, there to receive gifts for men, to raise up our affections thither, and to prepare a place for us, where himself is, and shall continue till his second coming at the end of the world.

Q. 54. How is Christ exalted in his sitting at the right hand of God?

A. Christ is exalted in his sitting at the right hand of God, in that as God-man he is advanced to the highest favour with God the Father, with all fulness of joy, glory, and power over all things in heaven and earth; and doth gather and defend his church, and subdue their enemies; furnisheth his ministers and people with gifts and graces, and maketh intercession for them.

Q. 55. How doth Christ make intercession?

A. Christ maketh intercession, by his appearing in our nature continually before the Father in heaven, in the merit of his obedience and sacrifice on earth, declaring his will to have it applied to all believers; answering all accusations against them, and procuring for them quiet of conscience,notwithstanding daily failings, access with boldness to the throne of grace, and acceptance of their persons and services.

Q. 56. How is Christ to be exalted in his coming again to judge the world?

A. Christ is to be exalted in his coming again to judge the world, in that he, who was unjustly judged and condemned by wicked men, shall come again at the last day in great power, and in the full manifestation of his own glory, and of his Father's, with all his holy angels, with a shout, with the voice of the archangel, and with the trumpet of God, to judge the world in righteousness.

Q. 57.What benefits hath Christ procured by his mediation?

A. Christ, by his mediation, hath procured redemption, with all other benefits of the covenant of grace.

Q. 58. How do we come to be made partakers of the benefits which Christ hath procured?

A. We are made partakers of the benefits which Christ hath procured, by the application of them unto us, which is the work especially of God the Holy Ghost.

Q. 59.Who are made partakers of redemption through Christ?

A. Redemption is certainly applied, and effectually communicated, to all those for whom Christ hath purchased it; who are in time by the Holy Ghost enabled to believe in Christ according to the gospel.

Q. 60. Can they who have never heard the gospel, and so know not Jesus Christ, nor believe in him, be saved by their living according to the light of nature?

A. They who, having never heard the gospel, know not Jesus Christ, and believe not in him, cannot be saved, be they never so diligent to frame their lives according to the light of nature, or the laws of that religion which they profess; neither is there salvation in any other, but in Christ alone, who is the Saviour only of his body the church.

Q. 61. Are all they saved who hear the gospel, and live in the church?
A. All that hear the gospel, and live in the visible church, are not saved; but they only who are true members of the church invisible.

Q. 62. What is the visible church?
A. The visible church is a society made up of all such as in all ages and places of the world do profess the true religion, and of their children.

Q. 63. What are the special privileges of the visible church?
A. The visible church hath the privilege of being under God's special care and government; of being protected and preserved in all ages, notwithstanding the opposition of all enemies; and of enjoying the communion of saints, the ordinary means of salvation, and offers of grace by Christ to all the members of it in the ministry of the gospel, testifying, that whosoever believes in him shall be saved, and excluding none that will come unto him.

Q. 64. What is the invisible church?
A. The invisible church is the whole number of the elect, that have been, are, or shall be gathered into one under Christ the head.

Q. 65. What special benefits do the members of the invisible church enjoy by Christ?
A. The members of the invisible church by Christ enjoy union and communion with him in grace and glory.

Q. 66. What is that union which the elect have with Christ?
A. The union which the elect have with Christ is the work of God's grace, whereby they are spiritually and mystically, yet really and inseparably, joined to Christ as their head and husband; which is done in their effectual calling.

Q. 67. What is effectual calling?

A. Effectual calling is the work of God's almighty power and grace, whereby (out of his free and special love to his elect, and from nothing in them moving him thereunto) he doth, in his accepted time, invite and draw them to Jesus Christ, by his Word and Spirit; savingly enlightening their minds, renewing and powerfully determining their wills, so as they (although in themselves dead in sin) are hereby made willing and able freely to answer his call, and to accept and embrace the grace offered and conveyed therein.

Q. 68. Are the elect only effectually called?

A. All the elect, and they only, are effectually called; although others may be, and often are, outwardly called by the ministry of the Word, and have some common operations of the Spirit; who, for their wilful neglect and contempt of the grace offered to them, being justly left in their unbelief, do never truly come to Jesus Christ.

Q. 69. What is the communion in grace which the members of the invisible church have with Christ?

A. The communion in grace which the members of the invisible church have with Christ, is their partaking of the virtue of his mediation, in their justification, adoption, sanctification, and whatever else, in this life, manifests their union with him.

Q. 70. What is justification?

A. Justification is an act of God's free grace unto sinners, in which he pardoneth all their sins, accepteth and accounteth their persons righteous in his sight; not for any thing wrought in them, or done by them, but only for the perfect obedience and full satisfaction of Christ, by God imputed to them, and received by faith alone.

Q. 71. How is justification an act of God's free grace?

A. Although Christ, by his obedience and death, did make a proper, real, and full satisfaction to God's justice in the behalf of them that are justified; yet inasmuch as God accepteth the satisfaction from a surety, which he might have demanded of them, and did provide this surety, his own only Son, imputing his righteousness to them, and requiring nothing of them for their justification but faith, which also is his gift, their justification is to them of free grace.

Q. 72.What is justifying faith?

A. Justifying faith is a saving grace, wrought in the heart of a sinner by the Spirit and Word of God, whereby he, being convinced of his sin and misery, and of the disability in himself and all other creatures to recover him out of his lost condition, not only assenteth to the truth of the promise of the gospel, but receiveth and resteth upon Christ and his righteousness, therein held forth, for pardon of sin, and for the accepting and accounting of his person righteous in the sight of God for salvation.

Q. 73. How doth faith justify a sinner in the sight of God?

A. Faith justifies a sinner in the sight of God, not because of those other graces which do always accompany it, or of good works that are the fruits of it, nor as if the grace of faith, or any act thereof, were imputed to him for his justification; but only as it is an instrument by which he receiveth and applieth Christ and his righteousness.

Q. 74.What is adoption?

A. Adoption is an act of the free grace of God, in and for his only Son Jesus Christ, whereby all those that are justified are received into the number of his children, have his name put upon them, the Spirit of his Son given to them, are under his fatherly care and dispensations, admitted to all the liberties and privileges of the sons of God, made heirs of all the promises, and fellow heirs with Christ in glory.

Q. 75.What is sanctification?

A. Sanctification is a work of God's grace, whereby they whom God hath, before the foundation of the world, chosen to be holy, are in time, through the powerful operation of his Spirit applying the death and resurrection of Christ unto them, renewed in their whole man after the image of God; having the seeds of repentance unto life, and all other saving graces, put into their hearts, and those graces so stirred up, increased, and strengthened, as that they more and more die unto sin, and rise unto newness of life.

Q. 76.What is repentance unto life?

A. Repentance unto life is a saving grace, wrought in the heart of a sinner by the Spirit and Word of God, whereby, out of the sight and sense, not only of the danger, but also of the filthiness and odiousness of his sins, and upon the apprehension of God's mercy in Christ to such as are penitent, he so grieves for and hates his sins, as that he turns from them all to God, purposing and endeavouring constantly to walk with him in all the ways of new obedience.

Q. 77.Wherein do justification and sanctification differ?

A. Although sanctification be inseparably joined with justification, yet they differ, in that God in justification imputeth the righteousness of Christ; in sanctification his Spirit infuseth grace, and enableth to the exercise thereof; in the former, sin is pardoned; in the other, it is subdued: the one doth equally free all believers from the revenging wrath of God, and that perfectly in this life, that they never fall into condemnation; the other is neither equal in all, nor in this life perfect in any, but growing up to perfection.

Q. 78.Whence ariseth the imperfection of sanctification in believers?

A. The imperfection of sanctification in believers ariseth from the remnants of sin abiding in every part of them, and the perpetual lustings of the flesh against the spirit; whereby they are often foiled with temptations, and fall into many sins, are hindered in all their spiritual services, and their best works are imperfect and defiled in the sight of God.

Q. 79. May not true believers, by reason of their imperfections, and the many temptations and sins they are overtaken with, fall away from the state of grace?

A. True believers, by reason of the unchangeable love of God, and his decree and covenant to give them perseverance, their inseparable union with Christ, his continual intercession for them, and the Spirit and seed of God abiding in them, can neither totally nor finally fall away from the state of grace, but are kept by the power of God through faith unto salvation.

Q. 80. Can true believers be infallibly assured that they are in the estate of grace, and that they shall persevere therein unto salvation?

A. Such as truly believe in Christ, and endeavour to walk in all good conscience before him, may, without extraordinary revelation, by faith grounded upon the truth of God's promises, and by the Spirit enabling them to discern in themselves those graces to which the promises of life are made, and bearing witness with their spirits that they are the children of God, be infallibly assured that they are in the estate of grace, and shall persevere therein unto salvation.

Q. 81. Are all true believers at all times assured of their present being in the estate of grace, and that they shall be saved?

A. Assurance of grace and salvation not being of the essence of faith, true believers may wait long before they obtain it; and, after the enjoyment thereof, may have it weakened and intermitted, through manifold distempers, sins, temptations, and desertions; yet are they never left without such a presence and support of the Spirit of God as keeps them from sinking into utter despair.

Q. 82. What is the communion in glory which the members of the invisible church have with Christ?

A. The communion in glory which the members of the invisible church have with Christ, is in this life, immediately after death, and at last perfected at the resurrection and day of judgment.

Q. 83. What is the communion in glory with Christ which the members of the invisible church enjoy in this life?

A. The members of the invisible church have communicated to them in this life the first-fruits of glory with Christ, as they are members of him their head, and so in him are interested in that glory which he is fully possessed of; and, as an earnest thereof, enjoy the sense of God's love, peace of conscience, joy in the Holy Ghost, and hope of glory; as, on the contrary, sense of God's revenging wrath, horror of conscience, and a fearful expectation of judgment, are to the wicked the beginning of their torments which they shall endure after death.

Q. 84. Shall all men die?

A. Death being threatened as the wages of sin, it is appointed unto all men once to die; for that all have sinned.

Q. 85. Death, being the wages of sin, why are not the righteous delivered from death, seeing all their sins are forgiven in Christ?

A. The righteous shall be delivered from death itself at the last day, and even in death are delivered from the sting and curse of it; so that, although they die, yet it is out of God's love, to free them perfectly from sin and misery, and to make them capable of further communion with Christ in glory, which they then enter upon.

Q. 86. What is the communion in glory with Christ, which the members of the invisible church enjoy immediately after death?

A. The communion in glory with Christ, which the members of the invisible church enjoy immediately after death, is, in that their souls are then made perfect in holiness, and received into the highest heavens, where they behold the face of God in light and glory, waiting for the full redemption of their bodies, which even in death continue united to Christ, and rest in their graves as in their beds, till at the last day they be again united to their souls. Whereas the souls of the wicked are at their death cast into hell, where they remain in torments and utter darkness, and their bodies kept in their graves, as in their prisons, till the resurrection and judgment of the great day.

Q. 87. What are we to believe concerning the resurrection?

A. We are to believe, that at the last day there shall be a general resurrection of the dead, both of the just and unjust: when they that are then found alive shall in a moment be changed; and the self-same bodies of the dead which were laid in the grave, being then again united to their souls forever, shall be raised up by the power of Christ. The bodies of the just, by the Spirit of Christ, and by virtue of his resurrection as their head, shall be raised in power, spiritual, incorruptible, and made like to his glorious body; and the bodies of the wicked shall be raised up in dishonour by him, as an offended judge.

Q. 88. What shall immediately follow after the resurrection?

A. Immediately after the resurrection shall follow the general and final judgment of angels and men; the day and hour whereof no man knoweth, that all may watch and pray, and be ever ready for the coming of the Lord.

Q. 89. What shall be done to the wicked at the day of judgment?

A. At the day of judgment, the wicked shall be set on Christ's left hand,

and, upon clear evidence, and full conviction of their own consciences, shall have the fearful but just sentence of condemnation pronounced against them; and thereupon shall be cast out from the favourable presence of God, and the glorious fellowship with Christ, his saints, and all his holy angels, into hell, to be punished with unspeakable torments, both of body and soul, with the devil and his angels forever.

Q. 90. What shall be done to the righteous at the day of judgment?

A. At the day of judgment, the righteous, being caught up to Christ in the clouds, shall be set on his right hand, and there openly acknowledged and acquitted, shall join with him in the judging of reprobate angels and men, and shall be received into heaven, where they shall be fully and forever freed from all sin and misery; filled with inconceivable joys, made perfectly holy and happy both in body and soul, in the company of innumerable saints and holy angels, but especially in the immediate vision and fruition of God the Father, of our Lord Jesus Christ, and of the Holy Spirit, to all eternity. And this is the perfect and full communion, which the members of the invisible church shall enjoy with Christ in glory, at the resurrection and day of judgment.

Having seen what the Scriptures principally teach us to believe concerning God, it follows to consider what they require as the duty of man.

Q. 91. What is the duty which God requireth of man?

A. The duty which God requireth of man, is obedience to his revealed will.

Q. 92. What did God at first reveal unto man as the rule of his obedience?

A. The rule of obedience revealed to Adam in the estate of innocence, and to all mankind in him, besides a special command not to eat of the fruit of the tree of the knowledge of good and evil, was the moral law.

Q. 93. What is the moral law?

A. The moral law is the declaration of the will of God to mankind, directing and binding everyone to personal, perfect, and perpetual conformity and obedience thereunto, in the frame and disposition of the whole man, soul and body, and in performance of all those duties of holiness and righteousness which he oweth to God and man: promising life upon the fulfilling, and threatening death upon the breach of it.

Q. 94. Is there any use of the moral law to man since the fall?

A. Although no man, since the fall, can attain to righteousness and life by the moral law; yet there is great use thereof, as well common to all men, as peculiar either to the unregenerate, or the regenerate.

Q. 95. Of what use is the moral law to all men?

A. The moral law is of use to all men, to inform them of the holy nature and will of God, and of their duty, binding them to walk accordingly; to convince them of their disability to keep it, and of the sinful pollution of their nature, hearts, and lives; to humble them in the sense of their sin and misery, and thereby help them to a clearer sight of the need they have of Christ, and of the perfection of his obedience.

Q. 96. What particular use is there of the moral law to unregenerate men?

A. The moral law is of use to unregenerate men, to awaken their consciences to flee from wrath to come, and to drive them to Christ; or, upon their continuance in the estate and way of sin, to leave them inexcusable, and under the curse thereof.

Q. 97. What special use is there of the moral law to the regenerate?

A. Although they that are regenerate, and believe in Christ, be delivered from the moral law as a covenant of works, so as thereby they are neither justified nor condemned; yet, besides the general uses thereof common to them with all men, it is of special use, to show them how much they are bound to Christ for his fulfilling it, and enduring the curse thereof in their stead, and for their good; and thereby to provoke them to more thankfulness, and to express the same in their greater care to conform themselves thereunto as the rule of their obedience.

Q. 98. Where is the moral law summarily comprehended?

A. The moral law is summarily comprehended in the ten commandments, which were delivered by the voice of God upon Mount Sinai, and written by him in two tables of stone; and are recorded in the twentieth chapter of Exodus. The four first commandments containing our duty to God, and the other six our duty to man.

Q. 99. What rules are to be observed for the right understanding of the ten commandments?

A. For the right understanding of the ten commandments, these rules are to be observed:

1. That the law is perfect, and bindeth everyone to full conformity in the whole man unto the righteousness thereof, and unto entire obedience forever; so as to require the utmost perfection of every duty, and to forbid the least degree of every sin.

2. That it is spiritual, and so reacheth the understanding, will, affections, and all other powers of the soul; as well as words, works, and gestures.

3. That one and the same thing, in divers respects, is required or forbidden in several commandments.

4. That as, where a duty is commanded, the contrary sin is forbidden; and, where a sin is forbidden, the contrary duty is commanded: so, where a promise is annexed, the contrary threatening is included; and, where a threatening is annexed, the contrary promise is included.

5. That what God forbids, is at no time to be done; what he commands, is always our duty; and yet every particular duty is not to be done at all times.

6. That under one sin or duty, all of the same kind are forbidden or commanded; together with all the causes, means, occasions, and appearances thereof, and provocations thereunto.

7. That what is forbidden or commanded to ourselves, we are bound, according to our places, to endeavour that it may be avoided or performed by others, according to the duty of their places.

8. That in what is commanded to others, we are bound, according to our places and callings, to be helpful to them; and to take heed of partaking with others in what is forbidden them.

Q. 100. What special things are we to consider in the ten commandments?

A. We are to consider, in the ten commandments, the preface, the substance of the commandments themselves, and several reasons annexed to some of them, the more to enforce them.

Q. 101. What is the preface to the ten commandments?

A. The preface to the ten commandments is contained in these words, *I am the Lord thy God, which have brought thee out of the land of Egypt, out of the house of bondage*. Wherein God manifesteth his sovereignty, as being

JEHOVAH, the eternal, immutable, and almighty God; having his being in and of himself, and giving being to all his words and works: and that he is a God in covenant, as with Israel of old, so with all his people; who, as he brought them out of their bondage in Egypt, so he delivereth us from our spiritual thraldom; and that therefore we are bound to take him for our God alone, and to keep all his commandments.

Q. 102. What is the sum of the four commandments which contain our duty to God?

A. The sum of the four commandments containing our duty to God is, to love the Lord our God with all our heart, and with all our soul, and with all our strength, and with all our mind.

Q. 103. Which is the first commandment?

A. The first commandment is, *Thou shall have no other gods before me.*

Q. 104. What are the duties required in the first commandment?

A. The duties required in the first commandment are, the knowing and acknowledging of God to be the only true God, and our God; and to worship and glorify him accordingly, by thinking, meditating, remembering, highly esteeming, honouring, adoring, choosing, loving, desiring, fearing of him; believing him; trusting, hoping, delighting, rejoicing in him; being zealous for him; calling upon him, giving all praise and thanks, and yielding all obedience and submission to him with the whole man; being careful in all things to please him, and sorrowful when in anything he is offended; and walking humbly with him.

Q. 105. What are the sins forbidden in the first commandment?

A. The sins forbidden in the first commandment are, atheism, in denying or not having a God; idolatry, in having or worshipping more gods than one, or any with or instead of the true God; the not having and avouching him for God, and our God; the omission or neglect of anything due to him, required in this commandment; ignorance, forgetfulness, misapprehensions, false opinions, unworthy and wicked thoughts of him; bold and curious searching into his secrets; all profaneness, hatred of God; self-love, self-seeking, and all other inordinate and immoderate setting of our mind, will, or affections upon other things, and taking them off from him in whole or inpart; vain credulity, unbelief, heresy, misbelief, distrust, despair, incorrigibleness, and insensibleness under judgments, hardness of heart, pride, presumption, carnal security, tempting of God; using unlawful means, and trusting in lawful means; carnal delights and joys; corrupt, blind, and indiscreet zeal; lukewarmness, and deadness in the things of God; estranging ourselves, and apostatizing from God; praying, or giving any religious worship, to saints, angels, or any other creatures; all compacts and consulting with the devil, and hearkening to his suggestions; making men the lords of our faith and conscience; slighting and despising God and his commands; resisting and grieving of his Spirit, discontent and impatience at his dispensations, charging him foolishly for the evils he inflicts on us; and ascribing the praise of any good we either are, have, or can do, to fortune, idols, ourselves, or any other creature.

Q. 106. What are we specially taught by these words before me *in the first commandment?*

A. These words *before me*, or before my face, in the first commandment, teach us, that God, who seeth all things, taketh special notice of, and is much displeased with, the sin of having any other God: that so it may be an argument to dissuade from it, and to aggravate it as a most impudent provocation: as also to persuade us to do as in his sight, whatever we do in his service.

Q. 107. Which is the second commandment?

A. The second commandment is, *Thou shalt not make unto thee any graven image, or any likeness of anything that is in heaven above, or that is in the earth beneath, or that is in the water under the earth: Thou shalt not bow down thyself to them, nor serve them: for I the Lord thy God am a jealous God, visiting the iniquity of the fathers upon the children unto the third and fourth generation of them that hate me; and showing mercy unto thousands of them that love me, and keep my commandments.*

Q. 108. What are the duties required in the second commandment?

A. The duties required in the second commandment are, the receiving, observing, and keeping pure and entire, all such religious worship and ordinances as God hath instituted in his Word; particularly prayer and thanksgiving in the name of Christ; the reading, preaching, and hearing of the Word; the administration and receiving of the sacraments; church government and discipline; the ministry and maintenance thereof; religious fasting; swearing by the name of God, and vowing unto him: as also the disapproving, detesting, opposing, all false worship; and, according to each one's place and calling, removing it, and all monuments of idolatry.

Q. 109. What are the sins forbidden in the second commandment?

A. The sins forbidden in the second commandment are, all devising, counselling, commanding, using, and anywise approving, any religious worship not instituted by God himself; tolerating a false religion; the making any representation of God, of all or of any of the three persons, either inwardly in our mind, or outwardly in any kind of image or likeness of any creature whatsoever; all worshipping of it, or God in it or by it; the making of any representation of feigned deities, and all worship of them, or service belonging to them; all superstitious devices, corrupting the worship of God, adding to it, or taking from it, whether invented and taken up of ourselves, or received by tradition from others, though under the title of antiquity, custom, devotion, good intent, or any other pretence whatsoever; simony; sacrilege; all neglect, contempt, hindering, and opposing the worship and ordinances which God hath appointed.

Q. 110. What are the reasons annexed to the second commandment, the more to enforce it?

A. The reasons annexed to the second commandment, the more to enforce it, contained in these words, *For I the Lord thy God am a jealous God, visiting the iniquity of the fathers upon the children unto the third and fourth generation of them that hate me; and showing mercy unto thousands of them that love me, and keep my commandments*; are, besides God's sovereignty over us, and propriety in us, his fervent zeal for his own worship, and his revengeful indignation against all false worship, as being a spiritual whoredom; accounting the breakers of this commandment such as hate him, and threatening to punish them unto divers generations; and esteeming the observers of it such as love him and keep his commandments, and promising mercy to them unto many generations.

Q. 111. Which is the third commandment?

A. The third commandment is, *Thou shalt not take the name of the Lord thy God in vain: for the Lord will not hold him guiltless that taketh his name in vain.*

Q. 112. What is required in the third commandment?

A. The third commandment requires, That the name of God, his titles, attributes, ordinances, the Word, sacraments, prayer, oaths, vows, lots, his works, and whatsoever else there is whereby he makes himself known, be holily and reverently used in thought, meditation, word, and writing; by an holy profession, and answerable conversation, to the glory of God, and the good of ourselves, and others.

Q. 113. What are the sins forbidden in the third commandment?

A. The sins forbidden in the third commandment are, the not using of God's name as is required; and the abuse of it in an ignorant, vain, irreverent, profane, superstitious, or wicked mentioning, or otherwise using his titles, attributes, ordinances, or works, by blasphemy, perjury; all sinful cursings, oaths, vows, and lots; violating of our oaths and vows, if lawful; and fulfilling them, if of things unlawful; murmuring and quarrelling at, curious prying into, and misapplying of God's decrees and providences; misinterpreting, misapplying, or any way perverting the Word, or any part of it, to profane jests, curious or unprofitable questions, vain janglings, or the maintaining of false doctrines; abusing it, the creatures, or anything contained under the name of God, to charms, or sinful lusts and practices; the maligning, scorning, reviling, or any wise opposing of God's truth, grace, and ways; making profession of religion in hypocrisy, or for sinister ends; being ashamed of it, or a shame to it, by unconformable, unwise, unfruitful, and offensive walking, or backsliding from it.

Q. 114. What reasons are annexed to the third commandment?

A. The reasons annexed to the third commandment, in these words, *The Lord thy God*, and, *For the Lord will not hold him guiltless that taketh his name in vain*, are, because he is the Lord and our God, therefore his name is not to be profaned, or any way abused by us; especially because he will be so far from acquitting and sparing the transgressors of this commandment, as that he will not suffer them to escape his righteous judgment, albeit many such escape the censures and punishments of men.

Q. 115. Which is the fourth commandment?

A. The fourth commandment is, *Remember the sabbath day, to keep it holy. Six days shalt thou labour, and do all thy work: but the seventh day is the sabbath of the Lord thy God: in it thou shalt not do any work, thou, nor thy son, nor thy daughter, thy manservant, nor thy maidservant, nor thy cattle, nor thy stranger that is within thy gates: For in six days the Lord made heaven and earth, the sea, and all that in them is, and rested the seventh day: wherefore the Lord blessed the sabbath day, and hallowed it.*

Q. 116.What is required in the fourth commandment?

A.The fourth commandment requireth of all men the sanctifying or keeping holy to God such set times as he hath appointed in his Word, expressly one whole day in seven; which was the seventh from the beginning of the world to the resurrection of Christ, and the first day of the week ever since, and so to continue to the end of the world; which is the Christian sabbath, and in the New Testament called the Lord's day.

Q. 117. How is the sabbath or the Lord's day to be sanctified?

A. The sabbath or Lord's day is to be sanctified by an holy resting all the day, not only from such works as are at all times sinful, but even from such worldly employments and recreations as are on other days lawful; and making it our delight to spend the whole time (except so much of it as is to be taken up in works of necessity and mercy) in the public and private exercises of God's worship: and, to that end, we are to prepare our hearts, and with such foresight, diligence, and moderation, to dispose and seasonably dispatch our worldly business, that we may be the more free and fit for the duties of that day.

Q. 118.Why is the charge of keeping the sabbath more specially directed to governors of families, and other superiors?

A. The charge of keeping the sabbath is more specially directed to governors of families, and other superiors, because they are bound not only to keep it themselves, but to see that it be observed by all those that are under their charge; and because they are prone oft times to hinder them by employments of their own.

Q. 119.What are the sins forbidden in the fourth commandment?

A.The sins forbidden in the fourth commandment are, all omissions of the duties required, all careless, negligent, and unprofitable performing of them, and being weary of them; all profaning the day by idleness, and doing that which is in itself sinful; and by all needless works, words, and thoughts, about our worldly employments and recreations.

Q. 120. What are the reasons annexed to the fourth commandment, the more to enforce it?

A. The reasons annexed to the fourth commandment, the more to enforce it, are taken from the equity of it, God allowing us six days of seven for our own affairs, and reserving but one for himself, in these words, *Six days shalt thou labour, and do all thy work*: from God's challenging a special propriety in that day, *The seventh day is the sabbath of the Lord thy God*: from the example of God, who *in six days made heaven and earth, the sea, and all that in them is, and rested the seventh day*: and from that blessing which God put upon that day, not only in sanctifying it to be a day for his service, but in ordaining it to be a means of blessing to us in our sanctifying it; *Wherefore the Lord blessed the sabbath day, and hallowed it.*

Q. 121. Why is the word Remember *set in the beginning of the fourth commandment?*

A. The word *Remember* is set in the beginning of the fourth commandment, partly, because of the great benefit of remembering it, we being thereby helped in our preparation to keep it, and, in keeping it, better to keep all the rest of the commandments, and to continue a thankful remembrance of the two great benefits of creation and redemption, which contain a short abridgment of religion; and partly, because we are very ready to forget it, for that there is less light of nature for it, and yet it restraineth our natural liberty in things at other times lawful; that it cometh but once in seven days, and many worldly businesses come between, and too often take off our minds from thinking of it, either to prepare for it, or to sanctify it; and that Satan with his instruments much labour to blot out the glory, and even the memory of it, to bring in all irreligion and impiety.

Q. 122. What is the sum of the six commandments which contain our duty to man?

A. The sum of the six commandments which contain our duty to man is, to love our neighbour as ourselves, and to do to others what we would have them to do to us.

Q.123.Which is the fifth commandment?

A.The fifth commandment is, *Honour thy father and thy mother; that thy days may be long upon the land which the Lord thy God giveth thee.*

Q. 124.Who are meant by father and mother in the fifth commandment?

A. By father and mother, in the fifth commandment, are meant, not only natural parents, but all superiors in age and gifts; and especially such as, by God's ordinance, are over us in place of authority, whether in family, church, or commonwealth.

Q. 125.Why are superiors styled father and mother?

A. Superiors are styled father and mother, both to teach them in all duties toward their inferiors, like natural parents, to express love and tenderness to them, according to their several relations; and to work inferiors to a greater willingness and cheerfulness in performing their duties to their superiors, as to their parents.

Q. 126.What is the general scope of the fifth commandment?

A.The general scope of the fifth commandment is, the performance of those duties which we mutually owe in our several relations, as inferiors, superiors, or equals.

Q. 127.What is the honour that inferiors owe to their superiors?

A.The honour which inferiors owe to their superiors is, all due reverence in heart, word, and behaviour; prayer and thanksgiving for them; imitation of their virtues and graces; willing obedience to their lawful commands and counsels; due submission to their corrections; fidelity to, defence and maintenance of their persons and authority, according to their several ranks, and the nature of their places; bearing with their infirmities, and covering them in love, that so they may be an honour to them and to their government.

Q. 128.What are the sins of inferiors against their superiors?

A.The sins of inferiors against their superiors are, all neglect of the duties required toward them; envying at, contempt of, and rebellion against, their persons and places, in their lawful counsels, commands, and corrections; cursing, mocking, and all such refractory and scandalous carriage, as proves a shame and dishonour to them and their government.

Q. 129.What is required of superiors towards their inferiors?

A. It is required of superiors, according to that power they receive from God, and that relation wherein they stand, to love, pray for, and bless their inferiors; to instruct, counsel, and admonish them; countenancing, commending, and rewarding such as do well; and discountenancing, reproving, and chastising such as do ill; protecting, and providing for them all things necessary for soul and body: and by grave, wise, holy, and exemplary carriage, to procure glory to God, honour to themselves, and so to preserve that authority which God hath put upon them.

Q. 130.What are the sins of superiors?

A.The sins of superiors are, besides the neglect of the duties required of them, an inordinate seeking of themselves, their own glory, ease, profit, or pleasure; commanding things unlawful, or not in the power of inferiors to perform; counselling, encouraging, or favouring them in that which is evil; dissuading, discouraging, or discountenancing them in that which is good; correcting them unduly; careless exposing, or leaving them to wrong, temptation, and danger; provoking them to wrath; or any way dishonouring themselves, or lessening their authority, by an unjust, indiscreet, rigorous,or remiss behaviour.

Q. 131.What are the duties of equals?

A. The duties of equals are, to regard the dignity and worth of each other, in giving honour to go one before another; and to rejoice in each other's gifts and advancement, as their own.

Q. 132.What are the sins of equals?

A. The sins of equals are, besides the neglect of the duties required, the undervaluing of the worth, envying the gifts, grieving at the advancement of prosperity one of another; and usurping pre-eminence one over another.

Q. 133. What is the reason annexed to the fifth commandment, the more to enforce it?

A.The reason annexed to the fifth commandment, in these words, *That thy days may be long upon the land which the Lord thy God giveth thee*, is an express promise of long life and prosperity, as far as it shall serve for God's glory and their own good, to all such as keep this commandment.

Q. 134. Which is the sixth commandment?

A. The sixth commandment is, *Thou shalt not kill.*

Q. 135. What are the duties required in the sixth commandment?

A. The duties required in the sixth commandment are, all careful studies, and lawful endeavours, to preserve the life of ourselves and others by resisting all thoughts and purposes, subduing all passions, and avoiding all occasions, temptations, and practices, which tend to the unjust taking away the life of any; by just defence thereof against violence, patient bearing of the hand of God, quietness of mind, cheerfulness of spirit; a sober use of meat, drink, physic, sleep, labour, and recreations; by charitable thoughts, love, compassion, meekness, gentleness, kindness; peaceable, mild and courteous speeches and behaviour; forbearance, readiness to be reconciled, patient bearing and forgiving of injuries, and requiting good for evil; comforting and succouring the distressed, and protecting and defending the innocent.

Q. 136. What are the sins forbidden in the sixth commandment?

A. The sins forbidden in the sixth commandment are, all taking away the life of ourselves, or of others, except in case of public justice, lawful war, or necessary defence; the neglecting or withdrawing the lawful and necessary means of preservation of life; sinful anger, hatred, envy, desire of revenge; all excessive passions, distracting cares; immoderate use of meat, drink, labour, and recreations; provoking words, oppression, quarrelling, striking, wounding, and whatsoever else tends to the destruction of the life of any.

Q. 137. Which is the seventh commandment?

A. The seventh commandment is, *Thou shalt not commit adultery.*

Q. 138. What are the duties required in the seventh commandment?

A. The duties required in the seventh commandment are, chastity in body, mind, affections, words, and behaviour; and the preservation of it in ourselves and others; watchfulness over the eyes and all the senses; temperance, keeping of chaste company, modesty in apparel; marriage by those that have not the gift of continency, conjugal love, and cohabitation; diligent labour in our callings; shunning all occasions of uncleanness, and resisting temptations thereunto.

Q. 139. What are the sins forbidden in the seventh commandment?

A. The sins forbidden in the seventh commandment, besides the neglect of the duties required, are, adultery, fornication, rape, incest, sodomy, and all unnatural lusts; all unclean imaginations, thoughts, purposes, and affections; all corrupt or filthy communications, or listening thereunto; wanton looks, impudent or light behaviour, immodest apparel; prohibiting of lawful, and dispensing with unlawful marriages; allowing, tolerating, keeping of stews, and resorting to them; entangling vows of single life, undue delay of marriage; having more wives or husbands than one at the same time; unjust divorce, or desertion; idleness, gluttony, drunkenness, unchaste company; lascivious songs, books, pictures, dancings, stage plays; and all other provocations to, or acts of uncleanness, either in ourselves or others.

Q. 140. Which is the eighth commandment?

A. The eighth commandment is, *Thou shalt not steal.*

Q. 141. What are the duties required in the eighth commandment?

A. The duties required in the eighth commandment are, truth, faithfulness, and justice in contracts and commerce between man and man; rendering to everyone his due; restitution of goods unlawfully detained from the right owners thereof; giving and lending freely, according to our abilities, and the necessities of others; moderation of our judgments, wills, and affections concerning worldly goods; a provident care and study to get, keep, use, and dispose these things which are necessary and convenient for the sustentation of our nature, and suitable to our condition; a lawful calling, and diligence in it; frugality; avoiding unnecessary lawsuits and suretyship, or other like engagements; and an endeavour, by all just and lawful means, to procure, preserve, and further the wealth and outward estate of others, as well as our own.

Q. 142. What are the sins forbidden in the eighth commandment?

A. The sins forbidden in the eighth commandment, besides the neglect of the duties required, are, theft, robbery, man-stealing, and receiving anything that is stolen; fraudulent dealing, false weights and measures, removing land-marks, injustice and unfaithfulness in contracts between man and man, or in matters of trust; oppression, extortion, usury, bribery, vexatious lawsuits, unjust inclosures and depopulations; ingrossing commodities to enhance the price; unlawful callings, and all other unjust or sinful ways of taking or withholding from our neighbour what belongs to him, or of enriching ourselves; covetousness; inordinate prizing and affecting worldly goods; distrustful and distracting cares and studies in getting, keeping, and using them; envying at the prosperity of others; as likewise idleness, prodigality, wasteful gaming; and all other ways whereby we do unduly prejudice our own outward estate, and defrauding ourselves of the due use and comfort of that estate which God hath given us.

Q. 143.Which is the ninth commandment?

A. The ninth commandment is, *Thou shalt not bear false witness against thy neighbour*.

Q. 144.What are the duties required in the ninth commandment?

A. The duties required in the ninth commandment are, the preserving and promoting of truth between man and man, and the good name of our neighbour, as well as our own; appearing and standing for the truth; and from the heart, sincerely, freely, clearly, and fully, speaking the truth, and only the truth, in matters of judgment and justice, and in all other things whatsoever; a charitable esteem of our neighbours; loving, desiring, and rejoicing in their good name; sorrowing for, and covering of their infirmities; freely acknowledging of their gifts and graces, defending their innocency; a ready receiving of a good report, and unwillingness to admit of an evil report, concerning them; discouraging talebearers, flatterers, and slanderers; love and care of our own good name, and defending it when need requireth; keeping of lawful promises; studying and practising of whatsoever things are true, honest, lovely, and of good report.

Q. 145.What are the sins forbidden in the ninth commandment?

A. The sins forbidden in the ninth commandment are, all prejudicing the truth, and the good name of our neighbours, as well as our own, especially in public judicature; giving false evidence, suborning false witnesses, wittingly appearing and pleading for an evil cause, out-facing and over-bearing the truth; passing unjust sentence, calling evil good, and good evil; rewarding the wicked according to the work of the righteous, and the righteous according to the work of the wicked; forgery, concealing the truth, undue silence in a just cause, and holding our peace when iniquity calleth for either a reproof from ourselves, or complaint to others; speaking the truth unseasonably, or maliciously to a wrong end, or perverting it to a wrong meaning, or in doubtful and equivocal expressions, to the prejudice of truth or justice; speaking untruth, lying, slandering, backbiting, detracting, tale-bearing, whispering, scoffing, reviling, rash, harsh, and partial censuring; misconstructing intentions, words, and actions; flattering, vain-glorious boasting, thinking or speaking too highly or too meanly of ourselves or others; denying the gifts and graces of God; aggravating smaller faults; hiding, excusing, or extenuating of sins, when called to a free confession; unnecessary discovery of infirmities; raising false rumours, receiving and countenancing evil reports, and stopping our ears against just defence; evil suspicion, envying or grieving at the deserved credit of any, endeavouring or desiring to impair it, rejoicing in their disgrace and infamy; scornful contempt, fond admiration; breach of lawful promises; neglecting such things as are of good report, and practising, or not avoiding ourselves, or not hindering what we can in others, such things as procure an ill name.

Q. 146.Which is the tenth commandment?

A.The tenth commandment is, *Thou shalt not covet thy neighbour's house, thou shalt not covet thy neighbour's wife, nor his man-servant, nor his maid-servant, nor his ox, nor his ass, nor any thing that is thy neighbour's.*

Q. 147.What are the duties required in the tenth commandment?

A. The duties required in the tenth commandment are, such a full contentment with our own condition, and such a charitable frame of the whole soul toward our neighbour, as that all our inward motions and affections touching him, tend unto, and further all that good which is his.

Q. 148.What are the sins forbidden in the tenth commandment?

A.The sins forbidden in the tenth commandment are, discontentment with our own estate; envying and grieving at the good of our neighbour, together with all inordinate motions and affections to anything that is his.

Q. 149. Is any man able perfectly to keep the commandments of God?

A. No man is able, either of himself, or by any grace received in this life, perfectly to keep the commandments of God; but doth daily break them in thought, word, and deed.

Q. 150. Are all transgressions of the law of God equally heinous in themselves, and in the sight of God?

A. All transgressions of the law of God are not equally heinous; but some sins in themselves, and by reason of several aggravations, are more heinous in the sight of God than others.

Q. 151. What are those aggravations that make some sins more heinous than others?

A. Sins receive their aggravations, From the persons offending: if they be of riper age, greater experience or grace, eminent for profession, gifts, place, office, guides to others, and whose example is likely to be followed by others. From the parties offended: if immediately against God, his attributes, and worship; against Christ, and his grace; the Holy Spirit, his witness, and workings; against superiors, men of eminency, and such as we stand especially related and engaged unto; against any of the saints, particularly weak brethren, the souls of them, or any other, and the common good of all or many. From the nature and quality of the offence: if it be against the express letter of the law, break many commandments, contain in it many sins: if not only conceived in the heart, but breaks forth in words and actions, scandalize others, and admit of no reparation: if against means, mercies, judgments, light of nature, conviction of conscience, public or private admonition, censures of the church, civil punishments; and our prayers, purposes, promises, vows, covenants, and engagements to God or men: if done deliberately, wilfully, presumptuously, impudently, boastingly, maliciously, frequently, obstinately, with delight, continuance, or relapsing after repentance. From circumstances of time and place: if on the Lord's day, or other times of divine worship; or immediately before or after these, or other helps to prevent or remedy such miscarriages: if in public, or in the presence of others, who are thereby likely to be provoked or defiled.

Q. 152. What doth every sin deserve at the hands of God?

A. Every sin, even the least, being against the sovereignty, goodness, and holiness of God, and against his righteous law, deserveth his wrath and curse, both in this life, and that which is to come; and cannot be expiated but by the blood of Christ.

Q. 153. What doth God require of us, that we may escape his wrath and curse due to us by reason of the transgression of the law?

A. That we may escape the wrath and curse of God due to us by reason of the transgression of the law, he requireth of us repentance toward God, and faith toward our Lord Jesus Christ, and the diligent use of the outward means whereby Christ communicates to us the benefits of his mediation.

Q. 154. What are the outward means whereby Christ communicates to us the benefits of his mediation?

A. The outward and ordinary means whereby Christ communicates to his church the benefits of his mediation, are all his ordinances; especially the Word, sacraments, and prayer; all which are made effectual to the elect for their salvation.

Q. 155. How is the Word made effectual to salvation?

A. The Spirit of God maketh the reading, but especially the preaching of the Word, an effectual means of enlightening, convincing, and humbling sinners; of driving them out of themselves, and drawing them unto Christ; of conforming them to his image, and subduing them to his will; of strengthening them against temptations and corruptions; of building them up in grace, and establishing their hearts in holiness and comfort through faith unto salvation.

Q. 156. Is the Word of God to be read by all?

A. Although all are not to be permitted to read the Word publicly to the congregation, yet all sorts of people are bound to read it apart by themselves, and with their families: to which end, the holy Scriptures are to be translated out of the original into vulgar languages.

Q. 157. How is the Word of God to be read?

A. The holy Scriptures are to be read with an high and reverent esteem of them; with a firm persuasion that they are the very Word of God, and that he only can enable us to understand them; with desire to know, believe, and obey the will of God revealed in them; with diligence, and attention to the matter and scope of them; with meditation, application, self- denial, and prayer.

Q. 158. By whom is the Word of God to be preached?

A. The Word of God is to be preached only by such as are sufficiently gifted, and also duly approved and called to that office.

Q. 159. How is the Word of God to be preached by those that are called thereunto?

A. They that are called to labour in the ministry of the Word, are to preach sound doctrine, diligently, in season and out of season; plainly, not in the enticing words of man's wisdom, but in demonstration of the Spirit, and of power; faithfully, making known the whole counsel of God; wisely, applying themselves to the necessities and capacities of the hearers; zealously, with fervent love to God and the souls of his people; sincerely, aiming at his glory, and their conversion, edification, and salvation.

Q. 160. What is required of those that hear the Word preached?

A. It is required of those that hear the Word preached, that they attend upon it with diligence, preparation, and prayer; examine what they hear by the Scriptures; receive the truth with faith, love, meekness, and readiness of mind, as the Word of God; meditate, and confer of it; hide it in their hearts, and bring forth the fruit of it in their lives.

Q. 161. How do the sacraments become effectual means of salvation?

A. The sacraments become effectual means of salvation, not by any power in themselves, or any virtue derived from the piety or intention of him by whom they are administered, but only by the working of the Holy Ghost, and the blessing of Christ, by whom they are instituted.

Q. 162. What is a sacrament?

A. A sacrament is a holy ordinance instituted by Christ in his church, to signify, seal, and exhibit unto those that are within the covenant of grace, the benefits of his mediation; to strengthen and increase their faith, and all other graces; to oblige them to obedience; to testify and cherish their love and communion one with another; and to distinguish them from those that are without.

Q. 163. What are the parts of a sacrament?

A. The parts of a sacrament are two; the one an outward and sensible sign, used according to Christ's own appointment; the other an inward and spiritual grace thereby signified.

Q. 164. How many sacraments hath Christ instituted in his church under the New Testament?

A. Under the New Testament Christ hath instituted in his church only two sacraments, Baptism and the Lord's Supper.

Q. 165.What is Baptism?

A. Baptism is a sacrament of the New Testament, wherein Christ hath ordained the washing with water in the name of the Father, and of the Son, and of the Holy Ghost, to be a sign and seal of ingrafting into himself, of remission of sins by his blood, and regeneration by his Spirit; of adoption, and resurrection unto everlasting life; and whereby the parties baptized are solemnly admitted into the visible church, and enter into an open and professed engagement to be wholly and only the Lord's.

Q. 166. Unto whom is Baptism to be administered?

A. Baptism is not to be administered to any that are out of the visible church, and so strangers from the covenant of promise, till they profess their faith in Christ, and obedience to him, but infants descending from parents, either both, or but one of them, professing faith in Christ, and obedience to him, are in that respect within the covenant, and to be baptized.

Q. 167. How is our Baptism to be improved by us?

A. The needful but much neglected duty of improving our Baptism, is to be performed by us all our life long, especially in the time of temptation, and when we are present at the administration of it to others; by serious and thankful consideration of the nature of it, and of the ends for which Christ instituted it, the privileges and benefits conferred and sealed thereby, and our solemn vow made therein; by being humbled for our sinful defilement, our falling short of, and walking contrary to, the grace of baptism, and our engagements; by growing up to assurance of pardon of sin, and of all other blessings sealed to us in that sacrament; by drawing strength from the death and resurrection of Christ, into whom we are baptized, for the mortifying of sin, and quickening of grace; and by endeavouring to live by faith, to have our conversation in holiness and righteousness, as those that have therein given up their names to Christ; and to walk in brotherly love, as being baptized by the same Spirit into one body.

Q. 168. What is the Lord's Supper?

A. The Lord's Supper is a sacrament of the New Testament, wherein, by giving and receiving bread and wine according to the appointment of Jesus Christ, his death is showed forth; and they that worthily communicate feed upon his body and blood, to their spiritual nourishment and growth in grace; have their union and communion with him confirmed; testify and renew their thankfulness, and engagement to God, and their mutual love and fellowship each with other, as members of the same mystical body.

Q. 169. How hath Christ appointed bread and wine to be given and received in the sacrament of the Lord's Supper?

A. Christ hath appointed the ministers of his Word, in the administration of this sacrament of the Lord's Supper, to set apart the bread and wine from common use, by the word of institution, thanksgiving, and prayer; to take and break the bread, and to give both the bread and the wine to the communicants: who are, by the same appointment, to take and eat the bread, and to drink the wine, in thankful remembrance that the body of Christ was broken and given, and his blood shed, for them.

Q. 170. How do they that worthily communicate in the Lord's Supper feed upon the body and blood of Christ therein?

A. As the body and blood of Christ are not corporally or carnally present in, with, or under the bread and wine in the Lord's Supper, and yet are spiritually present to the faith of the receiver, no less truly and really than the elements themselves are to their outward senses; so they that worthily communicate in the sacrament of the Lord's Supper, do therein feed upon the body and blood of Christ, not after a corporal and carnal, but in a spiritual manner; yet truly and really, while by faith they receive and apply unto themselves Christ crucified, and all the benefits of his death.

Q. 171. How are they that receive the sacrament of the Lord's Supper to prepare themselves before they come unto it?

A. They that receive the sacrament of the Lord's Supper are, before they come, to prepare themselves thereunto, by examining themselves of their being in Christ, of their sins and wants; of the truth and measure of their knowledge, faith, repentance; love to God and the brethren, charity to all men, forgiving those that have done them wrong; of their desires after Christ, and of their new obedience; and by renewing the exercise of these graces, by serious meditation, and fervent prayer.

Q.172. May one who doubteth of his being in Christ, or of his due preparation, come to the Lord's Supper?

A. One who doubteth of his being in Christ, or of his due preparation to the sacrament of the Lord's Supper, may have true interest in Christ, though he be not yet assured thereof; and in God's account hath it, if he be duly affected with the apprehension of the want of it, and unfeignedly desires to be found in Christ, and to depart from iniquity: in which case (because promises are made, and this sacrament is appointed, for the relief even of weak and doubting Christians) he is to bewail his unbelief, and labour to have his doubts resolved; and, so doing, he may and ought to come to the Lord's Supper, that he may be further strengthened.

Q.173. May any who profess the faith, and desire to come to the Lord's Supper, be kept from it?

A. Such as are found to be ignorant or scandalous, notwithstanding their profession of the faith, and desire to come to the Lord's Supper, may and ought to be kept from that sacrament, by the power which Christ hath left in his church, until they receive instruction, and manifest their reformation.

Q.174.What is required of them that receive the sacrament of the Lord's Supper in the time of the administration of it?

A. It is required of them that receive the sacrament of the Lord's Supper, that, during the time of the administration of it, with all holy reverence and attention they wait upon God in that ordinance, diligently observe the sacramental elements and actions, heedfully discern the Lord's body, and affectionately meditate on his death and sufferings, and thereby stir up themselves to a vigorous exercise of their graces; in judging themselves, and sorrowing for sin; in earnest hungering and thirsting after Christ, feeding on him by faith, receiving of his fulness, trusting in his merits, rejoicing in his love, giving thanks for his grace; in renewing of their covenant with God, and love to all the saints.

Q. 175.What is the duty of Christians, after they have received the sacrament of the Lord's Supper?

A. The duty of Christians, after they have received the sacrament of the Lord's Supper, is seriously to consider how they have behaved themselves therein, and with what success; if they find quickening and comfort, to bless God for it, beg the continuance of it, watch against relapses, fulfil their vows, and encourage themselves to a frequent attendance on that ordinance: but if they find no present benefit, more exactly to review their preparation to, and carriage at, the sacrament; in both which, if they can approve themselves to God and their own consciences, they are to wait for the fruit of it in due time: but, if they see they have failed in either, they are to be humbled, and to attend upon it afterwards with more care and diligence.

Q. 176. Wherein do the sacraments of Baptism and the Lord's Supper agree?

A. The sacraments of Baptism and the Lord's Supper agree, in that the author of both is God; the spiritual part of both is Christ and his benefits; both are seals of the same covenant, are to be dispensed by ministers of the gospel, and by none other; and to be continued in the church of Christ until his second coming.

Q. 177. Wherein do the sacraments of Baptism and the Lord's Supper differ?

A. The sacraments of Baptism and the Lord's Supper differ, in that Baptism is to be administered but once, with water, to be a sign and seal of our regeneration and ingrafting into Christ, and that even to infants; whereas the Lord's Supper is to be administered often, in the elements of bread and wine, to represent and exhibit Christ as spiritual nourishment to the soul, and to confirm our continuance and growth in him, and that only to such as are of years and ability to examine themselves.

Q. 178. What is prayer?

A. Prayer is an offering up of our desires unto God, in the name of Christ, by the help of his Spirit; with confession of our sins, and thankful acknowledgment of his mercies.

Q. 179. Are we to pray unto God only?

A. God only being able to search the hearts, hear the requests, pardon the sins, and fulfil the desires of all; and only to be believed in, and worshipped with religious worship; prayer, which is a special part thereof, is to be made by all to him alone, and to none other.

Q. 180.What is it to pray in the name of Christ?

A. To pray in the name of Christ is, in obedience to his command, and in confidence on his promises, to ask mercy for his sake; not by bare mentioning of his name, but by drawing our encouragement to pray, and our boldness, strength, and hope of acceptance in prayer, from Christ and his mediation.

Q. 181.Why are we to pray in the name of Christ?

A.The sinfulness of man, and his distance from God by reason thereof, being so great, as that we can have no access into his presence without a mediator; and there being none in heaven or earth appointed to, or fit for, that glorious work but Christ alone, we are to pray in no other name but his only.

Q. 182. How doth the Spirit help us to pray?

A. We not knowing what to pray for as we ought, the Spirit helpeth our infirmities, by enabling us to understand both for whom, and what, and how prayer is to be made; and by working and quickening in our hearts (although not in all persons, nor at all times, in the same measure) those apprehensions, affections, and graces which are requisite for the right performance of that duty.

Q. 183. For whom are we to pray?

A. We are to pray for the whole church of Christ upon earth; for magistrates, and ministers; for ourselves, our brethren, yea, our enemies; and for all sorts of men living, or that shall live hereafter; but not for the dead, nor for those that are known to have sinned the sin unto death.

Q. 184. For what things are we to pray?

A. We are to pray for all things tending to the glory of God, the welfare of the church, our own or others good; but not for anything that is unlawful.

Q.185. How are we to pray.?

A. We are to pray with an awful apprehension of the majesty of God, and deep sense of our own unworthiness, necessities, and sins; with penitent, thankful, and enlarged hearts; with understanding, faith, sincerity, fervency, love, and perseverance, waiting upon him, with humble submission to his will.

Q. 186.What rule hath God given for our direction in the duty of prayer?

A. The whole Word of God is of use to direct us in the duty of prayer; but the special rule of direction is that form of prayer which our Saviour Christ taught his disciples, commonly called the Lord's Prayer.

Q. 187. How is the Lord's Prayer to be used?

A. The Lord's Prayer is not only for direction, as a pattern, according to which we are to make other prayers; but may also be used as a prayer, so that it be done with understanding, faith, reverence, and other graces necessary to the right performance of the duty of prayer.

Q. 188. Of how many parts doth the Lord's Prayer consist?

A. The Lord's Prayer consists of three parts; a preface, petitions, and a conclusion.

Q. 189.What doth the preface of the Lord's Prayer teach us?

A. The preface of the Lord's Prayer (contained in these words, *Our Father which art in heaven*), teacheth us, when we pray, to draw near to God with confidence of his fatherly goodness, and our interest therein; with reverence, and all other childlike dispositions, heavenly affections, and due apprehensions of his sovereign power, majesty, and gracious condescension: as also, to pray with and for others.

Q. 190.What do we pray for in the first petition?

A. In the first petition (which is, *Hallowed be thy name*), acknowledging the utter inability and indisposition that is in ourselves and all men to honour God aright, we pray, that God would by his grace enable and incline us and others to know, to acknowledge, and highly to esteem him, his titles, attributes, ordinances, Word, works, and whatsoever he is pleased to make himself known by; and to glorify him in thought, word, and deed: that he would prevent and remove atheism, ignorance, idolatry, profaneness, and whatsoever is dishonourable to him; and, by his overruling providence, direct and dispose of all things to his own glory.

Q. 191.What do we pray for in the second petition.?

A. In the second petition (which is, *Thy kingdom come*), acknowledging ourselves and all mankind to be by nature under the dominion of sin and Satan, we pray, that the kingdom of sin and Satan may be destroyed, the gospel propagated throughout the world, the Jews called, the fulness of the Gentiles brought in; the church furnished with all gospel-officers and ordinances, purged from corruption, countenanced and maintained by the civil magistrate: that the ordinances of Christ may be purely dispensed, and made effectual to the converting of those that are yet in their sins, and the confirming, comforting, and building up of those that are already converted: that Christ would rule in our hearts here, and hasten the time of his second coming, and our reigning with him forever: and that he would be pleased so to exercise the kingdom of his power in all the world, as may best conduce to these ends.

Q. 192.What do we pray for in the third petition?

A. In the third petition (which is, *Thy will be done in earth, as it is in heaven*), acknowledging, that by nature we and all men are not only utterly unable and unwilling to know and do the will of God, but prone to rebel against his Word, to repine and murmur against his providence, and wholly inclined to do the will of the flesh, and of the devil: we pray, that God would by his Spirit take away from ourselves and others all blindness, weakness, indisposedness, and perverseness of heart; and by his grace make usable and willing to know, do, and submit to his will in all things, with the like humility, cheerfulness, faithfulness, diligence, zeal, sincerity, and constancy, as the angels do in heaven.

Q. 193.What do we pray for in the fourth petition?

A. In the fourth petition (which is, *Give us this day our daily bread*), acknowledging, that in Adam, and by our own sin, we have forfeited our right to all the outward blessings of this life, and deserve to be wholly deprived of them by God, and to have them cursed to us in the use of them; and that neither they of themselves are able to sustain us, nor we to merit, or by our own industry to procure them; but prone to desire, get, and use them unlawfully: we pray for ourselves and others, that both they and we, waiting upon the providence of God from day to day in the use of lawful means, may, of his free gift, and as to his fatherly wisdom shall seem best, enjoy a competent portion of them; and have the same continued and blessed unto us in our holy and comfortable use of them, and contentment in them; and be kept from all things that are contrary to our temporal support and comfort.

Q. 194.What do we pray for in the fifth petition?

A. In the fifth petition (which is, *Forgive us our debts, as we forgive our debtors*), acknowledging, that we and all others are guilty both of original and actual sin, and thereby become debtors to the justice of God; and that neither we, nor any other creature, can make the least satisfaction for that debt: we pray for ourselves and others, that God of his free grace would, through the obedience and satisfaction of Christ, apprehended and applied by faith, acquit us both from the guilt and punishment of sin, accept us in his Beloved; continue his favour and grace to us, pardon our daily failings, and fill us with peace and joy, in giving us daily more and more assurance of forgiveness; which we are the rather emboldened to ask, and encouraged to expect, when we have this testimony in ourselves, that we from the heart forgive others their offences.

Q. 195.What do we pray for in the sixth petition?

A. In the sixth petition (which is, *And lead us not into temptation, but deliver us from evil*), acknowledging, that the most wise, righteous, and gracious God, for divers holy and just ends, may so order things, that we maybe assaulted, foiled, and for a time led captive by temptations; that Satan, the world, and the flesh, are ready powerfully to draw us aside, and ensnare us; and that we, even after the pardon of our sins, by reason of our corruption, weakness, and want of watchfulness, are not only subject to be tempted, and forward to expose ourselves unto temptations, but also of ourselves unable and unwilling to resist them, to recover out of them, and to improve them; and worthy to be left under the power of them: we pray, that God would so over-rule the world and all in it, subdue the flesh, and restrain Satan, order all things, bestow and bless all means of grace, and quicken us to watchfulness in the use of them, that we and all his people may by his providence be kept from being tempted to sin; or, if tempted, that by his Spirit we may be powerfully supported and enabled to stand in the hour of temptation: or when fallen, raised again and recovered out of it, and have a sanctified use and improvement thereof: that our sanctification and salvation may be perfected, Satan trodden under our feet, and we fully freed from sin, temptation, and all evil, for ever.

Q. 196.What doth the conclusion of the Lord's Prayer teach us?

A. The conclusion of the Lord's Prayer (which is, *For thine is the kingdom, and the power, and the glory, forever. Amen.), teacheth us to enforce our petitions with arguments, which are to be taken, not from any worthiness in ourselves, or in any other creature, but from God; and with our prayers to join praises, ascribing to God alone eternal sovereignty, omnipotency, and glorious excellency; in regard whereof, as he is able and willing to help us, so we by faith are emboldened to plead with him that he would, and quietly to rely upon him, that he will fulfil our requests. And, to testify this our desire and assurance, we say, Amen.*

An Exposition of the Westminster Confession of Faith

Robert Shaw

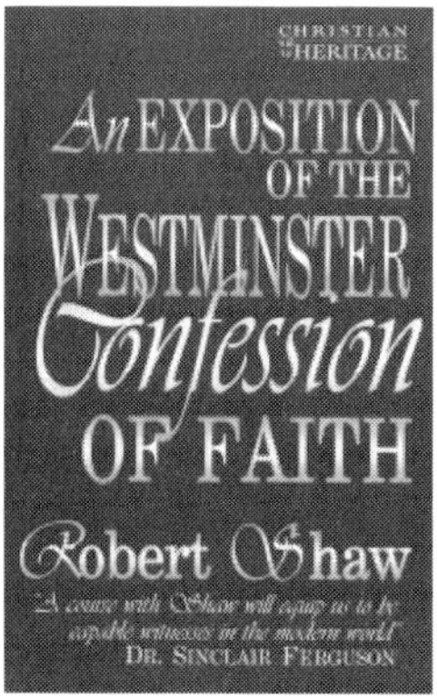

The Westminster Confession is the most comprehensive doctrinal credal statement of its kind. This classic explanation of the confession provides a thorough theological grounding. It is a practical aid to help us understand and apply the material in the Confession to our lives - making us live out our confession as individual Christians and as members of a worldwide church.

'His work provides a minature course in theology. More than that, it explains, expounds and applies the whole gospel in a way that will explain the message of Scripture, illumine understanding, stimulate worship and strengthen Christian living. A course with Shaw will equip us to be intelligent and capable witnesses to Jesus Christ in the modern world.'

Sinclair B. Ferguson

' . . . one of the best written and helpful expositions ever to appear. From 'Of the Holy Scripture' to 'Of the last judgement' each category of doctrine is opened up with clarity and applied with warmth and spirituality ... the value of the book is enhanced by the text of The Westminster Confession (together with Scripture proofs) given before each section is expounded... It is a handsome volume and is recommended highly.'

Evangelical Times

ISBN 0-906731-046

Bible Characters – People from the New Testament

Also includes characters from the parables of Jesus

Alexander Whyte

"Through the scriptures I first met the characters of the Bible. But only through Alexander Whyte have I come to know them... Without stretching the truth, he stretches our minds to embrace the character of the individuals revealed here. He is never superficial. He writes like a modern newspaperman – in terms of human interest and deep insight. It's just as though he had interviewed an individual and returned to the newspaper office to write up the feature. As a former newspaperman I deeply appreciate his thoroughness and his talent."

Ben Haden

This classic Bible character study book includes in this volume -

45 different real life characters from the New Testament
Plus 16 studies of the Apostle Paul
and 33 people from Jesus' parables

Alexander Whyte's well-researched compendium of biographies has been of great use to pastors, study group leaders and others for about 100 years. It is the most well respected source of material ever published for understanding the characters involved in the events of the Bible.

The material is here gathered into a handy hardback volume to continue its life of usefulness to the church today. Once you start dipping into Bible Characters, the people in the New Testament will leap from the page as real people – making the Bible relevant today, just as God intended it to be.

ISBN 1-85792-227-1

Christian Focus Publications

publishes books for all ages,
Our mission statement –

STAYING FAITHFUL
In dependence upon God we seek to help make His infallible Word, the Bible, relevant. Our aim is to ensure that the Lord Jesus Christ is presented as the only hope to obtain forgiveness of sin, live a useful life and look forward to heaven with Him.

REACHING OUT
Christ's last command requires us to reach out to our world with His gospel. We seek to help fulfill that by publishing books that point people towards Jesus and help them develop a Christ-like maturity. We aim to equip all levels of readers for life, work, ministry and mission.

Books in our adult range are published in three imprints.

Christian Focus contains popular works including biographies, commentaries, basic doctrine and Christian living. Our children's books are also published in this imprint.

Mentor focuses on books written at a level suitable for Bible College and seminary students, pastors, and other serious readers. The imprint includes commentaries, doctrinal studies, examination of current issues and church history.

Christian Heritage contains classic writings from the past.

Christian Focus Publications, Ltd
Geanies House, Fearn,
Ross-shire, IV20 1TW,
Scotland, United Kingdom
info@christianfocus.com

For details of our titles visit us on our website
www.christianfocus.com